RESEARCH IN
POPULATION
ECONOMICS

Volume 3 · 1981

RESEARCH IN POPULATION ECONOMICS

A Research Annual

Editors: JULIAN L. SIMON
Department of Economics
University of Illinois

PETER H. LINDERT
Department of Economics
University of California, Davis

VOLUME 3 · 1981

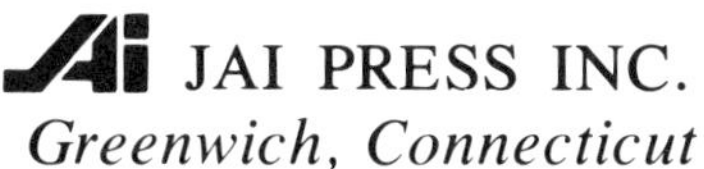 JAI PRESS INC.
Greenwich, Connecticut

CONTENTS

LIST OF CONTRIBUTORS

Lee E. Edlefsen   Department of Economic, University of Washington, and The University of Michigan

David D. Friedman   Department of Economics, University of California, Los Angeles

James W. Hughes   Center for Urban Policy Research, Rutgers University

Simon Kuznets   Professor of Economics, Emeritus Harvard University

Ronald Lee   Graduate Group in Demography University of California, Berkeley

Evelyn Lehrer   Department of Economics, Northwestern University

Andrew Mason   East-West Population Institute, University of Hawaii

Thomas W. Merrick   Center for Population Research, Georgetown University

Marc Nerlove   Department of Economics, Northwestern University

Alfred Sauvy   Institute National D'Études Démographiques, France

William Serow   Tayloe Murphy Institute, University of Virginia

Julian L. Simon	Department of Economics, University of Illinois
Stanley K. Smith	Department of Economics, University of Florida
Glenna D. Spitze	Department of Economics, State University of New York, Albany
Gunter Steinmann	The University of Paderborn West Germany
George Sternlieb	Center for Urban Policy Research Rutgers University
Daniel B. Suits	Department of Economics Michigan State University
Linda J. Waite	The Rand Corporation and University of Illinois

SIZE OF HOUSEHOLDS AND INCOME DISPARITIES

Simon Kuznets

I. THE ASSOCIATION ILLUSTRATED

In this paper we explore the relation between differentials in size of households, (preponderantly family households including one-person units) and disparities in income per household, per person, or per some version of consuming unit.[1] The relation is important, because, in size distributions of income among the population, the most common unit is the household—a group of persons, usually family members, related by blood, marriage, or adoption, residing together and sharing arrangements for living. Inequality in size of household may "produce," (be associated with) inequality in income per household, in income per person, in income per consuming unit, or in all three. Conversely, if we begin with inequality in income per person or per consuming unit, we shall observe association with size of household and with income per household. In either approach, one would find a connection between differentials in size

Research in Population Economics, Volume 3, pages 1–40.

ISBN: 0-89232-207-1

of household and disparities in income, the latter being substantial components in the observed size distributions of income among the population.

The treatment here can be only illustrative because of scarcity of relevant data and limitations of quality in the data available. Even the demographic data on the distribution of households by size are subject to undercount, differing for population subgroups with different household structure. The scarcer income data for households are far more defective. Most tests and comparisons (with the comprehensive national accounts for relevant totals) show that the available statistics on family income or consumption understate the totals by substantial margins, and margins that differ for different income sources and hence for different economic groups. Furthermore, the data refer to annual income or consumption rather than to longer-term levels, which are of more interest for many analytical purposes. But we had to use demographic and income statistics as they were available and for this reason the findings are at best suggestive. This warning, while necessary, does not mitigate the difficulties; these can be significantly overcome only with a large input of work on testing and revision with access to the original, unprocessed data—a task not feasible for an individual scholar.[2]

Table 1 provides a summary of data for six countries, bearing on the relation between size differentials among households and disparities in income per household and per person. The sample, while including both developed and less developed market economies, is small. Still, the nature of the association between size differentials among households and income disparities can be explored. We now consider the findings suggested by Table 1.

1. Inequalities among households in size, as measured by number of persons, are quite wide. A distribution like that for the United States in which the lower quintile of households (covered by the one-person class) accounts for only 7 percent of the population of persons whereas the top seventh (represented by households of five persons and over) accounts for a third of all persons, is clearly an unequal distribution. The same is suggested by the corresponding Gini coefficient of over 0.3 (see Panel B, line 46, column 4) and a total disparity measure, TDM (a simpler measure, but yielding results quite similar to the Gini coefficients) of well over 40.[3] An inspection of the percentage shares in columns 1 and 2 and the resulting size relative in column 4 of Panel A and the disparity measures in columns 1 and 4 in Panel B reveals that the size-of-household differentials are substantial in the other countries also, although they are of somewhat narrower amplitude in the three less developed countries—all of them in East Asia—than for the three more developed countries.

Table 1. Disparity Measures and Relatives of Income per Household and per Person by Size Classes of Households, Six Countries

A. Percentage Shares of Size-Classes, and Size- and Income-Relatives[a]

Classes of households by number of persons	Percentage in total			Relatives		
	House-holds (H) (1)	Persons (P) (2)	Income (Y) (3)	Size (P/H) (4)	Income per household (Y/H) (5)	Income per person (Y/P) (6)
United States, money income, 1975 (2.89)[b]						
1. One-person	20.6	7.1	10.0	0.345	0.49	1.41
2. Two-person	30.6	21.4	29.5	0.70	0.96	1.38
3. Three-person	17.2	18.0	19.6	1.05	1.14	1.09
4. Four-person	15.7	21.6	19.9	1.38	1.27	0.92
5. Five-person	8.6	14.8	11.6	1.72	1.35	0.78
6. Six-person	4.1	8.4	5.4	2.05	1.32	0.64
7. Seven-person-and-over (7.78)	3.2	8.7	4.0	2.72	1.25	0.46
Germany (FR), total income, 1970 (2.75)[c]						
8. One-person	22.6	8.2	11.6	0.36	0.51	1.41
9. Two-person	27.8	20.1	22.8	0.72	0.82	1.13
10. Three-person	22.2	24.2	24.6	1.09	1.11	1.02
11. Four-person	15.4	22.5	20.1	1.46	1.31	0.89
12. Five-person	7.2	13.2	11.3	1.83	1.57	0.86
13. Six-person	2.9	6.4	5.4	2.21	1.86	0.84
14. Seven-person-and-over (7.71)	1.9	5.4	4.2	2.84	2.21	0.80
Israel, Urban, total gross income, 1968–69 (3.65)[c]						
15. One-person	10.9	3.0	4.8	0.28	0.44	1.60
16. Two-person	23.0	12.6	19.8	0.55	0.86	1.57
17. Three-person	19.0	15.6	21.4	0.82	1.13	1.37
18. Four-person	21.4	23.4	27.9	1.09	1.30	1.19
19. Five-person	11.4	15.6	12.6	1.37	1.10	0.81
20. Six-person-and-over (7.2)	14.3	29.8	13.5	2.08	0.94	0.45

(Continued)

Table 1. (*Continued*)

Classes of households by number of persons	Percentage in total			Relatives		
	House-holds (H) (1)	Persons (P) (2)	Income (Y) (3)	Size (P/H) (4)	Income per household (Y/H) (5)	Income per person (Y/P) (6)
Taiwan, total household receipts, 1975 (5.27)[d]						
21. One-person	3.2	0.6	1.6	0.19	0.50	2.67
22. Two-person	5.2	2.0	4.1	0.38	0.79	2.05
23. Three-person	10.3	5.8	8.9	0.56	0.86	1.53
24. Four-person	16.8	12.7	16.0	0.76	0.95	1.26
25. Five-person	22.2	21.1	21.9	0.95	0.99	1.04
26. Six-person	19.0	21.6	19.6	1.14	1.03	0.91
27. Seven-person	11.3	15.0	11.9	1.33	1.05	0.79
28. Eight-person	5.9	9.0	7.2	1.53	1.22	0.80
29. Nine-person	2.7	4.7	3.4	1.74	1.26	0.72
30. Ten-person-and-over (11.7)	3.4	7.5	5.4	2.21	1.59	0.72
Philippines, total income, 1970–71 (5.77)[c]						
31. One-person	1.8	0.3	1.1	0.17	0.61	3.67
32. Two-person	6.9	2.4	4.6	0.35	0.67	1.92
33. Three-person	11.6	6.0	8.8	0.52	0.76	1.47
34. Four-person	14.9	10.3	13.6	0.69	0.92	1.32
35. Five-person	14.6	12.7	13.9	0.87	0.95	1.09
36. Six-person	13.5	14.0	13.2	1.04	0.98	0.94
37. Seven-person	11.6	14.0	12.3	1.21	1.06	0.88
38. Eight-person	11.0	15.4	13.1	1.40	1.19	0.85
39. Nine-person	5.6	8.7	6.4	1.55	1.15	0.74
40. Ten-person-and-over (11.0)	8.5	16.2	13.0	1.91	1.53	0.80
Thailand, money income, 1962–63 (5.53)[e]						
41. One-person	4.0	0.7	2.0	0.18	0.50	2.86
42. Two-to-three-person (2.6)	18.3	8.6	13.3	0.47	0.73	1.55
43. Four-to-five-person (4.5)	29.9	24.3	27.4	0.81	0.92	1.13
44. Six-to-seven-person (6.5)	27.1	31.9	29.4	1.18	1.08	0.94
45. Eight-person-and-over (9.2)	20.7	34.5	27.9	1.67	1.35	0.81

B. Measures of Disparity in Size of Household and in Income per Household and per Person, among Size Classes of Households[f]

	TDM			Gini Coefficient		
	Size (H-P) (1)	Income per household (H-Y) (2)	Income per person (P-Y) (3)	Size (H-P) (4)	Income per household (H-Y) (5)	Income per person (P-Y) (6)
46. United States, 1975	45.4	23.4	25.2	0.305	0.158	0.165
47. Germany, 1970	44.2	32.0	13.0	0.297	0.213	0.088
48. Israel, 1968/9	43.4	20.2	38.6	0.296	0.135	0.235
49. Taiwan, 1975	31.0	10.4	20.6	0.221	0.082	0.139
50. Philippines, 1970/1	36.2	16.2	20.6	0.251	0.119	0.133
51. Thailand, 1962/3	37.2	19.0	18.2	0.242	0.127	0.118

[a] Entries in parentheses in lines identifying the country refer to the average (arithmetic mean) number of persons per household. Entries in parentheses in the vertical stub of lines 42–45 refer to the average number of persons per household in the given size-class (provided in the source). The relatives in columns 4, 5, and 6 should equal ratios of the relevant percentage shares in columns 1, 2, and 3. The slight discrepancies are due to rounding. The relatives in column 6 should equal the ratio of the relatives in column 5 to those in column 4. The slight discrepancies are again due to rounding.

[b] *Source:* Lines 1–7: Taken or calculated from U.S. Bureau of the Census, *Current Population Reports, Series P-60, No. 104,* GPO, Washington 1977, Tables 3 and 15, pp. 13–20 and 48–57.

[c] *Source:* Lines 8–20 and 31–40: Taken or calculated from Table 13, pp. 45–46 of my paper, "Demographic Aspects of the Size Distribution of Income," in *Economic Development and Cultural Change,* Vol. 25, No. 1, October 1976. This paper provides detailed notes on the sources of data for these three countries (Germany, Israel, and the Philippines) as well as on United States and Taiwan and also provides discussion of related findings (referred to henceforth as Source I).

[d] *Source:* Lines 21–30: Taken or calculated from two sources, one covering Taipei City and the other covering Taiwan Province (the two comprising Taiwan). The former is by Bureau of Budget, Accounting and Statistics, Taipei City Government, *Report on the Survey of Family Income and Expenditure and Personal Income Distribution of Taipei City 1975,* 1976, Table 16, pp. 108–111. The latter is by Department of Budget, Accounting and Statistics, Taiwan Provincial Government, *Report on the Survey . . . . Taiwan Province 1975,* 1976, Table 25, pp. 538–549. The total and per household number of persons in the open-end, largest size group (line 30) was calculated from the other size groups and the population totals for all households given in other tables.

[e] *Source:* Lines 41–45: Taken or calculated from National Statistical Office, *Advance Report, Household Expenditure Survey, Whole Kingdom* (Bangkok 1963), Table 9.0, pp. 66–67. Money income was estimated at 81 percent of total income, the latter including value of goods produced and consumed at home (see *Ibid.,* Table H, p. 32).

[f] TDM is the sum of differences between percentage shares in the two relevant totals (households and persons, households and income, persons and income): signs are disregarded. They are calculated directly from the percentage shares in columns 1–3 for the six countries in Panel A. The Gini coefficients are calculated directly from the percentage shares arrayed by the order of the relatives in the corresponding columns (column 4 for households and persons, column 5 for households and income, and column 6 for persons and income): all are given in Panel A.

5

The size differentials just discussed are of interest in so far as they are associated with disparities in income per household, per person, or per consuming unit; and we shall indicate later that the magnitude of the differentials in size is the *minimum* to which the magnitudes of disparities in income per household and income per person add. If so, a wide amplitude of differentials in size of households would mean (with the same associations with disparities in income per household and income per person) a wider amplitude of disparities either in income per household, in income per person, or in both.

We can make one other comment on the differentials in size of households in comparison with those in income. Size of household may be subject to short-term disturbances, whether stochastic or of a different order. Thus a family household may, in a given year, be reduced by the death of a child, to be compensated for by quick response in terms of an additional birth. But it seems plausible to assume that such short-term changes are of lesser impact on the distribution of households by size than on their distribution by the current year's income. One tends to think of size of household as determined largely by long lasting life cycle and institutional patterns, in which the household unit remains at a given size for a number of years. If so, the amplitude of the size differentials is more clearly reflective of differences in longer-term levels than is the amplitude of income disparities in the conventional grouping of households by the current year's income.

2. The relatives of income per household for the successive size classes of households (column 5 of Panel A) show for all countries a *positive* association between total income of household and its size. In some cases (e.g., in the United States and particularly in Israel), the rise in the relative income per household reaches a peak at a size class well below the top and then declines. But these can be viewed as only partial limitations of the conspicuous positive association in which the rise in the size of household is, by and large, accompanied by a substantial rise in the household's total income.

The impressive positive association between size of household and its income suggested in Table 1 is not an arithmetic necessity or tautology. It is quite possible within a country for some socio-economic groups, which are characterized by large households, to show an average income per household distinctly lower than that for other groups with a smaller average household (e.g., the households in the United States in 1975 with employed heads who are blue collar workers compared with those whose employed heads are white collar workers; or in Taiwan in 1975, farmer households compared with nonfarmer households). In fact, a negative association between average income per household in occupational groups and the size of the average household by occupation is not uncommon; and some of the relevant data will be cited and discussed in a later section. If it is possible for a variety of subgroups within a country to show larger average household size associated with lower average per household income, the positive association for countrywide comparisons cannot be viewed as inevitable and obvious. It is rather the result of a balance of factors that make for a positive association dominating the factors that would otherwise make for a negative association—with outcomes that can differ among countries, or within countries over time, or at different ranges of the size-of-household differentials.

The disparity measures in columns 2 and 5 of Panel B reflect the magnitude of the component that size differentials among households contribute to the distribution of households by size of income per household. Thus within the total inequality among households by income per household in the United States in 1975, there is a component that is measured by a Gini coefficient of 0.158 and that reflects the inequality in the size of household in terms of number of persons—a component that presumably ought to be removed if households are to be used as comparable units in terms of persons. But the Gini coefficient just cited cannot be compared directly with that for the size distribution of income among households by income per household for two reasons. First, Gini coefficients (and the TDMs) are not additive, so the sum of two component measures may add to more or less than that for the total distribution. Second, and even more difficult, the size distribution of income is based on the size of annual income, with the transient and stochastic elements recorded in the income of each single household before it is classified in the size distribution. Such stochastic and other transient elements tend to be much reduced by cancellation for large groups of households that we average under the one-, two-, . . . , n-person class. The Gini coefficient for the total distribution of income among households by income per household would be substantially reduced with similar cancellation of stochastic and other transient components, were such cancellation possible. It is not feasible to attempt here a quantitatively meaningful comparison of the effects of size differentials among households on either income per household, per person, or per consuming unit, with the total size distribution of income among households by income per household, per person, or per consuming unit—the latter properly adjusted. We shall have to rely on a rough judgment resting on the absolute values of the disparity measures that we derive.[4]

3. Whatever factors limit the rise in per household income with increase in household size or even make for negative association between total income and household size, the combination of the two results in the rise in household income falling substantially short of the rise in the number of persons as we move from the smaller to larger households. This can

be observed in Panel A by comparing the levels and movements of the size relatives in column 4 with those of income per household in column 5; it can be observed more clearly in the ratio of the two, which represents the relatives of income per person in the successive size classes of households in column 6. This column reveals for each of the six countries a *decline* in per person income as we move from the smaller to the larger households, a decline that is quite substantial and continuous. In some cases (e.g., Taiwan and the Philippines, which are two countries with the most detailed grouping by size at the large levels), the decline in per person income slows down or ceases in the range of large households (above seven persons); but this is a minor qualification of what is an impressive *negative* association between size of household and household income per person.

The corresponding measures of disparity are given in columns 3 and 6 of Panel B. As already indicated, these measures represent the magnitude of the component that the size differentials among households contribute to the total distribution of income among households by income per person. Whereas the magnitudes differ among countries and relative to those for income per household, those in columns 3 and 6 are, on the whole, no less substantial than those in columns 2 and 5.

A more significant finding associated with the one just stated is the difference in *identity* of the households at low and high levels when we compare grouping by income per household with that by income per *person*.[5] As found in the paper cited, the higher levels of *per household* income are dominated by the larger households whereas the higher levels of *per person* income are dominated by the smaller households; and there is a similar contrast in identity at the lower levels, the latter dominated by smaller households in the distribution by income per household and by larger households in the distribution by income per person. Since for most purposes it is the distribution by income per person (or per consuming unit) that is the more significant, the use of income per household may lead to misleading identification of the better-off or the worse-off groups within the total population.

4. We come now to the relation between the measure of disparity for the size differentials among households and those for disparities in income per household and income per person. A glance at these measures in Panel B of the table shows that the sum of the two income disparity measures is never smaller than the size disparity measure. In the single case of Taiwan, the sum of the TDMs in columns 2 and 3 (10.4 and 21.6, respectively) equals the TDM in column 1 (31.0); the same is true of the two Gini coefficients in columns 5 and 6 relative to that in column 4. In most other countries, the sum of the disparity measures for income per household and income per person *exceeds* that disparity measure for the

size differentials but by relatively small margins (Germany, the Philippines, Thailand). For the United States, the excess in the sum of the disparity measures in columns 2 and 3 relative to 1 is of 48.5 to 45.4, with a similar excess in the sum of the Gini coefficients. This excess becomes striking in the case of Israel: the sum of the TDMs in columns 2 and 3 (58.3) is over a third larger than that for size differentials (43.4). There is a similar showing for the Gini coefficients.

Two comments are relevant. First, our finding that the disparity measure for household size is related to the sum of the measures for disparities in income per household and in income per person is dependent upon the finding of a *positive* response of household income to size but a response that falls short of the rise in household size and thus "leaves room," as it were, for the *negative* association between size and income per person. Were these two findings absent, the relation between the disparity measure for household size and the disparity measures for income per household and for income per person would have been different. Thus, if the association between size and household income remained positive, but the positive response of income were more than proportional to increase in size, the result would have been a measure of disparity in income per household alone greater than that for size, whereas the association between per person income and household size would have been positive. By contrast, were the association between size of household and income per household to become negative, the disparity measure for income per person would become the largest of the three disparity measures, it along exceeding that for size differentials among households. The summation in these two assumed cases would then be addition of the two smaller disparity measures to yield the *largest* of the three: it being for income per household in the former case and for income per person in the latter case.

Second, given a positive but incomplete response of household income to household size, the finding that the sum of the disparity measures for income per household and for income per person significantly exceeds the disparity for household size is presumably due to some additional factors that introduce elements affecting household income in ways *not associated* with size. In terms of the relatives and percentage shares shown in Panel A and related to TDM, one should view the size and income per household relatives as measures of proportional deviation from the countrywide average, so that 0.345 in line 1, column 4 becomes a proportional deviation of -0.655, whereas that in column 4, line 7 becomes $+1.72$ (being the relatives, as entered, minus 1.00). It will then be noted that, for the United States, the deviations in column 5 (income per household) are for each size class of the same *sign* as in column 4 (size of households) and that, for all size classes, the proportional deviation for household income is of smaller absolute magnitude than that for size, with one important exception. The exception is for the size class of three persons (line 3), for which the positive deviation for income per household ($+0.14$ in column 5) is much greater than that for size ($+0.05$ in column 4). If we remove this exception by setting the per household income relative for this size class at 1.025 (thus reducing the income share in column 3 from 19.6 to 17.6 percent) and compensate by adding two percentage points to the income share of one-person class in line 1, column 3 (thus making it 12.0, with resulting shifts in income relatives for this class), the new TDM for income per household becomes 19.4, that for income per person becomes 26.0, and the sum is now identical with TDM for size of 45.4. A different allocation of the two percentage points would yield a different pair of TDMs for income per household and income per person, but so long as the signs of the proportional deviations represented by the relatives in columns 4 and 5 are the same and those in column 5 are all absolutely smaller than those in column 4, the sum of the TDMs for income per household and income per person will be identical with the TDM for size differentials among households.

Even larger disturbances in the association between size and household income are observed for Israel. For the three-person class (line 17) (with a share of 19.0 percent of all households), a negative deviation for size (-0.18) is combined with a positive deviation for income ($+0.13$). For the six-and-over class (line 20) (with a share of 14.3 percent of all households), a positive deviation for size ($+1.08$) is associated with a negative deviation for household income (-0.06). Clearly, there are elements of heterogeneity in the structure of Israel's household population that disturb the positive association between size and household income; and we are aware of them from other sources because of the mixture of Jews and non-Jews, of immigrant and native populations, of the presence of different continent-of-origin stocks among the Jews, and different religious groups among the non-Jews.

II. SOME VARIANTS

In Section III, we consider some of the factors relevant to the associations between size of household and income disparities of the type observed in Table 1. But before doing so we should note, briefly, two other variants of size differentials among households.

The first is suggested by the large proportions in the developed countries today of one-person households, as illustrated in Table 1 for Germany and the United States—contrasted with the far more moderate proportions of one-person households in the less developed countries (e.g., Taiwan). This contrast is observed also for the larger number of countries for which we have data on size of households but no data on income. Since the one-person households may be viewed more easily as members of a larger family with which they may be associated than is true of larger households, one may ask what would be the effect on the size differentials and their association with income disparities if one-person households were excluded or transferred to the larger multiperson units.

An illustrative answer to this question is provided in Table 2, in which we use the data for the United States and Taiwan to perform the needed calculations. The effect of exclusion of one-person households, thus limiting the distributions to family households of two or more persons, naturally raises the average size of household and reduces both the size differentials and associated disparities in income per household (Panel A and columns 2 and 6 and of Panel C). Since we are eliminating one source of diversity among households with respect to size, the TDMs and the Gini coefficients for the size of household differentials and disparities in income per household should decline—and they do, appreciably more for the United States than for Taiwan. But the more significant finding is that the decline in *per person* income with rise in the size of household is still quite marked in Table 2, Panel A. The exclusion of one-person households leaves the TDMs and the Gini coefficients for the disparities in income per person about the same as they were for the complete size distributions of households in Table 1 (see Panel C of Table 2, columns 1 and 2, lines 33 and 36, and columns 5 and 6, lines 33 and 36).

If we try to transfer one-person households and their income to multiperson households, we need to have a reasonable scheme for allocating the former among the latter. One cannot claim that the schemes embodied in the two assumptions used for Panel B of Table 2 are realistic, but they are of interest as illustrations. Using Assumption 1, we allocate the one-person households to the other size classes proportionately to their relative weight, i.e., to their percentage proportion in the total of all households of two or more. Using Assumption 2, we follow a procedure that allocates the one-person households first to the largest size class in the distribution: one one-person household is assigned to each household of the largest size class; then, of the remaining one-person households, one is assigned to each household of the size class of next-to-largest size, and so on down, until all of the one-person households have been allocated. We should note that in Assumption 1, the additions of one-person households to the two-person size class yields a new group of three-person households, which is subtracted from the former two-person class and added to the former three-person class. In other words, transfer means shifts of the distribution along the full range from the earlier two-person household class to the top size class.

A glance at Panel B and the relevant parts of Panel C of Table 2 shows

Table 2. Effects of Exclusion or Transfer of One-Person Households, United States and Taiwan, 1975

A. Exclusion of One-Person Households

	Percentage in total			Relatives		
	H	P	Y	H/P	Y/H	Y/P
Classes of households	(1)	(2)	(3)	(4)	(5)	(6)
United States, 1975 (3.38)						
1. Two-person	38.5	23.0	32.8	0.60	0.85	1.43
2. Three-person	21.7	19.4	21.8	0.89	1.00	1.12
3. Four-person	19.8	23.3	22.1	1.18	1.12	0.95
4. Five-person	10.8	15.9	12.9	1.47	1.19	0.81
5. Six-person	5.2	9.0	6.0	1.73	1.15	0.67
6. Seven-person-and-over	4.0	9.4	4.4	2.35	1.10	0.47
Taiwan (5.41)						
7. Two-person	5.4	2.0	4.2	0.37	0.78	2.10
8. Three-person	10.6	5.8	9.1	0.55	0.86	1.57
9. Four-person	17.3	12.8	16.3	0.74	0.96	1.27
10. Five-person	23.0	21.2	22.2	0.92	0.97	1.05
11. Six-person	19.6	21.8	19.9	1.11	1.02	0.91
12. Seven-person	11.7	15.1	12.1	1.29	1.03	0.80
13. Eight-person	6.1	9.1	7.3	1.49	1.20	0.80
14. Nine-person	2.8	4.7	3.4	1.68	1.21	0.72
15. Ten-person-and-over	3.5	7.5	5.5	2.14	1.57	0.73

B. Transfer of One-Person Households to Multiperson Households

	Assumption 1				Assumption 2			
	Percentage in total			Income relative,	Percentage in total			Income relative,
	H	P	Y	Y/P	H	P	Y	Y/P
	(1)	(2)	(3)	(4)	(5)	(6)	(7)	(8)
United States (3.64)								
16. Two-person	28.6	15.7	21.9	1.39	38.5	21.2	29.5	1.39
17. Three-person	26.0	21.4	25.9	1.21	21.7	17.9	19.6	1.09
18. Four-person	20.2	22.3	22.0	0.99	13.9	15.3	13.9	0.91
19. Five-person	13.2	18.2	15.8	0.87	5.9	8.1	8.3	1.02
20. Six-person	6.6	10.8	8.1	0.75	10.8	17.9	15.8	0.82
21. Seven-person-and-over	5.4	11.6	6.3	0.54	9.2	19.6	12.9	0.66
Taiwan (5.44)								
22. Two-person	.5.2	1.9	4.0	2.11	5.4	2.0	4.1	2.05
23. Three-person	10.5	5.8	8.8	1.52	10.6	5.9	8.9	1.51
24. Four-person	17.1	12.5	15.9	1.27	17.3	12.7	16.0	1.26
25. Five-person	22.8	21.0	22.1	1.05	23.0	21.0	21.9	1.04

Table 2. (Continued)

	Assumption 1				Assumption 2			
	Percentage in total				Percentage in total			
				Income relative,				Income relative,
	H	P	Y	Y/P	H	P	Y	Y/P
	(1)	(2)	(3)	(4)	(5)	(6)	(7)	(8)
26. Six-person	19.7	21.7	20.1	0.93	19.6	21.6	19.6	0.91
27. Seven-person	11.9	15.3	12.4	0.81	11.7	15.0	11.9	0.79
28. Eight-person	6.3	9.2	7.6	0.83	6.1	9.0	7.2	0.80
29. Nine-person	2.9	4.8	3.6	0.75	2.8	4.6	3.4	0.74
30. Ten-person-and-over	3.6	7.8	5.5	0.71	3.5	8.2	7.0	0.85

C. Disparity Measures

	TDM				Gini Coefficient			
			Transfer				Transfer	
	Table 1	Excl.	Ass1	Ass2	Table 1	Excl.	Ass1	Ass2
	(1)	(2)	(3)	(4)	(5)	(6)	(7)	(8)
United States								
31. H—P	45.4	35.6	35.0	42.2	0.305	0.230	0.230	0.266
32. H—Y	23.4	11.4	13.6	22.2	0.158	0.073	0.110	0.138
33. P—Y	25.2	24.4	21.4	20.4	0.165	0.166	0.147	0.138
Taiwan								
34. H—P	31.0	29.0	28.8	29.4	0.221	0.203	0.202	0.207
35. H—Y	10.4	9.0	9.6	10.8	0.082	0.067	0.071	0.082
36. P—Y	20.6	20.0	19.2	18.6	0.139	0.136	0.131	0.125

Notes: All calculations use the percentage shares for households (H), person (P), and income (Y) shown for the two countries in Table 1.

The entries in parentheses following the name of the country are the arithmetic mean numbers of persons per household associated with the distributions by size given in the panel.

In both assumptions in Panel B, the allocation of the one-person households and their income uses the average income per household. In Assumption 1 (Ass1), the one-person households are allocated by the percentage shares of the size classes in column 1 of Panel A. In Assumption 2 (Ass2), one-person households are allocated to the larger multiperson households, assuming that each of them is assigned one extra person. This allocation, beginning at the top size-end of the distribution, is followed until all of the one-person households have been transferred.

that the assumed transfers have different effects on the size differentials among households and on the disparities in income per household—the latter particularly marked for the United States in Assumption 2. But, while raising the average size of the household even further (to 3.64 in United States and 5.44 in Taiwan), the transfers, in both assumptions, reduce the disparity in income per person. Thus, the TDMs in lines 33 and 36 tend to drift down in columns 3 and 4, and so do the Gini coefficients in columns 7 and 8. The reason is that the high per person income in the one-person household class is transferred to larger sized households, which originally had lower income per person. The effect, however, is limited, and the substantial disparity in income per person, which is negatively associated with size of household, tends to persist even with the experimental transfers of one-person households and their income to larger sized households.

Another variant of size differentials among households (different again from that used in Table 1) is suggested by the question whether the unweighted number of persons is a true measure of household size. As already noted, our interest is more in inequalities revealed by the relatives of income per person and not by those in the relatives of income per household since the latter are so dominated by inequalities in size of household. But is the shift from per household to per person bases the proper adjustment for inequalitites in size of household? If we are concerned with equivalent *consuming* units, the fact that the proportions of children are greater in the larger sized households suggests the possibility that division by the number of persons *overcorrects* for inequality in size of households. This possibility flows from the realistic hypothesis that the consumption needs of children are, on a per head basis, distinctly lower than those of adults. And there is the additional argument that suggests economies of scale in the larger household, even if all its members are adults.

The issues raised are complex and, indeed, are part of a wider group of issues—of differences in "needs" among members of the household, as distinguished by age and sex (and possibly other demographic and socio-economic characteristics), and of differences in living—working conditions, which may produce price differentials in the costs of a similar bundle of goods among groups of households. It is not feasible to explore these issues further here, nor do I feel competent to undertake the exploration. But it may suffice here to use whatever limited data on the topic could be assembled in Table 3 on an assumption (for three of the four countries) that persons under 18 years should be viewed as half-weight consuming units compared with a full weight for those 18 years of age and over.[6] This crude assumption probably overcorrects for difference in "needs," even including an allowance for economies of scale. For Israel, due to lack of relevant data on age structure by size classes of households, we adopted the conversion coefficients to "standard person" units derived in the Israeli statistics from the country's data on consumption patterns for households of different size. There is no full comparability between the results for Israel and for the three other countries; but the estimates are notional for all four.

Since the larger households usually have a higher proportion of children than the smaller households and since there may be a greater economy of scale in satisfying consumption needs for the former than for the latter, we would expect that the size differentials among households in terms of consuming units or "standard" persons would be narrower than in terms

Table 3.   Shift from Income per Capita to Income per Consuming Unit or per Standard Person, Four Countries

A. Shift to Income per Consuming Unit[a]

| Households by number of persons | Person per household | | | | Percentage of shares in | | Income relative, Y/C (7) |
	Under 18 (1)	18 and over (2)	Cons. Units (C) (3)	Ratio (2)/(3) (4)	C (5)	Y (6)	
United States, 1975[b]							
1. One-person	0	1.00	1.00	1.00	8.4	10.0	1.19
2. Two-person	0.06	1.94	1.97	0.98	24.7	29.5	1.19
3. Three-person	0.70	2.30	2.65	0.87	18.7	19.6	1.05
4. Four-person	1.61	2.39	3.20	0.75	20.6	19.9	0.97
5. Five-person	2.49	2.51	3.76	0.67	13.2	11.6	0.88
6. Six-person	3.34	2.66	4.33	0.61	7.3	5.4	0.74
7. Seven-person	4.81	2.97	5.38	0.55	7.1	4.0	0.56
8. Average	0.89	2.00	2.45	0.82			
Taiwan, 1975[c]							
9. One-person	0	1.00	1.00	1.00	0.8	1.6	2.00
10. Two-person	0.16	1.84	1.92	0.96	2.3	4.1	1.78
11. Three-person	0.77	2.23	2.61	0.85	6.5	8.9	1.37
12. Four-person	1.51	2.49	3.24	0.77	13.2	16.0	1.21
13. Five-person	2.24	2.76	3.88	0.71	20.9	21.9	1.05
14. Six-person	2.86	3.14	4.57	0.69	21.0	19.6	0.93
15. Seven-person	3.40	3.60	5.30	0.68	14.5	11.9	0.82
16. Eight-person	3.73	4.27	6.13	0.70	8.8	7.2	0.82
17. Nine-person-and-over	4.74	5.79	8.16	0.71	12.0	8.8	0.73
18. Average	2.27	3.00	4.14	0.73			
Philippines, 1970–71[d]							
19. One-person	0	1.00	1.00	1.00	0.4	1.1	2.75
20. Two-person	0.20	1.80	1.90	0.95	3.1	4.6	1.48
21. Three-person	0.95	2.05	2.52	0.81	6.9	8.8	1.28
22. Four-person	1.86	2.14	3.07	0.71	10.8	13.6	1.26
23. Five-person	2.75	2.25	3.63	0.62	12.5	13.9	1.17
24. Six-person	3.51	2.49	4.25	0.59	13.5	13.2	0.98
25. Seven-person	4.18	2.82	4.91	0.57	13.4	12.3	0.92
26. Eight-person	4.58	3.42	5.71	0.60	14.8	13.1	0.89
27. Nine-person-and-over	5.64	4.57	7.39	0.62	24.6	19.4	0.79
28. Average	3.06	2.71	4.24	0.64			

(*Continued*)

Table 3. (*Continued*)

B. Shift to Standard Person (SP)[e]

| | | Percentage of Shares in | | |
Households by number of persons	SP per household (1)	SP (2)	Y (3)	Income relative Y/SP (4)
Israel, urban households, 1968–69				
29. One-person	1.25	4.7	4.8	1.02
30. Two-person	2.00	15.9	19.8	1.25
31. Three-person	2.65	17.3	21.4	1.24
32. Four-person	3.20	23.6	27.9	1.18
33. Five-person	3.75	14.7	12.6	0.86
34. Six-person-and-over (7.2)	4.84	23.8	13.5	0.57

C. Disparity Measures[f]

| | TDM | | | Gini Coefficient | | |
	Size (H-C or H-SP) (1)	Income per household (H-Y) (2)	Income per C, SP (C, SP-Y) (3)	Size (H-C or H-SP) (4)	Income per household (H-Y) (5)	Income per C, SP (C,SP-Y) (6)
35. United States, 1975	36.2	23.4	14.6	0.244	0.158	0.090
36. Taiwan, 1975	28.0	10.4	17.6	0.200	0.082	0.120
37. Philippines, 1970/1	32.2	16.2	16.6	0.223	0.119	0.108
38. Israel, 1968/69	30.0	20.2	24.8	0.204	0.135	0.146

Sources: For the sources of underlying data, see the notes in Table 1 relating to the four countries covered here.

[a] The ratios in column 4, lines 8, 18, and 28 are computed from the arithmetic means in columns 2 and 3 of the same lines.

[b] The estimates in columns 1 and 2 are based on 1970 Census data on proportions of children under 18 in families of two to seven and over (see U.S. Bureau of the Census, *1970 Census of Population, Subject Report* PC(2) 4A, *Family Composition* (May 1973), Table 3, pp. 7–8. These proportions were applied to size classes of households used in Table 1 here (for March 1976, income for 1975). The results were adjusted proportionately so that the totals of under-18 and 18-and-over checked with the totals in the source used for Table 1. Numbers in column 3 are calculated from columns 1 and 2 by weighting the numbers aged below 18 by half. For discussion of this weighting se Source I cited for Table 1 above (Table 9, p. 31, and discussion, pp. 30–2). Numbers in columns 4–7 are calculated from columns 1–3 or taken directly from sources used for Table 1.

[c] The proportions given directly in the source are for persons under 21 and 21 and over (see Kuznets, "Size and Structure of Family Households: Exploratory Comparisons," *Population and De-*

of persons. In addition, since we are not regrouping the households by the consuming unit or standard person equivalent of each household, but retain size classes by number of persons, we underestimate the full range of size differentials in terms of consuming units (or standard persons): the spread in any variable is reduced if the data are classified by a criterion of size not directly reflecting the given variable. And, indeed, for these reasons, the size disparity measures in Table 3 for the four countries are all lower than the corresponding disparity measures in Panel B of Table 1. To use the TDMs for illustration: the measure drops from 45.4 to 36.2 for the United States; from 43.4 to 30.0 for Israel; from 31.0 to 28.0 for Taiwan; and from 36.2 to 32.2 for the Philippines.

The conversion to consuming units for the United States reduces the size differentials more sharply than for either Taiwan or the Philippines (the comparison with Taiwan being of most interest). This is despite the fact that for the household population as a whole, the proportion of persons below 18 is about 30 percent in the United States and over 40 percent for Taiwan. The explanation lies in differences in patterns of rise of the proportion of children in the larger households, combined with differences in distributions of household by number of persons. As Table 1 shows, in the United States over 51 percent of all households are in the one- and two-person classes, so that the population under 18 years of age is far more concentrated in what for that country are the larger households; whereas in Taiwan, with the shares of one- and two-person households small, no such concentration occurs. This can be seen by comparing the proportions of under 18 in the United States and Taiwan beginning with the class of four persons and more: in the four-person class, the entry for the United States (line 4, column 1) at 1.61 is already in excess of that for the same class in Taiwan (1.51: line 12, column 1). This greater proportion of members under 18 years of age in the United States than in Taiwan will be found also for the five-, six-, and seven-and-over size classes. Such differences in pattern and in relative reduction of size dif-

---

velopment Review, Vol. 4, No. 2, June 1978, Table 1, pp. 190–191). For the end of 1974, it is possible to estimate the ratio of total population under 21 to that under 18: it is 1.161 (see *Taiwan Demographic Fact Book 1974,* Taipei, Dec. 1975, Table 1, pp. 54). We applied this ratio to the total numbers in the successive size classes of households to approximate the distribution in columns 1 and 2.

 d The averages in line 28 are from the original Source I (Table 13). The distribution of members under 18 and of those 18 and over used in columns 1 and 2 follows the pattern established for Taiwan in lines 9–17, columns 1 and 2. This seemed to be a more plausible pattern than the one used in Table 13 of the 1976 paper (Source I).

 e For discussion of the scale of standard persons used in Israel for households of increasing size, see Source I (Table 9, p. 31, and discussion). Columns 2–4 are calculated using column 1 and the relevant data in Table 1.

 f See the notes on the measures of disparity, Panel B of Table 1.

ferentials among households in the shift from per person to per consuming unit, may be found in other comparisons between the more and the less developed countries.

With the reduction in size differentials among households and the disparities in income per household remaining unaffected, there is a reduction in the disparities in income per consuming unit when we compare them with disparities in income per person. The change, in TDMs, is from 25.2 to 14.6 in the United States (relatively, the largest change); from 38.2 to 24.8 in Israel; from 20.6 to 17.6 in Taiwan; and from 20.6 to 16.6 in the Philippines. Yet the disparities, even in income per consuming unit, remain substantial; and most interestingly, the negative correlation persists: this time between size of household as measured in consuming units and income per consuming unit. A glance at the relevant income relatives in Table 3 shows that with the exception of movement from the one- to two-person class in Israel, there is a marked and consistent decline in income per consuming unit as we move from the smaller to the larger households.

III. FACTORS RELEVANT TO THE ASSOCIATION

We may now ask why income per household increases with rise in household size and why this increase falls short of the rise in numbers (either of persons or consuming units) so as to yield a marked decline in income per capita or per consuming unit when we shift from smaller to larger households.

In considering the answers to the double question just posed, we may start at the beginning of the sequence—size of household, income per household, income per person or consuming unit—or reverse it and proceed from income per person or per consuming unit to size and then to income per household. In the first sequence, we begin with size differences among households (taking them as given) and then attempt to suggest the factors that, given the size differences, yield the observed disparities in income per household and in income per person or per consuming unit. But in this attempt, we must indispensably consider the demographic and socio-economic characteristics of households of differing size; and so come to view size differentials, in turn, as determined in part by other demographic and socio-economic groupings within the country (or within any other relevant total). In the second sequence, we begin with, and take as given, disparities among households in income per person or per consuming unit; and then attempt to suggest the factors that, given the income disparities, account for a negative association between the latter and size differentials among households and that do this in such a way as to make for a positive association between size and total income of households. But in this attempt, we must indispensably consider the associated demographic and socio-economic characteristics of households at low and high levels of income per person or per consuming unit. In this way, we come to view the income disparities, in turn, as determined in part by other demographic and socio-economic groupings within the relevant total of household population. While the analytical emphases will differ somewhat between the two sequences, the several demographic and socio-economic groupings whose different responses may account for the association between size-of-household differentials and income disparities will be the same.

The presentation in this section follows the first sequence because the available data center on the household as a unit, whereas those that center on the person or consuming unit are scarce. But it should be possible toward the end of the section to revert briefly to some aspects of the second sequence, referring to the illustrative findings in our discussion relating to those demographic and socio-economic groupings that we found to be of interest.

(a) The first and obvious reason for the positive association between size and income of household is that the larger number of members will, most likely, mean more members of working age. The latter can participate in earning activity (thus adding to the household's income) and may be induced to do so by the greater needs that a larger number of members represents. And, indeed, we find in Panel A of Table 3 that the number of adults per household increases with the rise in size of household, in each of the three countries covered.

Two comments are relevant to the just suggested factor in the positive association between size and income per household. First, for the present purpose the distinction between children and adults should not be with an eye to consumption needs as it was for the conversion in Table 3. The distinction should be between those too young or too old to be able to contribute to income as it is defined in the data and those who are of working age, i.e., capable of so contributing. This division line will differ among countries at the several stages of economic development and among socio-economic groups within a country. The effective application of such a criterion requires data on income earning capabilities at different ages in different situations. No such data are at hand, and as Table 3 indicates, data even on age distribution of members of families or households within the size classes of two members and above are extremely scarce. The approximations in Table 3 are, for the present purposes, crude indeed.

Second, the activities in which the properly defined working age members are assumed to be able to engage should be among those that are included in the income data. This requirement of consistency between the definition of income recipients within the household and the income covered in the data (or, still better, the income that should be covered) is obvious. Yet it needs to be noted, with the restriction of the United States and Thailand distributions to money income; and the bearing is even wider when we consider the variety of productive activities within the household (by the housewife and other members) that are excluded from the accepted definition of personal income of households in the standard economic accounts. Clearly, a wider definition of productive activity and income can significantly affect the pattern of relatives of income per household, perhaps making the rise with increasing size of household more substantial than it is now in column 5 of Panel A of Table 1 and thus moderating the associated decline in the relatives of income per person in column 6.

If we accept the crude approximations in Table 3, the rise in number of adults per household with increasing size of household provides one factor that makes for a rise in total income of household as the number of its members increases. But the moderate magnitude of the rise in total income thus attained, relative to increase in persons or consuming units, is also revealed. As already observed, the table shows a rapid rise in the proportion of children in total membership of household, once we pass the two-person level, in both the United States and Taiwan patterns. Hence, in all countries covered, the proportion of persons of working ages to total number of persons or of consuming units declines markedly, beginning with the size class of three persons and reaching a trough in the larger sized households. It follows that unless income per person of working age were to *rise* sharply to offset the decline in the proportion of potential workers to total of persons or consuming units, there would be a drop in household income per person or per consuming unit.

This finding of the rising proportion of children and declining proportion of adults as the size of the household increases beyond two persons is likely to be observed with a lower division line (say of 15 years of age), and the evidence on the importance of the children factor in explaining differentials in size of households (largely countrywide averages in cross-section and time comparisons) in Kuznets (1978; see Note 1) supports this inference. But in the present connection, one should stress that marriage and children mean not only a decline in the larger families of the proportions of members of working ages; they mean also the absorption of some of these members of working ages into activities within the household needed to take care of children and of living arrangements, activities the substantial returns on which bypass the markets and are not included in the personal income (or consumption) of the households in the data on size-distributions. If we assume that the absorption of worktime of working age adults is greater the larger the number of children in the household (particularly if the dividing line is set at a young age), the proportion of adults *available* for income securing pursuits in the total membership of the households declines even more sharply with the rise in household size.

(b) Another reason for the positive association between size of household and its income may be that size is associated with other characteristics that bear upon income. Assume that in both the countrywide total of households and within each size class we distinguish two subgroups, A and B, and that the proportions of A are smaller among the smaller households and greater among the larger households, whereas the opposite is true of the proportions of subgroup B. Assume further that, within each size class (or the overwhelming majority of them), the average income per household in subgroup A is significantly above that in subgroup B. This combination of a rising proportion of A households, with a significantly higher income per household for the A households within each or most size classes, would produce a rise in income per household, as we shift from smaller to larger size classes. The result would be a positive association between size and income of household, even if the number of adults of working age per household failed to rise in the shift from smaller to larger households.

An illustration of demographic characteristics associated with size (of the A-B type just conjectured) is provided in Table 4: the characteristics being sex of head of household, age of head of household, and a closely related economic characteristic of participation or lack of participation of the head in the labor force. The illustration is limited to the United States even though similar data are available for the same year for Taiwan Province (i.e., Taiwan, excluding Taipei City). But the proportions of households with female heads or with the head not participating in the labor force are quite small in Taiwan Province, and the data would yield only insignificant contributions to the positive association between size of household and its income. Likewise, household income differentials within size classes, by age of head, are far narrower in Taiwan Province than in the United States.

Table 4 provides the needed information for each of three sets of characteristics of head of household: (1) differences in percentage proportions of A and B within each size class and (2) the ratio of the lower income per household of the B subgroup to that of the higher income of the A subgroup [see lines 4, 8, and 12 on the percentage shares of the A subgroup (male heads, heads aged from 35 through 54, and heads in the labor force) and lines 5, 9, and 13, on the ratio of average household income of the B group to that of the A group (the B subgroup has female head households, households headed by persons under 35 or over 54 years of age, and

Table 4. Effect of Differences in Structure within Size Classes of Households on Income Relatives and Disparities: Structure by Sex, Age, and Labor Force Participation of Heads, United States, 1975

	Size classes of households (Number of persons)							All households
	1	2	3	4	5	6	7 and over	
	(1)	(2)	(3)	(4)	(5)	(6)	(7)	(8)
Countrywide measures as given[a]								
1. Percentage of shares in all households	20.6	30.6	17.2	15.7	8.6	4.1	3.2	45.4 (H − P)
2. Income relative, per household	0.49	0.96	1.14	1.27	1.35	1.32	1.25	23.4 (H − Y)
3. Income relative, per person	1.41	1.38	1.09	0.92	0.78	0.64	0.46	25.2 (P − Y)
Male- and female-headed households								
4. Percentage of male-headed households within size class[b]	36.9	83.4	83.2	90.2	93.8	89.4	86.4	75.8
5. Ratio, income per household, female head to male head[b]	0.64	0.64	0.56	0.49	0.50	0.46	0.49	
6. Income relative per household, constant percentage in line 4[c]	0.59	0.96	1.13	1.21	1.27	1.24	1.20	19.0 (H − Y)
7. Income relative per person, assumption of line 6[c]	1.72	1.38	1.08	0.88	0.74	0.61	0.44	29.4 (P − Y)
Age of head (35–54 age group versus others)								
8. Percentage of 35–54 year head households within size class[b]	17.0	19.7	37.1	48.7	63.1	69.6	77.7	34.2
9. Ratio, income per household, other age head households to 35–54[b]	0.63	0.79	0.81	0.78	0.74	0.73	0.81	
10. Income relative per household, constant percentage in line 8[c]	0.53	1.01	1.14	1.24	1.24	1.20	1.13	19.2 (H − Y)
11. Income relative per person, assumption of line 10[c]	1.55	1.44	1.09	0.90	0.72	0.58	0.41	29.8 (P − Y)
Head in labor force (L) and not in labor force (N)								
12. Percentage of L within size class[b]	49.2	64.6	83.3	90.5	91.8	88.0	84.8	72.7

Table 4.   (*Continued*)

	Size classes of households (Number of persons)							All households
	1 (*1*)	*2* (*2*)	*3* (*3*)	*4* (*4*)	*5* (*5*)	*6* (*6*)	*7 and over* (*7*)	(*8*)
13. Ratio, income per household, N/L[b]	0.46	0.54	0.63	0.59	0.54	0.47	0.50	
14. Income relative per household, constant percentage in line 12[c]	0.58	1.02	1.10	1.18	1.24	1.22	1.16	17.4 (H − Y)
15. Income relative per person, assumption of line 14[c]	1.68	1.45	1.06	0.86	0.72	0.60	0.43	31.0 (P − Y)

[a] The entries in columns 1–7 are from Panel A of Table 1, lines 1–7, columns 1, 5, and 6. Those in column 8 are the TDMs, from Panel B of Table 1, line 46, columns 1–3.

[b] Lines 4–5, 8–9, and 12–13 are calculated from the source for the United States referred to in the notes to Table 1 (Table 15, pp. 48–57). Lines 4, 8, and 12 refer to the percentage within each size class and for all households of households with male heads, with heads aged 35–54, and with heads in the labor force. The complementary percentage to 100 is then of households with female heads, with heads aged below 35 and above 54, and with heads not in the labor force. Lines 5, 9, and 13 refer to the ratio, within each size class, of the income per household with female heads to income per household with male heads; of the income per household with heads aged 35–54 to income per household with either younger or older heads; and of the income per household with heads not in the labor force to income per household with heads in the labor force.

[c] Lines 6–7, 10–11, and 14–15 are calculated by assuming (1) that *within* the size classes, percentages of male- and female-headed households are held constant at the countrywide proportions (i.e., 75.8 and 24.2 percent, respectively); (2) that a similar assumption is made with respect to percentages within each size class of households with heads aged 35–54 and of households with heads at younger or older ages (34.2 and 65.8 percent, respectively); and (3) that within each size class, percentages of households with heads in the labor force and with heads not in the labor force are the same (72.7 and 27.3 percent, respectively).

Given these assumptions and the within-size-class averages of income per household for the three comparisons of two groups each, it was possible to compute the average income per household for each size class. Then, having the common distribution in line 1 of households by size classes, we calculated the relatives of income per household in lines 6, 10, and 14 and the relatives of income per person in lines 7, 11, and 15.

The entries in column 8 of lines 6, 10, and 14 are the TDMs for inequality of income per household; those in column 8 of lines 7, 11, and 15 are for inequality in income per person—both sets resulting from size inequalities under the assumptions used.

households whose heads were not in the labor force)]. A glance at these lines shows that the A–B shares differ substantially among the size classes (the A shares rising markedly from low shares in the one-person class to much higher shares in the larger households), whereas the average household income for the A subgroup substantially exceeds that of the B subgroup within each of the several size classes.

Given the subgroup differentials in income per household, it is the pattern of differences in A–B shares in the successive size classes that are important (by contributing to the rise in income per household and then also in limiting that rise). The contribution of the differing A–B structure can be observed if we assume away these structural differences, i.e., posit the same A–B shares in the successive size classes and then compare with the result for the countrywide picture. The income relatives per household resulting from that assumption are in lines 6, 10, and 14, columns 1–7, and the disparity measures for income per household are in the same lines, column 8. These can be compared with the actual countrywide relatives of income per household, which reflect *variable* structure by size class and are given in line 2. The comparison shows that the differences in structure by A–B subgroups resulted in raising the positive response of income per household to size; this is shown by the finding that the TDM reflecting the differences in structure (23.4) exceeds those based on assumption of the same A–B structure in each of the size classes (19.0 in line 6; 19.2 in line 10; and 17.4 in line 14). The same result is observed when we compare the range of rise in the income per household from the lowest (at the one-person class) to the highest (at the five-person class). For the observed countrywide relative, the range is 0.49 to 1.35 or 2.8; with exclusion of differences in A–B structure, it is reduced to 2.2 for the subgroups by sex of head, to 2.3 for the subgroups by age of head, and to 2.1 for the subgroups by participation and nonparticipation of head in the labor force.

The assumptions used in lines 6, 10, and 14 imply that for the hypothetical distributions, the share of the size classes in total of all households are the same as in line 1, i.e., the one observed with variable structure of A–B subgroups. Hence, the TDM for size differentials among households in line 1 (45.4) is also the one for the hypothetical distributions implied in lines 6, 10, and 14. From what we have learned of the TDM for size differentials as the *minimum* to which the TDMs for income would add, we should infer that lower TDMs for income per household in lines 6, 10, and 14 (compared to line 2) would mean higher TDMs for income per person in lines 7, 11, and 15 (compared to line 3). In other words, the diversity of A–B structure, which made for stronger *positive* response of per household income to size, also made for a *weaker negative* response of per person income to size of household. And, indeed, the TDM in line 3 (25.2) is significantly smaller than those close to 30 in lines 7, 11, and 15.

If the diversity in A–B structure of the type revealed in lines 4, 8, and 12 contributes to the positive response of household income to household size, this contribution is limited if such diversity is reduced once the percentage share of A reaches high levels and leaves less room for further increases. It is therefore of interest that, for the structure by sex of head, a share of male-headed households as high as 83 percent already is reached in the two-persons class (see line 4, column 2) and that, for the structure by labor force participation, the share of households with heads in the labor force reaches 83 percent already in the three-persons class (see line 12, column 3). Only for the structure by age of head do we find (in line 8) that the rise in the share of households with heads between the ages of 35–54 is fairly continuous through the range of size classes, although even here the rise in the share is moderate beyond the five-persons class. Given variations in the A/B income-per-household ratios among the several size classes of relatively moderate range (see lines 5, 9, and 13), the diversity in A–B structure that diminishes rapidly as we pass to size classes beyond two or three persons can make only a limited contribution to *sustaining* the positive response of income to household size.

Illustrations of the effects of A–B structures similar to those provided in Table 4 can probably be found in a number of other countries; and what we know of the effects of sex and age of head on household income (directly and through influence on participation in labor force) would lead us to expect results in the economically developed countries similar to those that we found in the United States. We now turn to another kind of grouping in which the combination of diversity in structure within the successive size classes with per household income differentials between the subgroups within these size classes produces effects which are opposite in direction from those illustrated for the A–B type structure in Table 4, on the positive association between size of household and its income and on the negative association between household size and its income per capita.

(c) Assume another pair of subgroups, C and D (with the average income per household of C significantly larger than that of D) in each or most of the size-classes and assume the percentage proportions of C households to be greater among the smaller households and to decline substantially as we move toward the larger size classes. Thus, the major difference between the A–B and C–D structures is that, in the former, the percentage proportions of the higher income households *rise* as we move from the smaller to the larger households, whereas, in the latter, the percentage proportions of the higher income households *decline* as we move from the smaller to the larger households. One implication of this contrast is that in the A–B structure, the higher income households (A) are, on the average, larger in size than the lower income households (B), revealing, for the averages, a *positive* correlation between household income and size. Thus, to refer back to Table 4, the higher income households with male heads average 3.2 persons per household, whereas those with female heads average 2.0; those with heads between ages 35 to 54 average 3.8 persons per household, whereas those with heads below 35 or over 54 years average 2.4 persons; those with heads in the labor force average 3.2 persons per household compared with 2.1 persons for households with head not in the labor force. For the C–D structure, we will find the opposite, viz. that the higher income households (C) will, on the average, be smaller than the lower income households (D).

Two illustrations of the C–D structure are presented in Table 5: one for the United States and the other for Taiwan. The illustration for the United States (Panel A) distinguishes, among households with employed heads, those with white collar workers heads from those with blue collar heads, and treats the sum of the two (which excludes households with heads employed in agriculture or are service workers) as the total (in columns 1–3). White collar households (heads are professionals, administrators, sales, or clerical workers) are characterized by a per household income that is 30 to 50 percent higher than that of blue collar households (heads are craftsmen, operatives, or laborers, excluding those in agriculture; see column 5). The percentage share of the white collar households in the combined total declines from 70 percent in the one-person class to less than 40 percent in the seven-and-over-person class; column 4). It follows also that the average white collar household is smaller than the average blue collar household; the averages being 3.0 and 3.4 persons, respectively.

With this somewhat negative association between income and size of household, it is not surprising that our assumption [for columns 6 and 7 of Panel A (viz. that the percentage proportions of C and D households are the same for each size class: 55.1 and 44.9 percent, respectively, as indicated in line 8, column 4)] shows that the diversity in the C–D structure among the size classes *reduced* the positive association between size of household and its total income. Without such diversity, the TDM for disparity in income per household would have been 13.2; with the diversity, it drops to 12.0 (see line 8, columns 6 and 2). The effect on disparity in income per person is opposite: the diversity in structure *magnifies* this disparity, yielding a TDM of 29.8 compared to one without the diversity of 28.6 (see line 8, column 3 and 7).

The illustration for Taiwan distinguishes farmer households [those whose heads are substantially engaged in farming or related pursuits (fishing, hunting, and the like), even though income from agriculture may not be the dominant source of household income] from nonfarmer households. The countrywide proportions of nonfarmer households (this includes a tiny group of farmers in Taipei City) and of farmer households are 74 and 26 percent, respectively. As column 4 of Panel B shows, the proportion of nonfarmers is at a high level of about 80 percent in the households of one to five persons, but then declines rapidly in the larger size classes, down to 43 percent among households of ten and over. The countrywide average size of nonfarmer households (5.1 persons) is substantially below that of farmer households (6.0 persons). But, as one might have expected, the income per farmer household within each size class is distinctly below that per nonfarmer household, as is revealed, with some erratic disturbances, in column 5 of Panel B. The relative excess of the income of C-type household (nonfarmer) is between 30 and 60 percent.

The results of diversity here in the C–D structure can again be observed by comparing columns 6 and 7 with columns 2 and 3. The diversity results in moderating the positive response of household income to its size: TDM is reduced from 13.8 to 10.4, which is a relatively substantial reduction. It also results in magnifying the negative response of per person income to increasing size of household, with the TDM rising from 17.2 to 20.6. In terms of what we set out to discuss (viz., why the income per household rose with increasing size and why it rose so moderately as to yield a negative association between size of household and per person income), the C–D illustration for Taiwan (like that for the United States) helps to answer largely the second part of the double question.

The concentration on socio-economic subgroups in illustrating the C–D structure in Table 5, contrasted with the concentration on demographic subgroups of the A–B structure in Table 4, is a matter of choice. One could find socio-economic subgroups that would be of the A–B type and demographic subgroups that would be of the C–D type. And yet there is substance to the contrast. Size differentials among households are, realistically, associated with sex of head, given the concentration of a preponderant majority of households (at least in the statistical reporting) under male headship and given the female headship largely as a result of the "broken" status of the unit or of widowhood. Likewise, the larger households do tend to occur when the head is in the "central" rather than the extreme age phases of the typical life-cycle. It is not easy to find *demographic* characteristics that would distinguish significant sugroups of the C–D type unless one considers some characteristics (like urban versus rural residence) that are greatly affected by associated economic and social groupings.

Likewise, in recent times, when even the less developed countries have substantial modern economic and social components, the major socio-economic groupings do tend to be of the C-D type. With size differentials among households (preponderantly family households) reflecting differences in proportions of children and in the propensity of adults to live together or apart, it is the more modern components in the society and the economy that tend to reflect first the lower birth rates and the greater tendency to live apart that are the demographic hallmark of modern economic development, particularly under conditions of free markets and ef-

Table 5. Effects of Differences in Structure within Size Classes of Households on Income Relatives and Disparities, Structure by Economic Subgroups, United States and Taiwan, 1975

A. United States, White Collar Worker Heads (WW), Blue Collar Worker Heads (BW), and Combined Total (WBW)[a,b]

Size Classes	WBW					Income relative derived by assumption	
	Percentage of HH (1)	*Income relative per HH* (2)	*Income relative per P* (3)	*Percentage of WW in WBW HH* (4)	*Ratio of Y/H, BW/WW* (5)	*Per HH* (6)	*Per P* (7)
1. One-person	13.0	0.58	1.85	70.3	0.77	0.56	1.78
2. Two-person	27.1	0.98	1.57	57.2	0.72	0.97	1.55
3. Three-person	19.9	1.03	1.10	52.7	0.73	1.03	1.10
4. Four-person	20.0	1.10	0.88	52.9	0.71	1.10	0.88
5. Five-person	11.3	1.17	0.75	50.4	0.68	1.16	0.76
6. Six-person	5.1	1.18	0.63	44.5	0.67	1.22	0.65
7. Seven-person-and-over	3.6	1.17	0.51	39.2	0.63	1.25	0.54
8. Total or TDM	40.8	12.0	29.8	55.1		13.2	28.6
	(H − P)	(H − Y)	(P − Y)			(H − Y)	(P − Y)

B. Taiwan, Nonfarmer (NF), and Farmer (F) Households[a,c]

| | Countrywide | | | | | Income relative derived by assumption | |
	Percentage of HH (1)	Income relative per HH (2)	Income relative per P (3)	Percentage of NF in total (4)	Ratio of Y/H, F to NF (5)	Per HH (6)	Per P (7)
9. One-person	3.2	0.50	2.67	79.2	0.75	0.47	2.50
10. Two-person	5.2	0.79	2.05	78.1	0.42	0.79	2.05
11. Three-person	10.3	0.86	1.53	81.9	0.60	0.83	1.48
12. Four-person	16.8	0.95	1.26	82.5	0.59	0.91	1.20
13. Five-person	22.2	0.99	1.04	79.9	0.64	0.96	1.01
14. Six-person	19.0	1.03	0.91	72.3	0.67	1.04	0.92
15. Seven-person	11.3	1.05	0.79	65.0	0.70	1.08	0.81
16. Eight-person	5.9	1.22	0.80	56.9	0.66	1.29	0.84
17. Nine-person	2.7	1.26	0.72	52.4	0.68	1.37	0.79
18. Ten-person-and-over	3.4	1.59	0.72	42.9	0.73	1.74	0.79
19. Total or TDM	31.0	10.4	20.6	73.9		13.8	17.2
	(H − P)	(H − Y)	(P − Y)			(H − Y)	(P − Y)

[a] For both panels, see the notes on the data and assumptions in Table 4. For the nature of the assumptions (constant percentage shares within size classes of the two components, white and blue collar worker households for the United States and nonfarmer–farmer households in Taiwan) used to derive the income relatives in columns 6 and 7 in both Panels here, see the notes on similar assumptions in Table 4.

[b] The data for Panel A from the source used for Table 4. Note that the countrywide total here (in columns 1–3) includes only households whose heads are employed white collar and blue collar workers, accounting for 49.0 million households out of a total of 72.9 million. The white collar groups includes professional and technical workers; managers and administrators, except farm; sales workers; and clerical and kindred workers. Blue collar workers include craft and kindred workers; operatives, including transport workers (given separately); and laborers, except farm. All terms used here are from the source.

[c] In Panel B, the entries in columns 1–3 are directly from our Table 1 above. The additional data, needed to secure entries in columns 4 and 5, are from the two sources for Taiwan cited for Panel A of Table 1.

fective consumer sovereignty. But it is also the same modern groups that will show higher income per household for comparable size and on the average. The C–D structure is then associated with the contrast between the more modern, economically more advanced groups in society and those that are less "modern" and less advanced in the direction along which economic growth proceeds. This statement clearly applies to the nonfarmer–farmer distinction in the illustration for Taiwan, but, to a lesser degree, also, to the distinction between white collar and blue collar households in an economically developed country like the United States. While the bearing of it is particularly relevant to societies in the process of transition from older to more modern modes of production and life, one would argue that *every* society is in transition at the boundaries of *some* of its sectors and classes, even if the phases of major transition may already have been completed.

We are now at the end of a brief, illustrative discussion of the factors relevant to the positive association of size differentials among households with disparities in income per household and to the negative association of the same size differentials with household income per person (and, implicitly, per consuming unit, although we had no adequately cross-classified data at hand). Before we conclude this discussion, two general aspects of the analysis should be noted.

First, while we followed here the first sequence—from size differentials among households to disparities in income per household to those in household income per person—much of what was said of the effects of diversity of structure within size classes for the A–B and C–D subgroups would be relevant also to the second sequence. Were the data available to begin with a distribution of households by income per person (with the associated size and demographic and socio-economic characteristics), we would first observe the negative association between income per person (or per consuming unit) and size of household. Then, considering the factors relevant to this association, we would argue that low income per person is connected with large household size because of the large proportion of children and because of the propensity of adults to live separately in so far as income and absence of direct obligations to children permit. And we would be illustrating this by the C–D types of socio-economic groups that were covered in Table 5 and briefly discussed earlier. To proceed further, given the combination of disparities in per person or per consuming unit income with size differentials among households (revealed in the negative association between the two), the question would arise why it still allows room for a *positive* association between size and per household income; here the arguments about the greater absolute numbers of members of working ages and the effects of A–B types of largely demographic subgroups within size classes illustrated in Table 4 would be brought into play. In short, the second sequence would, in the process of establishing the links, rely also on the characteristics of the several demographic and socio-economic groups within the population—characteristics that would explain, if illustratively, the ties between size differentials and income disparities.

Second, the illustrations in Tables 1–5 refer to countrywide measures and to subgroups that comprise the countrywide household population (with the single exception of the white-collar–blue-collar dichotomy for the households in the United States). Yet the factors that are found to be relevant apply not only to countrywide household populations but also to connections between size differentials and income disparities *within* sub-country groups, whether they be distinguished by demographic economic, regional, ethnic, or similar criteria. So long as a subnational group includes households that differ substantially in size, these differences would be associated with differing proportions of children and adults, with differing structures within the size classes by sex and/or age of head, with further subdivisions with different economic and social characteristics that bear on income, and so on. And much of what was said of the factors relevant to the positive association between size differentials and disparities in income per household and to the negative association between size differentials and household income per person (or per consuming unit) could be repeated—changing the identity of some of the subgroups and of findings of such associations for *each* of a wide variety of subnational groupings. This must be the case, since the classifications that we can establish for the countrywide population are never so exhaustive of size differentials among households as to remove such differentials *within* the subnational groups themselves.

This last statement is true even of much finer classifications than the ones we used in Tables 4 and 5. But we illustrate it for the large subgroups (demographic and other) distinguished in Tables 4 and 5. In Table 6, we provide for each of five dichotomies used (three of the A–B type and two of the C–D type), the minimum of data needed to reveal the size differentials in association with relatives of income per household and income per person and to provide the basis for calculating the TDMs that are analogous to those used for the countrywide totals in Table 1 (for the two countries, United States and Taiwan).

Table 6 shows size differentials among households of substantial magnitude for all of the ten subgroups; these are revealed by TDMs ranging from about 30 to 54 (which would correspond to Gini coefficients ranging from about 0.2 to somewhat less than 0.4). Most of these measures of size disparities within the subgroups are somewhat below those for the countrywide populations of households (45.4 for the United States and 31.0 for Taiwan), but some (e.g., that for female-headed households in the

Table 6. Size Differentials and Income Disparities among Households *within* the Demographic and Economic Subgroups Distinguished in Tables 4 and 5, United States and Taiwan[a]

	Higher income per HH subgroup				Lower income per HH subgroup			
Size classes, totals, average TDMs	Percentage shares in total HHs (1)	Size relative (2)	Income relative per HH (3)	Income relative per P (4)	Percentage shares in total HHs (5)	Size relative (6)	Income relative per HH (7)	Income relative per P (8)
United States: Male Head and Female Head								
1. One-person	9.8	0.32	0.55	1.74	54.3	0.50	0.77	1.56
2. Two-person	33.7	0.63	0.89	1.42	21.1	1.01	1.26	1.25
3. Three-person	18.8	0.94	1.07	1.14	12.0	1.52	1.31	0.86
4. Four-person	18.6	1.26	1.16	0.92	6.3	2.02	1.27	0.63
5. Five-person	10.5	1.57	1.21	0.77	2.6	2.54	1.35	0.53
6. Six-person	4.9	1.90	1.20	0.63	1.8	3.06	1.22	0.41
7. Seven-person-and-over	3.7	2.38	1.16	0.49	1.9	4.37	1.24	0.28
8. Total or Average[b]	55.27	3.18	15.87	4.99	17.60	1.98	7.20	3.64
9. TDM[c]		40.6	16.2	27.0		53.8	25.2	39.2
		(H − P)	(H − Y)	(P − Y)		(H − P)	(H − Y)	(P − Y)
United States, HHs with Heads Aged 35–54 and HHs with Heads Aged below 35 or over 54								
10. One-person	10.2	0.26	0.55	2.07	26.0	0.41	0.52	1.25
11. Two-person	17.6	0.53	0.90	1.69	37.5	0.82	1.08	1.32
12. Three-person	18.6	0.80	1.01	1.26	16.5	1.23	1.23	1.00
13. Four-person	22.2	1.07	1.12	1.05	12.2	1.64	1.31	0.80
14. Five-person	15.8	1.33	1.16	0.88	4.8	2.04	1.29	0.63
15. Six-person	8.3	1.60	1.11	0.69	1.9	2.47	1.22	0.49
16. Seven-person-and-over	7.3	2.05	1.01	0.49	1.1	3.45	1.23	0.36
17. Total or Average[b]	25.05	3.75	17.66	4.71	47.82	2.44	11.74	4.81
18. TDM[c]		38.8	12.6	28.6		44.2	25.2	24.8
		(H − P)	(H − Y)	(P − Y)		(H − P)	(H − Y)	(P − Y)

United States, HHs with Heads in and not in the Labor Force

19. One-person	13.9	0.31	0.57	1.84	38.2	0.47	0.58	1.23
20. Two-person	27.2	0.63	0.98	1.56	39.6	0.95	1.17	1.23
21. Three-person	19.7	0.94	1.03	1.10	10.5	1.42	1.45	1.02
22. Four-person	19.5	1.26	1.12	0.89	5.5	1.90	1.46	0.77
23. Five-person	10.9	1.57	1.19	0.76	2.6	2.37	1.44	0.61
24. Six-person	5.0	1.88	1.19	0.63	1.8	2.84	1.25	0.44
25. Seven-person-and-over	3.8	2.35	1.14	0.49	1.8	4.29	1.25	0.29
26. Total or Average[b]	52.94	3.18	16.19	5.09	19.92	2.11	7.33	3.46
27. TDM[c]		41.6	13.0	29.8		44.2	32.0	26.4
		(H − P)	(H − Y)	(P − Y)		(H − P)	(H − Y)	(P − Y)

United States, Households of White Collar and Blue Collar Workers

28. One-person	16.6	0.33	0.56	1.70	8.6	0.29	0.57	1.97
29. Two-person	28.1	0.66	0.99	1.50	25.8	0.58	0.95	1.64
30. Three-person	19.0	0.99	1.04	1.05	21.0	0.87	1.01	1.16
31. Four-person	19.2	1.32	1.14	0.86	21.0	1.16	1.08	0.93
32. Five-person	10.4	1.66	1.23	0.74	12.4	1.45	1.12	0.77
33. Six-person	4.1	1.99	1.29	0.65	6.3	1.74	1.14	0.66
34. Seven-person-and-over	2.6	2.43	1.31	0.54	4.9	2.20	1.12	0.51
35. Total or Average[b]	23.5	3.02	19.66	6.51	19.17	3.44	14.69	4.27
36. TDM[c]		41.4	15.4	27.6		35.2	10.0	29.4
		(H − P)	(H − Y)	(P − Y)		(H − P)	(H − Y)	(P − Y)

Taiwan, Nonfarmer and Farmer Households

37. One-person	3.4	0.21	0.47	2.29	2.4	0.17	0.50	3.00
38. Two-person	5.4	0.41	0.85	2.09	4.3	0.33	0.49	1.50
39. Three-person	11.5	0.60	0.86	1.43	7.2	0.50	0.72	1.44
40. Four-person	18.8	0.80	0.95	1.19	11.4	0.67	0.77	1.15
41. Five-person	24.0	1.00	0.98	0.99	17.2	0.83	0.88	1.06
42. Six-person	18.5	1.20	1.05	0.88	20.0	0.99	0.99	1.00
43. Seven-person	9.9	1.39	1.09	0.78	15.1	1.16	1.06	0.91
44. Eight-person	4.6	1.59	1.33	0.84	9.9	1.32	1.21	0.92
45. Nine-person	1.9	1.84	1.37	0.73	4.9	1.49	1.29	0.87

(Continued)

Table 6. (Continued)

Size classes, totals, average TDMs	Higher income per HH subgroup				Lower income per HH subgroup			
	Percentage shares in total HHs (1)	Size relative (2)	Income relative per HH (3)	Income relative per P (4)	Percentage shares in total HHs (5)	Size relative (6)	Income relative per HH (7)	Income relative per P (8)
46. Ten-person-and-over	2.0	2.25	1.75	0.78	7.6	1.96	1.78	0.91
47. Total or Average[b]	2.25	5.01	119.9	23.9	0.79	6.03	86.1	14.3
48. TDM[c]		28.8	11.2	18.2		30.6	20.6	10.2
		(H − P)	(H − Y)	(P − Y)		(H − P)	(H − Y)	(P − Y)

[a] All the entries for the United States are taken or calculated from the source for the United States given in the notes to Tables 4 and 5. All the entries for Taiwan are taken or calculated from the two sources given for that country in the notes to Table 5.

[b] The entries in lines 8, 17, 26, and 35 are (1) columns 1 and 5, total of households, in millions; (2) columns 2 and 6, persons per household; (3) columns 3 and 7, income per household, $, U.S. 000s; (4) columns 4 and 8, household income per person, $ U.S., 000s. The entries in line 47 are (1) columns 1 and 5, total of households, in million; (2) columns 2 and 6, persons per household; (3) columns 3 and 7, income per household, $NT, 000s; columns 4 and 8, household income per person, $NT, 000s.

[c] The entries for TDM, lines 9, 18, 27, 36, and 48 are (1) in columns 2 and 6, for differentials among households in size (i.e., number of persons); (2) in columns 3 and 7, disparities in income per household among household size classes; (3) in columns 4 and 8, disparities in household income per person, among household size classes.

United States are substantially greater (see line 9, column 6). This probably reflects the greater heterogeneity within the female-headed households, with the contrast between the large group of one-person units headed mostly by widows and the various groups of larger households headed by a female in the absence of a resident husband.

In each subgroup, income per household shows positive association with size, as reflected in the relative income indexes in columns 3 and 7. In each subgroup, income per person is negatively correlated with size, as shown in the relative income indexes in columns 4 and 8. The magnitudes of the income disparities, whether in positive or negative correlation with size, are substantial. And one would expect that the negative relation would also be found between size measured in consuming units and income per consuming unit—although the magnitudes of size differentials and of disparities in income per consuming unit would be narrower than those shown now in columns 2 and 6 and in columns 4 and 8, respectively.

There are some interesting differences among the subgroups in the relative magnitudes of the disparities in income per household and in income per person. A good illustration is in the comparison of the nonfarmer and farmer households in Taiwan (lines 37–48; particularly the TDMs in line 48). The size differentials (in columns 2 and 6) are about the same for the two subgroups of households: the TDMs are 29 and 31, respectively. But the magnitude of the positive response of income per household to size of household is much more moderate among the nonfarmer households (with a TDM of 11.2) compared with that among the farmer households (with a TDM of 20.6; see line 48, columns 3 and 7). It may well be that the influence of the C–D type of subgroups, which limits the rise in per household income with increase in size of household, is greater for the more heterogeneous population of nonfarmer households than for that of farmer households. But because of this difference in the magnitudes of the *positive* response of income per household, there is an opposite difference in the magnitudes of the *negative* response of income per person. The TDM for disparities in per person income for the nonfarmer household (18.2) is almost twice that for the farmer households (10.2; line 48, columns 4 and 8). The size differentials among households thus contribute a larger component of inequalities in income per person to the population of nonfarmer households than they do to that of farmer households.

The number of such illustrations of different combinations of size differentials among households with disparities in income per household and in income per person (*within* demographic and socio-economic, intranational groups) could easily be multiplied. But the ones shown in Table 6 should suffice to indicate that a fuller study of the associations under discussion requires observing them not only for countrywide populations but for significant subnational groups—in cross section and over time.

IV. CONCLUDING COMMENTS

The discussion in the preceding sections of the connection between size differentials among households and disparities in income per household or in household income per person (or consuming unit) was based on data for a small number of countries. The view was focused on size alone, with other characteristics of households (also of bearing on income disparities) considered only as they were reflected in the size aspect. The narrow empirical base and scarcity of data that would reveal cross-relations among household characteristics limited the analysis to crude associations.

Yet it would be useful at this juncture, first, to summarize (in general terms unencumbered by qualifications) the major findings illustrated and discussed earlier and, then, to comment on the possible significance of the findings and on feasible directions of further inquiry to which they point.

1. Intracountry differences in size of households, whether size is measured by number of persons or of consuming units, are quite substantial. There is usually a positive association between income per household and size of household, in that larger households are found to secure larger total income. There is usually a negative association between size of household and household income per person or per consuming unit because the rise in per household income with greater size is not sufficiently large to compensate for the increase in persons or in consuming units.

2. Given the associations noted under (1), it follows that size differentials among households contribute to disparities in income per household and in household income per person or per consuming unit. Such income disparities, which are traceable to size differentials among households, may constitute substantial components in the overall inequalities in the countrywide (or other large collective-wide) distributions of income among households by income per household and in the overall inequalities of income among household population by household income per person or per consuming unit.

3. The magnitude of the size differentials among households, the measure of inequality in the size distribution of households, is the *minimum* to which the measures of inequality in associated disparities in income per household and in income per person (or per consuming unit) add. It is the *minimum* because the distribution of income per household or per person by size classes of households may also contain variance *not* associated with household size. Given this relation between, say, the Gini coefficient of the size differentials among households and those for associated disparities in income per household and in income per person (or per consuming unit), the following inference is suggested. With the signs of the

association as observed, the larger the Gini coefficient (or a similar measure of inequality) for the distribution of households by size, the larger should be the Gini coefficients either for the associated disparities in income per household, for disparities in income per person (consuming unit), or for both.

4. Since the distributions of households by size differ between developed and less developed market economies by the strikingly larger proportions in the former of one-person households, experimental calculations for the United States and Taiwan dealt with the effects of either omitting one-person households or shifting them under variant assumptions into the larger household size classes. The results, while indicating a reduction in size differentials that is appreciably greater among U.S. households than among Taiwanese households, still reveal a substantial magnitude of associated disparities in income per household and, particularly, in income per person.

5. The positive association of total household income with size of household is due partly to the inclusion of more work-and-earnings-capable adults in the larger households and partly to the greater preponderance among heads of larger households of heads with characteristics that make for higher income [e.g., of male rather than femal heads and of heads in the mature, higher earning ages rather than of heads too young (before their prime) or too old (after their prime)]. But the effects of these factors, which tend to raise overall income for the larger households, diminish rapidly as we rise above the small size classes. The larger the household, the lower the proportion of income-earning adults to children and the smaller the rise in the proportion of household with male heads or with heads in the more favorable ages.

6. The resulting shortfall in the increase of household's total income with greater size and the consequent negative association between size and household income per person (or per consuming unit) is sustained by the effect of socio-economic or ethnic characteristics of heads. In general, in developed, as well as in modernizing and developing countries, the socio-economic groups that are more advanced, more modern, and hence with a higher per person income tend to show a smaller average size of household (e.g., among professional white-collar employees) than the less modern, lower income groups (e.g., farm workers or lower-skilled blue collar employees). Such negative correlation between average household size and per person household income of the diverse socio-economic (or ethnic) groups contributes, within a country, to the negative association between size of household and its income per person (or per consuming unit).

7. While the associations between size differentials among households and disparities in income per household and per person were noted for

countrywide distributions and the relevant factors discussed in terms of the latter, such associations and the relevant factors would be observed also for subnational units (regions, socio-economic groups, and the like). So long as we find substantial size differentials among the households of a given group or collective, the effects on disparities in income per household and income per person are also likely to be found and sustained by demographic and socio-economic subgroupings of households within the given group or collective.

The significance of the findings just summarized depends, primarily, on our view as to the independence of households as they are commonly defined in the available data—independence as units deciding on acquisition and allocation of income or on raising claim to a share in the country's product. It also depends, secondarily, on our interest in income inequalities associated with size of household differentials alone, allowing for other income-affecting characteristics of households only as they are reflected in the size differentials.

If, on the first point (discussed briefly in the first of the four papers listed in Note 1), we were to find that separate households form clusters of close common interest that makes for joint economic decisions (as may be the case for a cluster that includes the parental households and those of their children or that comprises households of several siblings), then the approach that yielded these findings would have to be recast. Instead of treating the separate households in the data as independent units, we would have to group them into clusters of common interest (in action and in claims on national product) and only then consider whether size differentials among the clusters are of significant effect on inequalities in income per cluster or in cluster-income per person or per consuming unit. The identification of foci of common interest would, clearly, be difficult and would require a variety of additional data that are not now available on the interrelations of separate households. Still, we must recognize that our findings retain significance only to the extent that independence of interest and claim among the separate households actually prevails, and it may prevail in different degree in different societies and for different levels of economic decision. We followed the approach on the assumption that there is independence among separate households over a wide range of economic decisions. But this is an untested assumption, which, at present, limits the validity of findings for *all* income distributions that utilize households as independent units.

Second, our emphasis on the crude association between size of households and income disparities was initially meant as a warning—as a demonstration that conventional distributions of income by income per household conveyed a misleading impression of the more meaningful distribution of long-term incomes among roughly equivalent (in terms of need) consumer units (or equivalent producer units). For more reliable analysis, adequate data on long-term incomes would be most urgently needed, but it was not feasible to pursue this difficult goal. Even if we take the income data as given and concentrate on the recipient unit, the crude association observed could have been enriched by allowing other characteristics of households to be taken into account (phase of life cycle as reflected by age of head, occupation and industry attachment of head, and the like). But with the scarcity of relevant cross-classified data, this attempt would have reduced coverage below the small number of countries included in the tables in the preceding sections. We chose to limit the discussion to size and related structure of household in its division between children and adults because size differentials are the most obvious and general characteristic of households affecting intranational income disparities; we hoped to use the rather consistent findings as a departure point for further exploration.

The direction suggested for such exploration is that of observing size distributions of households, without the scarce and often more defective income data, for a large number of countries and over long periods for some of them. If inequality in the distribution of households by size contributes to inequality in the distribution of income among households (per household) or among the household population per person (or per consuming unit), differences or trends in inequality in the size distribution of households may contribute to differences and trends in income disparities. Consequently, it would be of interest to observe international or other cross-sectional differences in inequality in the size distributions of households and to observe trends over time in the latter. These cross-sectional and temporal comparisons are the subject of a later paper.

NOTES

1. This paper is a sequel to two earlier papers that touch upon this topic, among others bearing on demographic components in the size distribution of income: "Size and Age Structure of Households: Exploratory Comparisons." *Population and Development Review* 4:187–223 (1978); and of more direct relevance, "Demographic Aspects of the Size Distribution of Income: An Exploratory Essay." *Economic Development and Cultural Change* 25:1–94 (1976). Two other recent papers bearing on the findings and analysis here should be noted. One is by Pravin Visaria, "Demographic Factors and the Distribution of Income: Some Issues." in International Union for the Scientific Study of Population, *Economic and Demographic Change: Issues for the 1980's,* Helinski (1979), 1:289–320. The other is by Sheldon Danziger and Michael K. Taussig, "The Income Unit and the Anatomy of Income Distribution." *The Review of Income and Wealth,* Series 25, No. 4, December 1979, pp. 365–375.

2. The difficulties have grown with the rise in recent decades in the supply of basic socioeconomic statistics, for different population subgroups and for countries at widely different

levels of development. In the nature of the relation between the individual scholar and the data producing institutions, the results of scholarly analysis in the preponderant majority of cases are bound to be tentative, subject to revision with the needed improvements in the data base. One can only hope that the explorations by the individual analyst serve to call attention to some important connections, and thus lead to greater attention to the testing and improvement of the supply and quality of the relevant data.

3. For a discussion of this measure, see the 1976 paper listed in Note 1, pp. 12–13. TDM, as expressed here, is best viewed as the sum of deviations, signs disregarded, in relative size per unit (whether the size is number of persons, or income, or consumption, etc.) in the several classes, from the arithmetic mean, such deviations weighted by the percentage share of each class in the relevant total. Thus, in line 1 of Table 1, the entry for the TDM for size differentials among households by number of persons, would read 7.1 percent − 20.6 percent = −13.5 percent, the latter in turn being equal to $(0.345 − 1.00) \times 20.6$ percent, i.e., the relative deviation for the one-person class of households from the country-wide mean, weighted by the percentage share of this class in the total of all households. Expressed as a proper fraction (for United States, size of household inequality, it would then read 0.454), TDM is the ratio of the sum of class deviations, properly weighted, from the arithmetic mean, to the mean.

Both TDM and the slightly more sensitive Gini coefficient tend to understate the full range of differences in the distribution. But there are advantages of simplicity, and, in the case of TDM, ease in identifying the particular classes that are the major sources of inequality. We use the measures on the premise that they are adequate for rough comparisons of order of magnitude—in that substantial differences so revealed would be even greater relatively with more sensitive measures.

4. This means, to illustrate, that Gini coefficients of 0.1 and over and TDMs of well over 15, may be viewed as sufficiently large to assume that they contribute significantly to the inequality in the total distribution to whose component the cited disparity measures refer.

The nonadditivity difficulty could be overcome by converting the underlying distribution to near normal shapes (perhaps by taking logs of size or of income) and using variance measures that can then be assumed to be additive. While this requires elaborate calculations, the results will still be affected by inclusion in the measures for the total distribution by size of income of transient disturbances in their full magnitude—let alone the deficiencies in the income data referred to earlier.

Under the circumstances it seemed best to use simple and undemanding measures, applying them to as large a number of countries or subgroups as feasible, and tracing the relations to the specific size or other classes that could be more easily observed in these simple measures. The hope is that significant associations will be suggested that then may call for the application of the more elaborate measures to cases where the availability of reliable data warrants it.

5. See the 1976 paper cited in Note 1 above, Table 7, p. 25 and Table 17, pp. 57–58, and related discussion in the text.

6. See, in this connection, the 1976 paper referred to in Note 1, particularly Table 9, p. 31 and discussion, pp. 30 and 32.

THE EFFECT OF SAMPLE
TRUNCATION ON ESTIMATES
OF FERTILITY RELATIONSHIPS

Lee E. Edlefsen

ABSTRACT

It is commonly necessary to measure fertility before it is completed and to
base estimates of the effects of independent variables on completed fertility
upon such truncated measures. This paper analyzes the relationship
between such estimates and the true or desired estimates. Surprisingly
strong theoretical restrictions can be placed upon the relationships among
these estimates, and these restrictions are confirmed empirically. The
overall results of this paper are encouraging in terms of the use of truncated
samples. Such samples should in general circumstances provide relatively
good approximate estimates of the desired coefficients. However, the
estimates will be biased, and indeed can be extremely misleading in some
circumstances.

Research in Population Economics, Volume 3, pages 41–66
Copyright © 1981 by JAI Press Inc.
All rights of reproduction in any form reserved.
ISBN: 0-89232-207-1

41

I. INTRODUCTION

The dependent variable of primary interest in the economic theory of fertility is completed fertility. We are often interested in the effect of such independent variables as income and price on this variable. However, data on women who have finished bearing children are difficult to acquire, since childbearing is distributed over a reproductive span of thirty or more years. Even if such data are available they have the disadvantage of containing information on behavior which was for the most part completed long ago. For these and other reasons it is a common practice in fertility analyses to use samples of women who are younger than age 45, and thus for whom reproductive histories are truncated before completion.[1] Consequently, cumulative fertility must be used as a proxy for completed fertility. The question arises: what are the consequences of the use of such samples and such proxies? Despite the prevalence and potential importance of this question, it has received almost no systematic attention in the literature.[2] This paper analyzes some of the problems encountered in using such truncated samples.

If data on completed fertility (to be denoted by "*CEB*," measuring "children ever born" to women over age 45) were available, an equation of the form

$$CEB = \pi X + \epsilon_1 \tag{1}$$

could be estimated, where X is some independent variable such as income, education, race, religion or age at marriage.[3] The coefficient "π" measures the effect of X on *CEB* and is the desired or "true" coefficient.[4] However, if a truncated sample is used, this coefficient cannot be estimated. Imagine, for instance, that the sample used only contains information on the number of children ever born to women of some age (T) less than 45 (denote this measure of fertility by "*CF(T)*," which stands for "cumulative fertility by age T").[5] Then the equation that corresponds to Eq. (1) is

$$CF(T) = \delta(T)X + \epsilon_2 \tag{2}$$

where both cumulative fertility (*CF*) and the coefficient of X are shown as functions of T to emphasize the fact that they will vary by age. The central issue to be examined in this paper is: What is the relationship between the estimated coefficient(s) $\delta(T)$ and the desired coefficient π?

This issue is examined both theoretically and empirically. The most obvious and direct manner in which to ascertain the effects of truncation is to obtain samples in which both completed fertility (CEB) and cumulative fertility (CF) at different ages can be measured, and then to obtain and compare different estimates. This is one of the approaches followed

Table 1.   Definitions of Variables and Symbols

CEB	Children ever born by age 45; completed fertility
CF(T)	Children ever born by age T; cumulative fertility
X	Any independent variable
AM	Age of wife at marriage
AC	Age of wife at birth of first child
EDW	Years of schooling of the wife
YH	Husband's measured income
YHEST	Husband's estimated income at age 40 (see Note 11)
LFP	Wife's labor force participation (see Note 12)
π	The true or desired coefficient in a noncensored sample: $CEB = \pi X + \epsilon$
π_c	Same, but in a censored sample
$\delta(T)$	The observed coefficient in a noncensored, truncated sample: $CF(T) = \delta(T)X + \epsilon$
$\Theta(T)$	Same as $\delta(T)$, but in a censored sample
$\alpha(T), \beta(T)$	The coefficients in $CF(T) = \alpha(T)CEB + \beta(T)X + \epsilon$ in a noncensored sample
$\alpha_c(T), \beta_c(T)$	Same, but in a censored sample
$d(T)$	The coefficient measuring the relationship between X as measured at ages T and S: $X(S) = d(T)X(T) + \epsilon$
PI	π
DELTA	δ
THETA	Θ
PI·ALPHA	$\pi\alpha$
BETA	β
$f_1(T)$	The proportion of women at age T who have not had a child (Group 1)
$f_2(T), CF_2(T)$	The proportion of women at age T who have started but not finished reproduction, and cumulative fertility for these women, respectively (Group 2)
$f_3(T)$	The proportion of women at age T who have completed reproduction (Group 3)
g_2	Proportion of women in Group 2 in a sample censored on the basis of whether or not women have had a child: $g_2 = f_2/1 - f_1$
g_3	Same as g_2, but for Group 3: $g_3 = f_3/1 - f_1$

here.   In addition to this purely empirical approach, however, the relationships among the coefficients can be analyzed theoretically as well. It turns out that surprisingly strong theoretical results can be derived, and these can be used to explain and predict the empirical results.

There are three main reasons for bias in a truncated sample. First, cumulative fertility at any age less than 45 (which for practical purposes may be taken to be the age of menopause) reflects the timing and spacing as well as the ultimate numbers of births. Thus, cumulative fertility measures something very different from completed fertility. Indeed, it might be the case (in fact, it turns out to be the case empirically) that for some independent variables the effect on timing and spacing can be opposite in sign to the effect on completed fertility. In this situation, there is no reason to expect that the effect of the variable on cumulative fertility bears any simple relationship to its effect on completed fertility. Second, the independent variables as measured at an age less than 45 may be different from the "same" variables measured after age 45. And third, it may be the case that the sample of women observed at ages such as 20 or 25 is different from that that would be observed after age 45. The major reason for this difference is sample "censorship;" sometimes women are selectively excluded from the sample even though data are actually available for them. For instance, it is common practice to include in an analysis only those women who are married and/or who have had children. Other reasons for sample differences include mortality and migration.

The analysis that follows is divided into four parts. In the first part (Section II), the effect of sample truncation per se is examined. In the second part (Section III), the effect of measuring the independent variable differently at different ages is analyzed. In the third part (Section IV), the effect of sample censorship is investigated. In the fourth part (Section V), the effect of pooling together different age groups (for instance, of combining all women between the ages of 20 and 35) is examined. In Section VI, the results are summarized.

II. THE EFFECT OF TRUNCATION ALONE

The simplest situation to consider is that in which neither the independent variable nor the composition of the sample vary with age. Cumulative fertility (CF) is measured at successive ages of the mother for a fixed group of women and Eq. (2) can be estimated at each age [including age 45, at which point cumulative fertility becomes completed fertility and Eq. (2) becomes Eq. (1)]

$$CF(20) = \delta(20)X + \epsilon_{20}$$

$$CF(25) = \delta(25)X + \epsilon_{25}$$

$$\vdots$$

$$CF(40) = \delta(40)X + \epsilon_{40}$$

$$CEB = \pi X + \epsilon_{45} \tag{2a}$$

where 5-year age increments have been used and where $CEB = CF(45)$ and $\pi = \delta(45)$. The objective is to examine the way in which $\delta(T)$ varies with age and to compare these values with the desired value π.

It should be pointed out that the specific situation considered here is not commonly encountered in the literature because most samples there are censored (for instance, by including at any age only those women who have been married at least once) and also because different age groups are frequently pooled together. Nevertheless, this situation contains the basic elements that lead to bias in all truncated samples, and its analysis forms the basis of subsequent analyses of more complicated situations. Furthermore, analysis of this situation sheds considerable light on the appropriate procedures for utilizing truncated samples.

To analyze this situation, consider the following two equations

$$CF(T) = \alpha(T)CEB + \beta(T)X + \epsilon_3 \tag{3}$$

$$\delta(T) = \beta(T) + \pi\alpha(T) \tag{4}$$

where Eq. (4) relates the coefficients of Eqs. (1)–(3). (Indeed, this equation is a computational identity when least squares is used to estimate all the coefficients). Equation (4) states that the total effect $\delta(T)$ of an independent variable X on cumulative fertility at any age T can be decomposed into two parts. (1) The first part is $\beta(T)$, which is the coefficient of X in Eq. (3). This coefficient measures the "direct" effect of X on CF, holding CEB (completed fertility or final parity) constant. In other words, $\beta(T)$ measures the response of CF to a change in X within any group of women who end up with the same completed fertility. As an example, imagine that X measures education of the wife and that $\beta(30) = -.06$. This implies that, among women who end up with three children (or any other number of children), those with one more year of education have .06 fewer children by age 30. (2) The second part, $\pi\alpha(T)$, measures the "indirect" effect of X on CF as it acts through CEB. The term $\alpha(T)$ is the coefficient of CEB in Eq. (3) and measures the amount by which cumulative fertility increases (at age T) as completed fertility increases; π measures the total effect of X on CEB. Thus, a unit increase in X will increase CEB by π units, and a unit increase in CEB will increase $CF(T)$ by $\alpha(T)$ units; so a unit increase in X will have an indirect effect on $CF(T)$, through CEB, of $\pi\alpha(T)$ units. As an example, if $\alpha(30) = .40$, this implies that women who end up with one more child at age 45 have .40 more children (on average) at age 30. If an increase in X decreases CEB by $\pi = -.08$, then the indirect effect of X on CF, acting through CEB, is

$$\pi\alpha(T) = (-.08)(.40) = -.032$$

Combining this and the preceding result and using Eq. (4), the total effect of wife's education on cumulative fertility (CF) at age 30 is given by

$$\delta(30) = -.06 + (-.08)(.40) = -.092$$

Thus, in this example, the estimate of the effect of wife's education on cumulative fertility at age 30 [$\delta(30) = -.092$] is a slight overestimate (in absolute value) of the "true" or "desired" coefficient ($\pi = -.08$).

It is, of course, unnecessary to estimate $\alpha(T)$ and $\beta(T)$ in order to obtain $\delta(T)$; that coefficient can be estimated directly. Nevertheless, it is possible to place surprisingly strong theoretical restrictions on $\alpha(T)$ and $\beta(T)$ and thereby [through Equation (4)] on $\delta(T)$. It is convenient in continuing this analysis to generalize Eq. (4) to nonlinear relationships. Thus, Eq. (4) becomes[6]

$$\frac{dCF(T)}{dX} = \left.\frac{\partial CF(T)}{\partial X}\right|_{CEB} + \left(\frac{dCEB}{dX}\right)\left(\frac{\partial CF(T)}{\partial CEB}\right)\Big|_{X} \tag{5}$$

where $\beta(T)$ corresponds to $[\partial CF(T)/\partial X]|_{CEB}$ [this correspondence will be denoted by $\beta(T) \doteq \partial CF(T)/\partial X\,|_{CEB}$] and so on.[7] Notice that at any age T, some women will not yet have begun to reproduce, some will be in the midst of bearing children, and some will have completed childbearing. Let $f_1(T)$, $f_2(T)$, and $f_3(T)$ represent the proportions of women in each of these three groups, and let $CF_1(T)$, $CF_2(T)$, and $CF_3(T)$ represent cumulative fertility at age T in each group, respectively. Obviously, by the definition of the groups

$$CF_1(T) = 0$$

Thus

$$CF(T) = f_2(T) \cdot CF_2(T) + f_3(T) \cdot CF_3(T) \tag{6}$$

Note also that

$$CF_3(T) = CEB$$

Using Equation (6), the terms corresponding to $\alpha(T)$ and $\beta(T)$ can be expressed as follows

$$\alpha \doteq \frac{\partial CF}{\partial CEB} = \frac{\partial CF_2}{\partial CEB} \cdot f_2 + f_3 + \frac{\partial f_2}{\partial CEB} \cdot CF_2 + \frac{\partial f_3}{\partial CEB} \cdot CF_3 \tag{7}$$

$$\beta \doteq \frac{\partial CF}{\partial X} = \frac{\partial CF_2}{\partial X} \cdot f_2 + \frac{\partial f_2}{\partial X} \cdot CF_2 + \frac{\partial f_3}{\partial X} \cdot CF_3 \tag{8}$$

where explicit dependence upon T has been dropped for notational convenience. All partials with respect to CEB [Equation (7)] are taken holding X constant, and vice versa [Equation (8)]. Note that the partial of CF_3 with respect to X drops out of Eq. (8) because CF_3 equals CEB and CEB is being held constant. Consider the values of α and β at the beginning of the reproductive period. Before any women have begun to reproduce, $f_1 = 1$ and $f_2 = f_3 = 0$; in addition, $CF_2 = CF_3 = 0$ and the partials of f_2 and f_3 with respect to CEB and X are zero. Consequently, $\alpha = \beta = 0$. At the end of the reproductive period (age 45), $f_3 = 1$ and $f_1 = f_2 = 0$; in addition, the partials of f_2 and f_3 with respect to CEB and X are zero. Consequently, $\alpha(45) = f_3 = 1$ and $\beta(45) = 0$.

These results imply that α must go from 0 to 1 over the reproductive period, while β must begin and end at 0.[8] If the pace of childbearing is fairly even, then α and β can be expected to be fairly symmetric around the midpoint of the reproductive period.[9] That is

$$\alpha(A) \cong 1 - \alpha(45 - A)$$

$$\beta(A) \cong \beta(45 - A)$$

where A is age measured from the beginning of the reproductive period. Thus, it is reasonable to expect that $\alpha(T)$ will increase monotonically and symmetrically from 0 to 1, while $\beta(T)$ will have a fairly symmetric "U"-shaped path as age increases over the reproductive period.

The actual shapes of the age patterns of $\alpha(T)$ and $\beta(T)$ can easily be checked empirically. This is done using four samples: a sample of U.S. Whites, a sample of U.S. Blacks, and rural and urban samples from the Philippines.[10] Each sample contains reproductive histories for individual women who are aged 45 or older. Consequently, both completed fertility (CEB) and cumulative fertility [$CF(T)$] at every age are available, and all four coefficients $\alpha(T)$, $\beta(T)$, $\gamma(T)$, and π can be computed.[11] It turns out that in these samples very few women have begun to reproduce at age 20, so that $\alpha(20)$, $\beta(20)$, and $\gamma(20)$ are all close to zero. Consequently, age 20 has been used as the lower bound on the reproductive period in computing the coefficients.

The value of $\alpha(T)$ is plotted in Plot 1 against age for each of the four samples. As can be seen, the relationships are all very close to being linear and rise from 0 to 1 between the ages of 20 and 45. The results in this plot are taken from ordinary least squares regressions in which age of marriage of the wife is the independent variable (X). However, the pattern is not sensitive to the X variable used.

Included in Plots 2–7 are plots of the age patterns of β for six different, commonly encountered independent variables (using data from the U.S. White population): the level of education of the wife (EDW), husband's measured income at the time of the sample (YH), husband's estimated income at age 40 ($YHEST$),[12] wife's labor force participation (LFP),[13] age of the wife at marriage (AM), and age of the wife at birth of the first child (AC).[14] In each case, the basic U-shaped pattern of β is quite distinct, as β moves from about 0 at age 20 to 0 at age 45.[15] Similar patterns are observed for the coefficients of these types of variables in the other samples as well (these plots are not included here).

The age pattern of $\delta(T)$ [which, again, is the coefficent of X in Eq. (2) and is the coefficient that would be observed in a truncated sample] is the sum of age patterns of $\beta(T)$ and $\pi\alpha(T)$. Consequently, $\delta(T)$ is approximately the sum of a U-shaped curve and a straight line. Since $\alpha(T)$ is

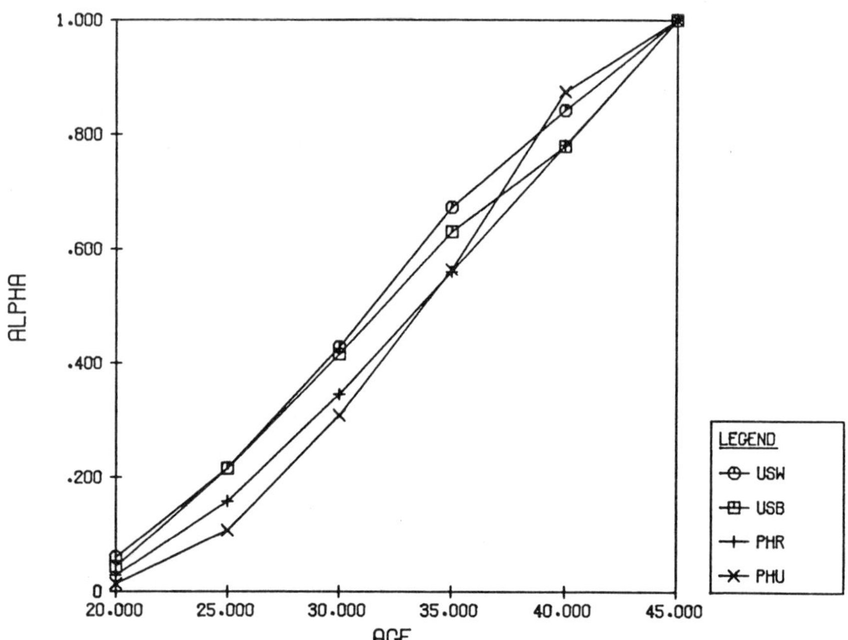

Plot 1. Alpha versus Age

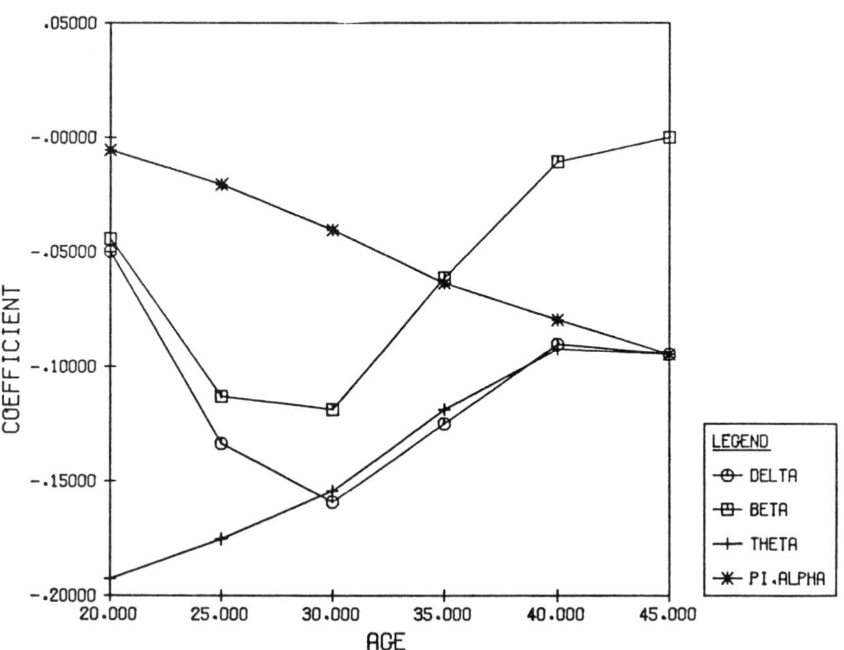

Plot 2. Coefficients of AM versus Age, U.S. White Sample

Plot 3.   Coefficients of AC versus Age, U.S. White Sample

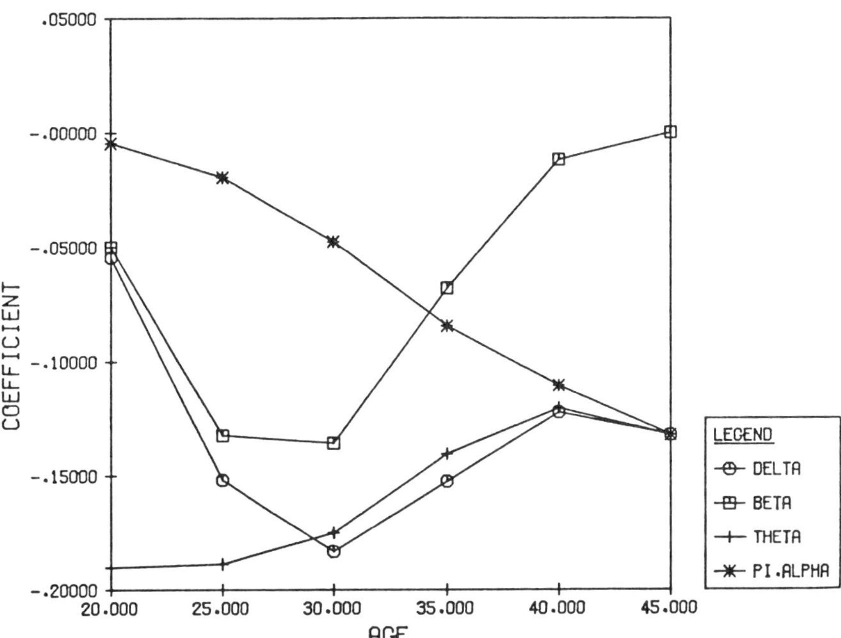

Plot 4.   Coefficients of EDW versus Age, U.S. White Sample

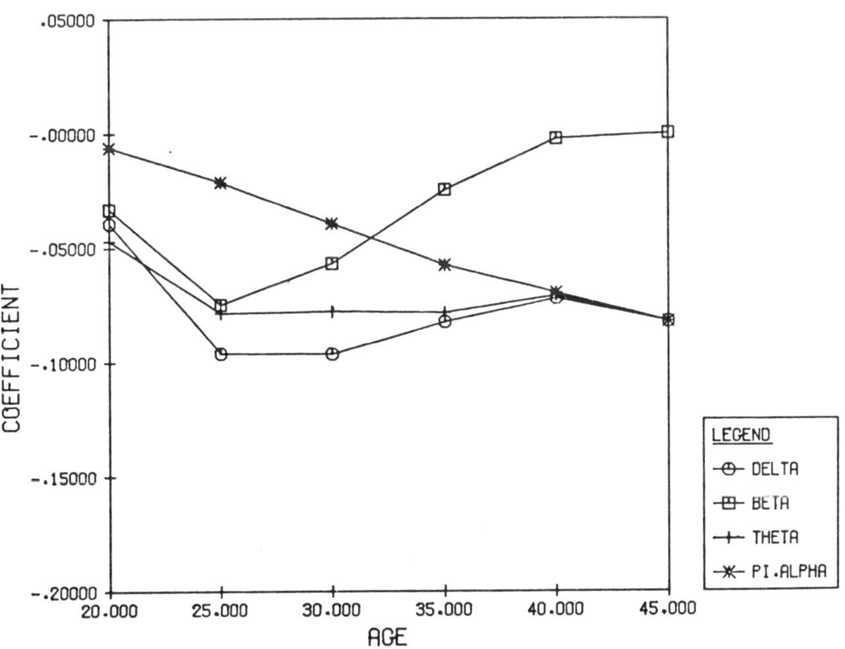

Plot 5.   Coefficients of YH versus Age, U.S. White Sample

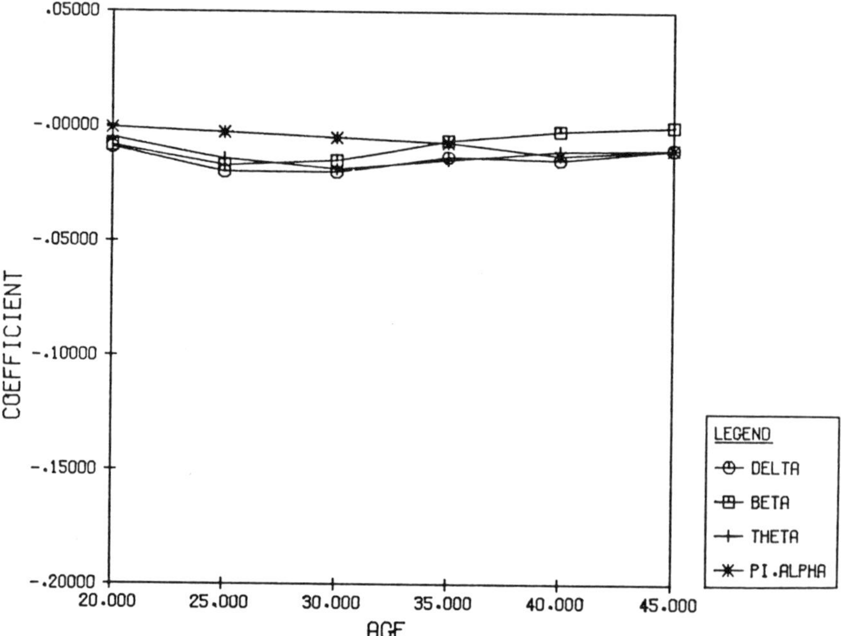

Plot 6.   Coefficients of YHEST versus Age, U.S. White Sample

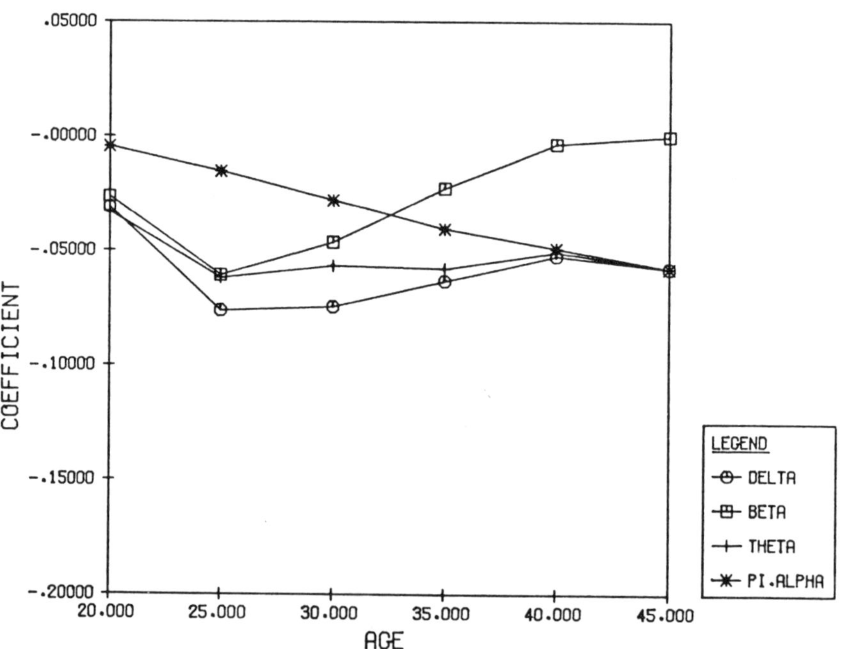

Plot 7. Coefficients of LFP versus Age U.S. White Sample

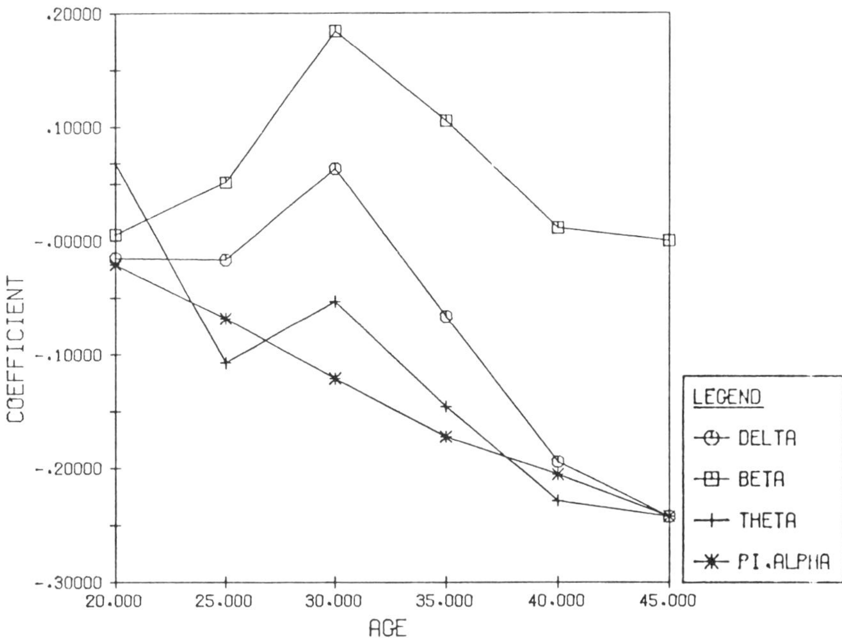

always positive, with a magnitude between 0 and 1, the sign of $\pi\alpha(T)$ is determined by sign of π, which is the effect of X on CEB. The term $\beta(T)$ measures the effect of X on cumulative fertility holding CEB constant and thus reflects the effects of X on the timing and spacing of births. This can be made more explicit. Note first that for those women who are in the midst of bearing children (Group 2), cumulative fertility (CF_2) at age T can be expressed as the product of the length of time since childbearing started ($T - AC$, where AC is age at first birth) and the average number of children born per unit of time, which is the reciprocal of average spacing (S). Thus

$$CF_2 = (T - AC)\frac{1}{S}$$

Note also that $f_1 + f_2 + f_3 = 1$. Consequently, the expression corresponding to β can be rewritten as

$$\beta \doteq \frac{\partial CF}{\partial X} = - \left(\frac{\partial AC}{\partial X} \cdot \frac{1}{S} + \frac{\partial S}{\partial X} \cdot \frac{T - AC}{S^2} \right) \cdot f_2$$

$$- \frac{\partial f_1}{\partial X} \cdot CF_2 + \frac{\partial f_3}{\partial X} (CF_3 - CF_2) \tag{8a}$$

where all partials are conditioned upon *CEB*. Thus, for example, if an increase in X induces later childbearing and longer birth intervals, it will also induce an increase in f_1 and a decrease in f_3, and β will be negative at every value of T. In this case, it would usually be expected that π would also be negative, so that β and $\pi\alpha(T)$ would have the same sign. However, it is quite possible for an independent variable X to increase *CF* at every age (conditional upon *CEB*) while decreasing *CEB*, so that β and $\pi\alpha(T)$ have opposite signs.

In Plots 2–7 are plotted the values of $\beta(T)$, $\pi\alpha(T)$, and their sum, $\delta(T)$, for six independent variables (as discussed earlier) using U.S. White data. (The coefficients Θ refer to censored samples and will be discussed later). Note again that $\delta(45) = \pi$, where π is the "desired" coefficient. For all but one of the variables (*LFP*), the two terms $\beta(T)$ and $\pi\alpha(T)$ have the same sign and thus augment each other. Consequently, $\gamma(T)$ tends to increase (in absolute value) until age 25 or 30 and then begins to decline. This rise and fall is determined by the rise and fall of $\beta(T)$, and so the maximum (minimum) falls near the center of the reproductive period. The decline in $\delta(T)$ continues until about age 40, at which point the shape of $\delta(T)$ comes to be dominated by $\pi\alpha(T)$. At this point, there tends to be a fairly sharp jump or change in slope, and $\delta(T)$ rises again (in absolute value) until it reaches the value π at age 45.

In the U.S. White sample for those variables for which β and π have the same sign, the value of δ at its peak is greater (in absolute value) than is the desired value π. However, this is probably unusual. Since α varies between 0 and 1, $\pi\alpha(T)$ is less than π at all ages less than 45. Furthermore, this term tends to increase linearly. Thus, the relation between $\delta(T)$ and π will depend primarily upon the magnitude of $\beta(T)$. In the U.S. White sample, timing and spacing are fairly responsive (at least to the variables examined), and the peak magnitudes of β approximate the magnitude of π. Consequently, $\delta(T)$ at its peak tends to overestimate π. However, in the other samples, timing and spacing are not so responsive; $\beta(T)$ is small relative to π, and $\delta(T)$ tends to underestimate π (or at least not to overestimate it) even at its peak. This is illustrated in Plots 8 and 9 in which $\delta(T)$ is plotted for each of the four samples (for the independent variables *AM* and *AC*, respectively).

The results presented in Plots 2–9 present a fairly optimistic picture of the effects of sample truncation as long as the timing and spacing effect, $\beta(T)$, has the same sign as the desired coefficient π. Particularly within the center of the childbearing period (ages 25–35), the extent of underestimation or overestimation does not seem large. Consequently, truncated samples probably give a good idea of the sign and approximate magnitude of the desired coefficient in this age range. However, when $\beta(T)$ and π differ in sign, this is no longer the case. This is illustrated by Plot 7,

Plot 8.   DELTA of AM versus Age (Noncensored Samples)

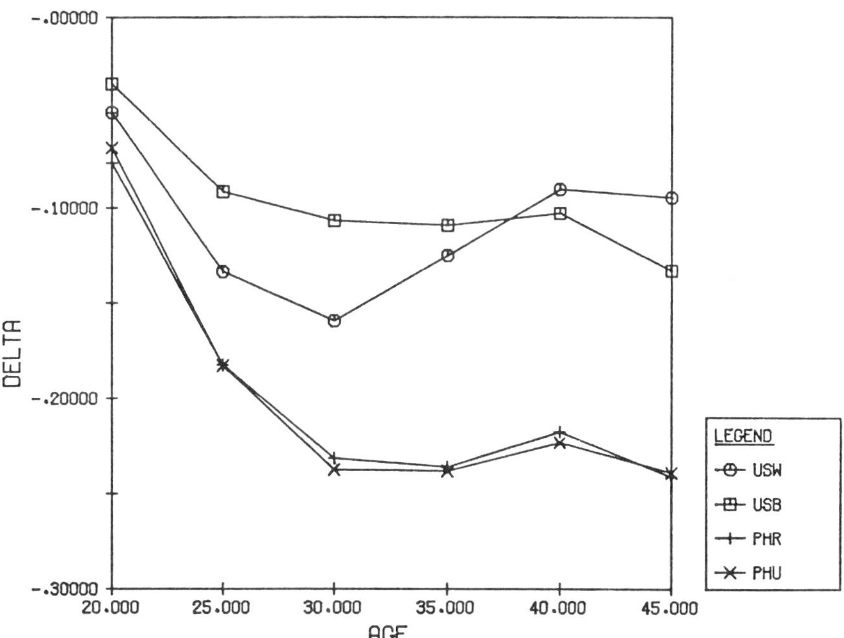

Plot 9.   DELTA of AC versus Age (Noncensored Samples)

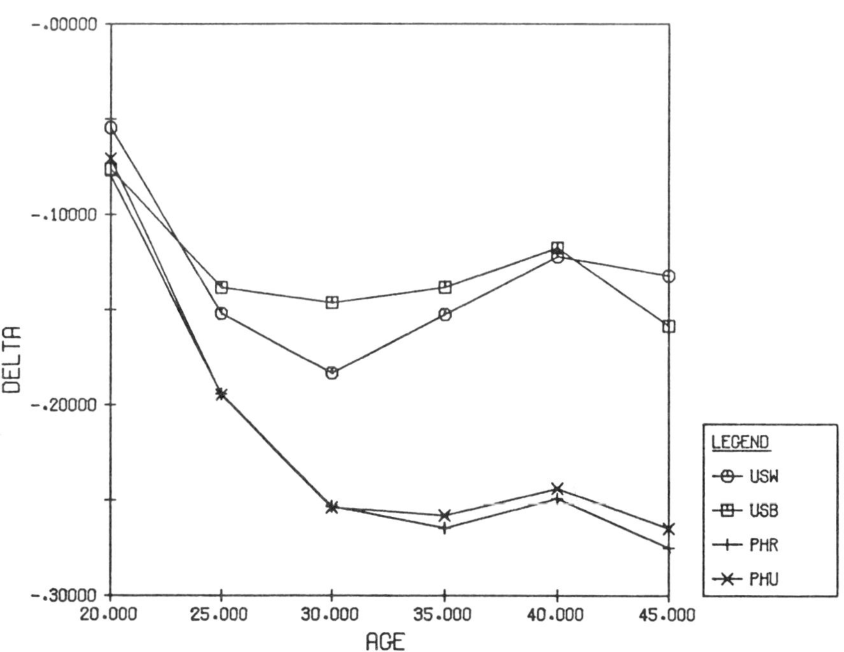

53

which shows the effect of labor force participation (*LFP*) in the U.S. White sample. The coefficient $\beta(T)$ is positive for all T while $\pi\alpha(T)$ is negative, and their sum $\delta(T)$ bears no relation to π. In this situation, the results from truncated samples are meaningless as approximations to π.

III. THE EFFECT OF DIFFERING MEASURES OF THE INDEPENDENT VARIABLES

The preceding analysis considered the situation in which the measured independent variable X did not vary with age. For instance, variables like age at marriage (*AM*), age at first birth (*AC*), and education (*EDW*) will normally (though not always) be established early in the life cycle and remain fixed thereafter. Similarly, the estimated income of the husband at age 40 (*YHEST*) is typically based upon variables that remain fixed. However, such variables as husband's measured income (*YH*) and wife's labor force participation (*LFP*) will tend to change from year to year.

The effect of using independent variables that change over time (with age) can easily be analyzed by extending the previous analysis. The objective is to determine the effect, for instance, of using *YH* as measured at some age such as 30 instead of *YH* as measured at some age after age 45. Designate the former value as *YH*(*T*) and the latter as *YH*(*S*). Analysis of the effect of using *YH*(*T*) instead of *YH*(*S*) requires the addition of one equation to the set [Eqs. (1)–(3)] previously considered

$$CEB = \pi X(S) + \epsilon_2 \tag{9}$$

$$CF(T) = \delta X(T) + \epsilon_1 \tag{10}$$

$$CF(T) = \alpha CEB + \beta X(T) + \epsilon_3 \tag{11}$$

$$X(S) = dX(T) + \epsilon_4 \tag{12}$$

The last equation gives the relationship between $X(S)$ and $X(T)$. Combining these equations, the new bias formula is

$$\delta(T) = \beta(T) + \pi\alpha(T)d(T) \tag{13}$$

This corresponds to the basic Eq. (4).

The fact that $X(S)$ differs from $X(T)$ introduces a new source of bias, in the form of the term d. This term measures the extent to which $X(S)$ changes as $X(T)$ changes. If a one unit change in X at age T is usually associated with a similar change at age S, then d will be close to 1. In this situation (which is approximately the case for income), no additional bias will be introduced by the use of differing measures of the independent variables.

The coefficient d is itself a function of T, and as T approaches S it will go to 1. On these grounds, the effect of d should generally grow less as T

increases. At the same time, d affects δ only after it is multiplied by $\pi\alpha$, and $\pi\alpha$ approaches 0 as age declines. These considerations together suggest that for many variables the effect of d will be small at every age, with the largest effect coming in the middle of the reproductive period.

Note that even when d does have a significant effect on δ, it may either lessen or worsen the extent to which δ is a biased estimate of π, depending upon the circumstances. With the data available for this paper, unfortunately, it was not possible to test empirically this type of effect.

IV. THE EFFECT OF SAMPLE CENSORSHIP

It is fairly common to exlude from an anlysis women who have not married and/or have not borne children.[16] Because of such censorship, proportionately fewer and fewer women are included in samples as age declines. This has the effect of introducing an additional source of bias into studies that use truncated samples.

The easiest such situation to analyze is that in which women who have not borne children (Group 1) are excluded at each age. Of the women who remain in the sample, let g_2 be the fraction who have started but not finished reproducing and let g_3 be the fraction who have finished. Thus

$$g_2 = \frac{f_2}{1 - f_1} \tag{14}$$

$$g_3 = \frac{f_3}{1 - f_1} \tag{15}$$

and

$$CF = g_2 CF_2 + g_3 CF_3 \tag{16}$$

(The effect of censorship based upon marital status is very similar to this and will not be considered separately.)

Let α_c, β_c, and π_c be the coefficients in a censored sample that correspond to α, β, and π, respectively, in an uncensored sample. Similarly, let $\Theta(T)$ be the observed effect of X on $CF(T)$ in a censored, truncated sample, corresponding to $\delta(T)$ in an uncensored, truncated sample. Thus

$$\Theta = \alpha_c \pi_c + \beta_c \tag{17}$$

In this and the following section, it will again be assumed that X does not vary with age.

Given Eqs. (14)–(16), the terms corresponding to α_c and β_c can be expressed as

$$\alpha_c \doteq \frac{\partial CF}{\partial CEB} = \frac{\partial CF_2}{\partial CEB} \cdot g_2 + g_3 + \frac{\partial g_2}{\partial CEB} \cdot CF_2 + \frac{\partial g_3}{\partial CEB} \cdot CF_3 \tag{18}$$

$$\beta_c \doteq \frac{\partial CF}{\partial X} = \frac{\partial CF_2}{\partial X} \cdot g_2 + \frac{\partial g_2}{\partial X} \cdot CF_2 + \frac{\partial g_3}{\partial X} \cdot CF_3 \tag{19}$$

As T changes, α_c and β_c will change for two reasons: (1) For any fixed sample of women, the components of the above expressions change with age, as in the case of α and β; and (2) the samples themselves change, and it may be that the components of the above expressions change with the sample. This would occur if women who begin bearing children early behave differently (in the sense of having different coefficients of response to independent variables) than those who begin late.[17] The first effect can be evaluated fairly easily; the second is more difficult to evaluate theoretically but does not appear too important empirically.

Note that the estimate of the effect of X on CEB (i.e., π_c) may itself be a function of age in a censored sample (it is, of course, a constant in an uncensored sample). This is due solely to reason (2) above: the behavioral response may vary among samples of women.

The age pattern of $\delta(T)$ has already been analyzed; thus it is convenient to anlyze $\Theta(T)$ by comparing it with $\delta(T)$. This is best done by comparing each term in turn: α_c with α, π_c with π, and β_c with β. Note first that censored samples become more and more similar to uncensored samples as age increases. Consequently $\Theta(T)$ will approach $\delta(T)$ as T approaches 45. Indeed, since nearly all women who will ever do so have begun to reproduce by age 30, the results from censored and uncensored samples may be very similar by that age, or at least by age 35. Consequently, the effects of censorship are most pronounced in the first half of the reproductive period.

The coefficient α_c must go to 0 as T declines, just as does α. (Note that g_3 and the partials of CF_2, g_2, and g_3 must all go to 0 at the lower end of the reproductive period.) However, the manner in which α_c goes to 0 might be expected to be somewhat different from the way in which α does. This is because f_2 goes to 0 as T declines while g_2 goes to 1. Nevertheless, empirically α_c and α seem to be very similar, although α_c has a tendency to underestimate α at low values of T (in the samples examined). Fortuitously, this is offset by the fact that π_c tends to overestimate π at low values of T and to decline monotonically toward π as T increases. As a consequence, the product $\pi_c\alpha_c$ tends to be close to $\pi\alpha$ at all values of T.

Since $\pi_c\alpha_c$ and $\pi\alpha$ tend to be close, the differences between $\delta(T)$ and $\Theta(T)$ must for the most part arise from differences between β and β_c. Note that β_c must be 0 at both ends of the reproductive period, as does β. However, because of the difference between g_2 and f_2 (as discussed earlier), the age patterns of β_c and β might be expected to differ. To analyze these differences, it is useful to consider the following expression

$$\beta_c - \beta \doteq \left(\frac{f_1}{1 - f_1}\right)\beta + \left(\frac{f_2 \cdot CF_2 + f_3 \cdot CF_3}{(1 - f_1)^2}\right)\frac{\partial f_1}{\partial X} \tag{20}$$

Since f_1 represents the proportion of women at every age who have not begun to reproduce, it will nearly always be the case that $\partial f_1/\partial X$ and β (which represents the effect of X on CF, given CEB) will have opposite signs. For instance, increasing wife's education (EDW) will generally decrease cumulative fertility and increase the proportion of women who have not begun to reproduce (conditional upon CEB, at every T). Thus, $\beta_c - \beta$ is the sum of terms of opposite sign. It appears empirically that the first term dominates at low values of T, since f_2, f_3, CF_2, and CF_3 all go to 0 fairly rapidly as T declines. Thus, at low values of T, β_c tends to exceed β in absolute value. As is shown in Eq. 20, the extent by which β_c exceeds β as age declines will depend upon the relative speeds at which $f_1/1 - f_1$ goes to infinity and β goes to 0. In the U.S. White sample, the average age at which women begin reproduction is fairly high, and the proportion who have not begun to reproduce (f_1) is correspondingly high at ages 20 and 25. Thus, the extent by which β_c exceeds β at these ages tends to be large. As is shown in Plots 6 and 7, for this sample and for the variables AM and AC, the coefficient $\Theta(T)$ actually increases in absolute value as T declines below the age of 30 (of course, ages below 20 are not represented). In the other samples, the value of f_1 is smaller at ages 20 and 25 than it is in the U.S. White sample, and consequently the differences between Θ and δ are not as great at these ages.

Plot 10.   THETA of AM versus Age (Censored Samples)

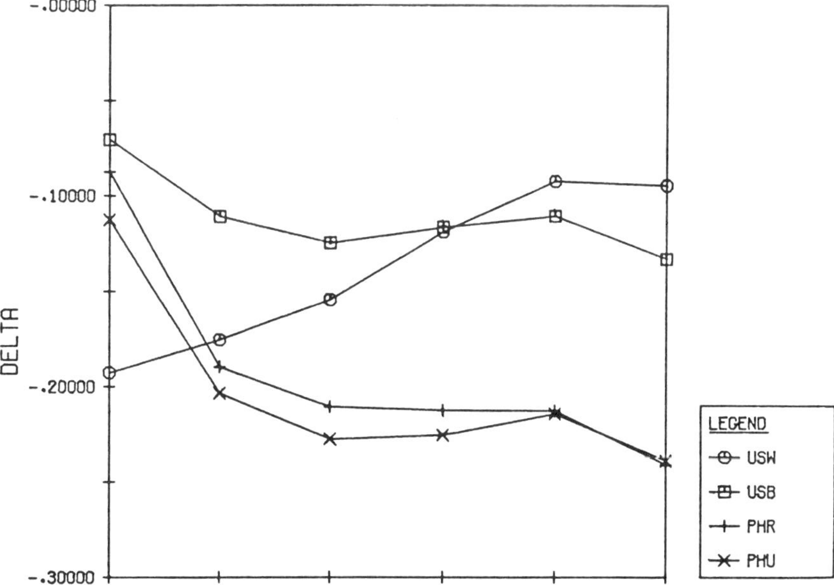

Plot 11. THETA of AC versus AGE (Censored Samples)

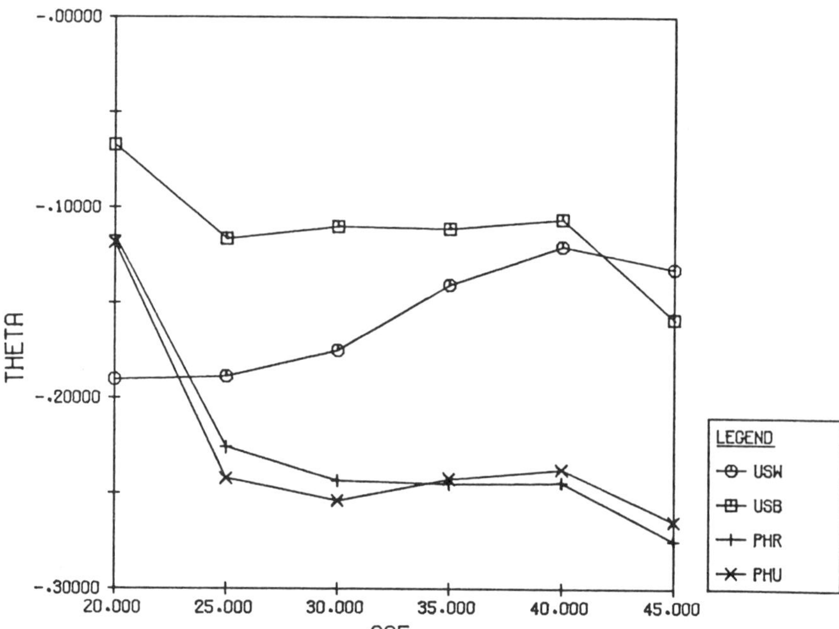

As age increases, the second term in Eq. (20) comes to dominate the difference between β_c and β. Thus, in general, β_c will tend to overestimate β (in absolute value) at low values of T but to underestimate it at high values of T (though equality will be reached by age 45, of course). This pattern is observed in nearly all of the variables examined for this paper. The switchover point generally occurs before the age of 30, and the amount by which Θ underestimates δ above age 30 is generally not large, as was pointed out previously. In Plots 2–7, the values of Θ are plotted along with δ (and β and $\pi\alpha$) for the six variables for the U.S. White sample. The values of Θ for age at marriage (AM) and age at first birth (AC) are plotted for all samples in Plots 10 and 11 and may be compared with the values of δ for the uncensored samples in Plots 8 and 9.

As may be seen in the plots, the fact that Θ tends to overestimate δ at low ages (below about 30) and to underestimate it at high ages gives Θ a flatter age pattern than δ. Because of this, Θ tends to provide better estimates of π than does δ. This is particularly true in the samples other than the U.S. White (see Plots 10 and 11). Between the ages 25 and 40, the estimates from truncated, censored samples tend to be fairly good approximations to the desired values.[18]

V. THE EFFECT OF POOLING OF DIFFERENT AGE GROUPS

The results of this paper have so far referred only to the situation in which cumulative fertility $[CF(T)]$ at one specific age is regressed upon the independent variables. A more common situation in practice is one in which women of different ages are "pooled" or grouped together and a single relationship is estimated.[19] This situation can be analyzed by combining results developed previously.

The analysis of the preceding sections has shown that in both uncensored and censored samples, the estimated coefficients $\delta(T)$ and $\Theta(T)$, respectively, have a systematic age pattern. In other words, two successive age groups will have coefficients [e.g., $\delta(T)$, $\delta(T + 1)$] that will in general be different. If these two age groups are pooled together and a single coefficient is estimated (label this coefficient δ_p), an implicit restriction being made is that the coefficients in the different age groups are the same. Clearly, this restriction will not be correct. Thus there is a sense in which pooling is fundamentally inappropriate. At least, some attempt should be made to allow the coefficient of X (e.g., δ or Θ) to vary with T. For instance, this might be done by using dummy variables to allow the coefficients to vary in a nonlinear pattern across age groups. Or it might be done by pooling only within fairly small age groups.

However, what is the effect of ignoring the fact that the coefficients vary with age and of simply pooling and estimating a single coefficent? This is not easy to answer exactly because there is no simple computational relationship between the coefficient obtained from a pooled regression (using a linear estimator such as least squares) and the coefficients obtained at each single year of age. Nevertheless, on average, over repeated random samplings, the coefficient of the pooled regression will equal the sum of the single-year coefficients weighted by the proportions of women in each age group. For instance, if all women between the ages 20 and 35 are grouped together, the expected value of the coefficient of X is the average of the single-year coefficients between the ages 20 and 35 (weighted by the proportions at each age group). This is true for both censored and uncensored samples. (Of course, while this relationship will hold on average, in any particular sample it will not hold exactly. Indeed, sometimes the observed relationship can be very different from this.)

The above consideration suggests that a single coefficient estimated from a pooled sample will frequently be a good approximation to the desired coefficient. This should be true for both censored and uncensored samples, and should especially be true if the samples include ages near the middle of the reproductive period (since the single-year coefficients in these ages tend to be good approximations to the desired values). The effect of pooling can be tested empirically, and in Table 2 are reported the results of pooled estimates for the six variables in the U.S. White sample. The pertinent results are reported in the odd-numbered columns. These are estimates taken from equations of the form

$$CF = \delta_p X + \epsilon \tag{21}$$

for censored and uncensored samples, as indicated (the remaining columns will be discussed later). Two age groupings (20–35 and 30–45) are used. As can be seen, in most cases the pooled estimates are approximately an average of the unpooled estimates (which are shown in Plots 2–7). Furthermore, they are on the whole fairly good approximations to the desired estimates. The major exception to the rule that the pooled estimates are weighted averages of unpooled estimates arises for labor force participation (*LFP*). Surprisingly, for this variable, the pooled estimates are better approximations to the desired value than are any of the unpooled results (however, it would probably not be wise to trust this result to hold in other samples).

Since the dependent variable, cumulative fertility, clearly varies with the age of the woman in a pooled truncated sample, it is tempting to include age (T) as a control variable and to estimate an equation of the form[20]

$$CF = \delta_p' X + \beta T + \epsilon \tag{22}$$

However, when the objective is to obtain an estimate δ_p' as an approximation to the desired coefficient π, there is no reason why this procedure should be appropriate. Indeed, it may do considerable harm. Note that introducing T will affect the coefficient of X only if there is some correlation between X and T. In an uncensored sample, there are two reasons for such a correlation: (1) X varies with age for each individual, or (2) X changes over time across cohorts. The types of X variables considered in this paper do not change rapidly with either age or cohort, and consequently inclusion of T will have very little effect on their coefficients in uncensored samples. In censored samples, T and X may in addition be correlated because of the way in which the sample is censored. For instance, when women who have not married are excluded from the sample at each age, AM and T will be positively correlated. In this circumstance, inclusion of T may have substantial effects on the estimate of δ_p', and there is no reason why this effect should be beneficial. The even-numbered columns in Table 2 present pooled estimates when T is included as a regressor. As expected, the inclusion of T has very little effect in uncensored samples (except in the case of *LFP*, which has fairly strong age variation). In the younger pooled group (20–35), T has a strong effect

Table 2. Pooled Estimates of Delta and Theta, U.S. White Sample, All Variables

| | Ages 20–35 | | | | Ages 30–45 | | | | |
| | Censored (Θ) | | Uncensored (δ) | | Censored (Θ) | | Uncensored (δ) | | |
	No T (1)	T (2)	No T (3)	T (4)	No T (5)	T (6)	No T (7)	T (8)	"True" estimate (π)
AM	−.11 (−9)	−.17 (−16)	−.12 (−20)	−.13 (−26)	−.11 (−13)	−.11 (−14)	−.12 (−16)	−.12 (−17)	−.095 (−10)
AC	−.11 (−10)	−.18 (−19)	−.14 (−29)	−.14 (−37)	−.13 (−18)	−.14 (−20)	−.15 (−23)	−.15 (−25)	−.132 (−16)
EDW	−.084 (−8)	−.089 (−9)	−.10 (−13)	−.090 (−13)	−.082 (−8)	−.078 (−8)	−.090 (−9)	−.084 (−9)	−.082 (−7)
YH	−.022 (−3)	−.023 (−4)	−.025 (−6.0)	−.021 (−5.6)	−.015 (−3)	−.014 (−3)	−.017 (−3)	−.015 (−3)	−.010 (−1.6)
YHEST	−.066 (−6)	−.071 (−6)	−.079 (−10)	−.071 (−10)	−.059 (−6)	−.057 (−6)	−.067 (−7)	−.064 (−7)	−.058 (−5)
LFP	−.19 (−2)	−.12 (−1.3)	−.17 (−2.3)	−.066 (−1.0)	−.18 (−2)	−.14 (−1.5)	−.048 (−.5)	−.0008 (−.009)	−.24 (−2.2)

Notes: (1) *t*-statistics in parentheses. (2) For a description of these variables, see Table 1. (3) Censored samples are censored by excluding women who have not yet borne children at every age. (4) "T" and "No T" refer to models that include and exclude, respectively, *T* (age) as a control variable.

on the coefficients of *AM* and *AC* (and biases them away from the desired coefficients), reflecting the effect of censoring. Otherwise *T* has little effect.[21]

VI. SUMMARY

Estimates from truncated samples of the effects of independent variables (*X*) on cumulative fertility will tend to differ from similar estimates of effects on completed fertility. The extent of this bias depends especially upon the age at which cumulative fertility is measured. Indeed, the effects of independent variables on cumulative fertility have age patterns whose general shapes depend primarily upon the way in which the estimates are obtained, rather than upon the independent variables or upon the sample.

In situations in which truncation alone is the issue, the observed coefficient $\delta(T)$ will be the sum of two terms, $\pi\alpha(T)$ and $\beta(T)$. The term $\alpha(T)$ measures the relationship between cumulative fertility (*CF*) and completed fertility (*CEB*) at each age, holding *X* constant. It moves from 0 to 1 over the reproductive period and tends to have a linear age pattern, regardless of *X* or of the sample. The term π measures the effect of *X* on *CEB* and is thus the true or "desired" coefficient. It is a constant with respect to age; consequently, $\pi\alpha$ varies linearly between 0 and π and the sign of $\pi\alpha$ is determined always by π. The term β measures the effect of *X* on *CF*, holding *CEB* constant, and thus reflects the effects of *X* on the timing and spacing of births. It must take on the value 0 at both ends of the reproductive period, and it follows a fairly symmetric U-shaped path in between. Consequently, in general, the age pattern of the observed coefficient δ will be the sum of a straight line ($\pi\alpha$) and a U-shaped curve (β).

When the effect of *X* on timing and spacing (as measured by β) has the same sign as the effect on completed fertility (π), then δ will be the sum of two terms that augment each other. Over the first half of the reproductive period, δ will thus tend to increase in absolute value. The peak value of δ will occur somewhere in the center of the reproductive period; beyond this, δ will tend to fall until about age 40, at which point it will rise again to take on the value π at age 45. As a general rule, under these circumstances δ will tend to underestimate π except in the center of the reproductive period. The smaller β is (the responsiveness of timing and spacing to *X*), the greater will be the amount by which δ underestimates π, at any age. As a general rule, when β and π have the same sign, δ seems to be a fairly good estimator of the sign and approximate magnitude of π within the age range 25–35.

When π and β have different signs for some independent variable (as they do for labor force participation in the U.S. White sample), δ will in general bear no relation at all to π.

The use of different independent variables at different ages will introduce an additional source of bias into the relationship between δ and π. However, this type of effect should usually not be large for most commonly used variables. When it is large, it may either increase or decrease the bias of δ as an estimate of π.

When samples are censored by excluding women who have never borne children, the effect will usually be to raise the estimate (Θ) at lower ages relative to what it would be in a noncensored sample (δ) and to lower the estimate at higher ages. Thus, Θ will frequently have a more flat time path than will δ. In the samples examined for this paper, the estimates of effects from censored samples (Θ) tend to be somewhat better than estimates from noncensored samples (δ) as estimates of π, at least within the middle of the reproductive period. However, the difference is not great in this age range. The effect of excluding unmarried women will be very similar to that of excluding women who have not had children.

Because of the fact that the coefficients from truncated samples vary with age, there is a sense in which it is fundamentally inappropriate to pool age groups together and to estimate only a single coefficient. At least, an attempt should be made to allow the coefficient of X to vary with age. Nevertheless, if a single coefficient is estimated, it will tend to be (on average over repeated random samples) equal to the weighted average of the single-year coefficients. Consequently, if the pooled age groupings are concentrated in the center of the reproductive period (ages 25–35), the pooled estimate may be a fairly good approximation to the desired coefficient (π). This is true for both censored and uncensored samples. There is never any good justification for the common practise of including age or marital duration as control variables in a pooled anlysis when only a single coefficient is being estimated.

The overall results of this paper are fairly encouraging in terms of the use of truncated samples. That is, such samples should give fairly good approximate estimates of the desired coefficients, at least in the common circumstance in which the signs of β and π are equal. Nevertheless, the results are still biased. Indeed, they can be extremely biased, and such samples should not be used when more appropriate data are available.

ACKNOWLEDGMENTS

I am indebted to the able research assistance of Prapan Tianwatenada in helping to prepare the data tapes to be analyzed, of Gerrit van der Wees in preparing the plots, and of Terry Wayment in helping with the programming. This research was supported by a grant from the Graduate School Research Fund at the University of Washington. I have benfited greatly from comments by Margaret Moody Marini, Tom Pullum, and Nicole Urban on an earlier draft. I would like to thank Dr. Mercedes Concepcion, Dean of the Population Institute at the University of the Philippines for permission to use the 1973 Philippine National Demographic Survey.

NOTES

1. As an illustration of the prevalence of this problem, a sampling of articles in the journals *Demography* and *Population Studies* for the years 1973–1977 revealed 14 studies which used truncated samples to ascertain the effects of independent variables on numbers of children ever born, and none in which the samples were not truncated. The articles which used truncated samples are Bean and Wood, 1974, Ben-Porath, 1975, Boyd, 1973, Cain and Weininger, 1973, Chamie, 1977, Chadhury, 1977, Goldstein, 1973, Hull and Hull, 1977, Jiobu and Marshall, 1977, Kim, *et al.*, 1974, Pitcher, *et al.*, 1974, Ritchey, 1975, Snyder, 1974, and Weller, 1977. Some of these studies use aggregated data, although most use micro data; some use tabular reporting techniques instead of estimating regression coefficients. The analysis in this paper uses regression coefficients estimated from micro data, but the basic issues are not affected by the level of aggregation or by the means of estimating the relationship between the variables.

As a further illustration of the use of truncated samples, in the NBER conference volume edited by Schultz (1974), the only article which includes regressions on completed fertility (defined as children ever born to women 45 and older) is that by Hashimoto (1974).

2. Marini, 1978, addressed this issue by examining empirically the way in which coefficients vary with age. However, in the sample available to her, ages varied only within a narrow range in the late 20's and early 30's.

3. The following analysis will be conducted in terms of a single independent variable. However, that is an unimportant restriction. None of the essential analysis is changed by the addition of more variables. In this and all subsequent equations the constant term is suppressed.

4. In this equation, and in all of the analysis which follows, it is not necessary that the observed relationships be causal, though of course, they could be.

5. Cumulative fertility at age T is equivalent to a woman's parity at that age.

6. The approach used in this paper was motivated by a study of the timing patterns of childbearing conditional upon completed fertility. See Edlefsen, 1979. In that analysis equations similar to (3) and (4) also play a central role. Evidence is presented in that paper that coefficients like $\alpha(T)$ and to a lesser extent $\beta(T)$ may be fairly stable across populations. That fact is not necessary to any of the analysis in this paper, but it obviously adds to its appeal.

7. This "correspondence" is not an equality because β denotes the estimated value of the partial derivative when linearity is imposed on the relationship, while the right hand side of the expression denotes the true value of the partial. While this notation leaves some things to be desired, it has the advantage of simplicity and serves the purposes of this paper.

8. It is easy to see that these restrictions must hold computationally. Consider equation (3). At the beginning of the reproductive period, CF has no variation and the coefficients of all independent variables must be zero. At the end of the reproductive period, $CF = CEB$, and so the coefficient of CEB must be unity and all other coefficients zero.

9. Indeed, the timing pattern of reproduction appears to be quite symmetric around the mean age of childbearing (see Edlefsen, 1979).

10. The U.S. White and Black samples were taken from the 1967 Survey of Economic Opportunity (SEO). For a description of this survey, see Reed and Sadowsky, 1969. The subsamples used consist of mothers currently-married at the time of the sample and between the ages of 45 and 59.

The Philippine Rural and Urban Samples were taken from the National Demographic Survey of May, 1973. This survey is a national representative sample conducted by the University of the Philippines Population Institute with the cooperation of the National Census and Statistics Office. See Population Institute, University of the Philippines, 1974, for a further description of this survey. Currently married mothers between the ages of 45 and 59 in 1973 were included in the sample.

11. The use of retrospective data introduces biases due to errors of recall. This type of bias is not explicitly analyzed in this paper, nor can it be investigated empirically with the available data.

12. These estimates are taken from a regression of the log of income in each major occupational category on a quadratic function of experience, education, size of place, and region of country.

13. The coefficient of *LFP* measures the difference in behavior between those women who were full-time workers at the time of the sample and those who did not work at that time and said that they did not do so because of household duties.

14. Since these samples are not censored—e.g., women who do not marry until age 25 are included in the sample at age 20 and so on—the reported results for the last two variables could never be observed in a true truncated sample. However, these results are included for comparison with the results for censored samples, (which are included in the same plots and which will be discussed below), and also because they illustrate the basic theoretical considerations.

15. As can be observed in the plots included here, the values of β at age 20 are generally not as close to zero as are the values of α (this is true in the other samples as well). If the plots began at age 15 the symmetry of the pattern of β would be more pronounced. However, data for age groups younger than 20 are not very reliable and so these estimates have not been included.

16. All of the articles listed in Note 1 use censored samples. In general, only currently married women are included in those samples.

17. There are really two completely separate reasons why the latter coefficients may change as the sample changes: (1) The true causal effects may vary with the sample. (2) Even if the true causal effects do not vary, the estimated effects may vary. In other words, there may be differential bias across the samples, resulting from a different correlation between the included and the omitted variables. One source of such differential bias has recently been considered by Heckman, 1979, among others. If the objective of the analysis is to estimate causal effects, as it usually is, then the biasing effects of sample censorship need to be dealt with explicitly. This issue is beyond the scope of this paper, but the techniques proposed by Heckman, 1979, should provide an adequate means of dealing with this problem in many situations.

18. Again, however, this holds true only as long as β and π have the same sign.

19. All of the articles referred to in Note 1 pool to some extent. However, some of them break the total sample into smaller age groupings (15–19, 20–24, etc.) and pool only within these. Clearly, as the age groupings become smaller this procedure more and more closely approximates the procedure of single-year age groupings which has already been analyzed.

20. Of the articles listed in Note 1, those by Ben-Porath, 1974, Gardner, 1974, Jiobu and Marshall, 1977, and Willis, 1974, use this procedure.

21. The effect of including marital duration $(T - AM)$ as a control variable is similar to the effect of including T. Indeed, when AM is included in the regression, addition of T or $(T - AM)$ have computationally identical effects on the coefficient of X.

REFERENCES

Bean, Frank D. and Charles H. Wood. 1974. Ethnic variations in the relationship between income and fertility. *Demography 11*:629–640.

Ben-Porath, Yoram. 1975. First generation effects on second generation fertility. *Demography 12*:397–405.

Ben-Porath, Yoram. 1973. Economic analysis of fertility in Israel: point and counterpoint. *Journal of Political Economy 81* (2), Part 2.

Boyd, Monica. 1973. Occupational mobility and fertility in metropolitan Latin America. *Demography 10*:1–8.

Cain, Glen and Adriana Weininger. 1973. Economic determinants of fertility: results from cross-sectional aggregate data. *Demography 10*:205–221.

Chamie, Joseph. 1977. Religious differentials in fertility: Lebanon, 1971. *Population Studies 31*:365–382.

Chaudhury, Rafique Huda. 1977. Relative income and fertility. *Demography 14*:179–195.

Edlefsen, Lee E. 1979. The fundamental structure of fertility. Department of Economics, University of Washington, Discussion Paper No. 79-18.

Gardner, Bruce. 1973. Economics of the size of North Carolina rural families. *Journal of Political Economy 81*(2), Part 2.

Goldstein, Sidney. 1973. Interrelations between migration and fertility in Thailand. *Demography 10*:225–241.

Heckman, J., 1979, Sample Selection as a Specification Error, *Econometrica*, Vol. 47, No. 1. (January 1979):153–61.

Hull, Terence H. and Valerie J. Hull. 1977. The relation of economic class and fertility: an analysis of some Indonesian data. *Population Studies 31*:43–57.

Jiobu, R. and H. Marshall. 1977. Minority status and family size. *Population Studies 31*:509–517.

Kim, Mo-Im, Rowland V. Ryder, Paul A. Harper, and Jae-Mo Yang. 1974. Age at marriage, family planning practices and other variables as correlates of fertility in Korea. *Demography 11*:641–656.

Marini, M. M. 1978. Consequences of childbearing and childspacing patterns for parents. Final Report, Contract No. N01-HD-52840, Battalle Human Affairs Research Center, Seattle.

Pitcher, Brian L., Evan T. Peterson, and Phillip R. Hunz. 1974. Residence differentials in Mormon feritlity. *Population Studies 28*:143–151.

Populations Institute, University of the Philippines. 1974. *Weighted Marginals, National Demographic Survey*. University of the Philippines.

Reed, Marjorie and George Sadowsky. 1969. The 1966 and 1967 survey of economic opportunity files and relate software. Brookings Computer Center Memorandum No. 48.

Ritchey, P. Neal. 1975. The effect of minority group status on fertility: A re-examination of concepts. *Populations Studies 29*:249–257.

Snyder, Donald W. 1974. Economic determinants of family size in W. Africa. *Demography 11*:613–627.

Weller, Robert. 1977. Wife's employment and cumulative family size in the United States: 1970 and 1960. *Demography 14*:43–65.

Willis, Robert J. 1973. A new approach to the economic theory of fertility behavior. *Journal of Political Economy 81*(2), Part 2.

A STOCK ADJUSTMENT MODEL OF U.S. MARITAL FERTILITY

Ronald Lee

I. INTRODUCTION

As demographers have long realized, current fertility may be viewed as a stock adjustment process whereby couples attempt to achieve some desired completed fertility, given an initial stock of children already born (and still surviving). Current marital fertility should therefore reflect the proportion of couples who have not yet attained their desired completed family size and perhaps the average number of additional births desired by this group still wanting more.

Economic factors might affect current marital fertility either by altering desired completed fertility or by altering timing, i.e., the rate at which those still wanting more will have them. I would expect long-run economic factors to have the first effect and transitory changes to have the second.

Apart from these considerations concerning couples' planned fertility,

Research in Population Economics, Volume 3, pages 67–91

ISBN: 0-89232-207-1

there are several systematic ways in which plans may fail. The most obvious way is contraceptive failure, which is of two sorts: (1) conceptions that occur too soon, but are otherwise wanted (timing failures) and (2) conceptions that occur after the desired size is attained (number failures). Subfecundity and sterility are other ways in which plans may be thwarted, but I have made no attempt to incorporate them in the analysis. A final problem is that fertility is irreversible. Desired completed family size may decline in response to economic change, leaving many of those who were previously at their desired completed size now with no-longer-wanted children. These children, who may have been fully planned when conceived and who may not be reported by parents as "unwanted," would not have been planned had later conditions been foreseen.

The principal contribution of this paper is the development of a demographic stock adjustment model that incorporates these considerations and that permits empirical analysis of factors influencing desired completed fertility and the timing of fertility.

This model is used to examine the influence of relative income on aggregate marital fertility in the U.S., 1949–1974, for age groups 25–29 and 30–34. Due in part to severe limitations of available earnings data[1] and in part to my desire to make this analysis compatible with the needs of a growth model developed elsewhere, the economic aspects of the analysis are less well-developed than the demographic ones.

The plan of the paper is as follows: Section II develops the stock adjustment model; Section III develops the relative income hypothesis; Section IV develops the empirical model and reports on estimation and testing; Section V carries out the analysis with correction for contraceptive failure rates; and Section VI carries out the analysis with corrections for the irreversibility of fertility.

II. PLANNED MARITAL FERTILITY

Each married couple either wants to have more children or wants to stop childbearing. If it wants more children, then its desired completed fertility $\tilde{F}$ must exceed the number of children it already has $\tilde{C}$. [The tilde (˜) indicates individual level variables.] If the couple wants no more children, then desired completed fertility must be less than or equal to actual children, so $\tilde{F} \leq \tilde{C}$. In this section, I ignore unwanted fertility and assume that $\tilde{F} = \tilde{C}$ if the couple wants no more. Clearly for the individual couple, whether or not more births are wanted is a function of the "gap," $\tilde{G} = \tilde{F} - \tilde{C}$.

Now consider *all* married couples. A certain proportion p will have $\tilde{F} > \tilde{C}$ and therefore want more births. Let F and G be the averages over all couples of $\tilde{F}$ and $\tilde{G}$. Then it is reasonable to suppose that p will depend closely on $G = F - C$, i.e., it will depend on the average number of additional children wanted.

To test this hypothesis, I plotted p against G for age groups 18–24, 25–29, 30–34, and 35–39, using results from various fertility surveys for 1955 to 1974. The results are shown in Figure 1. These not only strongly confirm the hypothesis, but also suggest a surprisingly simple form for the relationship. For age groups 25–29 and above, G is a constant times p. Let us call this (age-specific) constant α, so that $\alpha p = G$. It has a simple interpretation: $G/p = \alpha$ is the average number of additional births wanted by those who want at least one more. Thus Figure 1 suggests that while there have been large changes in p, which is the proportion of couples wanting more births in an age group, there has been virtually no change in the average number of additional children wanted by this subgroup from 1955 to the present. Approximate values for α are

Age	α_a
18–24	—
25–29	1.67
30–34	1.52
35–39	1.20

Why should α be constant over time? Suppose that initially the number of additional children wanted by those wanting more is distributed as a declining exponential, so that for some λ, the proportion wanting i additional children is $\lambda^{i-1}/(1 - \lambda)$, and the average additional children wanted (α) is then $\alpha = 1/(1 - \lambda)$. Now suppose that there is some change in desired completed fertility such that a proportion q of the couples previously wanting one more now want no more; the proportion q of those wanting two more now want one more; and so on. In this case, α will remain unchanged, although desired completed fertility has fallen. In fact, the relevant distributions are approximately geometric for all age groups except 18–24, for which the constancy of α does not hold.

If people who want more births plan to have them at average intervals of I, then the planned birth rate for those wanting more will be $m = 1/I$. It is likely that I and m vary by age and by the number of additional children desired, as well as by transitory economic conditions. However, we have seen that the additional children desired (α) is quite invariant, so for our purposes m depends on age and transitory conditions alone.

The closed intervals can be estimated from published data; in 1971, the average interval for births of order 2 and above was 41 months for age

Figure 1. Additional Expected Births by Proportion Expecting More for U.S. Married Women, by Age Group, for Survey Years 1955 to 1978.

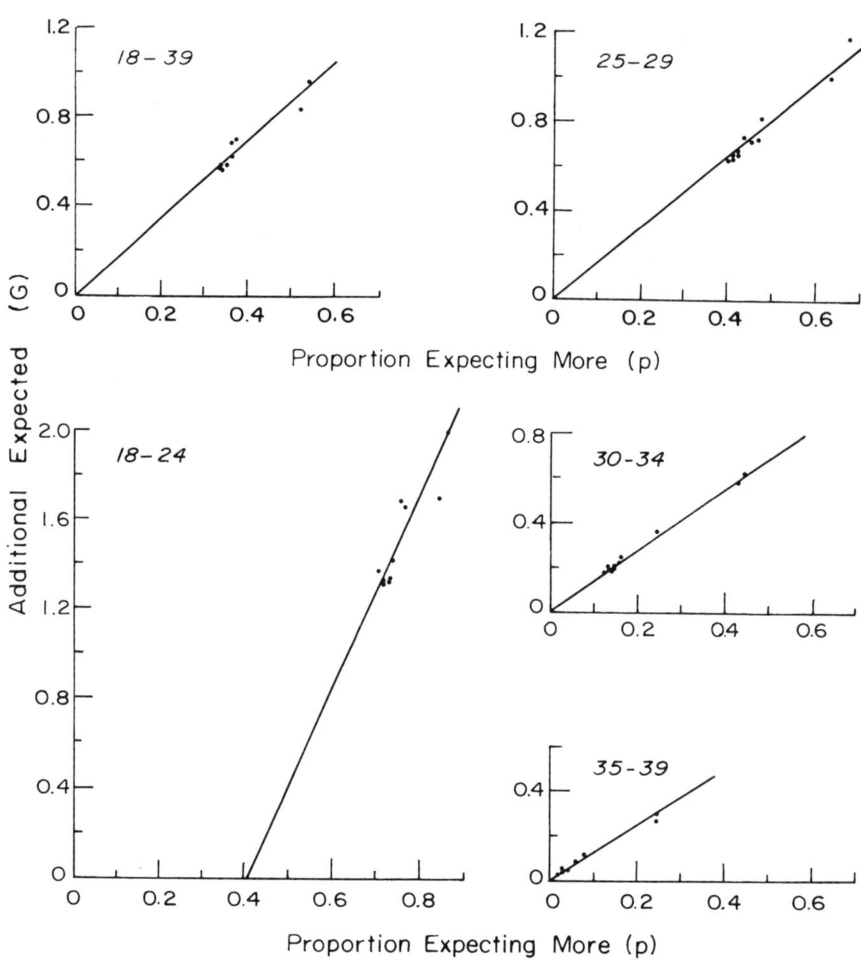

Note

The diagram shows data from 1955, 1960, 1962–64, 1967, 1971–1978, although not all of these years for each group. Sources are: Freedman and Bumpass (1955 to 1962–64); U.S. Bureau of the Census, 1978 (1967–1978). 1955 data refer to white women only.

25–29 and 55 months for age 30–34. These suggest corresponding values of *m* of .29 for age 25–29 and .22 for age 30–34. These mean intervals are biased by inclusion of unwanted births.

Another approach is to use survey responses on expected timing such as in which year the next birth is expected. Some figures on this are

Age	Percentage expecting next birth[2]	
	In first year	*In second year*
18–24	24.5	28.1
25–29	31.8	29.6
30–34	35.4	32.4
35–39	57.8	22.2

Figures for the first year are contaminated by responses of women already pregnant with an unwanted child. This bias is evaluated in Appendix 2 of Lee (1977a). The second year figure should be biased down for similar reasons. Since the difference is small for age groups other than the last, the bias cannot be large. In addition, respondents may underestimate the time necessary to conceive.

Marital fertility (denoted g) can now be expressed as the product of p and m: $g = pm$. This relationship is plotted for ages 25–29 to 35–39 in Figure 2. Note that the positive intercept reflects contraceptive failure, an issue that we will take up later.

Combining the relations $G = \alpha p$ and $g = mp$, it follows that $G = (\alpha/m)g$ and $F = (\alpha/m)g + C$. Consequently, desired completed family size can be estimated from current and cumulate marital fertility. Figure 3 plots calculated F for age groups 25–29 and 30–34, from 1947 to 1973, assuming that (α/m) equals 5. Also plotted are the survey estimates of expected completed fertility, which is a measure that, like F, includes contraceptive failures. The agreement is really very good, particularly considering that the survey questions were changed from time to time.

Having developed the demographic side of the stock adjustment model for marital fertility, I will anticipate the discussion of the next section by hypothesizing that desired completed family size F responds to economic changes that are perceived as being long-run. These are denoted Y^P, and $F = F(Y^P)$. Similarly, the rate m at which those couples wanting more children choose to have them depends on economic conditions perceived as transitory. These are denoted Y^T, and $m = m(Y^T)$. Of course it is also possible that Y^P also affects the spacing strategy chosen; if so, then this analysis would have to be altered somewhat.

At this point it will be useful to recapitulate the variables and equations of the model. These may be grouped as follows (note that age subscripts have been dropped).

Identies:

$$g = pm \tag{1}$$

$$G = p\alpha \tag{2}$$

$$G = F - C \tag{3}$$

Figure 2. Marital Fertility by Proportion Expecting More Births for U.S. Married Women with Husband Present, 1955 to 1974, for Age Groups 25–29, 30–34 and 35–39.

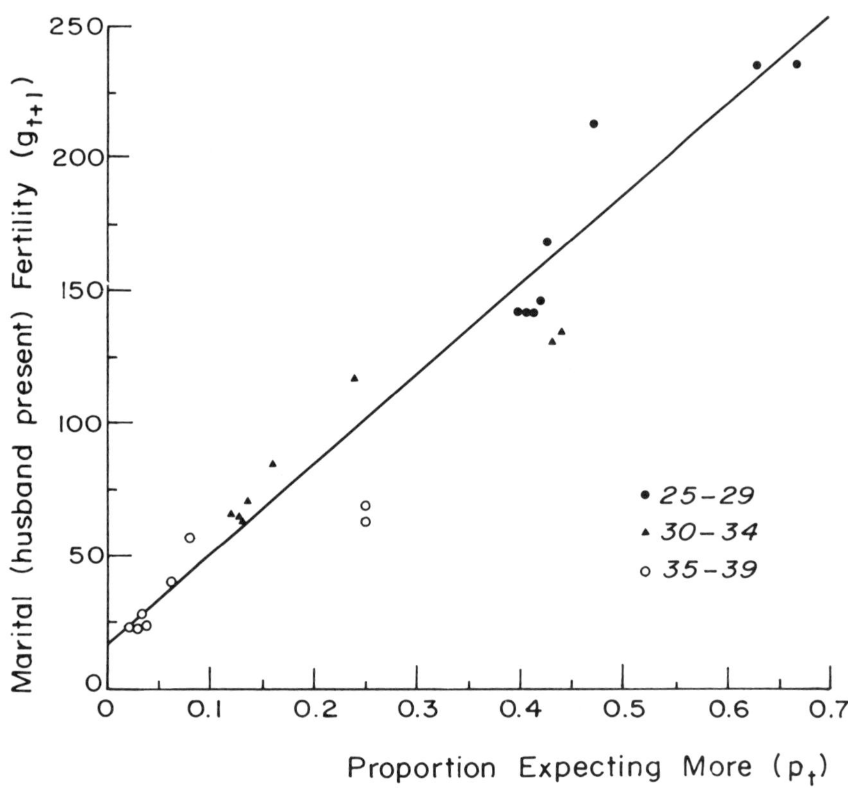

Note

Marital Fertility is adjusted for proportion of husbands present in the previous year. The basic data are from U.S. Public Health Service, 1979. Fertility is plotted against the proportion expecting more in the previous year; these proportions are for 1955, 1960, 1962–64, 1967, 1971–1974; sources are given in the note to Figure 1.

Behavioral equations:

$$\alpha = \bar{\alpha} \qquad \text{i.e., } \partial\alpha/\partial p = \partial\alpha/\partial G = 0 \tag{4}$$

$$F = F(Y^\text{P}) \tag{5}$$

$$m = m(Y^\text{T}) \tag{6}$$

Derived equations:

$$g = [m(Y^\text{T})/\alpha][F(Y^\text{P}) - C] \tag{7}$$

$$g = \lambda(Y^\text{T})[F(Y^\text{P}) - C] \tag{8}$$

Figure 3. Expected Completed Fertility as Measured by Surveys and as Inferred from Aggregate Data, U.S. Married Women, 1947 to 1978.

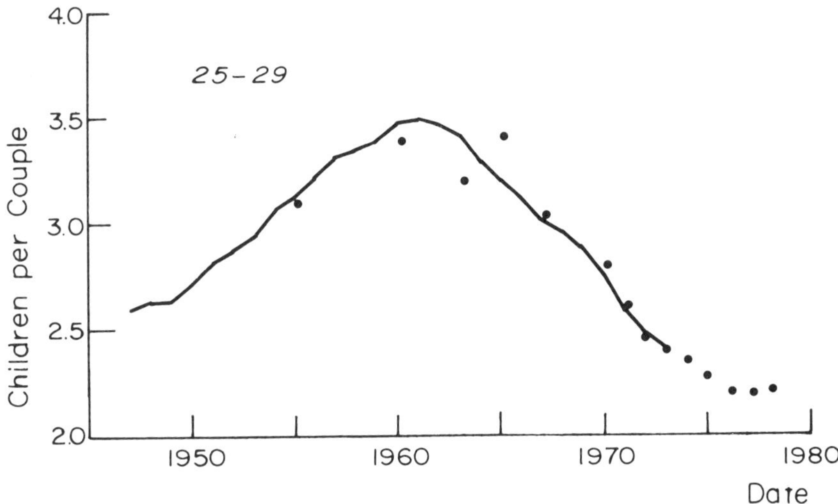

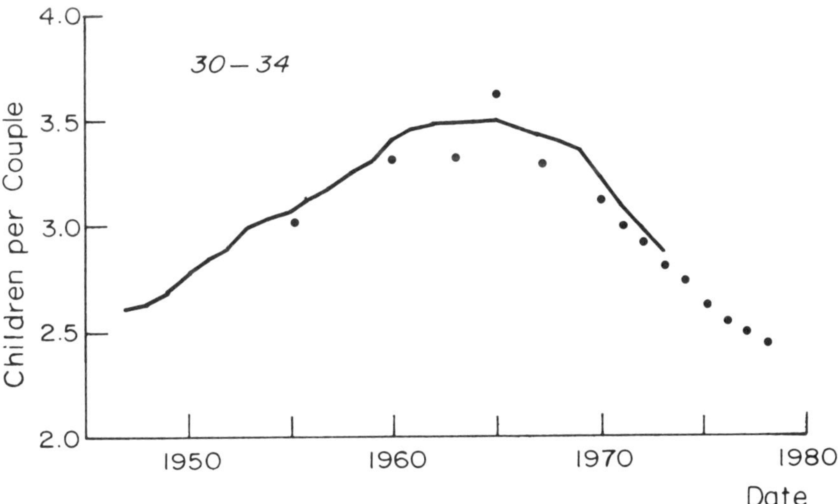

Note

Dots indicate survey estimates; for sources see the note to Figure 1; data for 1965 and 1970 are from Westoff and Ryder, 1977. The estimates from aggregate data are calculated as: $F_t = 5g_{t+1} + C_t$.

Definitions of variables (all are age-specific averages over all married women):

F = desired completed fertility
C = cumulated fertility to all ever-married women
G = additional desired children
g = marital fertility rate
m = fertility rate for those wanting additional births
α = number of additional births wanted by those wanting more
p = proportion of couples wanting more births[4]
λ = rate of adjustment, or proportion of desired additional births made up in each year
Y^P = measure of "Permanent" economic conditions
Y^T = measure of "Transitory" economic conditions

Since Eq. (8) is a simple stock adjustment model, one might wonder what was gained by the elaborate argument. Actually there have been a number of advantages to this approach. First, I have shown that the aggregate stock adjustment model makes sense at the individual level and is compatible with individual level survey responses. Second, I have derived estimates of λ (the rate of adjustment) via survey responses. Third, I have found that λ is independent of G, which was not expected *a priori*. Fourth, we will see that there are major gains to this formulation when we take into account contraceptive failures and the downward irreversibility of fertility decisions.

III. THE RELATIVE INCOME HYPOTHESIS

At this point, a descussion of the "permanent economic conditions" Y^P is in order. It seems obvious to me that the value of consumption in relation to both leisure and children is not determined absolutely, but rather is relative to some conventional standard or aspiration level that evolves through historical experience. This is the argument made recently by Easterlin (1973) and made long ago by those classical economists who invoked the "moving standard" in population theory; in addition, it is quite similar to Duesenberry's theory of consumption.

It is also plausible that parents' notion of the appropriate commodity inputs per child is closely linked to this changing standard. These two ideas can easily be incorporated in the Becker or Willis type of micromodel, as is illustrated in Appendix A.

This "relative income" theory implies that if the rates of change of aspirations, men's wages and women's wages are all equal, as may well be the case over the broad course of secular economic growth, then the desired number of children will not change and neither will the incentive for women to join the labor force. Only variations in wages relative to aspirations will lead to income and substitution effects on consumption, fertility, and labor force participation.

How can the theory be operationalized? Easterlin (1973), Lindert 1978), and Wachter (1975) have used ratios of current to past income with differing lags and age groupings; the method I use here is somewhat different and is motivated largely by its compatability with a growth model in which I elsewhere embed it (see Lee, 1977b; for a similar treatment of relative income, see Denton and Spencer, 1975).

Let $Y_{a,t}$ denote the income of age group a at time t. I assume that for each age a, the time path of $Y_{a,t}$, over the long run, can usefully be viewed as a series of fluctuations about an exponential growth path; i.e., $Y_{a,t}$ tends to follow $d_a e^{rt}$. Here d_a describes the steady-state relative position of the age groups' incomes, and r is their common rate of growth. I assume that cohorts somehow develop income aspirations $Y_{a,t}^*$ based on these underlying historical trends. A couple, age a, regards as its due an income stream described by $Y_{a,t}^* = d_a e^{rt}$ for each age a and time period t that it passes through. The aspired-to total future lifetime income, as assessed at age a_0 and time t_0, is given by

$$YL^* = \sum_{i=a_0}^{w} d_i e^{r(t_0+i-a_0)} \tag{9}$$

where w is the upper limit of the life span. (We could easily take account of discounting and mortality risks without altering the argument.)

On the other hand, the income a cohort actually *expects* to receive is determined by more recent experience. A cohort observes its actual position $Y_{a,t}$ relative to aspirations $Y_{a,t}^*$ for a number of previous years and then extrapolates its relative position over its remaining life cycle. The relative position as assessed at age a and time t is given by

$$R_{a,t} = \prod_{i=0}^{a} (Y_{a-i,t-i}/Y_{a-i,t-i}^*)^{c_{i,a}} \tag{10}$$

where the c_i are weights used to summarize previous experience. Future expected income, as assessed at age a and time t is then expected to be $R_{a,t} Y_{a+i,t+i}^*$ for each future year. Consequently, the ratio of future lifetime income (YL) to aspirations (YL^*) is also given by $R_{a,t}$. $R_{a,t}$ is the Y^P variable to which desired completed fertility $F_{a,t}$ will be related.

I will assume that the weights c_i decline exponentially and sum to unity, so that $c_{i,a} = \lambda_a^{\,i}(1 - \lambda_a)/(1 - \lambda_a^{a+1})$. Note that the c_i vary by age. Substituting this expression for $c_{i,a}$ in Eq. (10) and taking natural logarithms yields

$$\ln R_{a,t} = X_a - Y_a rt + Z_a \sum_{i=0}^{a} \lambda_a^{\,i} \ln Y_{a-i,t-i} \tag{11}$$

so that for fixed a, $\ln R_{a,t}$ is linear in $\ln Y_{j,s}$.[5]

Alternatively, defining $\eta_{a,t}$ by $Y_{a,t} = Y^*_{a,t}e^{\eta_{a,t}}$ gives the simpler expression

$$\ln R_{a,t} = Z_a \sum_{i=0}^{a} \lambda_a{}^i\,\eta_{a-i,t-i} \tag{12}$$

Here the $\eta_{a,t}$ could be estimated as the residuals from a regression of $\ln Y_{a,t}$ on an age-specific constant and t.

Nothing has been said so far of the measure of $Y_{a,t}$. In principle, it should be a full income measure including both male and female earning potential. Unfortunately, reliable data exist only for males; the data on female earnings are seriously distorted by the changing composition of the female labor force. Comparisons of results from the 1960 and 1970 censuses show deterioration, improvement, or no changes in male–female earnings ratios, depending on what standardizations are made.

It is also very important to include some form of long-run expectations about women's potential earnings as a price variable. However, because of the data problems mentioned earlier, this was not possible.

It remains to operationalize transitory economic conditions Y^T. Possibilities include the unemployment rate, the index of consumer sentiment, and $\eta_{a,t} - R_{a,t}$; I have tried each of these.

IV. ESTIMATION AND TESTING

The basic equation to be estimated is Eq. (7). However, it must first be specified in more detail. First, note that $m[Y^T]/\alpha \doteq .2$ has already been empirically established. Y^T may be measured or transformed in such a way that it has a mean of zero; then the following specification is convenient: $m(Y^T) = \overline{m(Y^T)}(1 + \gamma Y^T)$. Substituting this into Eq. (7) and rearranging yields

$$5g_{t+1} + C_t = (1 + Y_t^T)\, F(Y_p^P) - \gamma Y_t^T C_t \tag{13}$$

Now specify $F(Y_t^P) = \beta_0 + \beta_1 \ln R_t$ where R is defined as in Eq. (11) or (12). This yields

$$5g_{t+1} + C_t = (1 + \gamma Y_t^T)\,[\beta_0 + \beta_1 Z \sum_{i=0}^{a} \lambda^i \eta_{i,t-i}] - \gamma Y_t^T C_t \tag{14}$$

This equation may be estimated in its present nonlinear form, or the linear approximation can be derived by taking partial derivatives of $5g_{t+1} + C_t$ and evaluating at the sample means. This procedure yields

$$5g_{t+1} + C_t \doteq \beta_0 + \beta_1 Z \sum_{i=0}^{a} \lambda^i \eta_{i,t-i} + \gamma \overline{G} Y_t^T + u_t \tag{15}$$

where $\overline{G}$ (the mean gap between F and C) equals $\beta_0 - \overline{C_t}$, and an additive disturbance u_t has been appended. Since Z can be calculated from λ (see Note 5), all parameters in both the linear and nonlinear equations can be estimated.

These specifications are implied by the stock adjustment model developed earlier; however, it is also of interest to estimate a less constrained version of these equations in which g_{t+1} is estimated as a linear function of Y_t^{T}, Y_t^{P}, and C_t.

Actual estimation involves several problems; λ_a, which is the weight used to form income expectations based on past experience, must be determined empirically. This can be done using maximum likelihood techniques or it can be done approximately after a Koyck transform (the result is only approximately right because the geometric distribution of weights is truncated in this specification). If the Koyck transform is used, then the presence of variables with only a single lag (Y^{T} and C) requires nonlinear estimation techniques. Additionally, there are problems with the error term. The simplest assumption is that the error in Eq. (15) has autocorrelation λ, so that after a Koyck transform, the error is independently distributed. There is ample precedent in the econometric literature for such an assumption, although it is difficult to justify.

The empirical equations can be estimated in a single step, based on the expression for $R_{a,t}$ in Eq. (11) or in two steps, based on Eq. (12). I have done both, but I prefer the two-step procedure, using income data for all age groups in the first step to estimate the residuals $\eta_{a,t}$. In this way, r is constrained to reflect the income experience of all age groups rather than the fortunes of a particular age group, over the relatively short sample period (1947–1973).

Annual age-specific median income data are available only since 1947 and are usable only for age groups 25–29 and above. The analysis here is confined to age groups 25–29 and 30–34. Marital fertility is defined as legitimate births per married woman with husband present in the preceding year. Cumulative fertility is per ever-married woman and includes illegitimate births on the premise that these are perfect substitutes for legitimate births if the mothers later marry.

The equation to be estimated for current fertility therefore looks like

$$g_t - \lambda g_{t-1} = \beta_0 (1 - \lambda) + [\beta_1/(1 - \lambda)]\eta_t + \beta_2 (U_t - \lambda U_{t-1}) + \beta_3(C_t - \lambda C_{t-1}) + \epsilon_t \tag{16}$$

where η_t is the relative income residual for the age group, as estimated in a previous step, and U is the unemployment rate, taken to measure Y^{T}. The disturbance ϵ_t is assumed serially uncorrelated, as discussed earlier. The equation for desired fertility F is similar.

Equation (16) for current marital fertility, and the equivalent with desired completed fertility, were estimated by OLS for various values of λ between .1 and .95 to locate the least squares solution. The results are

Table 1.   Regressions with No Correction for Contraceptive Failure

Dependent variable	Constant	$\ln R_{a,t}$ (Y^p)	U.E. (Y^T)	Cumulative fertility (C)	λ	R^2 for transformed dependent variable
Marital fertility						
25–29	5.48	6.14	0.53	0.0177	0.95	0.33
	(1.40)	(1.95)	(0.41)	(0.51)		
30–34	5.83	4.56	0.247	--0.0172	0.95	0.26
	(1.49)	(2.27)	(0.33)	(0.67)		
Desired completed fertility						
25–29	288	21,800	16.7	—	0.90	0.61
	(22.7)	(6.03)	(1.62)	—		
30–34	166	30,800	6.32	—	0.95	0.65
	(20.9)	(6.56)	(0.97)	—		

Note: *t*-statistics are given in parentheses below each estimated coefficient.   The sample period is 1947 to 1974.

reported in Table 1, which shows that for three of the four equations, the minimizing solution was not found since it required $\lambda > .95$.   Such large values of λ are clearly in conflict with the theoretical role it plays; a λ of .95 implies a mean of 20 years in the formation of relative income expectations.   In the fourth equation, a λ of .9 minimizes squared errors; this implies a lag of 10 years in the formation of relative income expectations, which also seems a bit long.

The other parameter estimates (which are *not* least squares solutions except in the third equation) support the relative income hypothesis since both current marital fertility and desired completed fertility depend positively and significantly on it.

Adverse transitory conditions, as measured by unemployment, uniformly have an insignificant but *positive* effect on fertility, which is inconsistent with an enormous volume of empirical findings, although not necessarily with theory (see Ben-Porath, 1973).   Cumulative marital fertility was unconstrained in the current fertility equations, and its estimated effect was vitually nil.

Although these results do provide some support for the relative income hypothesis, they are rather discouraging for the other aspects of the stock adjustment approach.   We will see in the next section whether correction for contraceptive failure improves them.

V. PLANNED FERTILITY AND CONTRACEPTIVE FAILURE

It is widely believed, and with good reason, that improvements in contraceptive technology and more liberal legal and social attitudes toward contraception and abortion have played an important role in the fertility decline of the 1960s and 1970s (Westoff and Ryder, 1977a). However, even with no change in technology, a decline in relative income would lead couples not only to reduce desired completed fertility but also to contracept more assiduously and to choose less frequent coitus.

Declines in rates of contraceptive failure would therefore be expected even without legal, social, and technical changes; consequently, viewing all change in observed failure rates as exogenous overstates its role. Nonetheless, it is impossible to deny the effects of the pill, the IUD, sterilization, and liberalized abortion, and some adjustment of the data is therefore required. In this section, I (incorrectly) treat all change in contraceptive efficacy, other than exposure to risk, as exogenous.

The first correction to consider, and the simplest, is to purge cumulative fertility of "number" errors, i.e., unwanted births. Since these affect (by definition) only the woman wanting no more births and since (planned) current fertility occurs only to women who *do* want more children, the unwanted births should be removed. For this purpose, I have interpolated and extrapolated from data on unwanted births gathered in fertility surveys between 1955 and 1970. The estimates used are given in Appendix 1 of Lee (1977a).

The problem of adjusting current fertility is more complex. Suppose we know the (age-specific) rate for number failure to those at risk (q_1) and the rate for timing failure to those at risk (q_2). After making appropriate adjustments for the proportion of time spent *not* at risk in each category, due to pregnancy, postpartum amenorrhea, and efforts to conceive, we can derive rates Q_1 and Q_2, which apply to *all* women wanting to terminate on the one hand and all women wanting additional children on the other. Then the overall failure rate Q, including both number and timing failures, is

$$Q = (1 - p)Q_1 + pQ_2 \qquad (17)$$

Let g^* represent planned marital fertility and g represent actual marital fertility, including contraceptive failure. Then

$$g = g^* + Q = g^* + (1 - p)Q_1 + pQ_2 \qquad (18)$$

Alternatively, recalling that $g^* = pm^*$, this can be rewritten

$$g = p(m^* + Q_2 - Q_1) + Q_1 \qquad (19)$$

Note that when Q_1 and Q_2 are different, the overall contraceptive failure rate Q is endogenous in this model.

I have tried two different approaches empirically. The first and simplest assumes that $Q_1 = Q_2 = Q$; in which case, the only adjustment necessary is to subtract the numbers failure rate from marital fertility. In fact, it appears that q_2 is greater than q_1 by, say, 40 to 100 percent. However, women trying to terminate are almost always at risk, whereas women who are spacing are at risk only about one-half of the time (the remainder is spent pregnant, trying to conceive, or in amenorrhea). So in the end, Q_1 and Q_2 may actually be very close and assuming them equal is probably not far wrong.

The second approach I have taken is to ignore timing failure rates (Q_2) completely and correct only for number failure rates (Q_1). My reasoning is that improved contraception for timing should lengthen birth intervals; however, observed parity-specific intervals have shortened. Therefore any effects of improved contraception on timing have been more than offset by other factors working in the opposite direction. This is not the case for number failure rates, so these should be included.

Assuming $Q_2 = 0$, Eq. (16) reduces to

$$g = p(m^* - Q_1) + Q_1 \tag{20}$$

which suggests

$$\alpha(g - Q_1)/(m^* - Q_1) + C = F \tag{21}$$

This is a rather different, but easily estimable, specification.

Table 2 shows estimates paralleling those of Table 1 in method, but allowing for contraceptive failure. The correction used assumes all failures are number failures and so follows Eqs. (20) and (21).

For all four equations, the value of λ that minimized squared errors fell in the region .1 to .95, with implied average lags ranging from 4 to 10 years (see Figures 4 and 5 for comparison of predicted and actual data).

Once again, the relative income variable does very well, and this time the level and significance of the estimated relative income parameters in the current fertility equations are substantially increased. These esti-

Table 2. Regressions with Correction for Contraceptive Failure

Dependent variable	Constant	$\ln R_{a,t}$ (Y^P)	U.E. (Y^T)	Cumulative fertility (C)	λ	R^2 for transformed dependent variable
Marital fertility						
25–29	41.9	49.2	1.14	−0.024	0.75	0.49
	(3.98)	(4.34)	(1.21)	(1.08)		
30–34	30.3	22.9	.35	−0.037	0.80	0.58
	(4.72)	(5.32)	(.58)	(2.79)		
Desired completed fertility						
25–29	263	20,000	13.8	—	0.90	0.60
	(22.2)	(5.89)	(1.44)	—		
30–34	284	11,700	2.69	—	0.90	0.57
	(38.2)	(5.49)	(.44)	—		

Note: t-statistics are given in parentheses below each estimated coefficient. The sample period is 1947 to 1974.

mates provide strong support for the relative income hypothesis as applied both to current fertility and to desired completed fertility.

Adverse transitory conditions are again positively and insignificantly associated with fertility—a puzzling result. Cumulative fertility now has a negative estimated effect, although it is much smaller than the $-.2$ required by the strict stock adjustment theory.

The development of the model so far has implicitly assumed that the cumulated fertility of terminators can be altered when desired completed fertility changes; this is, of course, false. It is only the relatively few couples wanting additional children who can respond to deteriorating economic conditions. In the next section, I deal with this problem explicitly.

VI. CORRECTION FOR THE IRREVERSIBILITY OF FERTILITY

Current economic and social conditions may affect fertility through both desired completed family size F and the timing and spacing of births. Conventional measures of desired completed fertility, however, are seriously flawed reflections of the influence of current conditions on family size orientations. The reason is that they include the actual completed fertility of couples who terminated childbearing some time previous under possibly quite different social and economic conditions. In this section, I develop a method for adjusting F to make it more appropriate as a period measure of changing cohort desires.

During the course of its married life, a couple may revise its desired completed family size $\tilde{F}$ in response to changes in its tastes, social pressures, or its imperfectly foreseen economic situation. Nonterminators are able to implement either upward or downward changes in F. Because fertility is irreversible, however, and children once born cannot be discarded, terminators can implement only upward changes in F; downward revisions entail only regret and frustration. Presumably under these circumstances, most terminators do not make downward revisions in F, even though with perfect foresight or current nonterminator status, they would have chosen fewer children. The hypothetical excess children are in some sense "unwanted," even though their parents may not regard them so. Such couples are currently out of equilibrium, since their decisions were based on expectations not born out by subsequent events.

In a period of constant or rising average cohort F, the proportion of couples in this category should be fairly constant. However, when average F declines (as it has since 1963 or so), there is an *additional systematic* accumulation of "unwanted" children. While the equation $F^* = G^* + C^*$ still holds for nonaccidental completed fertility, it no longer holds for desired completed fertility, since C^* includes currently "un-

Figure 4. Predicted and Actual Marital Fertility, Corrected for Contraceptive Failure, for Age Group 25–29, 1949 to 1974

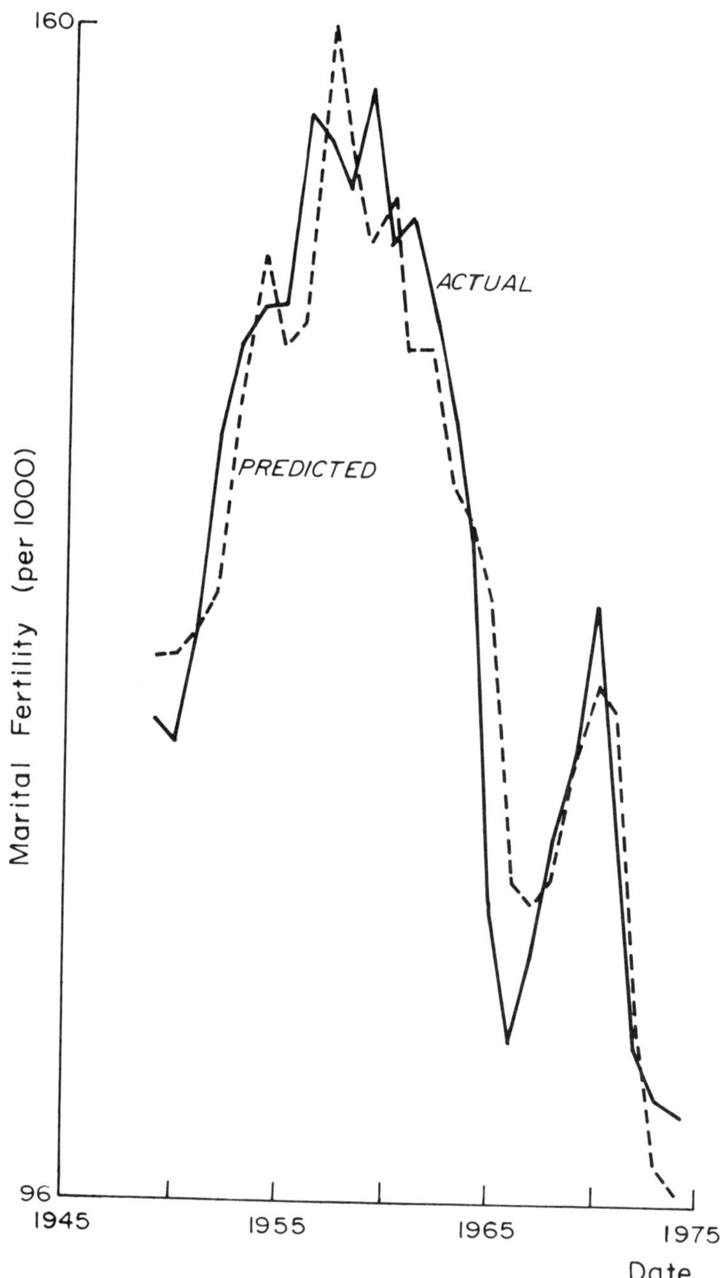

Note

The "actual" fertility is for married women with husband present in the previous year. The "predicted" is calculated using the estimates in the top panel of Table 2.

82

Figure 5. Predicted and Actual Marital Fertility, Corrected for Contraceptive Failure, for Age Group 30–34, 1949 to 1974

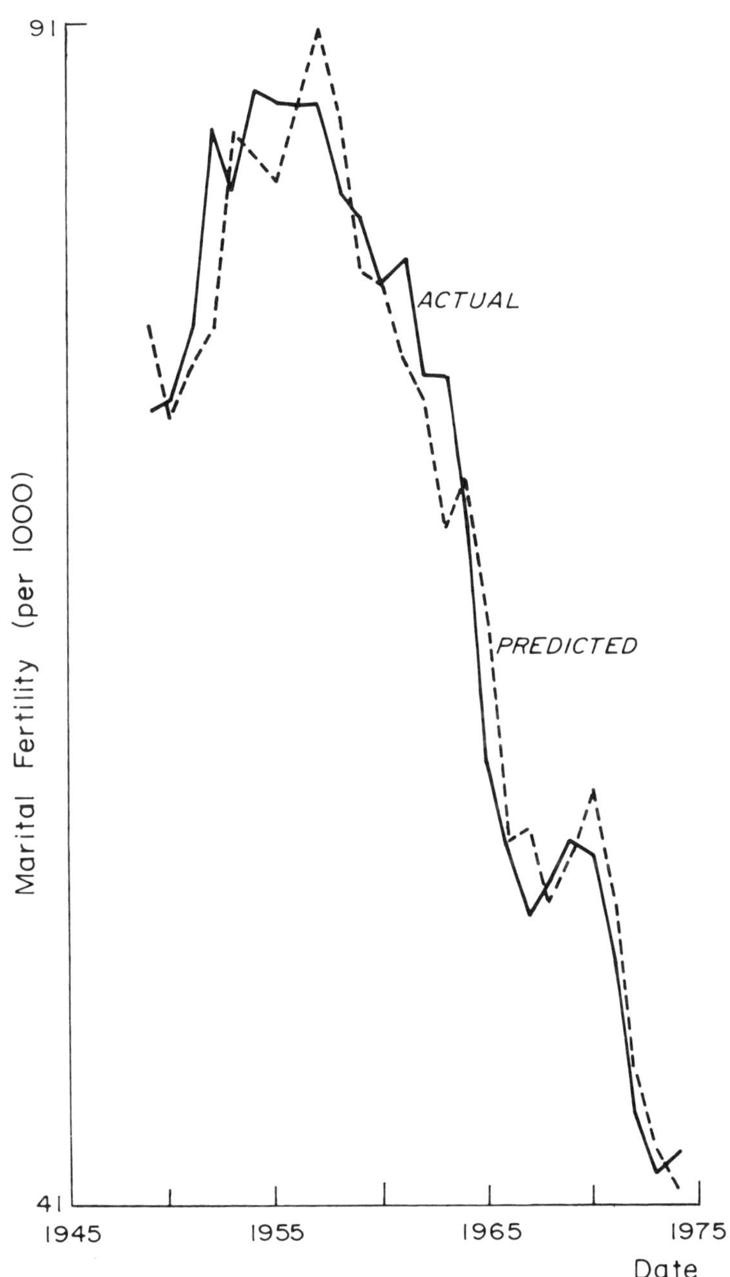

Note

   The "actual" fertility is for married women with husband present in the previous year. The "predicted" fertility is calculated using parameter estimates from the top panel of Table 2.

wanted'' births. The purpose of this part is to devise a method of correction.

An obvious starting point is to consider the desired completed family size of nonterminators alone, since they are free to revise their plans in response to changing situations. Is the average F of nonterminators likely to be very different from that of terminators? Nonterminators include those couples who married late and have lower than usual F, as well as those who married at the usual age and are still nonterminators because they have higher than usual F. It may not be far wrong to assume that these biases are offsetting and that terminators and nonterminators would have similar average desired completed family sizes under similar external conditions. Unfortunately, it is impossible to test this hypothesis since survey results are not tabulated in a way that allows the comparison to be made.

If we assume that the desired completed fertility of nonterminators would equal that of terminators, provided that terminators could reformulate their plans under current conditions, then we can adjust the measure of current F by purging it of no-longer-wanted births.

Let U_t be the average unwanted stock per terminator at time t [i.e., over the interval $(t, t + 1)$]. Since, by definition, nonterminators hold no unwanted stocks, the corrected equation is

$$F_t = G_t + C_t - (1 - p_t)U_t \tag{22}$$

Now, although it is true that U is never observed directly, we do know that U must be zero after a sustained period of constant or increasing F. So the problem is to derive an expression for U_{t+1} in terms of U_t and changes in F_t. To a first approximation, if the average unwanted stock held by terminators at time t is U_t, then at $t + 1$ it will have changed to $U_t + F_t - F_{t+1}$, increasing if F decreases and decreasing if F increases. But the changing composition of a given age group's terminators complicates the story. The details of the fuller analysis are given in Appendix B. Here, I will just briefly summarize the conclusions.

After taking into account the effects of aging, the expression for U_{t+1} is shown to be

$$U_{t+1} = [.8(1 - p_t)\, U_t + (.95 - p_t)(F_t - F_{t+1})]/(1 - p_{t+1}) \tag{23}$$

This can be combined with Eq. (19) and solved for F to yield

$$F_{t+1} = [\alpha P_{t+1} + C_{t+1} - .8(1 - p_t)U_t - (.95 - p_t)F_t]/(p_t + .05) \tag{24}$$

This equation permits calculation of the "true" F_{t+1} when U_t is known. Given this estimate, U_{t+1} is readily obtained from Eq. (22), and the procedure can be reiterated for F_{t+2}.

There is a further problem of dealing with a rise in desired completed fertility following a decline, since the procedure outlined above is not symmetric. The appropriate algorithm is developed in Appendix B.

Using the procedures developed in this section, I calculated the "true" desired completed family size by correcting for both irreversibility and contraceptive failure. The results are shown in Table 3 and Figure 6. Throughout the 1960's and early 1970's, terminators in both age groups came to hold stocks of no-longer-wanted children, which at their peak in 1971 averaged close to one-half child per terminator. While I don't suggest that these children were regarded as unwanted by their parents,

Table 3. Total Expected Fertility, with Adjustment for Contraceptive Failure and Irreversibility, by Age and Period

Date	Age 25–29				Age 30–34			
	F	F*	F**	U	F	F*	F**	U
1947	2594	2076	(No entry means	0	2613	2152	(no entry means	0
48	2633	2101	same as F*)	0	2634	2174	same as F*)	0
49	2635	2111		0	2687	2225		0
1950	2723	2164		0	2781	2298		0
51	2824	2268		0	2849	2398		0
52	2883	2351		0	2905	2431		0
53	2954	2417		0	2992	2518		0
54	3067	2494		0	3033	2569		0
55	3130	2616		0	3064	2592		0
56	3224	2667		0	3130	2634		0
57	3311	2721		0	3183	2660		0
58	3352	2789		0	3251	2697		0
59	3389	2781	2744	13	3307	2737		0
1960	3475	2861		0	3389	2804		0
61	3494	2887		0	3453	2864		0
62	3472	2874	2860	24	3480	2924		0
63	3422	2843	2799	72	3482	2915	2894	27
64	3292	2718	2538	271	3483	2910	2891	23
65	3199	2658	2476	265	3485	2946		0
66	3119	2653	2546	159	3454	2946		0
67	3022	2622	2520	155	3423	2950		0
68	2969	2577	2456	186	3398	2944	2924	24
69	2885	2541	2428	183	3343	2897	2743	189
1970	2753	2412	2183	352	3234	2807	2493	378
71	2588	2286	1982	441	3091	2696	2274	497
72	2470	2200	1913	412	2975	2605	2241	423
73	2399	2123	1857	n.a.	2868	2527	2213	n.a.

Key to symbols
F = total expected fertility
F* = total expected fertility corrected for contraceptive failure
F** = total expected fertility corrected for contraceptive failure and irreversibility
U = average stock of no-longer wanted fertility per terminator

Figure 6. Total Expected Births With Corrections for Contraceptive Failure and Irreversibility, Ages 25–29 and 30–34, 1947 to 1978.

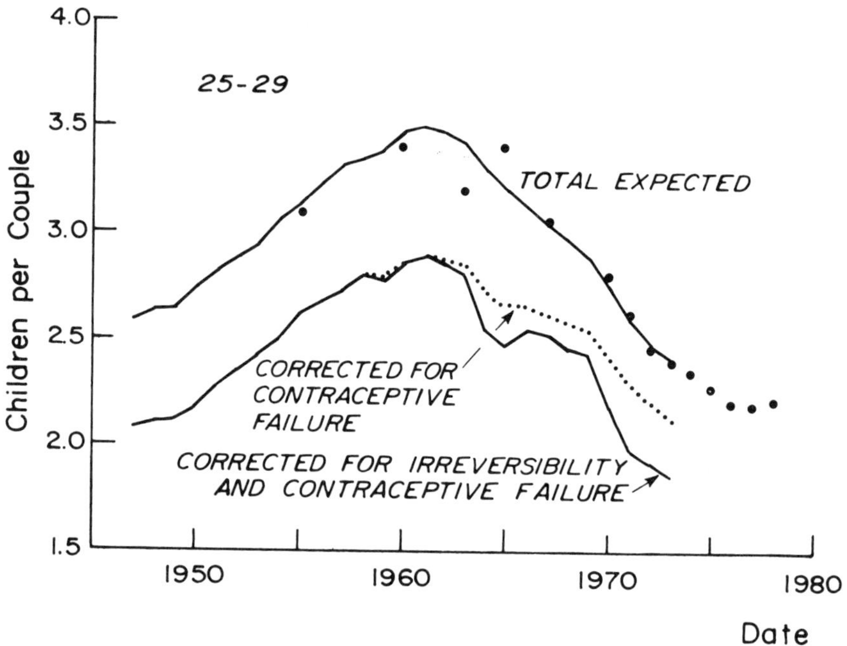

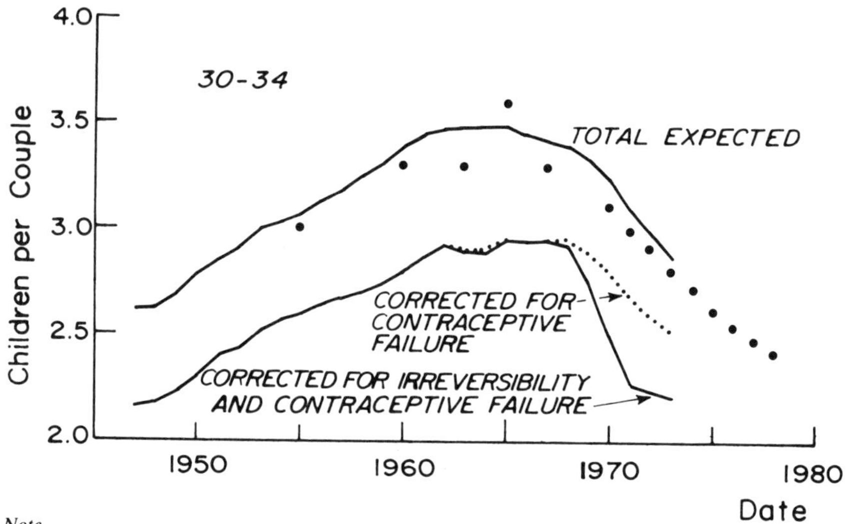

Note

    Survey estimates are indicated by solid circles; for sources, see the notes to Figures 1 and 3. The upper solid line is inferred from aggregate data using: $F_t = 5g_{t+1} + C_t$. The dotted line is estimated using equation (21) and data from the appendix to Lee, 1977a. The lower solid line is estimated using the procedure detailed in Appendix B of this paper.

Table 4. Regressions with Correction for Contraceptive Failure and Irreversibility

Dependent variable	Constant	$\ln R_{a,t}$ (Y^{P})	U.E. (Y^{T})	Cumulative fertility (C)	λ	R^2 for transformed dependent variable
Desired completed fertility						
25–29	353	16,355	14.4	—	0.85	0.58
	(15.9)	(5.68)	(1.15)	—		
30–34	365	15,600	−4.5	—	0.90	0.41
	(18.5)	(3.80)	(−.39)	—		

Note: *t*-statistics are given in parentheses below each estimated coefficient. The sample period is 1947 to 1974.

their presence presumably displaced parents from life cycle equilibrium. In particular, these excess children must have been supported at the expense of commodity consumption and leisure, and this could have been a factor behind the dramatic increases in labor force participation of married women with young children.

Finally the Table 3 and Figure 6 show that by 1973, desired completed fertility had fallen to 1.86 for women 25–29 and to 2.21 for women 30–34. These numbers are about .3 less than those corrected only for contraceptive failure and .5 to .6 less than those not corrected at all.

Regressions for desired completed fertility, corrected for irreversibility as well as contraceptive failure, were run as in the previous sections. The results are shown in Table 4. Once again the permanent relative income variable is strongly positive, with elasticities in the range of 5 to 6 and highly significant *t*-statistics. Unemployment again has an insignificant effect on desired completed fertility. The average lag of the coefficients is 6 to 10 years.

VII. CONCLUSIONS

I have attempted to explain the changes over time in the marital fertility of certain age groups in the U.S., 1947 to 1974, using a stock adjustment model in conjunction with a version of the relative income hypothesis. The stock adjustment model shows that the initiation of the decline in marital fertility in the late 1950s was *not* due to a decline in desired completed fertility but rather to its leveling off, together with an increase in children ever born. This reduced the *additional* desired fertility and hence the flow of marital fertility. However, the desired stock did not begin to fall until much later (for an elaboration of this argument, see Lee, 1980).

The stock adjustment model also was used to refine the measure of desired completed fertility by correcting for births that were unwanted when conceived due to contraceptive failure and for births that may have become unwanted *ex post* due to the emergence of unforeseen socioeconomic conditions.

The empirical results support the view that desired completed fertility is strongly influenced by permanent relative income, with positive elasticities in the range of 3 to 7. The rate at which desired completed fertility is achieved, measured as the birth rate to couples wanting additional children, was found to be insignificantly related to transitory economic conditions.

These results must be viewed with considerable caution, however; the analysis is very far from conclusive. A brief review of the uncertainties is in order. First, there are severe data limitations. I think currently available earnings series for females are badly distorted by compositional changes, as are income series for males under 25; therefore, I have restricted the empirical analysis.

Second, the amount of variation in the data series over this period probably does not permit a decisive test of rival hypotheses. For example, in this study, fairly strong results were found with five different versions of the dependent variable, some of which I have argued were quite inappropriate. This should not be taken as indicative of the robustness of the hypothesis but rather as a sign of the difficulty in discriminating among various hypotheses. Indeed, Butz and Ward's (1979) explanation of the baby boom and baby bust in terms of a time series version of the Willis (1972) model also appears to fit the historical experience quite well.

Third, while I feel that the stock adjustment model is an advance, it would be more useful if *direct* measures of the stock variable (F) and timing variable (m) were available for individual estimation and testing. In the present empirical work, identification of the influences affecting F and m rested on strict identifying assumptions (F depends only on Y^P; m depends only on Y^T), which are questionable. For example, in some contexts, m is clearly a function of F. In summary, this paper has told a story that is consistent with such data as are now available; to this extent, it supports the relative income hypothesis.

APPENDIX A

Microlevel Formulation of the Relative Income Hypothesis

Any of the microlevel formulations of the economic theory of fertility can easily be modified to incorporate the relative income hypothesis. Probably the simplest model incorporating time inputs to children would be

$$\max U(X,N)$$

$$\text{S.T.} \qquad Y = p_x X + N(p_y y + w_F t)$$

$$Y = (w_F + w_H)T$$

where X are commodities and N is the number of children. Children are produced by fixed inputs per head of commodities y, with price vector p_y, and a proportion t of wife's time, valued at her wage rate w_F.

To introduce relative income, assume there is a consumption standard S relative to which actual commodity consumption X is valued. Then the utility function becomes $U(X/S,N)$. Also, the couple's perception of the required commodity inputs per child depends on S, so that the budget constraint becomes

$$Y = p_x X + (S p_y y + w_F t)N$$

Now if S is determined by historical experience, it may well be that $\dot{S}/S = \dot{w}_H/w_H = \dot{w}_F/w_F$. In this case, the optimizing N will be constant, while X and Y will also grow at the rate $\dot{S}/S$. Only when w_H or w_F varies in relation to S do income and substitution effects occur. Thus one obvious consequence is that the parallel secular increase in men's and women's wage rates would have no tendency to induce substitution away from children and toward goods, and consequently, there would be no tendency toward rising female labor force participation rates.

APPENDIX B

Correction for the Irreversibility of Fertility

The excess stocks held by an age group's terminators at time $t + 1$ can be divided into two components: those carried over from time t and those resulting from the change in F between t and $t + 1$. I will treat these separately.

First consider those who had terminated by time t, given by the proportion $1 - p_t$. Of these, some have aged out of the interval by time $t + 1$. With 5-year age groups, about 20 percent will leave the age group every year, so I assume that a proportion $.8(1 - p_t)$ of those in the interval at $t + 1$ carry average excess stocks of U_t. This assumption involves two partially offsetting biases: (1) some of those couples aging into the interval will have terminated by t and will carry excess stocks; and (2) those couples aging out of the interval make up more than 20 percent of the interval's couples who had terminated by t, since the proportion of terminators increases with age. Assigning a value of $.8(1 - p_t)U_t$ to this component of U_{t+1} probably errs on the low side.

Now consider the effect of a decline in F from t to $t + 1$. This will apply to all those who had terminated by t who are in the age group at $t + 1$. Here account must be taken of the different proportions of terminators aging into and out of the interval. Since p_t is an average of the p's by single years of age and since there is little difference in numbers married across the relevant ages, the effect of aging on the p_t is $(p_t^{29} - p_t^{34})/5$ for age group 30–34, for example, and similarly for the others. Inspection of p by age shows that the change in p_t over 5 years is roughly .25 and doesn't vary much by age group or period. Thus the proportion at time $t + 1$ of those who have terminated by time t is $1 - (p_t + .25/5) = .95 - p_t$. Each of these couples acquires an additional unwanted stock of $F_t - F_{t-1}$ over the year.

To get U_{t+1}, the total excess stock at $t + 1$ must be divided by the total number of terminators at $t + 1$, or $1 - p_{t+1}$. It follows that the expression for U_{t+1} must be

$$U_{t+1} = [.8(1 - p_t)U_t + (.95 - p_t)(F_t - F_{t+1})]/(1 - p_{t+1}) \qquad (A2.1)$$

However, since neither U_{t+1} nor F_{t+1} is directly observable, one of these unknowns must be eliminated. This can be done by using the equation

$$F_{t+1} = \alpha p_{t+1} + C_{t+1} + (1 - p_{t+1})U_{t+1} \qquad (A2.2)$$

Substituting from Eq. (A2.1) for U_{t+1} in Eq. (A2.2) and rearranging, yields

$$F_{t+1} = [\alpha p_{t+1} + C_{t+1} - .8(1 - p_t)U_t - (.95 - p_t)F_t]/(p_t + .05) \qquad (A2.3)$$

This expression permits calculation of F_{t+1} provided U_t is known. The value of U_{t+1}, that is needed for the next iteration can be found from

$$U_{t+1} = (\alpha p_{t+1} + C_{t+1} - F_{t+1})/(1 - p_{t+1}) \qquad (A2.4)$$

Equations (A2.3) and (A2.4) should be applied, starting in the first year for which the estimated F declines.

Calculation of $F_{t+1} - F_t$ from Eq. (A2.3) shows that so long as $U_t = 0$, $F_{t+1} \gtrless F_t$ as $\alpha p_{t+1} + C_{t+1} \gtrless F_t$; however, the size of the change in F is magnified by a factor between two and ten depending on p. Therefore the initial turning point can be picked up by the simple calculation of F; once a decline is initiated, the complicated formula should be used.

There is a further problem of making the correct adjustment when desired completed fertility should rise following a decline, indicating that some previously unwanted births become wanted. In this case, the only component of change in unwanted fertility is the reduction in unwanted for terminators by t. This amounts, in total, to $.8(1 - p_t)(U_t + G_t - F_{t+1})$, so we have

$$(1 - p_{t+1})U_{t+1} = .8(1 - p_t)(U_t + F_t - F_{t+1}) \qquad (A2.5)$$

Solving for F_{t+1}, this gives

$$F_{t+1} = [\alpha p_{t+1} + C_{t+1} - .8(1 - p_t)(U_t + F_t)]/(.2 + .8p_t) \qquad (A2.6)$$

However, this is only correct when $U_{t+1} \le F_t - F_{t+1}$; if $U_t > F_t - F_{t+1}$, then we simply set $U_{t+1} = 0$, and have $F_{t+1} = \alpha p_{t+1} + C_{t+1}$.

ACKNOWLEDGMENTS

Research on this project was supported by NICHHD under contract HD-42857 and grant HD-14649. The work was carried out at the Population Studies Center at the University of Michigan and the Program in Population Research of the University of California, Berkeley. I am grateful to Mark Browning for research assistance.

NOTES

1. I consider the income series for males below age 25 and for all females to be unusable due to compositional biases.

2. For U.S. married women in 1974. *Source:* U.S. Bureau of the Census, 1975.

3. For ages 25–29, I have taken $\alpha = 5/3$ and $m = 1/3$ (or $I = 36$ months); thus $\alpha/m = 5$. For ages 30–34, I take $\alpha = 3/2$ and $m = .3$ (or $I = 40$ months); thus again $\alpha/m = 5$.

4. Note that since F is a function of Y^P, and $p = (F - C)/\alpha$, p is also a function of Y^P.

5. Where $X_a = Y_a(1 - \lambda_a) \Sigma_{i=0}^{a} \lambda_a^i \ln d_{a-i} \ln d_{a-i}/(1 - \lambda_a^{a+1})$; $X_a = Z_a r \Sigma i \lambda_a^i \ln d_{a-i}$ and $Z_a = (1 - \lambda_a)/(1 - \lambda_a^{a+1})$.

REFERENCES

Ben-Porath, Yoram. 1973. Short-term Fluctuations in Fertility and Economic Activity in Israel. *Demography 10*(2): 185–204.

Becker, Gary. 1960. An Economic Analysis of Fertility, *Demographic and Economic Changes in Developed Countries*, National Bureau for Economic Research. Princeton: Princeton University Press.

Butz, W. P. and M. P. Ward. 1979. The Emergence of Countercyclical U.S. Fertility, *American Economic Review 69*(3): 318–328.

Denton, Frank T. and Byron G. Spencer. 1975. *Population and the Economy.* Westmead, Farnborough, Hants., England: Saxon House, D.C. Heath Ltd.

Easterlin, Richard. 1973. Relative economic status and the American fertility swing. *Family Economic Behavior*, Eleanor Sheldon (ed.), Philadelphia: J. B. Lippincott. pp. 170–223.

Freedman, Ronald and Larry Bumpass. 1966. Fertility expectations in the U.S.: 1962–64. *Population Index 32*(2): 181–197.

Freedman, Ronald, Pascal Whelpton, and Arthur Campbell. 1959. *Family Planning, Sterility and Population Growth.* New York: McGraw-Hill.

Lee, Ronald. 1977. Target fertility, contraception and aggregate rates: toward a formal synthesis. *Demography 14*(4): 455–479.

Lee, Ronald. 1977b. *Fluctuations in U.S. Fertility, Age Structure and Income.* Contract Report to NICHHD NO1-HD-42857.

Lee, Ronald. 1980. Aiming at a moving target: period fertility and changing reproductive goals. *Population Studies 34*(2): 205–226.

Lindert, Peter. 1978. *Fertility and Scarcity in America.* Princeton: Princeton University Press.

U.S. Bureau of the Census. 1978. Fertility of American women: June 1977. *Current Population Reports.* Series P-20 No. 325, Washington: U.S. Government Printing Office.

U.S. Bureau of the Census. 1975. Fertility expectations of American women: June 1974. *Current Population Reports.* Series P-20, No. 277. Washington: U.S. Government Printing Office.

U.S. Public Health Service. 1979. Natality, *Vital Statistics of the United States 1975 vol. 1*, Washington: U.S. Government Printing Office.

Wachter, Michael. 1975. A time-series fertility equation: the potential for a baby boom in the 1980s. *International Economic Review 16*: 609–624.

Westoff, Charles and Norman Ryder. 1977a. *The Contraceptive Revolution.* Princeton: Princeton University Press.

Whelpton, Pascall, Arthur Campbell, and John Patterson. 1966. *Fertility and Family Planning in the U.S.* Princeton: Princeton University Press.

Willis, Robert. 1973. A New Approach to the Economic Theory of Fertility Behavior, *Journal of Political Economy 81*(2, supp.): S14–64.

LAND AVAILABILITY AND RURAL FERTILITY IN NORTHEASTERN BRAZIL

Thomas W. Merrick

I. INTRODUCTION

Clarification of relations between land and demographic variables in rural areas of the developing countries is important for policies seeking closer integration of population and rural deveopment. This is true especially for countries with large land areas such as Brazil, whose policies on population and development are premised on the assumption that untapped land resources will provide an escape valve for mounting rural population pressure in more densely settled coastal regions. This paper examines the relation between land and demographic factors in two regions of Brazil: the Northeast and the Amazon. The former is Brazil's poorest region, with a tradition of export-oriented plantation agriculture combined with subsistence farming. For the last three decades, it has experi-

Research in Population Economics, Volume 3, pages 93–121

Copyright © 1981 by JAI Press Inc.

All rights of reproduction in any form reserved.

ISBN: 0-89232-207-1

enced a high rate of natural increase relative to its capacity to absorb additional population (Andrade, 1973). The Amazon is Brazil's last remaining agricultural frontier and has been the target of a number of recent government incentive programs and other initiatives aimed at increasing its utilization, including the Trans-Amazon Highway. Previous expectations regarding the Amazon's capacity to absorb population overflow from the Northeast have been scaled down in the face of growing questions about its suitability for labor intensive agricultural settlement (Mahar, 1978). The present discussion is an outgrowth of earlier work on the relation between land availability and fertility in more settled parts of southeastern and southern Brazil as they compared to frontier settlement areas in the Central–West (Merrick, 1978).

Relations between land and demographic change have been the subject of considerable study in Europe and in regions of overseas European settlement. Scarcity of land, especially when coupled with limitations on migration as an outlet for rural population increase, has been cited as a factor in delayed marriage and declining fertility within marriage in a number of historical instances.[1] The link is a complex one in that land is both a productive input and a store of wealth for farm families who own it or are seeking to obtain it. As a factor of production, it influences the capacity of rural populations to establish and maintain consumption levels for households of given size. As a store of wealth, it may, depending on inheritance systems, influence marriage customs and the number of children desired within marriage in accord with families' concerns about dilution of their wealth through excessive subdivision of their holdings. These considerations led Easterlin (1976a, 1976b) to formulate a bequest hypothesis as an explanation for the relation between declining rural fertility and the degree of settlement in the United States during the last part of the nineteenth century.

Another link between land and demographic processes relates to the size of farm holdings, with variation in farm size hypothesized as an influence on fertility through the demand for child labor. Studies of rural demographic behavior in LDCs that include a consideration of land have emphasized this aspect, though conclusions about the strength and direction of the relationship vary according to the influence of such collateral factors as the type of crop, technology, use of nonfamily labor, and other aspects of the mode of production in particular settings.[2]

A number of other qualifications are required in order to specify adequately the links between land and the demographic behavior of rural households. Differences in land availability and farm size may vary in significance for a number of reasons.[3] Establishing the degree of land availability or scarcity may be difficult even if the total area is known in regions in which land settlement is still occurring. Not all land is used for agriculture, and the land available for agriculture may vary in quality according to terrain, soil fertility, rainfall, and accessibility. Lands suited to forest products or grazing may be of comparatively little value for intensive cropping or may be capable of supporting farm families at little more than the subsistence level. Differences in land tenure arrangements and other institutional factors determining access to land (land use policies and colonization schemes) are an additional and important condition in the land–population relationship. Wealth, income, and/or child labor considerations may weigh quite differently in a family farm situation than for families whose livelihood depends on low wage labor in latifundia and for sharecroppers and subfamily minifundia units.[4]

II. CONCEPTUAL FRAMEWORK

The household production approach to fertility provides some useful guideposts for sorting out and testing empirical relations between land and family size in the Northeast (Brazil), although the limitations of the theory in dealing with poor rural populations must also be recognized. By bringing the increased cost of mother's time and consideration of the child quality into focus in the analysis of fertility control, this theory has proved itself to be a powerful tool in establishing economic–demographic relationships in industrialized countries. In poor rural areas, women have considerably more time available for child care, and the opportunity cost of this time is limited by illiteracy and the scarcity of off-farm employment opportunities. Children are more highly valued for their numbers as farm workers, and investments in child quality are limited.

At the same time, household economic theory has strong appeal in the rural setting because it does take account of the allocation of time in household production and consumption through the concept of full income, in which the role of time and goods in nonmarket as well as market activities are recognized. Full income is especially important because such a high proportion of household economic activity is not monetized. It also creates special problems of measuring and interpreting prices that are imputed to different aspects of these activities, particularly when jointness in production and consumption is recognized. The capacity of poor farm households to rationalize family decisions is often doubted, especially when their awareness of and access to the means of fertility control are limited.

An important qualification to the demand oriented household decision framework as an explanation of fertility differences among low income households in developing countries relates to the comparative importance of conscious individual control of fertility vis-a-vis social and physiological limitations that affect exposure to intercourse and to risk of conception. Sociologists have long emphasized the importance of the latter set of variables, with the Davis–Blake intermediate variables framework being its most significant formal expression (Davis and Blake, 1956).

In response, Easterlin (1978) extended demand-oriented economic theory to incorporate much of the Davis–Blake framework on the "supply" side of the household reproductive model. Supply factors relate to determinants of natural fertility, which refers to variation in family size that results from physiological or cultural influences on the capacity to reproduce rather than conscious individual control. Such differences could occur because of infecundity or high mortality, as well as temporary disruptions due to migration (especially during early phases of frontier settlement), which would lead to decreased exposure to the risk of conception, less likelihood of occurrence of conception, and reduced survival of children who are born. The comparative importance of supply and demand determinants of family size could vary according to the type of social and economic context in which reproductive choices occur. Easterlin has developed a taxonomy of reproductive choice situations to account for such differences and these will be summarized in Section IV. In the early stages of modernization, increases in living standards that reduce demand for children would also be associated with an overriding slackening of "supply" limitations, leading to an actual increase in the number of children. Sustained fertility decline in response to changes in the demand for children is likely to occur after the phase of supply limitations has been passed, although the peak level that is attained may vary according to the interaction of supply and demand factors in particular circumstances.

A parallel view of this transition is provided by J.C. Caldwell, whose theory of the onset of declining fertility in traditional societies rests on the direction and magnitude of intergenerational wealth flows ["or the net balance of the two flows—over the period from when people become parents until they die" (1976:344)]. In pretransition societies, the net balance is child-to-parent, through unpaid family labor, remittance of a share of the earnings from wage labor, old age care, and other aspects of the value of children in such societies. The shift to "child centeredness," with the net balance becoming parent-to-child, is essential for economic influences such as the costs of investment in children through education and bequests to have an impact that will lead to declining fertility. Caldwell stresses that though economic motivation for having children is operative in both pre- and posttransition societies, the shift to this child-centered orientation is more likely to be related to cultural and institutional forces than to economics.

Caldwell's observation reinforces the importance of determining the institutional context in which the influence of economic factors on fertility is assessed. His view of pretransition societies is consistent with Easterlin's description of the early stages of modernization: one in which children have considerable economic value through farm labor, etc., and in which the demand for children could actually exceed supply. In such circumstances, variation in fertility would relate more systematically to variation in supply factors.

Thus, the relation of land availability and other aspects of rural socioeconomic structure to fertility in farm households could vary according to the position of particular rural populations in this cultural and institutional matrix. The bequest hypothesis clearly suggests a balance favoring children in the intergenerational flow of wealth, and land scarcity could well be a factor limiting fertility to the extent that it raises the cost of investment in children. If, on the other hand, children were valued primarily for their contribution as family workers, then a number of outcomes would be possible. If land and children were substitutes, then land scarcity could raise the demand for children. If demand for children were high, but capacity to have children limited by supply factors, land availability could affect fertility through its influence on the supply side.

Since the rural Northeast is Brazil's poorest region, it is very possible that one could find an excess-demand, limited-supply scenario reflected in relations between fertility and land variables there, in contrast to a land-scarcity, declining-fertility situation found in southern Brazil. Data for rural microregions in northern and northeastern Brazil appear to confirm this, and it is to a more detailed empirical examination of the question that we now turn.

III. DATA AND DESCRIPTION OF SOCIOECONOMIC CHARACTERISTICS

The analysis that follows will employ data that have been assembled from published tables in Brazil's 1970 population and agricultural censuses and from unpublished tables made available by Brazil's Census Bureau, the Fundação IBGE (1975). These tables provide information on demographic and socioeconomic characteristics of the rural population for 106 microregions in eight Brazilian states selected from the northeastern and amazonian macroregions (Amazonas, Pará, Maranhão, Piaui, Ceará, Rio Grande do Norte, Paraiba, Pernambuco). Microregions are geographical units intermediate in size between states and municipalities (counties) and have been devised by the Fundação IBGE (1970) to be the basis for more detailed analysis of sample data in the census. The clusters of municipalities that form individual microregions were grouped to insure that these microregions were comparatively homogeneous units of analysis in terms of population size, social structure, economic activities, climate, type of soil, terrain, vegetation, et cetera.

In order to facilitate a summary of the main demographic and socioeconomic differences among rural populations of the Northeast and the Amazon, the microregions have been grouped into six subregional categories. These categories attempt to capture geographic differences in ecological and socioeconomic characteristics and are used in place of state-by-state comparisons because political boundaries mask a number of important shifts in land use and settlement patterns.[5] The categories and their main features are as follows (see map for location): (1) *Zona da Mata*—a narrow, densely populated coastal plain where sugar plantations as well as most of the larger cities of the Northeast are located. (2) *Agreste*—a comparatively narrow transitional region between the coast and high plain in the interior that is well suited to the production of agricultural staples for the coastal region. (3) *Sertão*—a semiarid plain that accounts for most of the land area of the Northeast but is poorly suited to agriculture (with most of the population working in subsistence units) and is subjected to periodic devastating droughts. (4) *Cerrado*—a transition region between the Northeast and the Amazon, in which rainfall and vegetation are more abundant; the region is less settled and, except for areas of extractive forest products, most of the population is engaged in subsistence agriculture and/or cattle grazing. (5) *Frontier*—a group of microregions in the western Cerrado and eastern Amazon subregions, in which agricultural settlement was most intense during the 1960s; it is an area transversed by the Belem-Brasília Highway, which had a significant influence on settlement of the region. (6) *Amazon*—the entire Amazon macroregion except for the frontier areas, in which settlement is very sparse and most of the population and agricultural activities are concentrated along the rivers and clustered near the main cities.

Table 1 presents average measures for a number of demographic characteristics in these subregions. All measures are based on unpublished tabulations of 25 percent sample questions in the 1970 population census, which included children surviving by age of mother. Analysis of microregion data in the next section of the paper will focus on married women aged 30 to 34. This group was selected because sufficient births were recorded to minimize sampling error and because reporting for this group is comparatively less subject to recall error, which increases with age. While this group had not yet completed its reproductive cycle, variation in the number of children born (CEB) and surviving (SURV) to these women is viewed to be representative of differences in fertility and child mortality patterns in the regions.

The question on age at marriage that was asked in the 1960 census was not included in 1970, so that no direct measure of duration of marriage was available. An indirect measure (DUR) was derived from data on the

Map. Regions and Subregions of Northeastern and Amazonian Regions
of Brazil

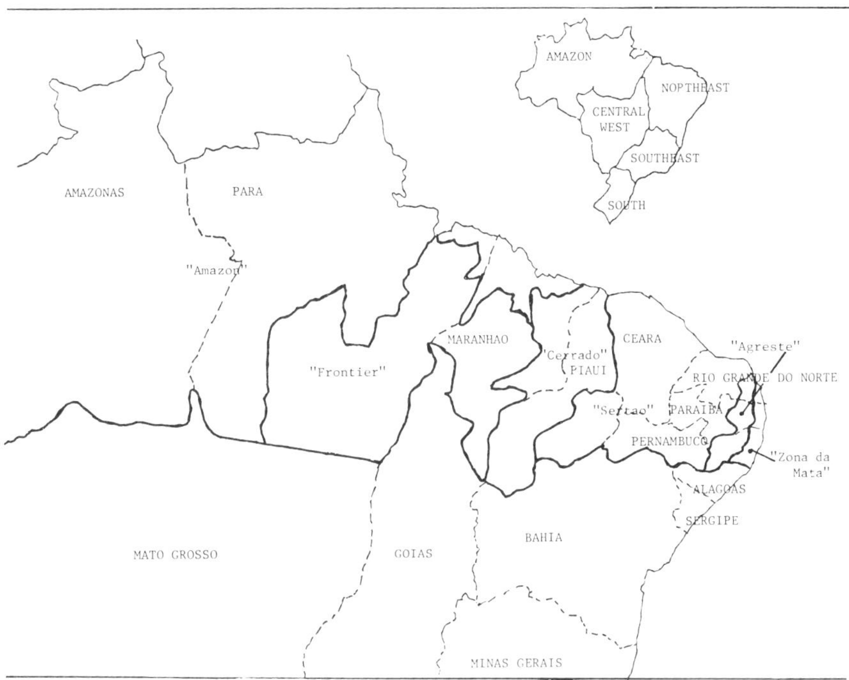

proportions of women aged 15–34 reported as married or in censensual unions in 1970. For this measure to approximate duration of marriage in a particular region up to 1970, it was necessary to assume that the average age at marriage did not change and that migration had not affected the composition of the of the regions' populations. Data on the proportion of women who are migrants (also reported in Table 1) suggest considerable variation across regions in the impact of migration. To reduce bias introduced by migration, the indirect measure of marital duration shown in Table 1 was derived from data on women who were natives to their region. This measure is closely correlated to a measure for all women, but the former was chosen for the reasons just stated.

Data on the proportion of women aged 30–34 reported as literate (LIT) and the proportion of children aged 5–14 attending school (SCHL) are also presented. In the absence of sex-specific rural wage data, literacy will be employed as an approximation for the value of women's time, which is not entirely satisfactory because it reflects a number of other potential influences (including income) on the demographic behavior of farm households. Averages of other demographic measures (total fertility, crude birth rates) are presented in the table but were calculated by sum-

Table 1. Demographic Characteristics of the Northeast and Amazon, by Subregions, in 1970

Characteristic	Symbol	Zona da Mata	Agreste	Sertão	Cerrado	Frontier	Amazon	Total
Children ever born per married rural women, aged 30–34	CEB[a]	6.54	6.53	6.05	5.47	4.98	5.63	5.84
Percent of children surviving from births to women 30–34	SURV	73.3	71.5	77.6	83.5	81.7	85.0	79.6
Average number of years married, women 30–34	DUR	12.3	12.0	11.8	10.6	10.5	10.1	11.2
Percent of rural women aged 30–24 reported as literate	LIT	36.8	39.9	42.9	35.1	37.3	51.3	42.4
Percent of children aged 5–14 attending school	SCHL	31.9	30.8	24.7	27.9	26.1	33.9	27.9
Percent migrants among women in ages 30–34	—[b]	30.9	14.8	16.3	21.4	58.5	16.7	22.4
Coale–Trussell index of fertility level	—[b]	1.04	1.09	1.05	0.80	0.73	0.93	0.96
Coale–Trussell index of fertility control	—[b]	0.20	0.10	0.00	0.07	0.07	0.08	0.04
Crude birth rate	—[b]	55.6	52.5	53.8	52.7	38.4	51.9	51.5
Total fertility rate	—[b]	8.82	8.74	8.54	7.47	6.91	8.67	8.33
N		5	8	47	13	12	21	106

[a] These symbols will be used to identify variables in the regression analysis in Section IV.
[b] Included here for descriptive purposes but not employed in the regression analysis.

ming microregion data and applying the Brass technique to the totals.[6] Sampling error at the microregion level in other age categories made interpretation of microregion results difficult, hence the restriction to the 30–34 age group in the detailed analysis. Averages for the Coale–Trussell indices of the level of fertility and of fertility control are shown. While indirect, these indices are particularly useful in suggesting the extent to which fertility differentials result from conscious control and/or the supply factors mentioned earlier.

Comparison of fertility measures across subregions reveals a pattern of differentials that contrasts with results reported elsewhere for the Southeast (Merrick, 1978). These averages were about 15 percent higher in areas of recent settlement in the Southeast than in the older, more settled regions, and fertility control among farm families adjusting their reproductive behavior to land scarcity appeared to be a partial explanation for the observed behavior. In comparing northeastern and amazonian microregions, the average is *highest* in the more densely settled regions (Zona da Mata, Agreste, and Sertão) and *lowest* in the frontier microregions. These differences show up both in current fertility measures (total fertility and crude birth rates) and in the number of children-ever-born for married women aged 30–34. Another contrast is provided by the two Coale–Trussell indices, which suggest that fertility differences are not related to fertility control. In no case shown in Table 1 does the index of fertility control exceed 0.2, which is suggested by Coale and Trussell as a cutoff point for even minimal control. What the Coale–Trussell measures do suggest is that the differences are related to the *level* of the fertility schedule vis-a-vis the natural fertility standard. Such differences could arise either from fertility control being practiced more vigorously by younger women, which implies that the natural fertility model is inappropriate for the population in question, or from supply factors affecting the whole schedule or some combination of both.

Another supply consideration is marital duration, which varies positively with the number of children ever born. The extent to which age of entry into sexual unions (a main determinant of marital duration— dissolution of unions through mortality and separation being the other) is a culturally determined supply factor or a conscious mechanism for controlling the number of children within marital unions in response to demand is an important question for the interpretation of its relation to fertility differences. Coale argues that earlier or later marriage is a different kind of response from the voluntary reduction of marital fertility and arises from a different set of social forces: ''Couples marry within a range of socially accepted ages, and postpone marriage within that range because of inability to satisfy the current norms (e.g., of dowry, property ownership, or income) for marriage. Few couples marry at 25 instead of

24 because of the calculation that they will have one birth less''
(1975:349). Demand theorists would probably disagree with the last
statement, though their arguments would be more valid in societies in
which fertility is also controlled within marriage and less applicable to
those in which conscious individual control is limited.

Another aspect of the relation between exposure to intercourse and fertility relates to migration. Delay of entry into unions and/or temporary
separation during early stages of frontier settlement could also lower the
number of children reported for the frontier category, since its migrant
share is particularly high there. Interestingly, the coastal Zona da Mata
microregions show the next highest migrant share, but with high fertility
levels, suggesting that the migration factor, if operative, depends upon the
nature of the migration flow.[8]

Subregional means for economic variables relating to the demographic
behavior of rural households are shown in Table 2. The ratio of agricultural land to total land area is presented as an index of the comparative
scarcity of land (LRAT), which decreases as one moves from the densely
settled coastal regions toward the Amazon. Median farm size (SIZE), on
the other hand, increases. The average value of farm land reflects both
its scarcity and quality, as is illustrated in the Sertão, where land is scarce
but low in quality, and in the Amazon, where land in farm establishments
in 1970 represented a small portion of the total but was comparatively
high in value. Variables indicating the utilization of machinery (value of
farm equipment; EQPT) and hired labor (salaries per employed worker;
SAL) are utilized as measures of other farm inputs that are potential substitutes for child labor. Differences in land tenure arrangements are reflected in the proportion of farms with owner–operators (OPER), who
represent a much larger share of total operators in the less settled regions
than in the coastal regions. Since only a small portion (less than 2 percent) of the reported work of children was market labor, analysis of child
labor will concentrate on unpaid family work, measured as the proportion
of children aged 5–14 reported as family laborers (UPFW) in the farm
operator's household.

The pattern of subregional differentials in Table 2 suggests that unpaid
labor is related to farm size and that farm machinery and hired labor
may be substitutes for child labor. A major question in analysis of relations between household investment in children (number of children,
schooling, leisure versus labor) and other economic variables is the extent
to which these substitution effects may be offset by income effects related
to these same variables, which would yield observed uncompensated
elasticities that are less than or opposite in sign to "true" compensated effects. Children are usually assumed to be "normal" goods (income elasticity positive but less than 1), and observed negative correlations

Table 2. Economic Characteristics of the Northeast and Amazon, by Subregion, 1970

Characteristic	Symbol	Zona da Mata	Agreste	Sertão	Cerrado	Frontier	Amazon	Total
Percent of total land area of region used by farm establishments	LRAT[a]	77.3	87.9	76.2	46.8	27.2	16.7	55.8
Median size of farm establishments, in hectares	SIZE	2.9	3.7	11.5	12.3	15.9	26.4	14.0
Value of farm land, cruzeiros per hectare[b]		597.2	386.3	97.6	25.8	31.8	101.5	127.5
Value of machinery, cruzeiros per hectare	EQPT	38.3	17.4	5.9	2.0	5.5	20.1	10.6
Salaries of employed farm labor, cruzeiros per month	SAL	121.9	97.9	105.1	316.8	116.6	184.2	148.3
Owner-operators as percent of all farm operators	OPER	40.2	71.3	60.6	91.8	76.3	84.2	70.7
Percent of children aged 5–14 reported as unpaid family workers	UPFW	9.7	24.6	22.8	25.5	41.7	34.1	27.0
Percent of children aged 5–14 reported as wage laborers[b]		1.1	0.7	2.5	0.6	0.7	0.2	1.4

[a] These symbols will be used to identify variables in the regression analysis in Section IV.

[b] Included here for descriptive purposes but not employed in the regression analysis.

between income and fertility, when they occur, are ordinarily interpreted as the composite of a "true" income effect and as offsetting substitution effects for such variables as the value of mother's time, which is positively associated with income. Analysis of the role of income in these data is complicated by the lack of information on rural household income. Brazilian national accounts provide data on agricultural income and on the population dependent on agriculture, but provide no way of determining what share to attribute to farm families. Since no suitable measure was found, it will be necessary to discern income efforts indirectly as they emerge in other variables.

IV. ANALYSIS

Quantitative specification of the structure of relations between observed fertility differentials and socioeconomic variables in northern and northeastern Brazil must deal with several problems in addition to the one just mentioned. Data limitations put major constraints on the level of analysis since neither the population census nor the agricultural census data that are available permit matching of information at the level of individual households. Care must therefore be taken to avoid drawing inferences about household behavior from the available microregion data that are, in fact, valid only for such aggregates.

Recognition that both supply and demand factors can determine the outcome of childbearing decisions raises the problem of identifying their separate contributions to observed differentials among regions. Demand considerations should account for variation in income, costs of children, and the satisfaction the parents derive from having children. The latter is a difficult concept to capture in quantitative terms since a variety of considerations, many of them transcending quantifiable measure, enter into the valuation of children, and the relative weight of these considerations varies according to particular socioeconomic and cultural contexts. Measurements are feasible for some dimensions (e.g., the number of children born and surviving, their education, and to some extent their contribution of labor to household and market production) but not others.

Since background variables relating to rural socioeconomic structure and to characteristics of rural households may also influence the supply of children, care is required in identifying the causal structure of models attempting to explain the observed number of surviving children. A variable such as education of women could be a proxy for the value of a mother's time in analysis of the effect of variation in the opportunity costs of children on demand and at the same time be a determinant of supply because of its relation to child survival, marital duration, and other supply variables (see Cochrane, 1979).

One way to deal with the identification problem is to establish particular subsets of variables as being uniquely supply or demand related. This approach is suggested in Easterlin's analytical framework, in which the observed number of surviving children could reflect either supply or demand or neither, depending on the type of reproductive regime in which the society that is being studied finds itself. Four such regimes are identified in the Easterlin framework:

1. Demand exceeds supply and there is no conscious control of fertility. In this case, the observed number of surviving children is equal to supply by virtue of the supply constraint.

2. Supply exceeds demand, but there is still no conscious individual control of fertility. The situation is now one of excess supply, and without control, the actual number of children continues to track on the supply curve.

3. Supply exceeds demand, and there is a conscious but incomplete control of fertility by individual couples. This is the most common case in societies experiencing a demographic transition and also the most difficult one to analyze since the actual number of children falls between supply and demand and neither curve can be determined on the basis of the observed number of children alone.

4. Supply exceeds demand, and there is conscious and complete control of fertility. In this case, the observed number of children is identical with demand.

Easterlin's breakdown permits identification of differences in supply if analysis of fertility variation is restricted to situations (1) and (2) in which there is no conscious individual control of fertility. Demand variation may also exist but would relate to other dimensions of the satisfaction deriving from children than the number of children actually observed.

Can such a strategy validly be used to interpret observed fertility differentials in Brazil's rural Northeast around 1970? While no direct evidence of fertility control practice is available for this period, the indirect Coale–Trussell indices presented in the previous section suggest that practice of fertility limitation within marriage was limited or nonexistent. In such circumstances, the assumption that differences in the observed number of surviving children reflects variation in supply is a reasonable one. This assumption does not imply anything about the relation of supply to demand [e.g., whether demand exceeds supply, as in situation (1) above, or whether supply exceeds demand as in (2)]; it implies only that all of the observed differences lie within the range of the first two of the four possible regimes described in the Easterlin framework. Demand, if it is to be identified, will be related to such aspects of the satisfaction from surviving children as child labor and investments in child quality. Separate analyses of supply and demand for surviving children are thus possible, and we will proceed first with the question of supply.

The supply of surviving children is composed of two main components: the number of births and the proportion of children born alive who survive to the time at which differences are observed. To control for variation relating to age composition and to avoid the problems of sampling error and recall mentioned earlier, the analysis is restricted to observations pertaining to married women aged 30–34 years. Since surviving children are the product of births and the proportion of survivors, the operational dependent variables in the analysis are the latter. In the absence of fertility control, the number of births is determined by intermediate variables such as fecundity and exposure to intercourse, and these are determined in turn by socioeconomic characteristics that could influence these intermediate variables. Child survival similarly would be related to environmental variables and other socioeconomic characteristics.

Particular attention to the relation between the number of births and child survival is required since it is likely that they are mutually independent. The number of children already born could affect the survival chances of new arrivals, whereas high levels of infant mortality could also affect fecundity by way of its effect on postpartum amenorrhea. One infant mortality–fertility relation that is precluded by there being no conscious individual control of fertility is the child-replacement motive for having additional births, since this would imply that parents who had *not* experienced loss of children were regulating the number of additions. Thus, in the path structure of relations in Figure 1, the number of births and child survival are shown as jointly dependent variables rather than with one of the two being casually prior to the other. The one intermediate variable that could be measured (and only indirectly) was marital duration. The remaining variables pertain to socioeconomic characteristics of the rural Northeast that could influence child survival and the number of births either directly or through the intermediate variables. These include female literacy, median farm size, the proportion of operators who owned their own land, and the ratio of land used for agriculture to total land area in each microregion.

Path analysis has been utilized to determine the direct and indirect effects of independent variables on births and proportions surviving. Figure 1 shows the structure of significant paths that were estimated. Because of simultaneity in the structure, two-stage least squares regression was employed as the estimating technique. In the second stage regressions, the birth equation was identified by excluding the land use ratio variable, while land ownership was excluded in the survivorship equation.[9]

Figure 1.　Path Analysis of Microregion Differentials in Children Ever Born and Children Surviving for Married Women Aged 30–34, 1970 Census Data

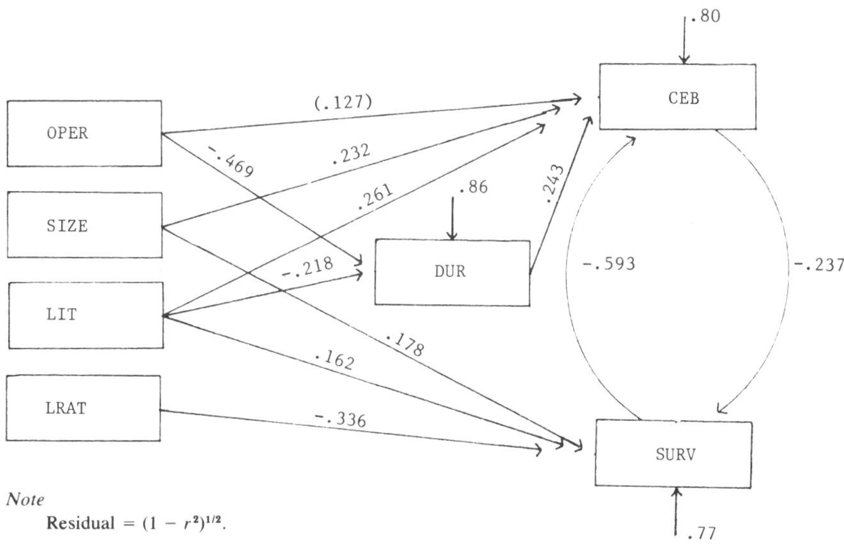

Note
　Residual $= (1 - r^2)^{1/2}$.

The paths shown in Figure 1 indicate that there are mutually reinforcing negative effects between child survival and the number of live births. Longer marriage duration increases the number of births and is itself influenced by other socioeconomic variables. A more complex set of relations between socioeconomic variables and births pertains to female literacy. Its direct effect is positive, suggesting that it is a proxy for positive effects relating to the standard of living. However, it also has negative influence on births through the mediation of marital duration and child survival. Increased literacy has a negative impact on marital duration and a positive impact on child survival, both of which would tend to offset its direct positive effect. The other two variables in the births equation have contrasting effects on births. The effect of farm ownership is indirect and negative. Farm owners have shorter marriage duration, which would reduce the number of births. The significance of the direct path between farm ownership and fertility was marginal. Farm size has a positive effect on the number of births, but in this case, the indirect path by way of marital duration was not significant. As with literacy, the standard of living may be influential in the effect of the farm size variable.

The last point is reinforced when we examined the paths linking literacy and farm size to the number of births by way of child survival. Both variables have a positive effect on child survival, which would create an offsetting negative effect on births through the mediation of the latter variable. The positive relation between land availability and the number of births can also be interpreted in this way. The regions with the highest ratio of land in use to land available are also the most densely populated and have the largest proportion of population with incomes below the poverty level. The path linking the land use ratio to the number of births is a mediated one (by way of its negative effect on child survivorship) and has a positive impact on the number of births.

Conventional decomposition of direct and indirect effects in path analysis is not appropriate when one of the mediating variables (child survival in the birth equation and vice versa) is determined simultaneously rather than treated as a casually prior variable. Some insight into the relative importance of direct versus indirect effects of variables in the birth equation can be obtained in a decomposition that is limited to total and direct effects and treats all indirect effects as a residual.[10] Table 3 presents such a decomposition of the effects of farm size, farm ownership, and literacy into direct effects and effects mediated by marital duration and child survival.

Decomposition confirms an earlier speculation about the direct and indirect effects of literacy, farm size, and farm ownership. The total effect of literacy nets out to zero since the positive direct effect is offset by negative indirect effects through marital duration and child survival. The total effect of farm size is also insignificant since the positive direct effect is offset by negative direct effects. Finally, land ownership has a negative total effect on births, mainly because of the negative mediating effects of duration and survival. Its direct effect, while positive, is not statistically significant.

To sum up the discussion of supply differences, a plausible case can be made for linking observed differences in the number of surviving children (as the product of the number of births and the proportion of these births surviving) to a complex of socioeconomic factors affecting the capacity of farm families to have the number of children that has actually been observed. In the absence of conscious individual control of fertility within marriage, interregional variation in the number of surviving children depends on socioeconomic determinants of the capacity to reproduce, either directly or indirectly via mediating variables. In the case of a variable such as literacy, the structure of this relation is complex, with offsetting positive direct and negative indirect effects leading to an insignificant net influence on supply.

The fact that observed differences in the number of children identify supply differences in the particular set of circumstances observed here does not imply that variation in the demand for children is absent. However, the data are not particularly useful in showing how demand and

Table 3.　Decomposition of Paths for Children Ever Born,
Schooling, and Unpaid Family Workers

Dependent and independent variables	Total effect	Indirect effect	Direct effect
1. *CEB*			
LIT	0.007	−0.254	0.261
OPER	−0.296	−0.423	0.127
SIZE	−0.004	−0.236	0.232
2. *SCHL*			
LIT	0.771	0.078	0.693
OPER	−0.194	−0.043	0.237
SIZE	−0.242	−0.025	−0.217
3. *UPFW*			
LRAT	−0.210	0.105	−0.315
OPER	0.331	−0.030	0.316
SIZE	0.246	0.036	0.210

supply are related to each other. Identification of demand differences is difficult in this situation, because data on demand variables are either not available or only very loosely measured in available census data. A combination of questions in the agricultural and population censuses does permit measurement of two potentially important components of variation in the demand for children: child labor and schooling (the latter is a proxy for investment in child quality). Again, measures refer to microregional averages rather than variation among individual household, so that care is required in interpretation of observed patterns. Such measures, while suggestive of the magnitude and direction of these patterns, are not precise enough to permit very close specification of the underlying behavioral relations that have been hypothesized in the theoretical literature, which suggests that the demand for children will decline as their price (in terms of goods and the value of their mother's time) rises compared to other goods and to the extent that children are a time-intensive item in household production.[11] A corollary is that investments in child quality are substitutes for child quantity and will increase as income and as the price of child quantity rises.

A major problem of measurement arises in determining the value of children's time in situations in which a market for child labor is not well established due to seasonality of demand and for a high proportion of child labor being nonmonetized in the form of unpaid family labor. Elasticities of child schooling and leisure (or their complement, child labor) with respect to prices of other agricultural inputs have been suggested as proxies for the marginal economic contribution of children. Rosenzweig (1977) has shown that the signs of uncompensated elasticities for child labor with respect to the prices of other agricultural inputs such as machinery and hired labor depend first upon their being substitutes or complements in productions. If, under a reasonable assumption for LDCs, machinery and hired labor are substitutes for child labor, the signs are still ambiguous in that a change in the price of these inputs also affects farm income, introducing a possibly offsetting income effect on the demand for children. The magnitude of this depends upon the income elasticity of children and the relative share of the substituted factor in full farm income. The effect of an increase in farm size, which would raise demand for children (assuming complementarity), as well as income, would also be ambiguous in that it also raises the marginal value of other inputs.

Path analysis is employed here to study the relationship of the proportion of rural children in school and the proportion engaged in unpaid family labor to two sets of variables to which variation in these averages could be linked. The first set of variables relates to outlays on other farm outputs that are potential substitutes for child labor and/or complementary to investments in child quality. These variables are (1) average outlays for salaries paid per hired farm worker and (2) the average value of farm equipment per hectare of land in agriculture. The computation of path coefficients is analogous to computation of elasticities, except that the ratio of standard errors is used to weight the former, whereas the ratio of means is employed for the latter. Path analysis makes it possible to determine the influence of background variables on intermediate variables but does not show the responsiveness of the dependent variable to these variables as clearly as elasticities. The latter will be reported with respect to salaries and farm equipment.

The second set of variables consists of background variables relating to aspects of rural socioeconomic structure that could influence levels of schooling and child labor either directly or through the mediation of the alternative farm input/investment opportunities described in the previous paragraph. The variables that are considered include female literacy, median farm size, the proportion of farms that are owner operated, and the ratio of land used for agriculture to total land. Literacy is a very rough measure of the value of mother's time, reflecting farm households' standard of living as well, but it is the only index available in the absence of data on female wages. Variations in farm size may also reflect income differences. The land-use measure and the proportion of owners are both included as a means of introducing into the discussion the effects of differences among regions in the institutional setting and the degree of settlement.

Figure 2 presents the results of path regressions for unpaid family workers and school attendance. Only those independent variables for which significant paths exist are shown, although all the variables

Figure 2. Path Analysis of Microregion Differences in the Proportion of Rural Children Age 5–14 Attending School and Reported as Unpaid Family Workers, 1970 Census Data

A. Unpaid Family Workers

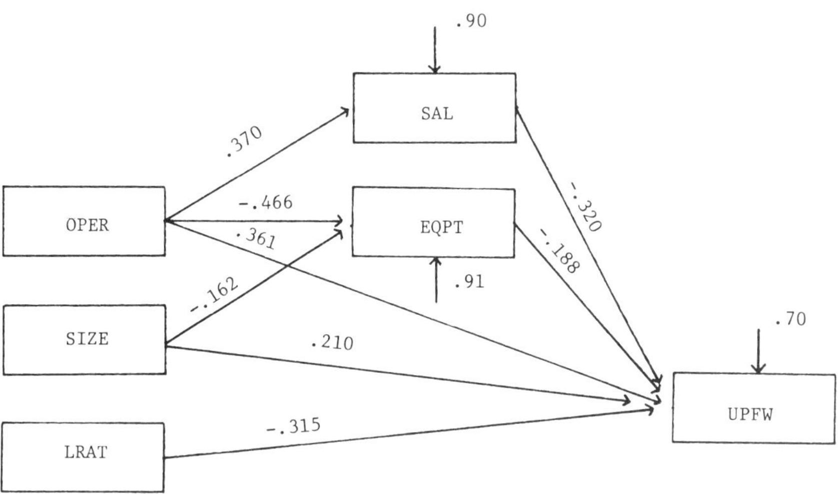

B. School Attendance

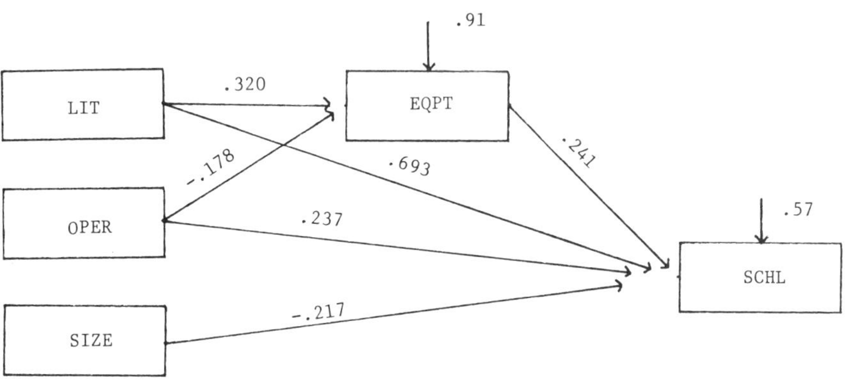

Note

Residual $= (1 - r^2)^{1/2}$.

111

described earlier were included at earlier stages of analysis. In the results for unpaid family workers (Figure 2A), the effects of variation in salary levels and farm equipment were negative, as earlier theoretical discussions suggested they would be.[12] The direct effect of farm size is also positive, but its total effect is mediated by its relation to farm equipment. Table 3 decomposes the effects of the size, ownership, and land use variables into direct and indirect effects. The indirect effect of farm size on unpaid family workers is also positive because of the negative relation between size and equipment per hectare and the latter's negative relation to unpaid family workers. It is important to recognize that the sign of the indirect effect for size relates to its association with equipment at the microregion level and does not necessarily imply that larger individual farm units would have a smaller stock of equipment per hectare, although it is quite likely that this would be the case since this variable is measured on a per hectare basis. If this is not done, farm size becomes the main component of differences in the stock of equipment.

The proportion of unpaid family workers declines as the land-use ratio increases. The land-use ratio also has an indirect effect via the farm equipment variable. This is positive because of the negative relation between land-use ratios and the stock of equipment. A third variable whose effect is mediated by farm investment is the proportion of owner–operators. Again the direct effect of this variable on the proportion of unpaid family workers is positive. At the same time, there is less equipment per hectare in regions where the proportion of owner–operators is high, which would lead us to expect a positive indirect effect. However the effect of ownership is mediated also by the salary per worker being higher where ownership is higher, which would have a negative effect on unpaid family workers. The latter appears to outweigh the effect mediated by farm equipment, so that the net indirect effect of ownership is negative.

Again, it is important in interpreting these relations to stress that averages for microregions rather than individual farm units are being observed. The picture that emerges is one in which the expected substitution effects between unpaid family labor vis-a-vis labor and farm equipment conform to theoretical expectations. The data also indicate that the strength of these relations depends on the rural economic structural variables, particularly land ownership, which has a strong influence on salaries and farm equipment stock in addition to its direct effect on unpaid family work. The level of disaggregation that can be achieved with published census data does not permit separate anlyses for owners and non-owners; such analyses would reveal much more of the nature of these differences. In addition, regional averages suggest that areas with a low degree of land utilization and with large average farm size are the most likely to have higher proportions of unpaid family workers and that the direct effect of these variables is reinforced through their influence on the levels of salaries and farm equipment.

Figure 2B presents a path analysis of microregion level data on the proportion of children in school. Preliminary analyses did not yield significant coefficients for the salary and land-use ratio, and only the variables with significant paths are shown. To the extent that the proportion of children in school and the stock of farm equipment per hectare are indicative of levels of investment (at either the farm or community level), the path regressions suggest that the two forms of investment are complementary. Female literacy, which reflects differences in the value of mothers' time as well as in the general standard of living, is also complementary with such investments. Most of the positive effect of female literacy is direct, but as the decomposition of the effects in Table 3 shows, about 10 percent of its total effect operates through its relation to the farm equipment variable. Farm size has an opposite effect. Proportions in school are lower where median farm size is higher, which suggests a substitution between child labor and schooling (at least with respect to this variable) because of the difference in signs of the size coefficient for the two dependent variables. The indirect effect of the size variable is negative, but not statistically significant.

The behavior of the owner–operator variable indicates that there may be important differences relating to the type of rural economic structure. The proportion of children in school is higher in regions in which the proportion of owner–operators is higher. The indirect effect of the owner–operator variable is negative because of its negative impact on farm equipment and the latter's positive relation to schooling. Except for the difference in sign in the indirect effect (which has to do with the effect of the equipment variable), the owner–operator variable relates in a very similar manner to both dependent variables: schooling *and* unpaid family workers. In both cases, the effect is positive and comparatively strong.

This suggests that demand forces may operate more strongly among owner–operators than other land tenure arrangements and landless laborers. It would be possible to test for this interaction if the regressions could be run separately for different types of tenure arrangements.

V. CONCLUSIONS

Returning to the question that was posed at the beginning of the paper about the impact of land availability and land tenure patterns on fertility in Brazil's rural Northeast and the Amazon, a few qualified conclusions can be drawn from the data analyzed here. In terms of the variability in indices of the number of children ever born, their survival, school attendance, and farm labor participation, the range in the Northeast and the Amazon is at least as great as that found in the rural Southeast, but the significance of differences varies in a number of important respects.

Evidence on the Southeast suggested a pattern of incipient fertility decline relating to conscious individual fertility control, i.e., a response to factors associated with increased costs of raising children (increased opportunity costs for mothers' time, as indicated by a negative relation of fertility to literacy and off-farm employment opportunities and by increased scarcity of land). In the Northeast and the Amazon, the links between land availability, land tenure patterns, and fertility are related to supply factors. There is no evidence that fertility differences in these regions are determined by conscious individual reproductive choices; so the observed number of children for rural married women aged 30–34 represent the maximum number that they could have within existing limits on their capacity to reproduce. This number could be less than, equal to, or possibly greater than the number that they desire, but in the absence of control, it is *supply* rather than demand that is identified by this number. The analysis of observed fertility therefore focuses on the impact of land availability, tenure, and literacy on supply.

Data limitations put important constraints on the precision with which these effects can be determined. Measurement of differences at the level of individual farm households was not possible, so analysis has been carried out using averages for each microregion of fertility levels, farm size, proportion of farm operators who were owners, tenants, etc. Clearly it would have been preferable to work with individual households or with averages for particular tenure/size groups, but the available data did not permit a matching of population and agricultural census data at these levels. This also reduced the number of indices that would be employed, since the proportion in one tenure class (e.g., operators) was generally a close complement of those in others (e.g., employees or tenants), making it statistically difficult to work with more than one of these variables at a time.

Despite these limitations, the analysis provides some useful insights into the links between land and reproductive patterns in the rural Northeast and Amazon. It shows, for example, that the direct effects are balanced or offset by indirect effects through mediating variables. The direct effect of the owner–operator variable on children ever born is positive, but the same variable is related also to shorter marital duration, which has a more powerful negative indirect effect on the number of children. The relation of farm size to the number of children is similar, except that the offsetting indirect effect is mediated by child survival, which is related to farm size. Indirect effects also help to explain the positive association between literacy and the number of children because higher literacy is related positively to increased survival and negatively to marital duration, both of which generate negative indirect effects on the number of children. No direct relation between land availability and the number of children is evident in the data, but an indirect effect was found in the positive relation between land availability (or negative with land scarcity) and child survival, which itself is related negatively to the number of children.

That supply rather than demand conditions are more influential in the *number* of children does not imply that other aspects of rural households' demographic behavior related to demand factors are inoperative for investment in child quality. In the case of the two factors examined here (schooling and child labor), behavior of rural households exhibits patterns that are consistent with demand theory. Again, the role of indirect effects is important for understanding these patterns. The owner–operator variable has a positive direct effect on both schooling and child labor but generates partially offsetting indirect effects through the farm equipment variable, to which it has a negative relation. The latter variable has a strong positive effect on schooling and a negative one on child labor, which is consistent with theoretical expectations about the relations of complementarity and substitution between these variables in farm households' investments and production decisions. Similar patterns of direct and indirect effects relate farm size positively to child labor and negatively to schooling. The negative relation between farm labor and land use is mediated also by the latter's negative relation to farm equipment, which generates a positive but not offsetting indirect effect. Female literacy strongly reinforces school attendance, both directly and through the farm equipment variable, indicating complementarity between human and physical capital investments in farm households.

The presence of these demand relations in school attendance and labor of children in rural households' suggests that efforts to increase conscious control of the number of children in these households could generate responses that are similar to those already occurring in rural areas of southern and southeastern Brazil if alternative outlets for child investments in the direction of child quality were also enhanced.

Recent developments suggest that analysis of 1980 census data will reveal patterns in the Northeast that more closely approximate the 1970 southeastern pattern. Programs to increase access to basic service (health, water, education) in the Northeast have been undertaken, and the Brazilian government has expressed a willingness to assist low income households in planning their families (though implementation has been limited to agreements between state governments and Brazil's IPPF affiliate, BEMFAM).

These positive signs should be balanced by recognition of a number of major structural problems confronting development efforts in the Northeast and Amazon. The combination of high natural increase up to 1970, decreasing land availability, and very unequal access to that land have put major pressures on poor farm households. Because of the region's long history of unequal social and economic opportunities, alternative forms of child investment are very limited for a large proportion of the poorest groups. The data presented here suggest that rural northeastern households may be capable of responding to alternatives, but that the degree to which they actually do it could depend to a major extent on the success of public policy efforts to extend and reinforce them.

APPENDIX A

Zero-Order Correlations

	SUR	*DUR*	*LIT*	*OPER*	*SIZE*	*LRAT*	*EQPT*	*SAL*	*SCHL*	*UPFW*
CEB	−0.64	−0.46	0.04	−0.30	−0.06	−0.43	0.03	−0.24	−0.06	−0.29
SURV		0.35	0.19	0.36	0.31	−0.60	−0.01	0.31	−0.01	0.29
DUR			−0.32	0.43	0.18	0.65	−0.04	0.20	−0.13	0.39
LIT				−0.11	0.04	−0.10	0.34	0.05	0.74	−0.06
OPER					0.20	−0.64	−0.24	0.42	0.06	0.51
SIZE						−0.31	−0.13	0.08	−0.16	0.38
LRAT							0.38	−0.31	−0.14	−0.50
EQPT								0.13	0.45	−0.32
SAL									0.03	−0.07
SCHL										−0.05

APPENDIX B

Summary of Regression Results for Dependent Variables
in Path Analysis

	CEB[a]	*SURV*[a]	*UPFW*[a]	*SCHL*[a]
CEB[b]	—	−0.036 (0.019)	—	—
SURV[b]	−9.968 (2.189)	—	—	—
DUR	0.121 (0.049)	—	—	—
LIT	1.415 (0.049)	0.082 (0.034)	—	0.546 (0.048)
OPER	0.429 (0.322)	—[d]	0.262 (0.076)	0.116 (0.029)
SIZE[c]	0.681 (0.257)	0.049 (0.019)	0.133 (0.047)	−0.093 (0.025)
SAL[c]	—	—	0.028 (0.006)	—
EQPT[c]	—	—	0.130 (0.055)	0.113 (0.029)
LRAT[c]	—[d]	−0.061 (0.023)	0.132 (0.042)	—
CONSTANT	11.433 (1.198)	1.000 (0.095)	0.095 (0.073)	0.034 (0.030)
R^2	36.5[e]	41.2[e]	50.6	67.1
F	11.5	14.0	20.5	51.4
MEAN SQUARE ERROR	0.217	0.001	0.009	0.008
MEAN (STANDARD DEVIATION) of DEPENDENT VARIABLE	5.84 (0.623)	0.796 (0.058)	0.270 (0.134)	0.279 (0.090)

[a] Standard errors of regression coefficients shown in parentheses.
[b] Values estimated in first stage of TSLS.
[c] Values divided by 100 for purposes of scaling.
[d] Variable excluded in second state of TSLS.
[e] From first stage of TSLS.

ACKNOWLEDGMENT

Research for this paper was conducted with partial support of an award (No. RF76102) by the Ford and Rockefeller Foundations under their Population and Development Policy Research Program.

NOTES

1. See Davis, 1963:355. "The common process by which reproduction was brought into equilibrium with the agrarian economy [in northwestern Europe] was the postponement or hastening of marriage according to the socially defined scarcity or abundance of land." More recent surveys are found in Tilly (1978) and Stokes *et al.* (1979). Tilly observed that the expansion of rural wage labor tends to weaken the peasant system of population control and that the poor, economically dependent populations of the Third World are more likely to repeat the experiences of the proletarian segments of rural population in Europe (pp. 22–23). For further evidence on Western Europe, see Demeny (1968), Goldscheider (1971), and Braun (1978).

2. Kleinman (1973) and Rosenzweig and Evenson (1977) report positive relationships between fertility and farm size in rural India. Ozorio de Almeida (1977) and Chernichovsky

(1976) report similar results for a small sample of farms in the Brazilian Northeast, pointing out that allotments of land to sharecroppers were often made on the basis of family size. On the other hand, Singh *et al.* (1978) found no significant relation between farm size and children ever born in the sample of 483 farm families that they drew from area of Ceará, Minas Gerais, and São Paulo. DeVany and Sanchez (1977) found a parallel type of institutional situation in studying *ejido* areas of Mexico, in which *ejiditarios'* usufruct rights to land depended upon having family labor to continue utilizing it. These situations points to the role of institutional and technological factors in conditioning the land fertility nexus, a point that is emphasized by Stokes *et al.* (1979:30). De Janvry (1975) suggests that the utilization of machinery and hired labor as substitutes for child labor may increase with farm size, reducing the marginal contribution of children, and Durham (1977) reports that data on El Salvador show that marginal contribution of children to be greatest under conditions of increasing rather than decreasing land scarcity.

3. Stokes *et al.* (1979) suggest that at least three dimensions of land availability need to be considered: (1) physical availability; (2) quality or use-capacity, which includes variation in productivity: (3) legal and informal institutional forces that govern the use of property and the distribution of the produce of land.

4. For a discussion of land use and land tenure in Brazil, see Schuh (1970) and Brant (1976). Ozorio de Almeida argues that under the share tenancy system found in many parts of the Northeast, tenants allocate resources to either children or to land rentals to maintain income, and that as the rents increase, they invest more in children.

5. Brazilian geographers often employ this type of breakdown instead of interstate comparisons because of the peculiarities of state boundaries. The state of Pernambuco, for example, cuts across three types of geographic areas. These subregions and divisions are discussed in Andrade (1973). Microregions were assigned to subregions using criteria found in Fundação IBGE (1970, 1973) and Lopes (1976).

6. Detailed description of techniques utilized to derive such standard demographic measures as the total fertility and crude birth rates from questions in censuses can be found in National Academy of Sciences, Committee on Population and Demography, *Demographic Estimation: A Manual of Indirect Techniques,* which will be published in 1981.

7. This method is described in Coale and Trussell (1974). Their measure derived from the ratios of a population's age-specific marital fertility rates to a standard representing natural fertility (therefore, no fertility control). Marital fertility at ages 20 to 24 is first compared to the standard rate for that cohort (yielding an index of the level of fertility), and then indexes of fertility control are determined for each of the remaining cohorts as a function of the degree to which they fall below the rates in the standard pattern. The fertility control index reported here was calculated using the procedure described in Coale and Trussell (1974), and refers to the pattern observed for married women aged 20 to 44.

8. Vehlo (1973) reports a high degree of temporary separation of spouses during early stages of frontier settlement in this region.

9. Residuals are not correlated with the total population of microregions, so weighted regression was not employed. The Fundação IBGE designed microregions (in 1968) to be approximately equal in total population.

10. This decomposition employs the method described in Alwin and Hauser (1975). Further discussion of decomposition of direct and indirect effects in simultaneous equations systems is found in Duncan (1975:73–75).

11. Following Schultz (1976), the elasticity of children with respect to the value of the wife's time (η_{CT}) is related to the own price elasticity of children ($\eta_{C\pi}$), the income elasticity of children (η_{CI}), the wife's relative value intensity on children (S_C) compared to other goods (S_G), and the relative importance of the time value of the wife's activities in total income (V). That is: $\eta_{CT} = \eta_{C\pi}(S_C - S_G) + V\eta_{CI}$. If children are normal goods ($0 < \eta_{CI} - 1$), V small, and children comparatively time intensive, then the negative $\eta_{C\pi}$ should dominate

η_{CT}. It is conceivable that $(S_C - S_G)$ could be small and V large enough for the income effect to dominate η_{CT}. Child care may not be competitive with women's time in home production, and the marginal contribution of the latter to full household income could well increase as the value of the wife's time increases. These arguments have been extended to include considerations appropriate for rural agricultural settings by Rosenzweig (1977), whose framework provides useful guidance here. In the application of this framework to data on rural India, Rosenzweig and Evenson (1977) tested a model in which the household decision process was restricted to four "commodities": the quantity of children, schooling of children (as investment in child quality), child leisure (with child labor as the complement of schooling and child leisure), and a composite representing the standard of living of the household. The model was further restricted on having only the wife make a time input to child quantity, and only children making an input to schooling and child leisure. They maximized a utility function defined in terms of these four commodities subject to full income constraint encompassing the value of the full-time of household members.

Their exercise yielded several combinations of compensated substitution elasticities of the three-child investment commodities with respect to the value of the children's time. The shadow price of children was a positive function of the value of the wife's time, goods used to produce children, and levels of child schooling and leisure, but negatively related to children's earnings. The only set of elasticities with unambiguous signs was one in which schooling and leisure were complements with each other but substitutes for child quantity. Compensated elasticities of schooling and leisure with respect to the value of the wife's time were unambiguously positive, but for the elasticity of child quantity to have a negative sign, the comparative intensity of the wife's time in raising children has to be greater than for the other activities in order to dominate the income effect deriving from the changes in time being made available for these other activities.

12. The elasticities of UFFW and SCHL with respect to SAL and EQPT are

	EQPT	SAL
UFFW	0.05	0.04
SCHL	0.15	–

While these magnitudes suggest a limited response, it is important to recognize that the range of variability in EQPT and SAL is large compared to UFFW and SAL.

REFERENCES

Alwin, Duane F. and Robert M. Hauser. 1975. The decomposition of effects in path analysis. *American Sociological Review 40*:37–47.

Andrade, Manual Correia de. 1973. *A Terra e o Homen no Nordeste*. São Paulo: Editora Brasiliense.

Brant, Vinicius Caldeira. 1976. Dinámica populacional, estructura agraria y desarrollo agrícola en Brasil. *Demografía e Economía 10*(2):119–126.

Braun, Rudolf. 1978. Early indutrialization and demographic change in canton of Zurich, *Historical Studies of Changing Fertility,* C. Tilly (ed.). Princeton: Princeton University Press. pp. 289–334.

Brazil, Fundação IBGE. 1970. *Divisão do Brasil em Mirco-Regiões Homogeneas 1968.* Rio de Janeiro: Fundação IBGE.

Brazil, Fundação IBGE. 1975. *Censo agropecuário, 1970* (Brasil and State Volumes). Rio de Janeiro: Fundação IBGE.

Brasil. Instituto Brasileiro de Geografia. 1973. *Novo Paisagens do Brasil.* Rio de Janeiro: Fundação IBGE.

Caldwell, John C. 1976. Toward a restatement of demographic transition theory. *Population and Development Review* 2:321–366.

Chernichovsky, Dov. 1976. Some socio-economic aspects of fertility behavior in Northeast Brazil. Population and Human Resources Division, The World Bank.

Coale, Ansley J. 1975. The demographic transition. *United Nations: The Population Debate, Vol. 1.* New York: The United Nations.

Coale, Ansley and T. James Trussell. 1974. Model fertility schedules: variation in the age structure of childbearing in human populations. *Population Index 40*:185–258 and *Erratum, Population Index 41*:572.

Cochrane, Susan H. 1979. *Fertility and Education: What Do We Really Know?* Boston and London: The Johns Hopkins University Press.

Davis, Kingsley. 1963. The theory of change and response in modern demographic history. *Population Index 29*:345–366.

Davis, Kingsley and Judith Blake. 1956. Social structure and fertility: an analytical framework. *Economic Development and Cultural Change 4*:211–235.

De Janvry, Alain. 1975. The political economy of rural development in Latin America: an interpretation, reply. *American Journal of Agricultural Economics 58*:590–591.

Demeny, Paul. 1968. Early fertility decline in Austria-Hungary: a lesson in demographic transition. *Daedalus 97*:502–522.

DeVany, Arthur and Nicholas Sanchez. 1977. Property rights, uncertainty, and fertility: an analysis of the effects of land reform on fertility in rural Mexico. *Weltwirtsch. Arch. 113*(4):741–764.

Duncan, Otis Dudley. 1975. *Introduction to Structural Equations Models.* New York: Academic Press.

Durham, William H. 1977. Land tenure and population policy in El Salvador. Paper at Joint National Meeting of Latin American and African Studies Associations. Houston, November 3, 1977.

Edmonston, Barry and Carl R. Zulauf. 1975. Modernization and fertility: an areal analysis of local areas in Brazil, Mexico and Columbia. Food Research Institute, Stanford University.

Easterlin, Richard A. 1976a. Population change and farm settlement in the northern United States. *Journal of Economic History 36*:45–75.

Easterlin, Richard A. 1976b. Factors in the decline of farm family fertility in the United States: some preliminary results. *Journal of American History 43*:600–614.

Easterlin, Richard A. 1978. The economics and sociology of fertility: a synthesis. *Historical Studies of Changing Fertility,* C. Tilly (ed.). Princeton: Princeton University Press. pp. 57–134.

Forman, Shepard. 1975. *The Brazilian Peasantry.* New York: Columbia University Press.

Goldscheider, Calvin. 1971. *Population, Modernization, and Social Structure.* Boston: Little, Brown, and Company.

Kleinman, David S. 1973. Fertility variation and resources in rural India. *Economic Development and Cultural Change 21*:679–696.

Lopes, Juarez Ruben Brandão. 1976. Do latifundio à empresa. *Cadernos Cebrap.* No. 26, São Paulo.

Mahar, Dennis J. 1978. *Desenvolvimento Econômico da Amazônia.* Rio de Janeiro: IPEA/INPES, Relatorio de Pesquisa No. 39.

Merrick, Thomas W. 1978. Fertility and land availability in rural Brazil. *Demography 15*:321–36.

National Academy of Sciences, Committee on Population and Demography. *Demographic Estimation: A Manual of Indirect Techniques.* In Press.

Ozorio de Almeida, Anna Luiza. 1977. Parceria e tamanho da família no nordeste Brasileiro. *Pesquisa e Planejamento Econômico 7*:291–332.

Robinson, Warren C. and Wayne A. Schutjer. 1979. Population change and agricultural development. Population Issues Research Center, Pennsylvania State University.

Rosenzweig, Mark R. 1977. The demand for children in farm households. *Journal of Political Economy 85*:123–145.

Rosenzweig, M.R. and R. Evenson. 1977. Fertility, schooling, and the economic contribution of small children in rural India: an econometric analysis. *Econometrica 45*:1065–1079.

Sawyer, Donald A. and Diana Oya Sawyer. 1975. Estrutura social e formação de famila numa frente de expansão agrícola da Amazônia. Rio de Janeiro: The Ford Foundation.

Schuh, G. Edward. 1970. *The Agricultural Development of Brazil.* New York: Praeger.

Schultz, T. Paul. 1976. Determinants of fertility: a micro-economic model of choice, *Economic Factors in Population Growth,* Ansley J. Coale (ed.), pp. 89–124. New York–Toronto:John Wiley and Sons.

Schultz, T.W. 1974. Fertility and economic values, *Economics of the Family: Marriage, Children and Human Capital* T.W. Schultz (ed.). Chicago: University of Chicago Press. pp. 3–22.

Singh, Ram D. *et al.* 1978. Economic analysis of fertility behavior and the demand for schooling among poor households in rural Brazil. University of Indiana, Department of Agricultural Economics, Agricultural Experiment Station Bulletin No. 218, West Lafayette, Indiana.

Stokes, C. Shannon *et al.* 1979. Land and human fertility: toward a synthesis of agricultural demographic development policy. Population Issues Research Center, Pennsylvania State University.

Tilly, Charles. 1978. The historical study of vital processes. *Historical Studies of Changing Fertility,* C. T. Tilly (ed.). Princeton:Princeton University Press. pp. 13–56.

Velho, Otavio G. 1973. *Modes of Capitalist Development: Peasantry and the Moving Frontier.* Dissertation, University of Manchester.

THE LABOR SUPPLY AND FERTILITY BEHAVIOR OF MARRIED WOMEN:

A THREE-PERIOD MODEL

Evelyn Lehrer and Marc Nerlove

I. INTRODUCTION

This paper adds to the literature on female time allocation by emphasizing the importance of dividing the family life cycle into various stages for the analysis of fertility and female labor supply.   Within the context of our model, we can explain what seem to be contradictory empirical findings in the literature.   Whereas some studies indicate a negative impact of fertility on labor supply (Cain, 1966; DaVanzo, 1972), others find an insignificant or positive effect (Cain and Dooley, 1976; Fleischer and Rhodes, 1979).   Our work suggests that these conflicting results may be due to differences in sample composition.   As shown herein, our estimates indicate

Research in Population Economics, Volume 3, pages 123–145
Copyright © 1981 by JAI Press Inc.
All rights of reproduction in any form reserved.
ISBN: 0-89232-207-1

a negative relationship between family size and female employment in the child-rearing stage, when small children are present in the household, but a weak, positive association when all children have reached school age.

Our work builds on a fairly large body of literature which, following Mincer's pioneering paper (1962), recognizes that the allocation of women's time is a substantially more complex phenomenon than the allocation of men's time. Some representative contributions include Bowen and Finegan (1969), Sweet (1973) and Schultz (1975). Largely because of deficiencies in the data, most of these studies follow Mincer and focus on female labor force participation as observed at the time of the survey. In Mincer's words (1962:68):

> In a broad view, the quantity of labor supplied to the market by a wife is the fraction of her married life during which she participates in the labor force. Abstracting from the temporal distribution of labor force activities over a woman's life, this fraction could be translated into a probability of being in the labor force a given period of time for an individual, hence into a labor force rate for a large group of women.

Fleischer and Rhodes (1979) improve on these papers by focusing on female lifetime labor supply rather than on current labor force participation. In the present paper, we take this one step further, by dealing with the *timing* of labor supply throughout the life cycle. Ours is a *period* analysis in which the life cycle is divided into three distinct stages: the pre-first-birth interval, the child-rearing stage, and a final period that begins when all the children have reached school age. To the best of our knowledge, our study is the first about life cycle phenomena in which life cycle stage is distinguished by the presence and age of children; previous studies represent life cycle stage by age, usually of the mother. We regard the presence and age of children, at least with respect to female labor supply decisions, to be a far more significant indicator of where a family is in its life cycle.

Section II presents our theoretical model. In Section III, using the retrospective information contained in our data, we examine empirically the determinants of fertility and female work in each period. A brief summary of our findings is offered in Section IV.

II. ANALYTICAL FRAMEWORK

This section presents a three-period theoretical model for the analysis of fertility behavior, female investment in human capital, labor supply, and wages. This provides a general framework within which to analyze the interactions among these various aspects of family decision-making.

To reduce the problem to manageable proportions, several simplifying assumptions are made. We assume the life cycle can be divided into three periods: the first period covers the wife's life between age 6 and the time when her first child is born; then comes the child-rearing stage, and, finally, the post-child-rearing interval, which starts when all of the children have reached school age and ends with the mother's retirement. This is certainly a crude specification, which abstracts from the problem of spacing and the timing of the first birth; however, it constitutes an improvement over the one-period static models encountered in the literature to date.[1]

The focal point of this model is the wife, and the possible endogeneity of many of the husband's actions is neglected. We assume his earnings plus any other family income in each period is fixed and known (for period i, we denote it by H_i).[2] This is perhaps not a very restrictive assumption, since husbands usually do work full time and exhibit little responsiveness to changes in their wives' wages (Ashenfelter and Heckman, 1974).[3] We also assume perfect capital markets in which unlimited lending and borrowing is possible.

The utility function is postulated to be intertemporally separable. In the first period, utility is derived from the consumption of market goods (x_1) and the wife's leisure (l_1). We assume the wife allocates her time among three competing activities: work in the labor force (L_1), which yields market goods; leisure, which directly yields utility, and the production of human capital (k). We assume she has a natural endowment of human capital K_0. (K_0 includes variables such as the wife's native ability and intelligence, as well as the human capital she acquires at home in the preschool years.) Then, she can increase this stock by spending time in education. The production of new capital follows the function $h(k,K_0)$, where the first and second partial derivatives are positive and negative, respectively. Also, the magnitude of $\partial h/\partial k$ varies positively with K_0. At the end of the first period, the wife's human capital stock is $K = K_0 + h(k,K_0)$. We assume that the wife's average wage in the first period may be expressed as some increasing function of the final stock of human capital: $w_1(K)$.

In the second period, the household derives utility from market goods (x_2), the wife's leisure (l_2), and child services. These absorb market goods $(x_2{}^c)$ and the wife's time $(t_2{}^c)$ according to a specified constant returns to scale production function, $f(x_2{}^c,K^\alpha t_2{}^c)$, where $0 \le \alpha \le 1$. This function allows for the possibility that the efficiency of the wife's time in the production of child services may be enhanced by her stock of human capital.

The wife may also spend some time working in the market in the second period. We denote this by L_2. The wage she can earn in this period is a function of her stock of human capital, K, and the amount of experience accumulated at the beginning of the period. Thus, her wage is $w_2(K,L_1)$, where the first partial derivatives are positive and the second ones are negative.[4] We further assume that the extent to which work experience raises the price of the wife's labor resources varies positively with the level of K. Thus, for very low levels of K, $\partial w_2/\partial L_1$ would be close to zero, whereas for high levels of K, $\partial w_2/\partial L_1$ would be very large.

This assumption is based on Jusenius' observation (1977) that those occupations that require a low skill level offer little reward to experience and little penalty to discontinuous labor-force participation. Thus, wages for occupations such as waitress, elevator operator, or sales clerk are likely to be quite insensitive to variations in the employees' experience. On the other hand, those occupations such as university professor, doctor, or lawyer, which demand a high skill level, are likely to require continuous maintenance and updating of knowledge and skills, to reward strongly those enriched by the experience and know-how acquired through on the job training, and to penalize similarly those whose skills have depreciated or suffered atrophy because of discontinuous labor force participation.

In the last period, the arguments of the utility function are leisure (l_3), market goods (x_3), and child services. These are produced according to the constant returns to scale function $g(x_3,K^\alpha t_3{}^c)$. We assume that the following inequalities hold:

$$\frac{\partial f}{\partial K^\alpha t^c} > \frac{\partial g}{\partial K^\alpha t^c} \qquad \text{for each level of } t^c$$

$$\frac{\partial f}{\partial x^c} < \frac{\partial g}{\partial x^c} \qquad \text{for each level of } x^c$$

These inequalities say that an increase in the amount of time, in efficiency units, devoted to the production of child services in the second period raises output more than a similar increase in the third period, whereas the opposite is true for increases in the market goods input. This assumption is inspired by the well-known fact that the most important input that children demand when they are young is time, whereas they become increasingly more goods intensive as they grow up.

The amount of time the wife devotes to the labor market in the third period is denoted by L_3. The wage she obtains is assumed to be $w_3(K,L_1 + L_2)$. This function shares the characteristics described above for w_2.

We assume that w_3 is substantially larger than w_2, specifically, that $w_3 > (1 + r)w_2 + L_3\,\partial w_3/\partial L_2$. Although this appears to be a strong assumption, it is not an implausible one. The relevant wage to the wife is that net of child care costs. While these are often negligible in the third period, they may be very large in the child-rearing stage. The upward long-term trend in wages lends some additional support to this assumption.

To conclude, we assume that all the conditions necessary to guarantee the negative definiteness of the bordered Hessian are satisfied. This involves, aside from the usual requirements that the second derivatives of the utility functions with respect to their arguments be negative, that diminishing returns be eventually encountered when the arguments of the w and h functions increase.

A. Mathematical Formulation

The model we have described can be formally written as follows:[5]

$$\text{maximize} \quad U(x_1,l_1) + U[x_2,l_2,f(x_2{}^c,K^\alpha t_2{}^c)] + U[x_3,l_3,g(x_3{}^c,K^\alpha t_3{}^c)]$$

subject to

(i) $\quad (1 + r)^2 px_1 + (1 + r)\, p(x_2 + x_2{}^c) + p(x_3 + x_3{}^c) =$
$\quad\quad (1 + r)^2 L_1 w_1 + (1 + r)L_2 w_2 + L_3 w_3 + (1 + r)^2 H_1 + (1 + r)H_2 + H_3$

(ii) $\quad l_1 + k\ + L_1 = 1$

$\quad\quad l_2 + t_2{}^c + L_2 = 1$

$\quad\quad l_3 + t_3{}^c + L_3 = 1$

(iii) $\quad L_1 \geq 0$

$\quad\quad L_2 \geq 0$

$\quad\quad L_3 \geq 0$

where $\quad w_1 = w_1(K)$

$\quad\quad w_2 = w_2(K,L_1)$

$\quad\quad w_3 = w_3(K,L_1 + L_2)$

$\quad\quad K = K_0 + h(k, K_0)$

B. Implications of the Model

1. The Optimal Level of Human Capital Accumulation. As shown in Appendix A, the first-order condition for k, the time allocated to the production of human capital, is the following:

$$\frac{\partial U}{\partial f}\,\frac{\partial f}{\partial K^\alpha t_2{}^c}\,\alpha K^{\alpha-1}\,\frac{\partial h}{\partial k}\,t_2{}^c + \frac{\partial U}{\partial g}\,\frac{\partial g}{\partial K^\alpha t_3{}^c}\,\alpha K^{\alpha-1}\,\frac{\partial h}{\partial k}\,t_3{}^c - \lambda_1$$

$$+ \lambda_4 \left[(1 + r)^2 L_1 \frac{\partial w_1}{\partial K}\frac{\partial K}{\partial k} + (1 + r)L_2 \frac{\partial w_2}{\partial K}\frac{\partial K}{\partial k} + L_3 \frac{\partial w_3}{\partial K}\frac{\partial K}{\partial k}\right] = 0 \quad (1)$$

where λ_1 is the opportunity cost of the time employed in the production of human capital and λ_4 is the marginal utility of market goods.

Equation (1) says that k should be chosen so as to equalize the marginal costs associated with an additional unit of capital, λ_1, with the incremental returns. These are represented by the first two and the last terms. The former indicate the marginal benefits of investment in human capital in the production of child services, which work through the enhanced productivity of the wife's time in that activity. The latter indicates the increase in market goods that the household can command throughout the life cycle due to the positive impact of K on the wife's wage in each period, weighted by the marginal utility of market goods. Thus, the optimal k must be such that these costs and benefits are balanced in the margin.

Equation (1) predicts that women with a high human capital endowment will invest heavily in their education, because all the terms that measure the benefits associated with such investment are larger the bigger K_0 is.

Another implication of Eq. (1) is that the wife's optimal level of investment in human capital is a function of the extent to which this capital is utilized in the various stages of the life cycle. Taking first the case in which $\alpha = 0$, we see from Eq. (1) that the larger the proportion of time the wife spends in the labor market rather than on children or consuming leisure, the greater becomes the last term, which measures the benefits from investment in human capital; thus the larger becomes the optimal level of accumulation, *ceteris paribus*. The same conclusion would follow if α were positive but very small.

If increases in K raise the productivity of the wife's time in the child-rearing activity, then it can easily be seen that the optimal k will be larger than in the case in which α is zero, for given paths of the other endogenous variables. This is shown in Appendix B. If this case is a realistic one, the college education acquired by many women who then become full-time mothers and housewives does not appear irrational.

This analysis has some bearing on the problem of determinism in the human capital models encountered in the literature. As Lydall (1976) remarks, referring to these models (pp. 21–22):

> The only reason for differences in lifetime earnings is differences in "ability," which affect both the earnings of those who have no human capital and the rate of return of those who have such capital. Paradoxically, therefore, a theory which purports to be "economic" rather than sociological leads inexorably to the conclusion that the really significant differences in earnings, i.e. differences in lifetime earnings, are not the result of "choice" but are entirely a reflection of differences in exogenously given "abilities."

In our model (assuming α is zero or close to zero), if we compare two women with the same ability, one who plans to devoate a substantial proportion of her life to rearing children and one who intends to spend most of her time actively participating in the labor force, the latter will find it optimal to invest more in human capital in the first period and will hence command a higher wage. Thus it is not only ability that matters; there is some room for personal choice. The effect this has on the interpretation of the empirical results is discussed in Section III,C.

2. The Optimal Level of Labor Supply

a. The participation decision. In this section, we focus our attention on the dichotomous variables related to the wife's decision in each period as to whether to participate in the labor market or not.

The conditions that must be satisfied for an optimal level of L_1, L_2, and L_3, respectively, are derived in Appendix A. They are the following:

$$\lambda_1 - \lambda_4 \left[(1 + r)^2 w_1 + (1 + r)L_2 \frac{\partial w_2}{\partial L_1} + L_3 \frac{\partial w_3}{\partial L_1} \right] \geq 0 \tag{2}$$

$$\lambda_2 - \lambda_4 \left[(1 + r)w_2 + L_3 \frac{\partial w_3}{\partial L_2} \right] \geq 0 \tag{3}$$

$$\lambda_3 - \lambda_4 w_3 \geq 0 \tag{4}$$

Let us consider Eq. (2). As stated before, λ_1 represents the opportunity cost of the wife's time in the first period. This can be measured in terms of the marginal utility of leisure or the value of an extra unit of time spent investing in human capital. The second term measures what we might call "the value of the wife's working." This is equal to the value, at the end of the third period, of the wife's wage in the first stage plus the increase in future earnings caused by the additional experience accumulated, all of this weighted by the marginal utility of market goods. If the shadow wage exceeds the "value of working," the wife will not participate in the labor force in the first period. Otherwise, she will choose a level of labor supply such that Eq. (2) holds as an equality.

A similar interpretation can be given to Eqs. (3) and (4). These conditions appear to be more general than those found in the literature. They suggest, for example, that a woman may work in the labor market in the second period, even if her current wage is small compared to the shadow price of her time at home, due to the presence of small children, if the increase in future earnings that she would otherwise sacrifice is sufficiently large. This, in turn, is higher the larger the wife's human capital stock and the larger her labor supply in the third period.

b. The impact of changes in K_0. A change in K_0 induces the usual income and substitution effects in each period. If K_0 increases, for example, the former would induce the wife to supply less labor. It can be seen from Eqs. (2), (3), and (4) that, given diminishing marginal utility of goods, λ_4 would fall, thereby decreasing the benefits of participating in the labor force. A substitution effect also arises, as can be seen from these three equations, since a higher K_0 leads to an increase in wages and also to an increase in the value of acquiring additional experience.

In our model, a change in K_0 affects not only the benefits from working but also the costs. In the first period, an increase in K_0 implies that the returns from investing in additional human capital become larger. In the second and third periods, the costs increase because as the capital stock rises, the wife becomes more efficient in the production of child services. This latter result may be referred to as a "child effect."

Due to the influence of these opposing effects, the outcome remains ambiguous *a priori*.

c. The impact of changes in exogenous income. We briefly consider here the impact of changes in the husband's earnings or other family income on the wife's labor supply. It is clear that changes in this "outside" income cause a pure income effect, so that if this variable increases, for example, the wife's labor supply will diminish, everything else being held constant.

This unambiguous effect can be seen from Eqs. (2), (3), and (4). A rise in exogenous income increases the cost of working, since the value of the wife's nonmarket time rises as more complementary goods become available to the household. Thus, λ_1, λ_2 and λ_3 rise. Further, the value of working declines, since λ_4 decreases in the presence of diminishing marginal utility of income. Since perfect capital markets have been assumed, changes in H_1, H_2 and H_3 play a parallel role.

Thus, we expect a negative sign on the coefficient of exogenous income in the equations explaining female labor supply.

d. Relationship between L_2 and L_3. In Appendix C, we show that, under certain specified assumptions, the wife will devote a smaller fraction of her time to market activity in the second period than in the post-child-rearing stage.

C. Summary of Conclusions

The major implications of this model are the following:

1. Women with a large human capital endowment are likely to invest more time in the acquisition of formal education in the first period than their more poorly endowed counterparts.

2. The wife's optimal level of human capital accumulation is a function of the extent to which this capital is utilized throughout the life cycle. If α is small or zero, the larger the proportion of time she devotes to market activity rather than to children or leisure, the more she has to gain from investing in human capital.

3. If increases in human capital augment the efficiency of time spent on children, the optimal level of investment in education will be larger than in the case in which α is zero, for given paths of the other endogenous variables.

4. The traditional models in the literature suggest that the wife's labor force participation decision depends on whether her market wage exceeds

the shadow price of her time. Our analysis implies that a woman may supply labor to the market in any given period, even if her current wage is smaller than the price of her time at home, if the increase in future earnings that she would otherwise forego is large enough.

5. Since changes in the husband's earnings are associated with a pure income effect, an increase in these earnings will have an unambiguous negative impact on female labor supply in each period.

6. Women tend to spend a larger proportion of their time in the labor market in the post-child-rearing period than in the child-rearing stage. If we look at a cross section, we expect to find a greater percentage of women working outside the home in the former than in the latter period.

III. THE ECONOMETRIC MODEL

The analysis in Section II implies that the wife's investment in human capital decision is an endogenous one. She chooses how much education to acquire at the same time that she makes her lifetime fertility and labor supply plans; the more market activity her plans involve, the more education she will acquire, if α is small. Unfortunately, because of data limitations, we must take her education level as exogenous in our econometric model. With this restriction, our endogenous variables are reduced to fertility and female labor supply in the various periods.

The literature on models of female labor supply and fertility ("new home economics" models) offers two basic econometric approaches. The first consists of formulating a "structural" model; the dependent variables are treated as jointly determined, and using simultaneous equations techniques, the direct relationship among them is quantified (see, e.g., DaVanzo, 1972; Hill and Stafford, 1978). As noted by Rosenzweig (1978), this procedure leads to some problems. First, inappropriate restrictions must often be imposed in order to obtain identification. Second, the information the resulting coefficients give us may be uninteresting for policy purposes. For example, if the coefficient of female work in a fertility equation is negative, this does not imply that, say, increasing employment opportunities for women will reduce family size. The negative coefficient may simply reflect the fact that certain exogenous variables have influences of opposite signs on each of the dependent variables.

The second approach, used by Rosenzweig (1978) and others, consists of estimating "reduced-form" equations, i.e., each dependent variable is regressed against all the exogenous variables in the system. Behind this procedure lies the notion that the household decision process is such that a common set of exogenous variables determines the values assumed by the dependent variables. Thus, what is important is to measure quantitatively the impact of each independent variable on each endogenous variable.

We will follow the latter approach in this paper. But, in addition, we will examine the correlations among the residuals of the reduced-form equations. As explained in the following paragraphs, this provides some information on the impact of *unobserved* exogenous variables on the dependent variables of interest.

As a very simple example, consider the following equation:

$$WORK = \alpha_0 + \alpha_1 X + \alpha_2 Y$$

$$FERTILITY = \beta_0 + \beta_1 X + \beta_2 Y$$

Let *WORK* represent the level of female labor supply in some given period, and let *FERTILITY* indicate complete family size. X is a vector of the exogenous variables on which we do have information. For simplicity, assume that there is only one independent variable on which we do not have information. Say it is Y, a dummy that equals 1 if the mother wished to work in the market in the given period but was unable to find an acceptable job, and is 0 otherwise. Thus $\alpha_2 Y$ is the residual of the *WORK* equation; $\beta_2 Y$ is the residual of the *FERTILITY* equation. Suppose we compute the correlation coefficient between these residuals and obtain a significantly negative number. This would imply that Y influences *WORK* and *FERTILITY* in opposite directions; while Y has a negative influence on *WORK*, it has a positive impact on *FERTILITY*.

In reality, the residuals involve not one but many unobserved variables, ranging from preferences (to the extent that these are not captured by the variables we do include) to sex and race discrimination in the labor market. The arguments above indicate that an analysis of the correlations among the residuals from the various regressions provides information as to whether these unobserved variables affect the dependent variables in the same or opposite direction, on average.

A. The Data

The 1973 National Survey of Family Growth was conducted by the National Center for Health Statistics, Department of Health, Education, and Welfare. The survey was addressed to civilian, noninstitutionalized women living in the United States, who, at the time of the survey, were currently married, previously married, or single with natural children living in the household. It contains pregnancy, contraceptive, marital status, and female employment histories, as well as information on health and family planning, religion, child care, location, and a number of socioeconomic variables.

In our analysis, we have restricted the sample in several ways. We have only considered women who were formally married, with at least one child, and in the third stage of the life cycle at the time of the survey. Thus, all the respondents in our sample had completed the formation of their families and none of them had children under 6 years of age. Further, we eliminated all of those cases in which the wife had been married more than once, as well as those in which twins or adopted children were reported. Cases in which the wife had raised the children of her husband from a previous marriage were also excluded. The resulting sample size was 1485.

B. Definitions of Variables

1. Dependent Variables.   Our endogenous variables consist of the levels of female labor supply in the various periods and the household's fertility.

   a. Female labor supply variables: L1A, L1B, L2, L3.   Since the richness of our data enables us to subdivide the first period into 2 parts, we do so in our econometric model.   Period 1A begins when the woman reaches school age and ends with her marriage; period 1B covers the interval between marriage and first birth; period 2 corresponds to the child-rearing stage, as defined in Section II, and period 3 represents the post-child-rearing interval.   L1A, L1B, L2 and L3 indicate the proportion of time the wife worked in the market in the corresponding period.   For example, if period 2 lasted 8 years and the wife reports that she worked 2 years in that time interval, L2 would be 0.25.[6]

   b. Fertility variable: NUM.   *NUM* represents the number of children born alive to the household.   Abstracting from infant and child mortality considerations, this measure indicates complete family size for the respondents in our sample.

2. Independent Variables.   Our main exogenous variables are the husband's income and the wife's education.   In addition, we include a number of background and religious variables, as well as some biological and demographic variables.   These are intended to serve as proxies for preferences, for the economic opportunities faced by the wife, and for the couple's contraceptive efficiency and physical limitations.

   a. Husband's permanent income: PERMINC.   In order to avoid the confounding effect of transitory income components, we use an instrumental-variable estimator as a proxy for the husband's permanent income. This is based on the equation in Table 1.

   The endogenous variable is the husband's income as observed at the time of the survey.   Some respondents reported an exact figure when asked about their spouse's earnings.   Those who did not wish to do so were shown a card containing various income categories and asked to select the most appropriate one.   For these latter cases, we follow Schultz

Table 1.   Dependent Variable: Husband's Income as
Observed at the Time of the Survey[a]

Constant	−10195.0	(2425.6)
Husband's education	1014.0	(87.239)
Median income earned in his occupation	0.68836	(0.10884)
Experience	447.62	(160.05)
$(Experience)^2$	−6.2312	(3.1745)
Nonwhite race	−2915.9	(559.51)
Residence in south	−863.75	(442.36)
Residence outside SMSA	−2116.7	(468.65)
R^2	0.2621	
N	1485	

[a] Standard errors in parentheses.

(1969), who, instead of using the midpoint as the average income level in each closed income interval, employs the geometric mean, in accordance with the approximately log-normal distribution of income. For the open-end interval ($25,000 or more), we follow Miller's (1963) suggestion by fitting a Pareto curve to the data.[7]

Turning to the exogenous variables, the husband's education is measured in terms of years of regular schooling. The median income earned in his occupation is based on figures reported in the 1970 Census (U.S. Summary, Part 1, p. 1–766). The experience variable is computed by subtracting 6 and the years of schooling from the husband's age at the survey date. The underlying assumption behind this procedure is that men work continuously after completing their education, a valid one in most cases. We also control for race and for residence in the South or outside a Standard Metropolitan Statistical Area. All the coefficients have the expected signs.

Following Willis (1973), we use the estimated coefficients to obtain the husband's predicted income at age 40. We divide this by 1000 to obtain our variable *PERMINC*, measured in thousands of dollars.

b. Wife's education: WEDUC, WED1. Because of the way the questionnaire was designed, we have two variables to represent the wife's education. *WEDUC* indicates the number of years of regular schooling completed by the wife; *WED1* is a dummy variable that equals 1 if the wife had some other training such as technical education.

c. Background variables: SOUTHC, LIVPAR, SIBL1. SOUTHC is a dummy variable that equals 1 if the respondent lived in one of the southern states most of the time during her childhood and adolescence. *LIVPAR* is a dummy variable that takes the value 1 if at the age of 14 the respondent was not living with her own father and mother, due to death, separation, or divorce. Finally, *SIBL1* is the number of siblings in the woman's family plus 1, i.e., the total number of children in her home.

d. Religion variables: RELED, CATH. RELED is a dummy variable that takes the value 1 to indicate that the wife received at least some of her education in a religious school. *CATH* equals 1 if she is Catholic.

e. Biological variables: CONTR, SUBF. CONTR is a dummy variable that equals 1 if the respondent ever used the pill or IUD since the last pregnancy. *SUBF* equals 1 if the wife reports it would be difficult or impossible for her to have another child, provided she had not reached the age of menopause, and had not had an operation for contraceptive purposes.

f. Demographic variables: RACE, AGE. RACE equals 1 to indicate that the respondent is nonwhite. *AGE* is a continuous variable that controls for the wife's age at the time of the survey.

C. Empirical Findings

Table 2 presents the reduced-form equations of our model, in which the labor supply and fertility variables are regressed against all the exogenous variables of the system. The equations for L1A, L1B, L2 and L3 are estimated using the Tobit procedure, since these dependent variables are truncated at 0 with many observations at that point. The equation for *NUM* is estimated by ordinary least squares. Our results are summarized below.

1. Husband's Permanent Income. Inspection of the first column of Table 2 indicates that whereas the husband's income has an insignificant effect on female labor supply prior to the birth of the first child, it has a strong negative impact on the wife's market work in periods 2 and 3. It is interesting to note that contrary to what one might have expected, the husband's earnings only depress female employment when children are present.

Our results also indicate that the husband's permanent income exerts a significant negative influence on fertility. This finding, which has emerged in a number of other studies, does not imply that children are inferior goods (see Becker and Lewis, 1973). An important aspect of this phenomenon has been emphasized in a review article by Birdsall (1977: 76). As she remarks, "high fertility . . . exacerbates the inequality of income distribution among families. . . . To the extent that there are social or economic restrictions on upward mobility, the relatively more rapid increase in numbers of the poor constitutes a drag on any income redistribution effort." A paper by Cramer (1974), using data from the Panel Study of Income Dynamics, presents some surprising evidence indicating that most low income families who fall into poverty by having large numbers of children do so voluntarily, not by having accidental births. Although on the surface this would seem to imply that no policy action is therefore required (since what really matters is utility, not income), this argument ignores the welfare of the children who did not

Table 2.   Reduced-Form Equations[a]

	PERMINC	WEDUC	WEDI	SOUTHC	LIVPAR	SIBLI	CATH
L1A	0.0008918	0.003280	0.009129	−0.06053	0.01508	−0.0005344	0.02907
	(0.001575)	(0.002721)	(0.01414)	(0.01152)	(0.01164)	(0.0007660)	(0.01257)
	[0.0784]	[0.262]					
L1B	0.0005050	0.1552	0.7331	−0.08840	−0.2825	−0.01219	0.3079
	(0.02409)	(0.04213)	(0.2102)	(0.1752)	(0.1799)	(0.01242)	(0.1902)
	[0.0127]	[3.55]					
L2	−0.01001	0.02739	0.07814	0.07589	0.01786	−0.0005727	0.02121
	(0.003530)	(0.006173)	(0.03151)	(0.02545)	(0.02593)	(0.001714)	(0.02865)
	[−0.755]	[1.88]					
L3	−0.01057	0.02938	0.1084	0.07815	−0.002262	0.001500	0.03843
	(0.004725)	(0.008133)	(0.04230)	(0.03421)	(0.03469)	(0.002166)	(0.03800)
	[−0.256]	[0.647]					
NUM	−0.04630	−0.08658	−0.1549	−0.1952	0.01774	0.01027	0.2661
	(0.01079)	(0.01841)	(0.09733)	(0.07828)	(0.07950)	(0.005084)	(0.08678)
	[−0.190]	[−0.321]					

[a] Standard errors in parentheses. Elasticities in brackets. $n = 1485$.

choose to be born into a large, poor family. Thus, even if further research with other bodies of data were to confirm Cramer's results, a policy issue would remain.

2. *Wife's Education.* The wife's education variables have insignificant coefficients in the L1A equation, reflecting the fact that at least in part of this period, investment in formal education and labor force participation are competing activities. In all of the other stages, *WEDUC* and *WEDI* have a strong positive influence on female work. The coefficients associated with these variables are substantially larger in period 1B than in the subsequent stages.[8] This is consistent with the hypothesis that α is positive, i.e., that human capital raises the productivity of the wife's time spent on child services. As expected, the wife's education has a significant negative impact on the number of children. Thus, *WEDUC* and *WEDI* strongly influence fertility and female labor supply in opposite directions.

3. *A Comparison between the Elasticities of the Husband's Income and the Wife's Education.* An examination of columns 1 and 2 of Table 2 reveals that in every equation, the elasticity associated with the wife's education is larger than that associated with the husband's income. To the extent that the former variable is a good proxy for her potential market wage, we may conclude that this is a more potent force than the husband's income in both the fertility and labor supply decisions.

This result must be qualified in two important respects. First, our mea-

Table 2. *(Continued)*

RELED	CONTR	SUBF	RACE	AGE	CONST	R^2	Percentage of observations at limit point
0.001229	−0.003037	0.01394	−0.01115	0.005822	−0.1361		22
(0.01409)	(0.01096)	(0.01172)	(0.01521)	(0.001174)	(0.05347)		
−0.07924	0.1367	0.02703	−0.05245	0.03319	−0.3626		42
(0.2120)	(0.1664)	(0.1779)	(0.2366)	(0.01801)	(0.8235)		
0.0003093	0.07125	0.06312	0.1182	−0.009543	0.1008		46
(0.03222)	(0.02437)	(0.02617)	(0.03259)	(0.002595)	(0.1180)		
−0.0005863	0.05328	0.03946	0.2027	−0.01019	0.5157		26
(0.04258)	(0.03275)	(0.03505)	(0.04454)	(0.003480)	(0.1584)		
0.1813	0.02152	−0.1987	0.7803	0.08072	1.587	0.1957	
(0.09748)	(0.07501)	(0.08025)	(0.1026)	(0.008004)	(0.3611)		

sure of the husband's income reflects only permanent income. Thus, our coefficients do not capture possible female labor supply responses to temporary variations in the husband's income (e.g., an unemployment spell or an unusually low level of earnings in the pre-first-birth stage, when the husband may be just beginning his career).

Second, holding constant the husband's education, the omission of tastes from our equations leads to a positive and negative bias, respectively, in the coefficients associated with the wife's education in the labor supply and fertility equations (see Nerlove, 1974; Nerlove and Razin, 1979a, Appendix B). As noted in these papers, the difference in educational attainment of husband and wife partly reflects the couple's preferences for children. Positive assortative mating by education in the marriage market leads men with very high education to marry women who also have high levels of schooling. Differences in tastes are not likely to be reflected in the educational attainment of men; however, it is very plausible that women with low tastes for market activities and high preferences for children will tend to seek smaller amounts of formal education, whereas those women with opposite preferences will tend to invest more in acquiring human capital. Given positive assortative mating by preferences for children, men with a given educational attainment with high preferences for children will tend to marry women with less schooling than the average associated with the level these men have achieved. If the husband's schooling level is associated primarily with an income effect, while his wife's education is associated mostly with a substitution effect, it follows that the negative impact of her opportunity cost of time on fertility will be exaggerated, holding male educational attainment constant, if tastes are not explicitly included in the statistical analysis. A similar argument holds for the labor supply equations.

4. Background Variables. As expected, *SOUTHC* has a negative effect on L1A, indicating the smaller opportunities for market work in the period before marriage. Curiously, this variable has a significant positive effect on L2 and L3, and a negative impact on *NUM.*

LIVPAR has a weak, positive coefficient in the L1A equation. This probably reflects the fact that girls who are not brought up by both parents have greater financial needs in the pre-marriage stage.

SIBL1 has a significant positive effect on *NUM:* women who come from large families tend to form large families themselves.

5. Religion Variables. As expected, the coefficients of *RELED* and *CATH* have positive signs in the fertility equations. The positive sign of *CATH* on female work in the pre-first-birth years is a puzzling result.

6. Biological Variables. Disappointingly, *CONTR* has an insignificant impact on our fertility variable.[8] It has, however, a strong positive effect on L2 and a weak, positive effect on L3, suggesting that women who have used modern contraceptives tend to work more in the market, perhaps because they have more liberal attitudes toward the role of women.

The subfecundity variable behaves as expected. It has a strong negative impact on fertility. It also has a strong positive effect on L2 and a weak positive influence on L3, reflecting the indirect impact through the number of children variable.

7. Demographic Variables. *RACE* has a strong positive impact on both fertility and labor supply in the second and third periods. Its influence on female work prior to the first birth is insignificant, however.

The *AGE* variable displays a puzzling pattern of coefficients. It has a positive influence on L1A and L1B, as ecpected, but a very strong negative impact on L2 and L3. Its effect on fertility is positive.

8. Timing of Female Labor Supply. The last column of Table 2 reports the percentage of observations on the labor supply variables at the truncation point. These figures can be translated into percentages representing the fraction of women who supplied some positive amount of labor to the market in each stage. These are 78, 58, 54, and 74 percent, for periods 1A, 1B, 2, and 3, respectively. The lowest percentage is associated with the child-rearing period; the peak participation rate occurs in the pre-marriage stage. As our model predicts, the percentage is higher in the third than in the second period.

Another dimension of the timing of labor supply may be obtained by examining some cross-sectional information contained in our data. Each respondent was asked whether or not she had worked in the market in the past 12 months. The answers to this question indicate participation rates of 85, 84, 44, and 64 percent, in the corresponding periods. These statistics are rather different from the former ones, reflecting in part a cohort effect; however, the qualitative conclusions stated earlier remain unchanged.

9. Analysis of Residuals. Table 3 presents the simple correlations of the residuals from the reduced-form equations.

As expected, the correlations among the residuals from the labor supply equations are positive. This suggests that those unobserved variables that influence female work positively in one period, operate in the same way in the other stages. The correlation between the residuals of the L2 and L3 equations is particularly large in magnitude and strong in significance. This is probably due to the fact that many of the women who work in the child-rearing period do so precisely because they intend to engage in market activity in the third period, and, therefore, wish to maintain their skills and wage levels.

The residual of the fertility regression is negatively correlated with the residual of L1A, L1B and L2; the unobserved forces that tend to increase fertility also decrease female work in these periods. This negative sign disappears in the third stage; the relationship becomes positive but insignificant at conventional levels.

10. Correlations among Dependent Variables. Table 4 shows the matrix of correlations among the dependent variables in the model. These correlations may be interpreted as resulting from the impact of observed and un-

Table 3.   Correlation Matrix of Residuals for Specified Equations[a]

	Res L1A	*Res* L1B	*Res* L2	*Res* L3	*Res NUM*
Res L1A	1.00	0.1997	0.0691	0.0010	−0.0766
		(0.001)	(0.008)	(0.970)	(0.003)
Res L1B		1.00	0.0264	0.0150	−0.0506
			(0.308)	(0.565)	(0.051)
Res L2			1.00	0.5587	−0.0307
				(0.001)	(0.237)
Res L3				1.00	0.0233
					(0.369)
Res *NUM*					1.00

[a] *p*-values in parentheses. A *p*-value indicates the probability of obtaining a sample value as extreme as that actually observed, assuming the null hypothesis (coefficient = 0) is true. The reported *p*-values are based on two-sided tests.

Table 4.   Correlation Matrix of Dependent Variables[a]

	L1A	L1B	L2	L3	NUM
L1A	1.00	0.1782	0.0444	−0.0280	−0.0440
		(0.001)	(0.087)	(0.281)	(0.090)
L1B		1.00	0.0567	0.0379	−0.0324
			(0.029)	(0.144)	(0.213)
L2			1.00	0.5901	−0.0335
				(0.001)	(0.197)
L3				1.00	0.0338
					(0.193)
NUM					1.00

[a] p-values in parentheses.

observed exogenous variables on each of the dependent ones. The results show that, in most cases, labor supply in one period is positively correlated with that in other periods. The figures also indicate that while at first the relationship between fertility and female work is negative, this becomes weakly positive in the final stage. This lends some additional support to the findings for Quebec reported by Lehrer (1978), which show that the negative association between fertility and the mother's employment vanishes when the children reach school age. This result probably reflects the goods intensiveness of children in this final period.

IV. SUMMARY AND CONCLUDING REMARKS

The model we have estimated in this paper emphasizes the importance of dividing the life cycle into various stages for the analysis of female labor supply and fertility. Our results show that the influence of exogenous variables on the former varies substantially among the life cycle stages. Whereas the husband's income has no impact on the wife's market work in the pre-first-birth interval, it has a significantly negative effect in the subsequent stages. With the exception of the pre-marriage period, in which investment in human capital and market work are competing activities, the wife's education is a potent force affecting labor supply. Our estimates suggest that this variable has the strongest positive influence prior to the birth of the first child. With some qualifications, the wife's education is a more important determinant of both market activity and fertility than the husband's income. Another important finding is that the association between fertility and female employment varies in sign across stages. Thus, an analysis of the relationship between these variables that does not distinguish among life cycle stages will result in some average measure that obscures the nature of the underlying process.

Because of data limitations, several implications of our theoretical model have remained untested.   It is hoped that future studies with richer bodies of data will provide empirical tests for these propositions.

In a forthcoming paper (Lehrer and Nerlove, 1980), an important *consequence* of women's life cycle time allocation decisions is explored.   We examine the impact that working wives have on the inequality of the income distribution across households at the various stages.   Our analysis reveals that family earnings are more equally distributed than husband's earnings in all periods.   We note, however, that female employment need not improve the distribution of a broader measure of welfare.   Wives who work in the market, must, because of the time constraint, devote less attention to other activities, especially child care.   A rigorous analysis of these issues is an important topic for future research.

APPENDIX A

We present below the Lagrangian function and first-order conditions associated with our model.

The Lagrangian function is:

$$\Phi = U(x_1, l_1) + U(x_2, l_2, f(x_2^c, K^\alpha t_2^c)) + U(x_3, l_3, g(x_3^c, K^\alpha t_3^c))$$
$$+ \lambda_1(1 - l_1 - k - L_1) + \lambda_2(1 - l_2 - t_2^c - L_2) + \lambda_3(1 - l_3 - t_3^c - L_3)$$
$$+ \lambda_4[(1 + r)^2 l_1 w_1 + (1 + r) L_2 w_2 + L_3 w_3$$
$$+ (1 + r)^2 H_1 + (1 + r)H_2 + H_3 - (1 + r)^2 p x_1 - (1 + r)p(x_2 + x_c)$$
$$- p(x_3 + x_c)] + \lambda_5 L_1 + \lambda_6 L_2 + \lambda_7 L_3$$

The first-order conditions are:

$$\Phi_{x_1} = U_{x_1} - \lambda_4(1 + r)^2 p = 0 \tag{A1}$$

$$\Phi_{l_1} = U_{l_1} - \lambda_1 = 0 \tag{A2}$$

$$\Phi_k = \frac{\partial U}{\partial f} \frac{\partial f}{\partial K^\alpha t_2^c} \alpha K^{\alpha-1} \frac{\partial h}{\partial k} t_2^c + \frac{\partial U}{\partial g} \frac{\partial g}{\partial K^\alpha t_3^c} \alpha K^{\alpha-1} \frac{\partial h}{\partial k} t_3^c$$
$$- \lambda_1 + \lambda_4 \left[(1 + r)^2 L_1 \frac{\partial w_1}{\partial K} \frac{\partial K}{\partial k} + (1 + r)L_2 \frac{\partial w_2}{\partial K} \frac{\partial K}{\partial k} + L_3 \frac{\partial w_3}{\partial K} \frac{\partial K}{\partial k} \right] = 0 \tag{A3}$$

$$\Phi_{L_1} = -\lambda_1 + \lambda_4 \left[(1 + r)^2 w_1 + (1 + r)L_2 \frac{\partial w_2}{\partial L_1} + L_3 \frac{\partial w_3}{\partial L_1} \right] + \lambda_5 = 0 \tag{A4}$$

$$\Phi_{x_2} = U_{x_2} - \lambda_4(1 + r)p = 0 \tag{A5}$$

$$\Phi_{x_2^c} = \frac{\partial U}{\partial f} \frac{\partial f}{\partial x_2^c} - \lambda_4(1 + r)p = 0 \tag{A6}$$

$$\Phi_{t_2^c} = \frac{\partial U}{\partial f} \frac{\partial f}{\partial K^\alpha t_2^c} K^\alpha - \lambda_2 = 0 \tag{A7}$$

$$\Phi_{l_2} = U_{l_2} - \lambda_2 = 0 \tag{A8}$$

$$\Phi_{L_2} = -\lambda_2 + \lambda_4 \left[(1 + r)w_2 + L_3 \frac{\partial w_3}{\partial L_2} \right]$$
$$+ \lambda_6 = 0 \tag{A9}$$

$$\Phi_{x_3} = U_{x_3} - \lambda_4 p = 0 \tag{A10}$$

$$\Phi_{x_3^c} = \frac{\partial U}{\partial g} \frac{\partial g}{\partial x_3^c} - \lambda_4 p = 0 \tag{A11}$$

$$\Phi_{t_3^c} = \frac{\partial U}{\partial g} \frac{\partial g}{\partial K^\alpha t_3^c} K^\alpha - \lambda_3 = 0 \tag{A12}$$

$$\Phi_{l_3} = U_{l_3} - \lambda_3 = 0 \tag{A13}$$

$$\Phi_{L_3} = -\lambda_3 + \lambda_4 w_3 + \lambda_7 = 0 \tag{A14}$$

$$L_1 \cdot \lambda_5 = 0 \tag{A15}$$

$$L_2 \cdot \lambda_6 = 0 \tag{A16}$$

$$L_3 \cdot \lambda_7 = 0 \tag{A17}$$

APPENDIX B

In this section we prove that, for given paths of the other endogenous variables, the optimal level of k will be larger if α is positive than if α is zero.

With the help of Eqs. (A7) and (A12), we can rewrite Eq. (A3) as follows:

$$\alpha \frac{\lambda_2}{K} \frac{\partial h}{\partial k} t_2^c + \alpha \frac{\lambda_3}{K} \frac{\partial h}{\partial k} t_3^c + \lambda_4 \left[(1 + r)^2 L_1 \frac{\partial w_1}{\partial K} \frac{\partial K}{\partial k} + (1 + r) L_2 \frac{\partial w_2}{\partial K} \frac{\partial K}{\partial k} + L_3 \frac{\partial w_3}{\partial K} \frac{\partial K}{\partial k} \right] = \lambda_1$$

If α is zero, then we must have:

$$\lambda_4 \left[(1 + r)^2 L_1 \frac{\partial w_1}{\partial K} \frac{\partial K}{\partial k} + (1 + r) L_2 \frac{\partial w_2}{\partial K} \frac{\partial K}{\partial k} + L_3 \frac{\partial w_3}{\partial K} \frac{\partial K}{\partial k} \right] = \lambda_1$$

For given paths of the other choice variables, the k that satisfies the second equation must be smaller, since the $\left(\frac{\partial w}{\partial K} \right)$'s and/or the $\left(\frac{\partial K}{\partial k} \right)$'s must be larger in this case, and the second partial derivatives are negative.

APPENDIX C

We show here that, under certain specified conditions, L_2 will be smaller than L_3 in equilibrium.

Assuming an interior solution for L_2 and L_3, Eqs. (A7), (A9), (A12) and (A14) imply the following equality:

$$\frac{\dfrac{\partial U}{\partial f} \dfrac{\partial f}{\partial K^\alpha t_2^c} K^\alpha}{(1 + r) w_2 + L_3 \dfrac{\partial w_3}{\partial L_2}} = \frac{\dfrac{\partial U}{\partial g} \dfrac{\partial g}{\partial K^\alpha t_3^c} K^\alpha}{w_3}$$

Since, by assumption, $(1 + r) w_2 + L_3 (\partial w_3 / \partial L_2) < w_3$, it follows that

$$\frac{\partial U}{\partial f} \frac{\partial f}{\partial K^\alpha t_2^c} K^\alpha < \frac{\partial U}{\partial g} \frac{\partial g}{\partial K^\alpha t_3^c} K^\alpha$$

If we restrict the form of the utility functions in such a way that $\partial U/\partial f = \partial U/\partial g$, it must be the case that at the optimal $t_2{}^c$ and $t_3{}^c$ (denoted by $t_2{}^{c*}$, $t_3{}^{c*}$), the following holds:

$$\frac{\partial f}{\partial K^{\alpha} t_2{}^{c*}} < \frac{\partial g}{\partial K^{\alpha} t_3{}^{c*}}$$

But we have assumed that the marginal productivity of the wife's time in the second period is larger than in the third stage when applied to child services. This implies, as shown in the following diagram, that $t_2{}^{c*} > t_3{}^{c*}$.

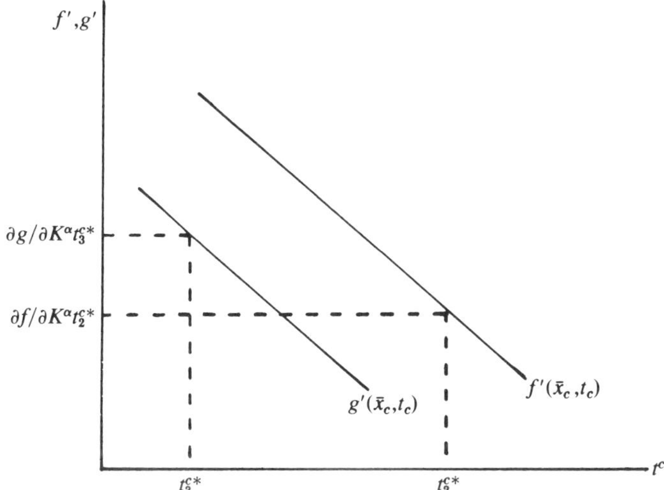

Thus, unless the function U_{l_2} lies below the function U_{l_3} (which is implausible), it may be concluded unambiguously that $L_2^* < L_3^*$, that is, the wife supplies a smaller fraction of her time to the market in the child-rearing stage than in the final period.

ACKNOWLEDGMENT

The authors gratefully acknowledge the support of the Health, Education and Welfare Department, Public Health Service, under Grant No. HD 12037-02. The opinions expressed herein are those of the authors and should not be construed as representing the opinions or policy of any agency of the United States Government.

NOTES

1. For a study that specifically addresses the issues of the timing and spacing of children, see Nerlove and Razin (1979b).

2. H_1 may be thought of as a weighted average of the husband's income in the period between marriage and first birth and some measure of the income of the wife's family in the period prior to marriage.

3. We also neglect the possibility that the husband's retirement decision may be endogenous.

4. It would perhaps be more rigorous to use some average of L_1 and L_2, but this would complicate matters without altering the nature of the results.

5. For simplicity of notation, we denote the three utility functions by U, although it is understood that this does not imply that they are all the same.

6. Since the oldest women in the survey was only 44 years of age, none of our respondents had completed the third period according to our definition. Thus, we use the post-child-rearing stage to date.

7. The Pareto fit was found to be appropriate to our data, according to the criterion indicated by Miller (1963). This procedure led us to use \$37,610 as the average income in the open-end interval.

8. This may be due to the fact that *CONTR*, our proxy for contraceptive efficiency, captures two effects. First, women who use more modern contraceptive techniques have fewer children, *ceteris paribus*, because they have a smaller number of unplanned pregnancies. But, second, it may also happen that those couples who have already had many children may seek better methods to avoid increasing their family size further. The insignificant result we obtained may be a result of the netting out of these two influences.

REFERENCES

Ashenfelter, O. and J. Heckman. 1974. The estimation of income and substitution effects in a model of family labor supply. *Econometrica 42*:73–85.

Becker, G. S. 1965. A theory of the allocation of time. *Economic Journal 75*:493–517.

Becker, G. S. and H. G. Lewis. 1973. Interaction between quantity and quality of children. *Journal of Political Economy 84*:S279–S288.

Birdsall, N. 1977. Analytical approaches to the relationship of population growth and development. *Population and Development Review 3*:63–102.

Bowen, W. G. and T. A. Finegan. 1969. *The Economics of Labor Force Participation.* Princeton: Princeton University Press.

Cain, G. G. 1966. *Married Women in the Labor Force: An Economic Analysis.* Chicago: University of Chicago Press.

Cain, G. G. and M. D. Dooley. 1976. Estimation of a model of labor supply, fertility and wages of married women. *Journal of Political Economy 84*:S179–S201.

Cramer, J. 1974. Births, expected family size, and poverty. *Five Thousand American Families—Patterns of Economic Progress, Volume II*, J. N. Morgan (ed.). Ann Arbor: The Institute for Social Research. pp. 279–317.

DaVanzo, J. 1972. *The Determinants of Family Formation in Chile, 1960: An Econometric Study of Female Labor Force Participation, Marriage and Fertility Decisions.* Santa Monica: The Rand Corporation.

Fleischer, B. M. and G. F. Rhodes. 1979. Fertility, women's wage rates, and labor supply. *American Economic Review 69*:14–24.

Hill, R. and F. Stafford. 1978. Lifetime fertility, childcare, and labor supply. Unpublished paper.

Jusenius, C. L. 1977. The influence of work experience, skill requirement, and occupational segregation on women's earnings. *Journal of Economics and Business 29*:107–115.

Lehrer, E. 1978. Women's allocation of time over the life cycle: an econometric study. Unpublished Ph.D. Dissertation, Northwestern University.

Lehrer, E. and M. Nerlove. 1980. The impact of female life cycle time allocation decisions on income distribution among families. *Proceedings of the International Economic Association, Volume IV* forthcoming.

Lydall, H. F. 1976. Theories of the distribution of earnings, *The Personal Distribution of Incomes*, A. B. Atkinson (ed.). London: George Allen & Unwin Ltd. pp. 15–46.

Miller, H. P. 1963. Trends in the income distribution of families and persons in the United States, 1947–1960. Technical Paper No. 8, United States Bureau of the Census. Washington: U.S. Government Printing Office.

Mincer, J. 1962. Labor force participation of married women: a study of labor supply. *Aspects of Labor Economics,* National Bureau of Economic Research. Princeton: Princeton University Press. pp. 63–105.

Nerlove, M. 1974. Toward a new theory of population and economic growth. *Journal of Political Economy 84*:S200–S216.

Nerlove, M. and A. Razin, assisted by W. Joerding and E. Lehrer. 1979a. Child spacing and numbers: an empirical analysis. Discussion paper No. 371. The Center for Mathematical Studies in Economics and Management Science, Northwestern University.

Nerlove, M. and A. Razin. 1979b. Child spacing and numbers: an empirical analysis, *Essays in the Theory and Measurement of Consumer Behavior* A. Deaton, (ed.). Cambridge: Cambridge University Press.

Rosenzweig, M. 1978. The value of children's time, family size and non-household child activities in a developing country: evidence from household data, *Research in Population Economics I,* J. L. Simon (ed.). Greenwich: JAI Press Inc. pp. 331–347.

Schultz, T. P. 1969. Secular trends and cyclical behavior of income distribution in the United States, 1944–1965. *Six Papers on the Size Distribution of Wealth and Income,* L. Soltow (ed.). New York and London: Columbia University Press pp. 75–100.

Schultz, T. P. 1975. *Estimating Labor Supply Functions for Married Women.* Santa Monica: The Rand Corporation.

Sweet, J. A. 1973. *Women in the Labor Force.* New York: Seminar Press.

Willis, R. 1973. A new approach to the economic theory of fertility behavior. *Journal of Political Economy 81*:514–564.

YOUNG WOMEN'S PREFERENCES FOR MARKET WORK:
RESPONSES TO MARITAL EVENTS

Glenna D. Spitze and Linda J. Waite

ABSTRACT

Using data from the NLS Young Women Survey, we examine how women's relative preferences for market work and home work are affected by three transitions: first marriage, marital dissolution, and first birth. We argue that all three events should affect market work preferences by changing levels of available resources such as time and money and by changing the level of personal fulfillment derived from family life. Probit analysis indicates that first marriage decreases market work preferences through age 24 but not beyond that age, perhaps because concomitant changes in resources are less unexpected after than before that age. Marital dissolution tends to increase preference for market work at ages 19 through 29, probably by exposing women to financial insecurity. A first birth has no immediate impact but is followed 1 to 2 years later by striking upward revisions in market work preferences. Implications of these results are discussed.

Research in Population Economics, Volume 3, pages 147–166

ISBN: 0-89232-207-1

I. INTRODUCTION

Individual "tastes" or preferences are an important theoretical component of economic models of such behavior as childbearing (Becker, 1960; Easterlin, 1969), educational attainment (Bowen and Finegan, 1969; Cohen *et al.*, 1970), and female labor force participation (Cain, 1966; Cain and Dooley, 1976; Lehrer and Nerlove, 1979). But measures of tastes rarely are included in empirical economic analyses of any of these subjects: economists tend to take tastes as a given, as data, to be explained by someone else (Stigler and Becker, 1977:76). This is especially the case in economic models of female labor supply. Since tastes are almost never measured directly or included (except through proxies) in economic analyses of women's labor force participation, we know relatively little about the role that these preferences play in determining the amount of labor women supply to the market. Although the importance of tastes for employment in female labor supply has never been established, there are a number of reasons that preferences for market work are of interest in and of themselves. First and most obviously, these preferences may have some effect on when and whether an individual woman works for pay. Second, there is considerable evidence that tastes for work have important implications for other aspects of women's lives: some work-related, some not. Women who prefer market to home work over the long run tend to invest more in their human capital, both formal schooling and job training, than those who prefer homework (Sandell and Shapiro, 1978). Polachek (1977; see also Doescher, 1979) argues that women chose their occupations at least in part on the basis of their long-run preferences for employment and childbearing, seeking to match the two to minimize conflict between the wife–mother and worker roles. And there is considerable evidence that tastes for market work affect timing and number of children (Waite and Stolzenberg, 1976; Ross, 1973). Thus it is important to understand as much as possible about women's preferences for work in the market, how these tastes develop, and the conditions under which they change. In this paper, we examine young women's stated, long-run preference for market versus home work; specifically, we explore the ways in which tastes for employment change in response to a first marriage, a first birth, or a marital dissolution.

The late adolescent and young adult years are important in women's lives because this is when decisions about many lifetime activities are made: young women decide when and whether to form families; they decide on the amount, timing, and kind of work they will do for much of their lives. Many of these decisions are irreversible and have important, long-term consequences. Tastes for market work held during the young adult years are one input into these lifetime decisions, and, we argue, change as a result of experiences during these years. Young women may revise their preferences for employment because of experience in school, as a result of the quality and extent of the early labor market experience (Spitze and Waite, 1980; Presser, 1971), or because of their reaction to the changes that occur when they first marry, become a mother, or have a marriage dissolve. In this paper, we focus on the effects on tastes for market work of the latter experiences, of what we call "marital events."

We expect these "marital events" to cause women to revise their relative preferences for work in the market and work in the home by altering (1) the psychic income or personal fulfillment that they receive from family life and (2) the level of resources and psychic income that we argue are associated with each marital event: a first marriage, a first birth, and a marital breakup, in turn. We begin our discussion with entry into wedlock.

Much of young girls' socialization in this society revolves around the anticipation of getting married and raising children. It would hardly be surprising if the wife and mother roles were less fulfilling than young women expect them to be. Bailyn (1970) hypothesizes that a "traditional dream" of fulfillment through marriage and motherhood may be destroyed by the reality. If young women expect more satisfactions from being married than they receive, then when their expectations are not met they may seek fulfillment in other spheres, one of which may include gainful employment. Married women, even those who are employed, tend to do the vast majority of the housework (Walker and Woods, 1976), receiving relatively little help from their husbands. Since a new bride is suddenly responsible for the household maintenance for two adults instead of one, marriage probably results in a decrease in leisure time for the wife. But personal fulfillment through family life may increase upon marriage, even if the increase is not as large as many young women expect it to be. An increase in fulfillment could increase preference for work in the home over work in the market.

Marriage may increase a young woman's sense of financial security by giving her access to the earnings of another person, one who probably earns considerably more than she does, or who will in the long run. She is no longer solely responsible for her own financial support, although this is a burden that she may have shared with her parents before her marriage. But marriage may increase the short-run felt need for income since the costs of setting up a new household are considerable.

The arrival of a first child causes many of the same changes that a first marriage does—an increase in the amount of work required in the home and the collision of the traditional dream of fulfillment through motherhood with the reality of childcare—but instead of increasing feelings of financial security, a first birth may decrease these feelings. The financial demands that parenthood places on a family, especially knowledge of the long-term costs of children, may make a woman cognizant of the future need for her earnings and thereby increase her taste for employment.

Marital dissolution tends to reduce a woman's financial security, we argue. On average, the economic situation of the wife worsens substantially following divorce whereas that of the husband improves (Hoffman, 1977). This occurs because the couple loses the economies of scale realized by living together (Lazear and Michael, 1980) and the wife usually retains custody of the children. The low probability that alimony or child support will be awarded and paid consistently (Eckhardt, 1968; Jones *et al.*, 1976) will tend to increase the woman's awareness that her own earnings are important for her financial security. Her long-term preferences for market work may increase as a result.

We will summarize our expectations about the responses of women's tastes for employment to marital events. We expect marital dissolution to increase relative preferences for market over home work since this event will tend to decrease women's financial security and the psychic income they receive from family life. Both of these changes should make gainful employment more attractive. Whether a first marriage or a first birth will raise or lower tastes for employment is an empirical question, since there are forces operating in both cases to make market work both more and less appealing. The effect of the event may depend on initial preferences. It may also depend on the age at which the event occurs. We expect that the older the woman, the more developed are her preferences for employment and work in the home and the less likely to change with a marital event. Older women should know more in general about the realities of marriage, parenthood, and the stresses of divorce than their younger counterparts because they have had time to observe others in these situations and to evaluate their reactions.

To this point, we have presented our reasoning about the responses of young women's market work preferences to marital events. In the next section, we present a causal model of this process.

II. THE MODEL

Thus far we have suggested that market work preferences will change with the occurrence of "marital events," that is, first marriage, first birth, or marital dissolution, due to resultant changes in available resources and sources of fulfillment. Levels of resources and amount of personal fulfillment are not explicitly measured in our analysis. Our model can be represented as shown in Figure 1.

In this paper, we focus only on the last stage of the model presented in Figure 1: the effect of a marital event on changes in tastes for paid em-

Figure 1. Causal Model of Effects of Marital Events on Young
Women's Preference for Market Work

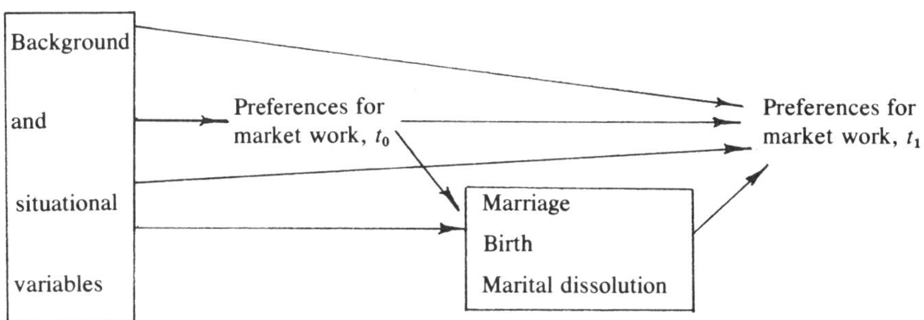

ployment. The occurrence of the marital events, initial preferences for
market work, and other characteristics of the woman are all taken as exogenous. Marital events are viewed as altering tastes directly. In fact,
these effects could occur in any of three ways. Events could alter *levels*
(means) of background variables; they could alter *effects* of background
or situational variables (i.e., interaction effects); or they could have their
own direct effects on preferences. Here we examine explicitly only the
direct effect of marital events on tastes for employment, although we recognize that more complex effects may be operating to a small degree.
Most background and situational variables measured here could not
change with the event, since they are permanent characteristics of the
woman or her family of origin. Situational variables such as employment
and school enrollment could change relatively quickly in response to a
marital event, and the effects of a marital event could vary according to
original employment or enrollment status. Since this is a first test of this
issue, we confine ourselves to the relatively simple model.

Our model is based on the further assumption that marital events are
not *caused* by changes in preferences that occur between the beginning of
the year and the time of the event, i.e., that causality runs only from the
marital event during a year to preferences for employment at the end of
the year. We feel that there are theoretical reasons for our causal specification. Most marital events are planned and anticipated at least to some
degree; their causes operate over a long time frame. A woman not planning a marriage, divorce, or first birth, who had a "sudden" change in
preferences for market work would be unlikely subsequently to plan and
execute any of these events within *less* than a year. Much more plausible
is a sequence in which the event occurs, perhaps partly as a result of preferences at the beginning of the year, which in turn may reflect anticipation
of the event. Preferences are then altered in response to *experience* in
the new state. In addition to these theoretical reasons, results for first

birth (presented later) provide empirical evidence against an alternative model. This is the underlying causal process on which our model is based.

Our model requires data on tastes for work at two times as well as information on timing of marital events and on other characteristics of the woman. This model can be estimated only with longitudinal data on young women of the ages to be experiencing a first marriage, a first birth, and marital dissolution. Large numbers of observations are required to provide enough cases with marital events. Fortunately data meeting these requirements are available and are described in the next section of the paper.

III. DATA AND PLAN OF ANALYSIS

As we discussed earlier, without longitudinal data one can only speculate about the effects of family formation on preferences for market activity. Presser (1971) points out that a woman may bear a child or avoid bearing a child at a given age *because* of her level of occupational or educational aspirations, but an unplanned early birth may curtail her job preparation prematurely. An analysis of the relation between age at first birth and later aspirations would not clarify which sequence of events had occurred. In order to test the impact of family formation events on preferences for employment, we need measures of these preferences before and after the period in question so we may determine what change has occurred due to the intervening event.

The necessary data are available in the National Longitudinal Survey of Young Women. Conducted by the Ohio State University Center for Human Resource Research, this survey includes yearly data on over 5000 young women over a recent 5-year period. Personal interviews were conducted with a national probability sample of the noninstitutionalized female population age 14–24 in 1968, with yearly reinterviews through 1973. Attrition rates were low; 85.5 percent of the original sample were still being interviewed as of 1973.

A measure of preferences for market work versus home work was included in every wave of this survey. The young woman was asked what she would like to be doing at age 35, to which she could respond with an occupation or with "housewife." We code this as a dichotomy indicating whether the woman would or would not prefer to be doing market work. We argue that this question expresses her true preferences in a discretionary situation. Women are generally expected to work before their first birth and to stay home with young children for the first few years of the child's life. By age 35, however, for the average woman, all children are in kindergarten or grade school and most other mothers will, at least, have no infants in the home (Glick, 1977). Any preschool-age children could be put in day care if the woman wants to hold a job, but since most women at this age will still have relatively young children, they have a legitimate "excuse" to stay home.

We wish to stress that this variable is interpreted here as a measure of *current* preferences. It is not known, nor is it crucial to know, whether it is a strong predictor of actual labor market participation at age 35. By referring to a time in the fairly distant future, we avoid responses that would reflect constraints in the woman's current situation (e.g., young children or a husband's low income), and we can tap the woman's true preferences in a hypothetical absence of such constraints.

Our strategy is to examine the effect on preference for market work of getting married, dissolving a marriage, or experiencing a first birth during a 1-year period,[1] with preferences and other relevant variables at the beginning of the year controlled.[2] Since we wish to examine these effects separately by age of the woman for whom the event occurs, we restructure the data onto observations on each respondent over a 1-year period. The periods are separated by age of respondent at the beginning of the year. The NLS women were age 14–24 in 1968 and 19–29 in 1973, so observations on 1-year transitions from 14–15 through 28–29 were available. The number of observations on each age differed considerably, since, for example, only those age 14 in 1968 experienced the 14-to-15 transition, while those anywhere from 14 to 18 in 1968 experienced the 18-to-19 transition sometime between 1968 and 1973.

Fifteen separate samples were created for two of the three transitions: those never married at each age and those childless at each age. For those currently married at each age in the divorce analysis, 12 age groups starting at age 17 were created, since so few women aged 14 through 16 were married. For economy and ease of reporting results, each of the three sets of samples of 12 to 15 age groups was then collapsed into seven groups (6 for divorce); for example, the 14-to-15 and the 15-to-16 transition samples were combined. To avoid problems of autocorrelation (Johnston, 1972), age groups were selected so that no woman was included in a given analysis more than once.[3]

The dependent variable in each of these analyses is preference for market work, which is coded as a dichotomy. An appropriate estimation technique for such equations is probit analysis (Hanushek and Jackson, 1977), which is a maximum likelihood technique based on the assumption that the underlying probability distribution is normal.[4] Given a probability interpretation of the predicted values of the dependent variable, a marginal change in probability should be most difficult to obtain when the probability is close to one of the limits, 0 or 1. Probit analysis allows the calculation of differing slopes (or differing levels of effects of independent variables) at varying levels of the predicted probability for the dependent variable (Vanneman and Pampel, 1977). It also constrains the predicted values of the dependent variable to fall between 0 and 1. Values outside this range are meaningless as probabilities but may be obtained when ordinary least squares is used with a dichotomous dependent variable.

For cross-equation comparability, probit slopes can be reported at the same point along the curve and can be interpreted similarly to unstandardized regression coefficients. Here we report all slopes at a probability level of .50, close to the mean level of preference for employment for all age groups and also the point of maximum slope along the curve.

The independent variables of major interest in all three analyses are dichotomies indicating whether or not a given event took place. For women never married at a given age, we examine the effect of a first marriage during the year on preference for market activity at the end of the year. For women married at the beginning of a given year, we examine the effect on preference for employment of a marital dissolution (separation or divorce) during the year. It should be noted that we know only marital status at each time point. If a woman separates from her husband during the year but is living with him at the end of the year, or gets divorced and remarried during the year, we are unable to detect this. This will make our estimates of the effects of marital dissolution slightly conservative. For women childless at the beginning of a given year, we examine the impact of bearing a first child during that year on preference for work at the end of the year. For reasons that will be described shortly, we also look at the effect of a first birth on preferences for market activity 2 years later.

Control variables in each model reflect two kinds of factors: the woman's family background, which may be a causal antecedent of both preference for work and the timing of the events examined here, and relevant characteristics of the woman and her current situation at the beginning of the year. All equations include a control for the year from which beginning-of-year data were taken (coded from 1 = 1968 to 5 = 1972).

A measure of preference for market versus home work at age 35 was included in every wave of the NLS data, as we mentioned earlier. This question was asked in precisely the same way in every year, with the exception of a minor wording difference between the 1968 survey and all other years. Tastes for employment at the beginning of the year in question were included as a control in every equation predicting preferences at the end of the year. In every case, preferences at t_0 and t_1 were obtained via precisely the same question, with the minor exception just stated. Thus, in our analysis, the effect of a marital event on tastes for employment at the end of a year measures the impact of a marital event on *change* in these tastes.[5]

Family background variables include mother's and father's education (coded in years), household head's occupational status (Duncan prestige scores), number of siblings, whether the mother worked when the woman was 14, whether two parents were present when she was 14 (both coded as dummy variables), region at age 14 (1 = south, 0 = other), and size of city in which she was reared (ranging from 1 = 3 million or more, to 8 = rural). Characteristics of the woman include race (coded 1 = black, 0 = other) and years of education completed. Employment and full-time school enrollment status are both dummy variables, coded 1 for employed or enrolled and 0 for other.[6] For the marital dissolution and marriage analyses, a dummy variable indicating the presence of children is included; and for the childbearing analysis, a dummy variable indicates whether the woman is currently married. For the marital dissolution analysis, four predictors, applicable to married women only, are included: age at marriage, own income, husband's income (coded in hundreds of dollars per year), and the ratio of own to husband's income. These latter four variables are not included in the childbearing analysis, since that analysis includes unmarried women.

IV. RESULTS

A. Transition to Marriage

As Table 1 indicates, the impact of a first marriage during a year on preference for market work at the end of that year is consistently negative from ages 14 through 23. Since the number of marriages in the 14- and 15-year-old group is small, results for that group will not be discussed further, but the effects for the other age groups are striking. The likelihood that a young woman prefers market to home work at age 35 decreases from 10 to 20 percentage points upon first marriage.

While it is impossible to determine from this analysis what specific factors enter into this drop, we can speculate that on balance women experience unexpected increases in financial security or decreases in time, the two major resources that both marriage and market work affect. Since between 80 and 90 percent of women who get married during a given year are going to school or working and since presumably very few quit either activity immediately, women may experience unexpected increases in total work responsibilities with the addition of housework to their other activities. Husbands typically do very little housework whether or not their wives work (Walker and Woods, 1976), although 80 percent of men will respond positively to a survey question stating that a man *should* share housework equally if his wife works full time.[7] Thus, women may be surprised by the actual division of household labor after marriage. If they foresee that the chances of increasing the husband's

Table 1. Effect of First Marriage and Control Variables on Preference for Market Work[a]

Independent variables	Age at beginning of year						
	14–15	16–17	18–19	20–21	22–23	24–25	26–28
Marriage during the year	−0.509*	−0.203*	−0.111*	−0.102*	−0.143*	−0.019	0.016
Earlier preference for market work	0.512*	0.611*	0.570*	0.633*	0.617*	0.594*	0.851*
Education	−0.067*	0.026*	0.001	−0.010	0.015*	0.023*	0.019
Enrollment	0.051	−0.039	0.133*	0.133*	0.276*	−0.064	1.128
Employment	−0.087*	−0.006	−0.032	−0.050	−0.101	−0.173**	0.074
Kids	0.087	−0.102	0.047	−0.042	−0.020	−0.107	−0.105
Intact	−0.065	0.035	−0.095*	−0.048	0.022	−0.061	0.246
Mother's education	−0.011*	0.011*	0.011*	0.010	−0.004	0.009	0.020
Father's education	0.015*	−0.005	−0.003	0.006	−0.018*	−0.015	0.035*
City size	0.009	−0.010*	0.011*	0.013*	0.017*	−0.008	−0.016
Head occupation	−0.001	−0.000	−0.001	−0.001	−0.000	0.002	−0.001
Race	0.313*	0.136*	0.116*	0.117*	0.129**	0.152	0.265
Number of siblings	−0.020*	0.001	−0.019*	0.002	0.012	0.022	0.011
Year	—	−0.106*	−0.034*	−0.027*	−0.041*	0.001	—
Region	−0.045	−0.002	−0.051	0.012	−0.141*	−0.045	0.073
Probability of marriage	0.01	0.08	0.16	0.20	0.20	0.12	0.14
Variance explained	0.35	0.37	0.39	0.42	0.44	0.40	0.64
N	904	1793	1975	1380	715	316	131

* $p < .05$.
** $.05 < p < .10$.
[a] Probit slopes at $p = .50$.

share of housework are small, they may begin to look forward to a time when they themselves will be responsible *only* for the housework and child care.

Marriage also complicates the woman's decision-making by creation of a new unit, the household. Her future work plans may become altered by unexpected positions taken by her husband. He may disapprove of market work for married women with young children, in a manner contrary to her own attitudes. His own work may require frequent moves, making the woman's career planning difficult.

Women who first marry beyond the age of 24 experience no change in preferences for labor force participation.[8] The explanation for this may lie in the increased knowledge women acquire regarding home and market work compatibilities as they age (Stolzenberg and Waite, 1977). As indicated by the effects of preferences for paid employment the previous year on current preferences, market work preferences remain somewhat consistent over time but are most stable beyond the age of 25. By this time, a woman probably has gained adequate knowledge of how employment, marriage, and childbearing can be combined and how she wishes to combine them. She has had time to participate in the labor force, and even if unmarried or childless herself, has watched friends make decisions in these areas. So apparently, by age 24, the amount of new information gained by actually marrying is small enough not to alter a woman's basic orientation toward market activity.

While our major interest here is in the effects of marriage on market work preferences, two other highly consistent effects in Table 1 merit brief discussion. Any effect here will reflect changes during the 1-year period in taste for employment, net of earlier tastes. Thus, the consistently positive coefficients of race reflect a tendency for black women to increase market work preferences *more rapidly* than do whites during the ages represented here. The negative impact of year (for all but one of the groups for which it is applicable) implies that market work preferences were increasing at faster rates earlier than later during the 1968–1973 period. This probably reflects a minor wording change in this item between 1968 and 1969, which increased favorable responses toward market work.

B. Transition out of Marriage

The positive impact of marital dissolution on a young woman's preference for labor force participation is substantial—between 18 and 29 percentage points (see Table 2)—and tends to be higher the later it occurs. Not only does the experience of marital dissolution cause women to *need* to work and to prepare for future work (Mott and Moore, 1977; Hoffman, 1977), these results suggest that it increases their *desire* to work, perhaps

Table 2. Effect of Marital Dissolution and Control Variables on Preference for Market Work[a]

	Age at beginning of year					
Independent variables	*17–18*	*19–20*	*21–22*	*23–24*	*25–26*	*27–28*
Divorce during the year	−0.021	0.173**	0.046	0.236*	0.208*	0.291*
Earlier preference for market work	0.487*	0.596*	0.574*	0.600*	0.702*	0.703*
Education	0.029	0.047*	0.011	0.017*	0.032*	−0.001
Enrollment	0.185	0.147	0.229*	0.250**	−0.405*	1.535
Employment	−0.252*	−0.047	0.013	−0.031	0.003	0.046
Kids	0.218*	0.101*	−0.045	0.141*	0.167*	0.137**
Intact	−0.009	−0.084	0.012	0.009	0.023	−0.008
Father's education	−0.005	0.004	0.010	0.006	0.010	0.006
City size	0.012	0.007	−0.018*	−0.006	−0.019*	0.014**
Race	−0.031	0.139	0.093	0.099	0.148	−0.062
Year	−0.021	−0.024**	−0.022**	−0.014	—	—
Age married	0.001	−0.002	0.001	0.000	−0.003	−0.002**
Income	0.008	0.002	−0.003*	−0.000	0.001	0.000
H income	0.002	0.001	0.001*	−0.000	0.000	0.000
Ratio own/H	0.006	0.009	0.040*	0.044*	0.013	0.006
Region	0.023	−0.046	−0.033	−0.030	−0.128	−0.193
Probability of divorce	0.09	0.04	0.06	0.04	0.04	0.03
Variance explained	0.35	0.39	0.40	0.40	0.51	0.50
N	221	726	904	1167	544	499

* $p < .05$.
** $.05 < p < .10$.
[a] Probit slopes at $p = .50$.

as a route to financial self-sufficiency and fulfillment outside the home. There is no significant change in preference for market work following marital dissolution during the teen years, although the small sample sizes make the results suspect.

C. Transition to Motherhood

A first birth leads to substantial changes in a young woman's life. Apart from experiencing an increased financial burden, she may stop work or school and spend much of the day at home for the first time in her adult life. The baby probably makes more demands on her time than the mother has ever experienced from any one source. Since we were unsure whether the full impact of this change would be apparent within a short period, and since the demands and rewards of childrearing change rapidly during the first year, we estimated the effects of a first birth during a given year on preference for market activity at the end of that year *and* at the end of the *next* year. We found no significant impact of a first birth during a given year on changes in preferences for labor force participation during that year. This probably reflects the fact that most births are planned and anticipated. Most women giving birth during a given year will either be pregnant at the beginning of the year before or plan to become so. Thus tastes immediately following a birth are not significantly different from those held while anticipating the birth. This does, however, provide evidence for the causal ordering in our model. If the birth were caused by changed preferences after the beginning of the period, these changes would be apparent after the first year.

We now turn to changes in a young woman's preferences for market work between 1 and 2 years after she experiences a first birth. By this point, presumably, she has a clearer picture of how the birth has affected her situation. For women between ages 16 and 27 who experience a first birth, the probability that they prefer paid employment to home work is increased by 10 to 15 percentage points. This effect is consistently positive and is significant for 6 out of 7 age groups (see Table 3). The coefficient for the 26- and 27-year age group is .13 and therefore consistent with those for other groups, although it is not significant due to sample size. A first birth is such a rare event for those in the youngest group that we have no confidence in the coefficient for that group.

Why should a first birth be followed by dramatically increased preference for market work while the impact of a first marriage is negative? Certainly the two events change a woman's life in different ways. Marriage generally increases a woman's financial security, whether she plans to work or be supported totally by her husband. Her economic situation is not solely her responsibility after marriage. On the other hand, the addition of children to the family increases financial demands on the parents

Table 3. Effect of First Birth and Control Variables on Preference for Market Work[a]

	Age at beginning of year						
Independent variables	*14–15*	*16–17*	*18–19*	*20–21*	*22–23*	*24–25*	*26–27*
First birth during the year	1.522*	0.150*	0.151*	0.122*	0.104*	0.121**	0.133
Earlier preference for market work	0.459*	0.343*	0.363*	0.381*	0.379*	0.406*	0.438*
Education	−0.050*	0.022*	0.025*	0.003	0.021*	0.023*	0.041*
Enrollment	0.209*	0.042	0.162*	0.106*	0.141*	0.296**	0.118
Employment	−0.066**	0.014	−0.038**	0.004	0.067*	0.124*	0.066
Intact	−0.105*	0.014	−0.042	−0.037	−0.034	−0.011	0.105
Mother's education	−0.019*	0.002	0.001	0.014*	0.004	−0.017*	0.013
Father's education	0.015*	0.003	0.003	0.012*	−0.004	0.012	0.010
City size	0.011**	0.002	0.012*	0.010*	0.008**	0.000	0.021
Head occupation	0.001	0.000	0.000	−0.001	−0.001	0.000	0.000
Race	0.319*	0.162*	0.098**	0.067	0.076	0.112	0.275**
Mother work	0.094*	0.060*	0.013	0.107*	−0.024	0.100*	0.001
Number of siblings	−0.019*	−0.007	0.002	−0.003	0.020*	0.007	−0.029
Year	—	−0.055*	−0.026*	−0.019**	−0.031*	0.042**	—
Region	−0.058	−0.012	−0.034	0.032	−0.112*	−0.114*	−0.249*
Marital status	−0.400**	0.056	−0.020	−0.054**	0.066**	0.056	−0.022
Probability of first birth	0.01	0.06	0.08	0.10	0.13	0.11	0.11
Variance explained	0.31	0.17	0.25	0.25	0.26	0.29	0.42
N	921	1803	1975	1484	984	471	147

* $p < .05$.
** $.05 < p < .10$.
[a] Probit slopes at $p = .50$.

and may make the woman more cognizant than before of the need to bring money into the household.

The occurrence of a first birth continues to have an impact on a woman's preference for labor force participation up to about age 25, whereas marriage has no impact beyond age 23. These results may indicate that young women are less prepared for motherhood than for marriage. By age 23, women may be cognizant of the changes involved in getting married, whereas a first birth may be such a major change that it is impossible for a young woman to be prepared fully or to anticipate her reactions simply by observing the experience of others.

The positive impact of a first birth on preference for paid employment is consistent with the positive coefficients for the effect of child presence for currently married women (Table 2).[9] These coefficients imply that the impact of a first birth is not temporary—mothers of young children are more likely than others to increase tastes for employment. The increase in preference may reflect desire to get away from full-time child care, a recognition of financial needs engendered by children's presence, or timing effects. However, the results in Table 3 would seem to contradict the last interpretation; women in the oldest age category experience the greatest increase in preference for market activity despite the high probability that the youngest child will not be in school when the woman is age 35.

Since these equations contain controls for preference for market work in the previous year, effects of other variables reveal only the circumstances under which women's preferences may be revised in a relatively short period. The most striking of these is school enrollment. Probability of prefering market work to home work increases substantially—anywhere from 10 to 30 percentage points—during a year in which a woman is enrolled in school. This is consistent with previous results on the effect of college attendance on market work preferences (Spitze, 1978). We also find that education tends to have a positive impact—smaller than that of school enrollment—on preference for employment.

V. DISCUSSION

In this paper, we have developed a causal model of changes in women's long-run tastes for paid employment. This model is based on the premise that women have a certain preference for market versus home work at the beginning of a year and that during the year some women experience a marital event, which may be a first marriage, a first birth, or the breakup of an existing marriage. This marital event may then cause some of the women experiencing it to revise their relative tastes for employment and work in the home. We argue that changes in the level of such resources as time and money and changes in feelings of personal fulfillment that occur as a result of marriage, first birth, or divorce are responsible for alterations in market work preferences. We test this model and our results are consistent with it. But the reader must keep in mind that we have not proved that this is the causal process that is operating; causation may run from changed preferences to marital events in some cases, although we argue that this causal ordering is quite unlikely. With that caveat in mind, we turn to a discussion of the implications of our results, if one accepts the causal model we have developed.

On the basis of results presented here, current trends toward postponement of marriage and childbearing and increased probability of divorce would lead one to expect increases in general levels of preference for market work in recent cohorts of women. The percentage of young women in their early twenties never married and the percentage in their late twenties still childless has nearly doubled since 1960 (U.S. Bureau of the Census, 1976; 1978). Increasing numbers of women postpone marriage to an age when it has no negative impact on preference for work and many postpone childbearing to the age range when the positive impact is relatively high, the overall result should be higher levels of preference for market activity in current cohorts than for their predecessors. Further reinforcement of this trend should occur due to the recent upward swing in the divorce rate: approximately 40 percent of marriages currently contracted by women in their twenties are expected to dissolve (Glick and Norton, 1977).

However, although we have indirect evidence that levels of preference for labor force participation are increasing for recent cohorts of young women, we have no direct support for this contention. Sex-role attitudes are changing among women at all socioeconomic and educational levels (Mason *et al.*, 1976), but whether these changes are reflected in preferences and plans for market behavior is an open question.

A related question concerns time lags for the measurement of change. In this research we have examined changes in preference for market work during a 1-year period in which a first marriage or a marital dissolution occurs or during a 2-year period in which a first birth takes place. While the changes measured here can be argued convincingly to be a direct result of the transition, we do not know whether the attitude change is permanent or even whether it is likely to change in direction at a later point. It is possible, for example, that after a short early period (1 or 2 years) of enjoyment of housework and increased preferences for home work, a woman who marries then revises her preference for labor force participation upwards. Similarly, the woman who divorces and experiences preference for paid employment may return to her previous preferences when, as is generally the case, she remarries (U.S. Bureau of the Census, 1976).

Finally, we should point out that the results of this research are only a beginning in understanding the actual process of women's changing preferences for market work.[10] For example, while the results from the childbearing analysis provide support for the existence of a "traditional dream" that is destroyed by the reality of a first birth, we do not know for sure that this is going on. Since our measure of preference for work is a dichotomy, it is impossible to determine whether market work preferences are "moderated" by the transition to marriage or motherhood. An interval-level measure would be necessary to detect this kind of effect.

The question that we address in this paper could be answered more convincingly by research that includes more detailed information on women's preferences and expectations before and after these events. If it were known what actually occurs during this transitional period, it might be possible to provide young women with information regarding family–work conflicts earlier in their lives so that they could consider alternative strategies. Since a decision to prepare for a career ideally is made early in a young woman's life, the question of how she will combine work and family roles without restricting later work prospects should be raised before family formation (for example, in high school courses or by high school guidance counselors). If these issues were raised early in a young woman's life, along with provision of the requisite information, the onset of marriage or motherhood might cause fewer sharp revisions in preference for labor force participation. Certainly the later in life these revisions occur, the more time is lost for job preparation or wasted in preparation for a career or job that is later discarded.

ACKNOWLEDGMENTS

This research was supported by the Employment and Training Administration, U.S. Department of Labor, under Grant Numbers 91-17-78-05 and 91-17-78-11. Since contractors performing research under government sponsorship are encouraged to express their own judgment freely, the report does not necessarily represent the department's official opinion or policy. Authorship of this paper is joint and shared equally by Spitze and Waite. We would like to thank Valerie Oppenheimer and two anonymous reviewers for their comments on an earlier version of this paper.

NOTES

1. Since early adulthood is a period when a variety of new experiences occur and since tastes and attitudes may change rapidly in response to these events, we chose a 1-year period over a larger period during which effects of various events might be difficult to determine.

2. This issue of the appropriate length of the lag between the occurrence of a marital event and preferences for market work is of theoretical and methodological importance. Marriages and births, and probably marital dissolutions, are planned in advance so that some adjustment of tastes for employment may take place in anticipation of the new status

and would be reflected in preferences at t_0. This would bias the effect of a marital event on preferences at t_1, net of preferences at t_0, toward being too small and make our estimate of this effect conservative. But we argue that it is the *experience* in the new status (either wife, mother, or divorcee) that causes changes in tastes for employment and that the experience may be quite different than was anticipated. We chose to focus on a 1-year period to (1) reduce the probability that intervening events cause changes in work preferences; (2) observe the short-run impact of a marital event. The long-run effect of a marital event on tastes for employment is of interest but is outside the scope of our analysis.

3. This section was not random, but the inclusion of data on a given women for one year rather than for another was unrelated to whether she married in either year. For example, in the analysis of the 20-to-21 transitions, data on the 20-to-21 transition was included for those women ages 16, 18, and 20 in 1968, and data on the 21-to-22 transition for those ages 17, 19, and 21 in 1968.

4. A similar technique, logit, assumes a logistic distribution. Logit and probit are very similar, with small differences in the tails of the distribution (Hanushek and Jackson, 1977:204).

5. One reader of this paper suggested that we estimate the model using first differences. This would involve using as the dependent variable the difference between preferences at t_0 and t_1 and as independent variables changes in circumstances (for example in marital status or parenthood) during the year. Regression of first differences is a solution to the problem of serial correlation in the error term of an equation estimated with ordinary least squares. Serial correlation of errors violates the assumption of independence of errors upon which OLS depends (Wonnacott and Wonnacott, 1970:136–140). However, we estimate our model with probit analysis, a maximum likelihood technique. It is not clear that estimating first difference equations is a solution to the problem of serially correlated error terms, if such a problem exists in this case. For this reason we have chosen to estimate the effect of a marital event on work preferences at t_1, net of the effect of work preferences at t_0.

6. While a measure of whether the woman is living independently of her parents would be desirable, this information is not available in these data. Women going to college away from home are coded as living with their parents.

7. Joan Huber found this result in a national probability sample of married men in 1978.

8. Results for women age 26–28 should be viewed cautiously due to small sample sizes.

9. It should be kept in mind here that these results are from two different sets of equations and samples.

10. We should also point out that preferences for market work are only one of a complex set of factors that influence women's labor market behavior. Other factors such as family income, child care availability, local labor market conditions, and husband's attitudes will affect employment decisions and may interact with preferences in affecting employment behavior. We recognize the complexity of this process; however, that complexity is not the focus of this study.

REFERENCES

Bailyn, Lotte. 1970. Career and family orientations of husbands and wives in relation to marital happiness. *Human Relations 23*:97–113.

Becker, Gary. 1960. An economic analysis of fertility. *NBER Demographic and Economic Change in Developed Countries*. Princeton: Princeton University Press. pp. 209–231.

Bowen, William and T. Aldrich Finegan. 1969. *The Economics of Labor Force Participation*. Princeton: Princeton University Press.

Cain, Glen C. 1966. *Married Women in the Labor Force.* Chicago: University of Chicago Press.

Cain, Glen C. and Martin D. Dooley. 1976. Estimation of a model of labor supply, fertility, and wages of married women. *Journal of Political Economy 84*:S179–S201.

Cohen, Malcolm, S. A. Rea Jr., and R. Lerman. 1970. *A Micro Model of Labor Supply.* BLS Staff Paper 4. Washington, D.C.: U.S. Government Printing Office.

Doescher, Tabitha Ann. 1979. Fertility and female occupational choice. Working paper. University of North Carolina, Chapel Hill.

Easterlin, Richard A. 1969. Towards a socioeconomic theory of fertility: a survey of recent research on economic factors in American fertility. *Fertility and Family Planning: A World View,* S. J. Behrman, L. Corsa, and R. Freedman (eds.). Ann Arbor: University of Michigan Press. pp. 127–156.

Eckhardt, Kenneth. 1968. Deviance, visibility, legal action: the ability to support. *Social Problems 15*:470–477.

Glick, Paul C. 1977. Updating the life cycle of the family. *Journal of Marriage and the Family 39*:5–14.

Glick, Paul C. and Arthur Norton. 1977. *Marrying, Divorcing and Living Together in the U.S. Today. Vol. 35,* No. 5. Washington, D.C.: Population Reference Bureau.

Hanushek, Eric A. and John E. Jackson. 1977. *Statistical Methods for Social Scientists.* New York: Academic Press.

Hoffman, Saul. 1977. Marital instability and the economic status of women. *Demography 14*:67–76.

Johnston, J. 1972. *Econometric Methods.* New York: McGraw-Hill.

Jones, Carol A., Nancy M. Gordon, and Isabel V. Sawhill. 1976. Child support payments in the United States. Working Paper 992-03. Washington, D.C.: The Urban Institute.

Lazear, Edward P. and Robert T. Michael 1980. Real income equivalent among one earner and two earner families. *American Economic Review 70:*203–9.

Lehrer, Evelyn and Marc Nerlove. 1979. Female labor supply behavior over the life cycle: an econometric study. Discussion paper No. 382. Northwestern University.

Mason, Karen Oppenheim, John L. Czoika, and Sara Arber. 1976. Change in U.S. women's sex role attitudes, 1964–1974. *American Sociological Review 41*:573–596.

Mott, Frank and Sylvia Moore. 1977. The socioeconomic determinants and short run consequences of marital disruption. Paper presented at the annual meetings of the Population Association of America, St. Louis.

Polachek, Solomon. 1977. Occupational segregation among women: a human capital approach. University of North Carolina Paper No. 77–4. Chapel Hill, NC.

Presser, Harriet B. 1971. The timing of the first birth: female roles and black fertility. *Milbank Memorial Fund Quarterly 49*:329–359.

Ross, Sue Goetz. 1973. The timing and spacing of births and women's labor force participation: an economic analysis. Ph.D. dissertation, Department of Economics, Columbia University, New York.

Sandell, Steven H. and David Shapiro. 1978. Work expectations, human capital accumulation, and the wages of young women. Columbus, Ohio: Center for Human Resource Research.

Spitze, Glenna D. and Linda J. Waite. 1980. Young women's early labor force experiences and work attitudes. Sociology of Work and Occupations. *7:*317–35.

Spitze, Glenna D. 1978. Role experiences of young women: a longitudinal test of the role hiatus hypothesis. *Journal of Marriage and the Family 40*:471–480.

Stigler, George J. and Gary S. Becker. 1977. De gustibus non est disputandum. *American Economic Review 67*:76–90.

Stolzenberg, Ross M. and Linda J. Waite. 1977. Age and the relationship between young women's plans for childbearing and employment. *American Sociological Review* 42:769–783.

U.S. Bureau of the Census. 1976. *Number, Timing, and Duration of Marriage, and Divorces in the United States: June 1975.* Current Population Reports, Series P-20, No. 297. Washington, D.C.: U.S. Government Printing Office.

U.S. Bureau of the Census. 1978. *Trends in Childspacing: June 1975.* Current Population Reports, Series P-20, No. 315. Washington, D.C.: U.S. Government Printing Office.

Vanneman, Reeve and Fred C. Pampel. 1977. The American perception of class and status. *American Sociological Review* 42:422–437.

Waite, Linda J. and Ross M. Stolzenberg. 1976. Intended childbearing and labor force participation of young women: insights from nonrecursive models. *American Sociological Review* 41:235–252.

Walker, Kathryn and Margaret E. Woods. 1976. *Time Use: A Measure of Household Production of Family Goods and Services.* Washington, D.C.: American Home Economics Association.

Wonnacott, Ronald and Thomas H. Wonnacott. 1970. *Econometrics.* New York: Wiley.

WOMEN'S WORK, FERTILITY, AND COMPETING TIME USE IN MEXICO CITY

Stanley K. Smith

ABSTRACT

The degree to which work and childcare are competing uses of time is suggested as a crucial determinant of the relationship between female labor force participation and fertility in less developed countries. Several variables are suggested as measures of competing time use. Using data from Mexico City, it was found that the fertility of women who had worked since marriage was very similar to the fertility of those who hadn't, but women who worked at jobs in which work and childcare were competing uses of time had considerably lower fertility than other workers and nonworkers.

I. INTRODUCTION

It is frequently suggested that higher rates of female labor force participation (FLFP) can play an important role in lowering fertility rates in less

Research in Population Economics, Volume 3, pages 167–187

ISBN: 0-89232-207-1

developed countries. Yet the theoretical justification for expecting such a relationship is not well established, and the empirical evidence supporting it is quite contradictory: some studies have found a negative relationship between FLFP and fertility, some a positive relationship, and some no relationship at all. What can account for the existence of so much contradictory evidence? The present study suggests that the degree to which work and childcare are competing uses of time is an important determinant of the FLFP–fertility relationship in less developed countries. If work and childcare can easily be done simultaneously, there is no time constraint forcing a trade-off between the two. If they cannot be done simultaneously, however, then a time constraint does exist and a trade-off between the two must be made. A negative relationship may thus be found where work and childcare are competing uses of time, and no relationship (or even a positive one) where they are not. Several measures of competing time use are developed, and the competing time use hypothesis is tested using sample survey data from Mexico City.

This study deals primarily with correlation, not causation. A basic assumption is that FLFP and fertility decisions are made jointly, and depend on income, prices, tastes, wages, employment opportunities, and current family size. The empirical work focuses on the direction and significance of partial correlations between FLFP and fertility and whether these correlations vary predictably according to the degree to which work and childcare are competing uses of time. It does not deal with the internal dynamics of the FLFP–fertility relationship over time or with the timing of births and market work. The FLFP and fertility variables used in this study are cumulative measures of market work and fertility over the life span since marriage.

II. REVIEW OF EVIDENCE

There is a vast literature concerning the existence and causality of the relationship between FLFP and fertility in more developed countries. Although its causal nature is still a moot issue, the existence of a negative relationship is widely accepted. Virtually all studies have found that women who work have fewer children than those who don't, and women who work more have fewer children than those who work less.[1] This result holds for many different measures of FLFP and fertility and after the effects of such variables as age, education, income, and fecundity status have been accounted for (Ridley, 1959; Freedman and Coombs, 1966; Whelpton *et al.*, 1966; Kiser *et al.*, 1968; Kupinsky, 1971; Groat *et al.*, 1976; Weller, 1977).

A similar consensus does not emerge from studies of less developed countries. Many studies have found a negative relationship. Tabah and Samuel (1962) found that the average number of live births in Santiago, Chile was over half a child less for workers than nonworkers. Miró and Rath (1965) obtained similar results in San Jose, Panama City, and Rio de Janeiro, and Miró and Mertens (1968) found a negative FLFP–fertility relationship in seven Latin American cities. Nerlove and Schultz (1970) found the demand for female labor had a significant negative effect on the crude birth rate in Puerto Rico, whereas the number of children under age five had a significant negative effect on the FLFP rate. Maurer *et al.* (1973) found that births per woman had a significant negative effect on FLFP for Thai women age 20–34. Jaffe (1959) found that women working in modern industries in Puerto Rico had considerably fewer births than nonworkers of the same educational attainment. Gendell *et al.* (1970) found workers in Guatamala City had fewer births than nonworkers; working as a domestic had a considerably stronger negative association with fertility than did other types of work. Davidson (1973) found a negative FLFP–fertility relationship in Caracas and Mexico City; she also found that whereas women working at home had slightly more births than nonworkers, those working away from home had considerably fewer births. Weller (1968) reported that white collar workers in San Juan had fewer births than other workers.

Other studies have found a positive relationship between FLFP and fertility in less developed countries. Driver (1963) found in India that currently employed wives have borne an average of 5 children while nonemployed wives average only 4.5. Goldstein (1972) found in Thailand that women in the labor force had about 15 percent more births than women not in the labor force. Bindary *et al.* (1973) found in aggregate data from Egypt that the child–woman ratio was positively related to female employment in rural areas. Snyder (1974) found a significant positive relationship between FLFP and family size in Sierra Leone. He suggested that women with large families were forced to work in order to supplement family income.

Some studies have found no significant relationship between FLFP and fertility. Mueller *et al.* (1971) found in Taiwan that labor force status had very little effect on family size ideals, after the effects of backgound variables were controlled. Using Turkish data, Stycos and Weller (1967) found no significant relationship between labor force status and births per woman, controlling for age, education, and rural-urban residence. Stycos (1965) found a small, insignificant negative relationship between live births and FLFP in Lima. Zarate (1967) found in Monterrey, Mexico that women who had worked since marriage had an almost identical average number of births as women who had not. Hass (1972) found little relationship between labor force status and fertility in a study of seven Latin American cities.

While the above is not an exhaustive survey of the literature, it does illustrate that the empirical evidence on the FLFP–fertility relationship in less developed countries is extremely contradictory. How can the existence of such disparate results be explained? Part of the explanation is that these studies mentioned differ in the degree to which the effects of other variables were controlled, employed different time references, and used different measures of fertility and FLFP. While each of these factors undoubtedly plays some role, I would like to suggest another explanation: the direction and significance of the FLFP–fertility relationship in less developed countries depends on the degree to which work and childcare are competing uses of time.

III. THEORETICAL FRAMEWORK

Recent work done by economists has placed FLFP and fertility behavior within a comparative statics framework of household decision-making (DeTray, 1972; Ben-Porath, 1973; Gardner, 1973; Michael, 1973; Willis, 1973). In this context, a husband and wife at the outset of their marriage adopt a utility-maximizing lifetime plan of fertility, market work, non-market activities, and consumption of goods and services. This plan depends on the wages, prices, and nonwage income expected by the couple, their relative preferences for the things that afford them utility, and time. In this model, it is assumed that market work and nonmarket activities cannot be carried out simultaneously. As a result, any nonmarket activity carries with it an implicit opportunity cost equal to the income foregone in order to pursue that activity.

This model doesn't stipulate that a negative relationship must exist between FLFP and fertility; whether it does or not depends on the cost of nonparental childcare, the time intensity of childcare, and the relative strengths of the income and substitution effects of changes in the wife's wage. However, the model does imply that a negative relationship is likely to exist. Since the total amount of time available to a woman is fixed, an increase in the amount of time devoted to market work necessarily implies a decrease in the time spent in nonmarket activites. Children, requiring a good deal of attention and supervision, are very time-intensive. As a result, childcare accounts for a substantial portion of nonmarket time, and childcare time will generally decrease as work time increases. Since the amount of time spent on childcare over the life cycle is highly correlated with the number of children in a family (see, for example, Hill and Stafford, 1974), it follows that couples who choose to have large families will choose lower levels of FLFP than couples who choose small families, other things being equal.

This expected negative relationship depends on the assumption that women's work and childcare are competing uses of time. In more developed countries, this is a reasonable assumption: virtually all market work is done in settings in which work and childcare are competing uses of time and cannot be carried out simultaneously. In less developed countries, however, this is not necessarily the case. There is a broad spectrum of work–childcare time use combinations. Some types of work (e.g., sewing garments at home) can be carried out simultaneously with childcare, with little loss in productivity. Other types of work (e.g., working on a factory assembly line) cannot. Work and childcare are competing uses of time for some types of work in less developed countries but not for others.

The idea that the type of work might affect the FLFP–fertility relationship has been raised before (Jaffe and Azumi, 1960; Weller, 1968; Hass, 1972; Davidson, 1973). The focus in these studies, however, has not been specifically on competing time use. Rather it has been on the broader concept of "role incompatibility," which includes price, wage, and taste factors as well as time use. For example, Weller included the costs of childcare, the ease with which employment can be interrupted to rear children, and normative attitudes toward female employment. Hass included financial remuneration and the amount of educational preparation and on-the-job training required. Price, wage, and taste factors are intermingled with the effects of competing time use, and it is impossible to determine whether the fertility differences reported are due to differences in attitudes, opportunity costs, or the fact that some jobs can be done while caring for children and others cannot. McCabe and Rosenzweig (1976) did consider time use specifically, but looked at the common determinants of FLFP and fertility rather than at the FLFP–fertility relationship *per se*.

The present study deals not with the broad issue of role incompatibility but rather with the more narrow issue of competing time use, or "time incompatibility." The FLFP–fertility relationship itself is treated as a variable. The focus is on how this relationship varies with the degree to which work and childcare are competing uses of time. If work and childcare can be performed simultaneously, there is no time constraint forcing a trade-off between the two. If they cannot be performed simultaneously, however, a time constraint does exist and a choice must be made between working and caring for children. Since the number of children in a family is positively correlated with the amount of time spent caring for children over the lifetime, a negative relationship would be expected between family size and types of FLFP that cannot be performed simultaneously with childcare. The specific hypothesis tested in this study is that a significant negative correlation between FLFP and fertility will exist only if work and childcare are competing uses of time.

The basic assumption regarding the causal nature of the FLFP–fertility relationship is that FLFP and fertility are jointly determined. Work and fertility decisions are not made independently of each other, but are made together with full knowledge of what one implies for the other. These decisions are based on income, prices, tastes, wages, employment opportunities, and current family size (which will generally be zero for decisions made at marriage). The empirical work focuses on the correlation between FLFP and fertility over the entire life span since marriage but does not delve into the timing of births and market work.

IV. DATA AND VARIABLES

A sample survey from Mexico City was used to test the competing time use hypothesis. Mexico City was chosen because of the large variations in fertility and the diversity in occupational opportunities found there and because good data were available. The data were drawn from a multistage, stratified, clustered probability sample of married Mexican women living in the Mexico City Metropolitan Area. All women were living with their husbands at the time of the interview. The survey was conducted in early 1971. Sample size was 798, representing a response rate of 96 percent. The sample was stratified by measures of housing structural–sanitary deficiencies, household monthly income, and household physical area. The data have been weighted to account for inequalities in the probability of selection of individual women.[2]

The primary problem in testing the competing time use hypothesis is the choice of measures. Categories such as rural versus urban, home versus away from home, part-time versus full-time, and white collar versus blue collar are commonly used in studies of the FLFP–fertility relationship. While these measures capture to a certain extent differences in the degree to which work and childcare can be carried out simultaneously, none is completely satisfactory as a measure of competing time use. Rural work may more often be carried out simultaneously with childcare than urban work, but within both the urban and rural sectors, there are some jobs that can be carried out simultaneously with childcare and some that cannot. Work at home may be carried out simultaneously with childcare, but it doesn't follow from this that work away from home cannot be. Full-time work presents more of a time use conflict with childcare than part-time work only if work and childcare cannot be performed simultaneously. White collar work cannot generally be carried out simultaneously with childcare, but blue collar work and childcare may be either competing or complimentary uses of time, depending on the specific job. In addition, the white collar versus blue collar dichotomy is strongly correlated with socioeconomic status, adding differences in income, education, and tastes to differences in time use.

Some of these measures are used in the present study. In addition, a measure is constructed that deals more directly with the degree to which work and childcare are competing uses of time. Work is divided by sector. Occupations in which hours and location of work are fairly flexible, in which relationships between employer and employee or proprietor and customer are quite informal, and in which work duties do not require full-time attention are classified as traditional sector jobs. In the traditional sector, work and childcare are not necessarily competing uses of time. It is quite possible that childcare and work in the traditional sector can be performed simultaneously. Occupations in which hours and location are quite rigid, in which work relationships are relatively formal, and in which work duties require full-time attention are classified as modern sector jobs. In the modern sector, it is quite likely that work and childcare cannot be performed simultaneously but rather are competing uses of time.[3]

The classification of occupations by sector is shown in Table 1. This classification was based on the consensus of several researchers familiar with the employment characteristics of less developed countries, particularly Mexico City. Although there may be some disagreement on the classification of a few occupations, in most cases, the choice is fairly obvious. All market work performed at home is classified in the traditional sector.

The labor force variables employed in this study are location (home or away from home), concentration (part-time or full-time), sector (traditional or modern), and duration (years worked since marriage as a proportion of total years married). It is assumed that work and childcare are more likely to be competing uses of time if work is away from home rather than at home, full-time rather than part-time, in the modern rather than the traditional sector, and the longer its duration since marriage. Two combination variables are also used, one combining sector with concentration (part-time and full-time in the modern and traditional sectors) and the other combining sector with duration (proportion of married years spent working in the modern and traditional sectors). These additional measures permit a more detailed analysis of fertility differences across labor force groups.

All labor force variables refer to work at any time since marriage rather than current labor force status. These are cumulative measures covering the entire married lifetime. Data on the timing of entrances and exits into and out of the labor force are not available in the present data set. When more than one job has been held since marriage, interview responses

Table 1. Wife's Occupation, by Sector

Sector	N^a	
Modern		
1. Doctor; Dentist	1	
2. Teacher	14	
3. Certified public accountant	1	
4. Nurse; Medical technician	7	
5. Chemist; Physicist; Geologist; etc.	4	
6. Artist; Musician; Writer	5	
7. Self-employed business person	8	
8. Business manager	1	
9. Other proprietor	1	
10. Secretary	29	
11. Bookkeeper	4	
12. Other office worker	13	
13. Salesworker, nonfood store	12	
14. Factory worker	22	
15. Barber; hairdresser	1	
Total		123
Traditional		
1. Farm worker	3	
2. Foodstore; Small restaurant owner	11	
3. Salesworker, foodstore	6	
4. Street vendor	10	
5. Traditional craft: Bakers; Tailors; etc.	34	
6. Business manager (home)	2	
7. Artist; Musician; Writer (home)	2	
8. Barber; Hairdresser (home)	1	
9. Cook; Waitress	17	
10. Maid; Servant; Laundress	49	
11. Janitor	4	
12. Other service worker	10	
13. Urban laborer, unspecified	1	
Total		150

a N, number of women.

regarding sector, concentration, and location of work refer to the primary job held. The dichotomous variables provide simple measures of market work experience in that they refer to work performed at any time since marriage regardless of the length of time involved. The continuous variables provide more refined measures by taking explicit account of differing lengths of time spent working.

The fertility variables are the number of children ever born to a woman (CEB) and the family size she expects by the time she has completed her childbearing years (EFS). The woman's age and education (years of schooling) and husband's education are employed as control variables.

Age is a control for years of potential childbearing, as all the women in the sample were married at the time of the interview and variation in age at marriage was fairly small. Wife's education controls for the opportunity costs of nonmarket activities and differences in family size preferences, whereas husband's education controls for income and social status differences.

The theoretical model implies that the availability and cost of non-parental childcare may affect the FLFP–fertility relationship. The availability of relatives for childcare has occasionally been used as a measure of nonparental childcare and has sometimes been found to have a positive effect on the fertility of workers (Weller, 1968:519) and other times been found to have no effect (Driver, 1963:82). Previous work with the present data set showed that living in an extended rather than a nuclear family had no perceptible effect on fertility or women's work (Smith, 1976:135, 152). The present study does not consider types or costs of nonparental childcare.

V. EMPIRICAL ANALYSIS

Tables 2 and 3 provide empirical evidence regarding the FLFP–fertility relationship in Mexico City. Table 2 shows the average fertility levels of women in various FLFP categories. The mean gives the average CEB and EFS for each FLFP category and the adjusted mean gives the average CEB and EFS for each category after adjustments have been made for differences in wife's age and education and husband's education. These adjustments are made using multiple classification analysis, an extension of dummy variable multiple regression analysis in which the explanatory variables may represent membership in categories rather than numerical values.[4]

While multiple classification analysis is useful in showing fertility differences among women in various FLFP categories, it cannot provide tests for assessing the significance of these differences. Partial correlation analysis can provide such tests. The fertility and FLFP variables are regressed on wife's age and education and husband's education and the residuals are saved from each regression. These residuals represent the parts of FLFP and fertility that are unrelated to wife's age and education and husband's education. The FLFP and fertility residuals are then correlated and tested to determine whether the correlations are significant. Partial correlation analysis is used rather than OLS regression analysis because it tests the direction and significance of the FLFP–fertility relationship without specifying the causal relationship between FLFP and fertility. The results of the partial correlation analysis are shown in Table 3.

Table 2.   Means and Adjusted Means[a] of CEB and EFS
for Seven FLFP Measures

Measure	N[b]	CEB[c]		EFS[d]	
		Mean	Adjusted mean	Mean	Adjusted mean
Never worked	525	4.23	4.48	6.00	6.11
Worked	273	4.78	4.40	5.92	5.71
Never worked	525	4.23	4.48	6.00	6.11
Home	49	5.49	4.83	6.52	6.09
Away	224	4.62	4.18	5.79	5.64
Never worked	525	4.23	4.48	6.00	6.11
Part-time	112	5.82	5.01	6.87	6.43
Full-time	161	4.05	3.81	6.26	5.22
Never worked	525	4.23	4.48	6.00	6.11
Traditional	150	6.14	4.92	7.21	6.24
Modern	123	3.10	3.55	4.34	5.07
Never worked	525	4.23	4.48	6.00	6.11
Home	49	5.49	4.83	6.52	6.12
PT-TRAD[e]	50	7.43	5.75	8.54	7.19
FT-TRAD[f]	61	5.27	4.13	6.37	5.43
PT-MOD[g]	29	2.97	3.51	3.76	5.01
FT-MOD[h]	85	3.07	3.54	4.45	5.06
Never worked	525	4.23	4.48	6.00	6.11
<33% YWSM[i]	155	5.87	4.78	6.71	6.26
≥33% YWSM	118	3.33	3.69	4.87	5.02
Never worked	525	4.23	4.48	6.00	6.11
<33% YWSM-TRAD	97	6.99	5.37	7.87	6.83
≥33% YWSM-TRAD	53	4.65	4.05	6.08	5.17
<33% YWSM-MOD	58	4.07	3.76	4.86	5.28
≥33% YWSM-MOD	65	2.25	3.40	3.88	4.90
Grand mean		4.42		5.97	

[a] Adjusted for wife's age, wife's education, and husband's education.
[b] *N*, Number of women.
[c] CEB, Children ever born.
[d] EFS, Expected family size.
[e] PT-TRAD, Part-time traditional.
[f] FT-TRAD, Full-time traditional
[g] PT-MOD, Part-time modern.
[h] FT-MOD, Full-time modern.
[i] YWSM, Years worked since marriage.

It is clear from the first panel of Tables 2 and 3 that fertility differences between workers and nonworkers are small and insignificant. When no controls are employed, the average CEB is half a child higher for workers than nonworkers, whereas EFS is slightly lower. When the effects of wife's age and education and husband's education are controlled, fertility differences between workers and nonworkers become very small and statistically insignificant. When all types of market work are lumped together and no allowance is made for competing time use, fertility does not vary by labor force status. If the analysis went no further, one would have to conclude that there is no significant relationship between FLFP and fertility in Mexico City.

When FLFP measures that account for competing time use are considered, however, a striking relationship emerges. The six lower panels of Tables 2 and 3 show FLFP–fertility relationships when other measures of FLFP are used. These data indicate that workers in jobs in which work and childcare are likely to be competing uses of time have considerably lower fertility than nonworkers, whereas workers in jobs in which work and childcare are less likely to be competing uses of time have similar or higher fertility than nonworkers.

When differences in wife's age and education and husband's education are accounted for, women who have worked away from home have lower CEB than nonworkers whereas women who have worked at home have

Table 3. Partial Correlation of CEB and EFS with Seven FLFP
Measures, Controlling for Wife's Age, Wife's Education,
and Husband's Education[a]

	CEB[b]	EFS[c]
Worked	0.038	−0.022
Home	0.054	0.025
Away	0.010	−0.037
Part-time	0.141*	0.104*
Full-time	−0.077**	−0.116*
Traditional	0.120*	0.058***
Modern	−0.068**	−0.084*
PT-TRAD	0.169*	0.124*
FT-TRAD	−0.017	−0.054
PT-MOD	0.002	−0.003
FT-MOD	−0.076**	−0.091*
%YWSM	−0.097*	−0.131*
%YWSM-TRAD	−0.031	−0.082**
%YWSM-MOD	−0.105*	−0.096*

* Significant at .01.
** Significant at .05.
*** Significant at .10.
[a] $N = 798$.
[b] CEB, Children ever born.
[c] EFS, Expected family size.

higher CEB. These fertility differences by location of work are not large, however, and are statistically insignificant.

Fertility differences by concentration and sector are large and significant. Part-time workers have an adjusted average CEB that is over half a child higher than nonworkers, whereas full-time workers have two-thirds lower CEB than nonworkers. Traditional sector workers have almost half a child higher adjusted average CEB than nonworkers whereas modern sector workers average almost a full child lower. All of these differences are statistically significant.

The fifth panel combines concentration and sector characteristics. It shows that part-time workers in the traditional sector have far higher CEB than any other group, both before and after controls are employed. Full-time traditional sector workers have somewhat lower CEB than nonworkers, but this difference is not statistically significant. Part-time modern sector workers do not have a level of CEB that is significantly different from that of nonworkers, but full-time workers in the modern sector have significantly lower CEB than nonworkers.

These are particularly interesting results. Workers in the FLFP category in which work and childcare are most likely to be competing uses of time (FT-MOD) display fertility levels significantly below nonworkers; workers in the category least likely to be competing uses of time (PT-TRAD) display levels significantly higher; and workers in categories midway on the spectrum (PT-MOD and FT-TRAD) display levels that are not significantly different from those of nonworkers. Even though these are dichotomous measures dealing with work at any time since marriage, they provide strong empirical support for the competing time use hypothesis.

The last two panels of Tables 2 and 3 deal with work duration i.e., the number of years worked since marriage as a proportion of the total number of years married (%YWSM). With these measures, it is possible to differentiate between the fertility levels of women who have worked only a short time since marriage and those who have worked a relatively long time. From Table 2 it can be seen that women who have spent more than 33 percent of their married lives in the labor force have considerably lower CEB than nonworkers, whereas those who have worked less than 33 percent have somewhat higher CEB than nonworkers, after adjustments have been made for wife's age and education and husband's education. This relationship holds for workers in both the modern and traditional sectors.

In Table 3, work duration is treated as a continuous rather than a categorical variable. The proportion of married life spent in the labor force is found to be negatively correlated with CEB. This correlation is only marginally significant, however. When %YWSM is correlated with CEB separately for modern and traditional sector workers, the correlations are found to be large and significant for modern sector workers, but small and insignificant for traditional sector workers. This is consistent with the competing time use hypothesis: the negative relationship between fertility and the proportion of married life spent working will be strong only if work and childcare are competing uses of time.

Virtually the same patterns exist for EFS as CEB. Home workers have about the same EFS as nonworkers whereas away-from-home workers have lower EFS; full-time workers have lower EFS than non-workers and part-time workers higher EFS; traditional sector workers have somewhat higher EFS than nonworkers and modern sector workers considerably lower EFS; part-time traditional sector workers have far higher EFS than any other group; and women who have worked more than 33 percent of their married lives have lower EFS than those who have worked less than 33 percent, for both modern and traditional sector workers. Levels of significance of the partial correlations of EFS with FLFP are very similar to those of CEB.

The results shown in Tables 2 and 3 provide substantial support for the hypothesis that the FLFP–fertility relationship in less developed countries is strongly affected by the degree to which work and childcare are competing uses of time. Workers for whom market work and childcare cannot be performed simultaneously have significantly lower fertility than nonworkers, whereas workers for whom market work and childcare can be performed simultaneously have similar or even higher fertility than nonworkers. These results help explain the seemingly contradictory evidence found in the literature on the FLFP–fertility relationship in less developed countries. Of the studies cited above finding a positive FLFP–fertility relationship, none differentiated among types of work. They lumped together occupations that can be carried out simultaneously with childcare (e.g., agriculture or home handcrafts) with occupations that cannot be (e.g., modern factory or office jobs). Of the studies finding no relationship, only Hass (1972) and Mueller *et al.* (1971) differentiated among types of work. Even these studies found negative relationships for some measures or some localities. Of the studies finding a negative relationship, on the other hand, most made some division among various types of work. These divisions included rural versus urban, home versus away, part-time versus full-time, white collar versus blue collar, and cottage versus factory industry. All these measures pick up differences in competing time use to one extent or another. A pattern thus emerges from the literature: women who work at jobs in which work and childcare are likely to be competing uses of time have lower fertility than non-workers, whereas women who work at jobs in which work and childcare are not necessarily competing uses of time do not.

While the present study is directed primarily toward testing the hypothesis that a significant negative FLFP–fertility relationship will exist only if work and childcare are competing uses of time, an interesting sidelight emerges from Tables 2 and 3. Some types of work actually have a significant positive correlation with fertility. In particular, part-time workers in the traditional sector are found to have far higher fertility than any other group, including nonworkers. It has been suggested that very high fertility may put such a strain on the budget that women are forced to work in order to supplement family income (Hass, 1972; Snyder, 1974). In such a case, women must either make nonparental childcare arrangements or find work that can be done while caring for children. If nonparental childcare arrangements are too expensive or otherwise unacceptable, the second option will have to be taken. Very high fertility may thus promote labor force participation in jobs that can be done while caring for children. Although the present study does not consider the direction of causation between FLFP and fertility over time, the evidence just cited is certainly consistent with such a hypothesis.

The question has been raised whether negative FLFP–fertility relationships might be caused by the self-selection of subfecund women for the labor force (Freedman *et al.*, 1959; Namboodiri, 1964; Stycos and Weller, 1967). If this were the case, the ability to conceive, rather than competing time use, would be the driving force behind the FLFP–fertility relationship. This hypothesis has been tested frequently for more developed countries, with a consensus that although working wives tend to have higher incidences of fecundity impairments than nonworking wives, a negative FLFP–fertility relationship exists for both fecund and subfecund women (Freedman *et al.*, 1959; Freedman and Coombs, 1966; Whelpton *et al.*, 1966). For less developed countries the effects of fecundity differences on the FLFP–fertility relationship have seldom been tested.

Such effects can be tested by examining the FLFP–fertility relationship for a subgroup of fecund women. Women under age 45 were classified as fecund if they reported that they were sure they were currently fecund. Since women over age 45 would be subfecund because of age, they were classified as fecund if they had had two or more children. This measure of fecundity understates the number of fecund women to the extent that women over age 45 had fewer than two children by choice rather than because of fecundity impairments. It therefore provides a conservative estimate of the number of fecund women.

The FLFP–fertility relationship for fecund women is shown in Table 4. The similarity of correlation coefficients and levels of significance to those in Table 3 indicates that the same FLFP–fertility relationship holds for fecund women as holds for the entire sample. The FLFP–fertility relation-

Table 4.   Partial Correlation of CEB and EFS with Seven FLFP
Measures, Controlling for Wife's Age, Wife's Education,
and Husband's Education, for Subgroup of Fecund Women[a]

	CEB[b]	EFS[c]
Worked	0.068***	0.009
Home	0.099*	0.063
Away	0.019	−0.023
Part-time	0.182*	0.140*
Full-time	−0.079**	−0.113*
Traditional	0.163*	0.103*
Modern	−0.066***	−0.082**
PT-TRAD	0.213*	0.161*
FT-TRAD	−0.014	−0.038
PT-MOD	0.008	0.006
FT-MOD	−0.077**	−0.094*
%YWSM	−0.063***	−0.101*
%YWSM-TRAD	0.067***	0.006
%YWSM-MOD	−0.109*	−0.112*

* Significant at .01.
** Significant at .05.
*** Significant at .10.
[a] $N = 674$.
[b] CEB, Children ever born.
[c] EFS, Expected family size.

ship reported in this study is not due simply to the self-selection of subfecund women for the labor force.

While multiple classification analysis and partial correlation analysis
are useful in netting out the effects of wife's age and education and husband's education, it may prove useful to investigate the FLFP–fertility
relationship within specific age and education categories. This is done in
Table 5, where three categories of wife's age and two categories of wife's
education are combined into six subgroups. The age caregories were
chosen in light of previous work (Smith, 1976), which showed fertility differences to be very small among women under age 30, while family size
was largely completed by age 40. Education was divided at 6 years, the
completion of primary school.

The top panel of Table 5 shows that among women with more than 6
years of schooling, workers have considerably lower fertility than nonworkers. These differences are shown by a *t*-test to be statistically significant at .05 for all but the oldest age group. Among women with 6 or
fewer years of schooling, however, this is not the case. In fact, among

Table 5.   Average CEB and EFS by Age, Education,
and Two FLFP Measures

Age	Education	N^a	CEB[b]		EFS[c]	
			Never worked	Worked	Never worked	Worked
<30	6	190	2.96	2.64	6.12	5.11
30–39	6	161	5.58	6.23	7.44	7.71
40+	6	202	6.57	6.90	6.68	7.24
<30	7+	119	1.94*	1.38*	4.60*	3.65*
30–39	7+	69	4.08*	2.76*	4.78*	3.45*
40+	7+	57	4.09	3.68	4.20	3.68
			TRAD	MOD	TRAD	MOD
<30	6	28	2.68	2.75	5.20	5.00
30–39	6	75	6.68*	4.70*	8.14*	6.10*
40+	6	78	7.47*	4.75*	7.74*	5.38*
<30	7+	37	1.00[d]	1.44	3.20[d]	3.72
30–39	7+	33	2.33[d]	2.90	2.67[d]	3.66
40+	7+	22	5.25[d]	3.28	5.25d	3.28

* Fertility differences between FLFP categories are significant at .05.
[a] N, Number of women.
[b] CEB, Children ever born.
[c] EFS, Expected family size.
[d] Five or fewer persons; all other categories had ten or more.

women over age 30, workers have higher fertility than nonworkers. Previous studies have found that workers with more education have lower fertility than nonworkers but workers with less education do not (e.g., Minkler, 1970). Why might trade-offs exist between FLFP and fertility for women with more education but not for women with less education? The reason suggested here is that the work performed by women with more education may be qualitatively different from that performed by women with less education. Specifically, more educated women may be more likely to work in the modern sector, whereas less educated women may be more likely to work in the traditional sector. If this were true, work and childcare would be largely competing uses of time for more educated women but not for less educated women.

Table 6 shows that women with more than 6 years of schooling are indeed much more likely to work in the modern sector whereas women with 6 or fewer years are more likely to work in the traditional sector. Of the 91 working women with more than 6 years of schooling, only 12 worked in the traditional sector. Of the 182 with 6 or fewer years, 138 worked in the traditional sector. The absence of a FLFP–fertility trade-off among women with little education can thus be explained by the type of jobs they

Table 6. Number of Working Women by Education
and Occupational Sector

	Education		
Sector	*Six or fewer years*	*Seven or more years*	*Total*
Traditional	138	12	150
Modern	44	79	123
Total	182	91	273

generally hold; namely, traditional sector jobs in which work and child-care are not necessarily competing uses of time.

If the hypothesis of competing time use is correct, workers in the modern sector should have lower fertility than nonworkers or workers in the traditional sector at all levels of educational attainment. The lower panel of Table 5 addresses this implication. For women with more than 6 years of schooling, those who have worked in the modern sector have considerably lower CEB and EFS than nonworkers for all three age groups. Since very few women with more than 6 years of schooling have worked in the traditional sector, a meaningful comparison with more educated traditional sector workers is not possible. For women with 6 or fewer years of schooling, a comparison of fertility levels of modern and traditional sector workers is possible. Whereas workers above age 30 have higher fertility than nonworkers, modern sector workers above age 30 have higher lower fertility than nonworkers or traditional sector workers. CEB for modern sector workers is 0.9–1.8 lower than for nonworkers and 2.0–2.7 lower than for traditional sector workers; EFS is 1.3 lower than for nonworkers and 2.0–2.4 lower than for traditional sector workers. These fertility differences between modern and traditional sector workers are statistically significant at .05 for women over 30. For women under age 30, the fertility of modern and traditional sector workers is quite similar.

Even among women with low levels of formal education, then, there is a trade-off between certain types of work and fertility. Women who have worked in the modern sector have considerably lower fertility than non-workers regardless of their educational level. The hypothesis of competing time use provides a plausible explanation of why a fertility difference exists between highly educated workers and nonworkers whereas none exists between less educated workers and nonworkers.

VI. SUMMARY AND CONCLUSIONS

The hypothesis tested in this study is that a negative FLFP–fertility relationship will exist only if work and childcare are competing uses of time.

The data used are from a sample survey conducted in Mexico City in 1971. Several variables were constructed to measure competing time use: location (home or away from home), intensity (part-time or full-time), sector (modern or traditional), and duration (years worked since marriage as a proportion of total years married). It is assumed that work and childcare are more likely to be competing uses of time if work is away from home rather than at home, full-time rather than part-time, in the modern rather than the traditional sector, and the longer its duration since marriage.

The empirical results provide strong support for the competing time use hypothesis. When no distinction is made regarding competing time use, no significant FLFP–fertility relationship is found: women who have worked at some time since marriage have very similar levels of fertility to women who have not. When distinctions regarding competing time use are made, however, large fertility differences become evident. Workers for whom market work and childcare cannot be performed simultaneously have significantly lower fertility than nonworkers, whereas workers for whom market work and childcare can be performed simultaneously have similar or higher fertility than nonworkers. Full-time workers have significantly lower fertility than nonworkers, but part-time workers do not. Modern sector workers have significantly lower fertility than nonworkers but traditional sector workers do not. The correlation between fertility and the proportion of married life spent working is large, negative, and significant for women working in the modern sector, but small and generally insignificant for women working in the traditional sector.

These results illustrate the obvious but often overlooked fact that work in less developed countries is not a homogeneous activity. It is rather an aggregation of many components, each with unique characteristics. Studies of the FLFP–fertility relationship in less developed countries must therefore take into account not only whether women work or not, but also the type of work they do; specifically, the degree to which work and childcare are competing uses of time.

The expansion of female employment is often suggested as a means of lowering fertility rates in less developed countries. The results of the present study suggest that such a policy may not be successful, at least in the short run. No significant negative correlation was found between fertility and FLFP in jobs that can be done while caring for children. The hypothesis that increased female employment in such jobs will have a significant negative impact on fertility must therefore be rejected. If increased female employment is primarily in jobs in which work and childcare can be performed simultaneously there is no time constraint forcing a trade-off between the two. There is consequently no reason for expecting a negative FLFP–fertility relationship. Although the long-run effects of increased FLFP on fertility may be negative regardless of the nature of the work (through changes in women's views of themselves, their relationships with their husbands, or their aspirations for their children) the short-run effects are not likely to be negative unless work and childcare are competing uses of time. Policies dealing with female employment in less developed countries must deal not only with levels of employment, but with the nature of that employment as well.

ACKNOWLEDGMENT

The author is grateful to Professor David Goldberg, Population Studies Center, University of Michigan, for the use of the data analyzed in this article; and to Professors Goldberg, Eva Mueller and Ronald Lee for helpful comments on an earlier draft.

NOTES

1. To simplify terminology, women in the labor force are referred to as "workers" whereas those not in the labor force are referred to as "nonworkers."

2. This survey was conducted under the supervision of David Goldberg, Population Studies Center, University of Michigan. Further information about the data is available upon request.

3. Ideally the division of occupations into sectors would be based directly on a time use survey. Unfortunately such data were not available in the present sample, and more informal criteria had to be used.

4. A detailed description of multiple classification analysis can be found in Andrews *et al.*, 1973.

REFERENCES

Andrews, Frank M., James N. Morgan, John A. Sonquist, and Laura Klem. 1973. *Multiple Classification Analysis.* Ann Arbor: Institute of Social Research, University of Michigan.

Ben-Porath, Yoram. 1973. Economic analysis of fertility in Israel: point and counterpoint. *Journal of Political Economy 81*, Part 2:S202–233.

Bindary, Aziz, Colin Baxter, and T. H. Hollingsworth. 1973. Urban–rural differences in the relationship between women's employment and fertility: a preliminary study. *Journal of Bio-Social Science 5:*159–166.

Davidson, Maria. 1973. A comparative study of fertility in Mexico City and Caracas. *Social Biology 20:*460–472.

DeTray, Dennis N. 1972. Child quality and the demand for children. Santa Monica: Rand Publication P4838.

Driver, Edwin D. 1963. *Differential Fertility in Central India.* Princeton: Princeton University Press.

Freedman, Ronald and Lolagene Coombs. 1966. Economic considerations in family growth decisions. *Population Studies 20:*197–222.

Freedman, Ronald, Pascal K. Whelpton, and Arthur A. Campbell. 1959. *Family Planning, Sterility and Population Growth.* New York: McGraw-Hill.

Gardner, Bruce. 1973. Economics of the size of North Carolina rural families. *Journal of Political Economy 81*, Part 2:S165–188.

Gendell, Murray, Maria Maraviglia, and Philip Kreitner. 1970. Fertility and economic activity of women in Guatemala City, 1964. *Demography 7*:273–278.

Goldstein, Sidney. 1972. The influence of labor force participation and education on fertility in Thailand. *Population Studies 26*:419–436.

Groat, H. Theodore, Randy L. Workman, and Arthur G. Neal. 1976. Labor force participation and family formation: a study of working mothers. *Demography 13*:115–125.

Hass, Paula H. 1972. Maternal role incompatibility and fertility in urban Latin America. *Journal of Social Issues 28*:111–127.

Hill, C. Russell and Frank P. Stafford. 1974. Allocation of time to preschool children and educational opportunity. *Journal of Human Resources 9*:323–341.

Jaffe, A. J. 1959. *People, Jobs and Economic Development.* Glencoe, Illinois: The Free Press.

Jaffe, A. J. and K. Azumi. 1960. The birth rate and cottage industries in underdeveloped countries. *Economic Development and Cultural Change 9*, Part I:52–63.

Kiser, Clyde V., Wilson H. Grabill, and Arthur A. Campbell. 1968. *Trends and Variations in Fertility in the United States.* Cambridge: Harvard University Press.

Kupinsky, Stanley. 1971. "Non-familial activity and socio-economic differentials in fertility." *Demography 8*:353–368.

Maurer, Kenneth, Rosalinda Ratajczak, and T. Paul Schultz. 1973. Marriage, fertility, and labor force participation of Thai women: an econometric study. Santa Monica: Rand Publication R-829-AID/RF.

McCabe, James and Mark Rosenzweig. 1976. Female employment creation and family size. *Population and Development,* Ronald Ridker (ed.). Baltimore: Johns Hopkins University Press.

Michael, Robert T. 1973. Education and the derived demand for children. *Journal of Political Economy 81*, Part 2:S128–164.

Minkler, Meredith. 1970. Fertility and female labor force participation in India: a survey of workers in Old Delhi area. *The Journal of Family Welfare 17*:31–43.

Miró, Carmen and Walter Mertens. 1968. Influences affecting fertility in urban and rural Latin America. *Milbank Memorial Fund Quarterly 46*:89–117.

Miró, Carmen and F. Rath. 1965. Preliminary findings of comparative fertility surveys in three Latin American countries. *Milbank Memorial Fund Quarterly 43*:36–62.

Mueller, Eva, Richard Cohn, and Stephany Reineck. 1971. Female labor force participation and fertility in Taiwan. Unpublished manuscript, University of Michigan.

Namboodiri, N. Krishnan. 1964. The wife's work experience and child spacing. *Milbank Memorial Fund Quarterly 42*:65–77.

Nerlove, Marc and T. Paul Schultz. 1970. A demographic–economic model of decision-making: love and life between the censuses. Rand Document No. 20187-AID.

Ridley, Jeanne C. 1959. "Number of Children Expected in Relation to Non-Familial Activities of the Wife." *Milbank Memorial Fund Quarterly 37*:277–296.

Samuel, T. J. 1965. Social factors affecting fertility in India. *Eugenics Review 57*:5–15.

Smith, Stanley K. 1976. Women's work and fertility in Mexico City. Ph.D. dissertation, University of Michigan.

Snyder, Donald. 1974. "Economic determinants of family size in West Africa." *Demography 11*:613–627.

Stycos, J. M. 1965. "Female employment and fertility in Lima, Peru." *Milbank Memorial Fund Quarterly 43*:42–54.

Stycos, J. M. and Robert Weller. 1967. Female working roles and fertility. *Demography 4*:210–217.

Tabah, Leon and Raul Samuel. 1962. Preliminary findings of a survey on fertility and attitudes toward family formation in Santiago, Chile. Clyde Kiser, (ed.), *Research in Family Planning*. Princeton: Princeton University Press.

Weller, Robert. 1968. "The Employment of Wives, Role Incompatibility and Fertility." *Milbank Memorial Fund Quarterly* 46:507–526.

Weller, Robert. 1977. Wife's employment and cumulative family size in the United States, 1970 and 1960. *Demography* 14:43–65.

Whelpton, P. K., A. A. Campbell, and J. E. Patterson. 1966. *Fertility and Family Planning in the United States*. Princeton: Princeton University Press.

Willis, Robert J. 1973. A new approach to the economic theory of fertility behavior. *Journal of Political Economy 81*, Part 2:S14–65.

Zarate, Alvan O. 1967. Differential fertility in Monterrey, Mexico: prelude to transition? *Milbank Memorial Fund Quarterly* 45:93–108.

SOME ECONOMIC EFFECTS OF RECENT MIGRATION PATTERNS ON CENTRAL CITIES

George Sternlieb and James W. Hughes

I. INTRODUCTION

The impact of selective migration from central cities in the United States has long been a topic of study. The bulk of the effort, however, has concentrated upon the sociological ramifications, initially of white flight and then of the more general shift of the middle class. In recent years, a counter element has been introduced: the potentials, both positive and negative, of gentrification—of the return of the middle class to selected areas. Somewhat slighted in these analyses have been the aggregate results of these flows of population in terms of their impact on resident incomes and purchasing power within central cities. And it is this element that provides motive power for much of the primary/secondary economic activity (and with it employment opportunities) that conventionally have been focused in urban areas.

Research in Population Economics, Volume 3, pages 189–207

Copyright © 1981 by JAI Press Inc.

All rights of reproduction in any form reserved.

ISBN: 0-89232-207-1

In this article, demographic data are analyzed in an effort to answer the questions: Has the departure of the middle-class ceased? Has the rise of the de facto central city new town, peopled by the more affluent, offset the earlier outmigration trends? Are there longer-term dynamics under way in terms of household configuration that give insight into probable futures for the urban core?

II. DEMOGRAPHIC CHANGES IN THE CENTRAL CITY

A. Population Losses

The central cities of the United States are losing population; in this retrenchment, it is the very largest of them—those central cities in metropolitan areas with a million or more population—that are the heaviest losers. As shown in Table 1, while the total population of the United States from 1970 to 1977 grew by 6.4 percent, the central cities in total lost 4.6 percent of their residents. The experience of the central cities in the largest metropolitan areas was a decline of 7.1 percent. In the central cities of smaller metropolitan areas, losses of 1.6 percent were evidenced.

B. Racial Population Shift

The overall data mask significant shifts in racial character. Central cities as a whole, in the 7-year period under consideration, lost nearly 1 in 12 of their white residents (−8.1 percent). Indeed, in the large metropolitan areas, the central city equivalent was nearly a 1 in 8 (−12.3 percent). But gains in black population only partially offset these losses, thus creating the absolute decline. For example, in central cities in metropolitan areas of one million or more, the increase in the number of black residents was only 2.3 percent. The latter resulted from the enormous level of out-migration of central city black residents to suburbia. Current census data indicate, for example, that in the last 2 years for which data is available (1976 to 1978), this amounted to a net out-migration of some 400,000 people. This process is mirrored by the fully one-third (33.9 percent) increase of black residents in suburban areas of our SMSAs.

C. Household Shifts

Yet within this pattern of population decline there is remarkably little equivalent shrinkage in the need for housing, at least as measured by total units. As shown in Table 2, the number of households has continued to grow even in the central cities most characterized by absolute population losses. It is particularly striking in this context to note the 15.2 percent increase in the number of black households within the central cities of

Table 1. Population by Type of Residence: 1970 and 1977[a]

	Total (all races)				White				Black			
			Change: 1970 to 1977				Change: 1970 to 1977				Change: 1970 to 1977	
	1970	1977	Number	Percent	1970	1977	Number	Percent	1970	1977	Number	Percent
U.S. total	199,819	212,566	12,747	6.4	175,276	184,335	9059	5.2	22,056	24,474	2418	11.0
Metropolitan areas	137,058	143,107	6,049	4.4	118,938	122,177	3239	2.7	16,342	18,048	1706	10.4
Central cities	62,876	59,993	−2,883	−4.6	48,909	44,951	−3958	−8.1	12,909	13,451	542	4.2
Suburban areas	74,182	83,144	8,932	12.0	70,029	77,226	7197	10.3	3,433	4,596	1163	33.9
Central cities in metropolitan areas of 1 million or more	34,322	31,898	−2,424	−7.1	25,007	21,939	−3068	−12.3	8,664	8,863	199	2.3
Central cities in metropolitan areas of less than 1 million	28,554	28,095	−459	−1.6	23,903	23,012	−891	−3.7	4,245	4,588	343	8.1

Source: Center for Urban Policy research analysis of data presented in U.S. Department of Commerce, Bureau of the Census, *Current Population Reports,* Special Studies P-23, No. 55, ''Social and Economic Characteristics of the Metropolitan and Nonmetropolitan Population: 1977 and 1970,'' November 1978.
[a] Numbers in thousands; 1970 metropolitan definition.

Table 2. Households by Type of Residence: 1970 and 1977[a]

	Total (all races)				White				Black			
			Change: 1970 to 1977				Change: 1970 to 1977				Change: 1970 to 1977	
	1970	*1977*	*Number*	*Percent*	*1970*	*1977*	*Number*	*Percent*	*1970*	*1977*	*Number*	*Percent*
U.S. total	63,447	74,142	10,695	16.9	56,609	65,353	8744	15.4	6178	7776	1598	25.9
Metropolitan areas	43,851	50,414	6,563	15.0	38,622	43,649	5027	13.0	4733	5981	1248	26.4
Central cities	21,401	22,741	1,340	6.3	17,254	17,712	458	2.7	3833	4566	733	19.1
Suburban areas	22,450	27,672	5,222	23.3	21,368	25,937	4569	21.4	900	1415	515	57.2
Central cities in metropolitan areas of 1 million or more	12,056	12,246	190	1.6	9,230	8,914	−316	−3.4	2625	3025	400	15.2
Central cities in metropolitan areas of less than 1 million	9,344	10,494	1,150	12.3	8,024	8,798	774	9.6	1207	1541	334	27.7

Source: Center for Urban Policy research analysis of data presented in U.S. Department of Commerce, Bureau of the Census, *Current Population Reports,* Special Studies P-23, No. 55, "Social and Economic Characteristics of the Metropolitan and Nonmetropolitan Population: 1977 and 1970," November 1978.

[a] Numbers in thousands; 1970 metropolitan definition.

larger metropolitan areas. This is seven times the increase (2.3 percent) in absolute population growth of this group. As we will note, this represents both a very positive tribute to upgrading in housing—but also a far-less salubrious fragmentation of households.

Part of the process of household growth in the context of population stability and decline is the actual shrinking size of families, as shown in Table 3. Much of the housing trauma of the post-World War II era involved the difficulties of housing large families and it is now particularly heartening to see the diminishing need for large facilities, as shown in Table 3 by the average size of families and most significantly, by the number of families in central cities with 5 persons or more.

But this is not merely a consequence of a declining birth rate, it is also due to the drastic change in the configuration of households—most importantly, to that of the single parent family.[1] In Table 4 are shown data on this point for the nation as a whole, for all central cities, and for central cities in metropolitan areas of one million or more people. Primary families as a group in central cities are shrinking both relatively and in absolute numbers. The case is most strikingly evident in terms of the decline (− 965,000 or − 7.6 percent) of husband–wife families for all central cities over the 1970 to 1977 period. For central cities in the larger metropolitan areas, a decline of 12.0 percent (813,000 families) was experienced. In the latter case, husband–wife families achieved minority status by 1977, with only 48.8 percent of households in this configuration.

Fully one out of seven (14.8 percent) of all households in the central cities in major metropolitan areas are female-headed (no husband present); moreover, the configuration is a dynamic growth element, with an increase of 22.9 percent in such incidence from 1970 to 1977. Indeed, if we were to sum primary individual households headed by females with families headed by females, they would represent virtually one in three of all central city households.

Central city populations, then, are increasingly dominated by household types that, as will be shown subsequently, are characterized by relatively low incomes—a major problem that cuts across racial partitions.

III. ECONOMIC EFFECTS OF DEMOGRAPHIC CHANGES IN THE CENTRAL CITY

A. Race and Household Configuration
The decline in primary families is largely a white phenomenon, undoubtedly in part as a function of select migration. The white resident who are increasing in number and proportion in the central city are largely in primary individual households. Indeed, husband–wife families de-

Table 3. Families by Size and Type of Residence: 1970 and 1977

	U.S. total				All central cities				Central cities in metropolitan areas of 1,000,000 or more people			
			Change: 1970–1977				Change: 1970–1977				Change: 1970–1977	
	1970	1977[b]	Number	Percent	1970	1977[b]	Number	Percent	1970	1977[b]	Number	Percent
Total families	50,967	56,710	5,743	11.3	15,816	15,529	−287	−1.8	8621	8144	−477	−5.5
Two persons	18,139	21,530	3391	18.7	6,033	6,334	301	5.0	3362	3336	−26	−0.7
Three persons	10,618	12,472	1854	17.5	3,407	3,497	90	2.6	1866	1837	−29	−1.6
Four persons	9,649	11,483	1834	19.0	2,798	2,888	90	3.2	1498	1468	−30	−2.0
Five persons	6,107	6,209	102	1.7	1,700	1,471	−229	−13.5	897	762	−135	−15.1
Six persons	3,328	2,800	−528	−15.9	936	720	−216	−23.1	497	387	−110	−22.1
Seven persons or more	3,126	2,216	−910	−29.1	943	619	−324	−34.4	502	353	−149	−29.7
Average size of family	3.57	3.38			3.47	3.30			3.44	3.31		

Source: Center for Urban Policy research analysis of data presented in U.S. Department of Commerce, Bureau of the Census, *Current Population Reports,* Special Studies P-23, No. 55, "Social and Economic Characteristics of the Metropolitan and Nonmetropolitan Population: 1977 and 1970," November 1978.

[a] Numbers in thousands; 1970 metropolitan definition.

[b] 1977 Family data include a relatively small number of secondary family heads who are not household heads.

[c] Numbers may not add due to rounding.

Table 4. Households by Type and Residence: 1970 and 1977

	U.S. total		Change: 1970 to 1977		All central cities		Change: 1970 to 1977		Central cities in metropolitan areas of 1,000,000 or more people		Change: 1970 to 1977	
	1970	1977	Number	Percent	1970	1977	Number	Percent	1970	1977	Number	Percent
Total	63,447	74,142	10,695	16.9	21,401	22,741	1,340	6.3	12,056	12,246	190	1.6
Primary families	50,967	56,472	5,505	10.8	15,816	15,444	−372	−2.4	8,621	8,092	−529	−6.1
Husband–Wife family	43,717	57,471	3,754	8.6	12,748	11,783	−965	−7.6	6,783	5,970	−813	−12.0
Male head (no wife present)	1,621	1,461	−160	−9.9	587	499	−88	−15.0	360	304	−56	−15.6
Female head (no husband present)	5,629	7,540	1,911	33.9	2,480	3,161	681	27.5	1,478	1,817	339	22.9
Primary individuals	12,480	17,669	5,189	41.6	5,584	7,298	1,714	30.7	3,435	4,155	720	21.0
Male	4,597	6,971	2,374	51.6	2,139	2,971	832	38.9	1,376	1,747	371	27.0
Female	7,883	10,698	2,815	35.7	3,445	4,327	882	25.6	2,059	2,408	349	16.9
Total	100.0	100.0			100.0	100.0			100.0	100.0		
Primary families	80.3	76.2			73.9	67.9			71.5	66.1		
Husband–wife family	68.9	64.2			59.6	51.8			56.3	48.8		
Male head (no wife present)	2.6	2.0			2.7	2.2			3.0	2.5		
Female head (no husband present)	8.9	10.2			11.6	13.9			12.3	14.8		
Primary individuals	19.7	23.8			26.1	32.1			28.5	33.9		
Male	7.2	9.4			10.0	31.1			11.4	14.3		
Female	12.4	14.4			16.1	19.0			17.1	19.7		

Source: Center for Urban Policy research analysis of data presented in U.S. Department of Commerce, Bureau of the Census, *Current Population Reports,* Special Studies P-23, No. 55, "Social and Economic Characteristics of the Metropolitan and Nonmetropolitan Population: 1977 and 1970," November 1978.

[a] Numbers in thousands; 1970 metropolitan definition.

clined both among white and black residents in central cities with the former showing a loss of nearly a million, the latter approximately 150,000 (Table 5). The only family type expanding in number within central cities among white residents was female-headed (no husband present), with an increase slightly under 250,000. The faster growing incidence of this phenomenon among black residents, however, is indicated by the 432,000 increase in black female-headed (no husband present) families. Nearly 60 percent of the total growth of black households over the 1970 to 1977 period was in this format.

Thus, the white population of central cities is decreasingly that of primary families and increasingly that of single individuals. The sum of these produce a relatively minor increase in total household numbers. Among black residents, there is an equivalent decline of husband–wife families to a level where they represent only 38.2 percent of total households; this figure is nearly matched by an incidence of 29 percent of female-headed (no husband present) households—nearly triple that of white central city households. One out of three (33.0 percent) white households now is in the primary individual group. The incidence among blacks is nearly as high: at the three in ten level (29.7 percent).

The vigor of the shift in household formation in terms of the percentage of primary families headed by females is emphasized by Table 6, which shows the ratios of such households in 1977 versus 1970. There is significant growth both for white and for black households; the level of absolute gain, however, in the latter group is nearly double that of the former. Indeed, in all central cities, the growth ratio for the 7 years under consideration among black residents is at the 1.34–1.35 level.

By 1977, more than four in ten of all black primary families in central cities were headed by a female.

B. Income and Family Configuration

There appears to be a significant relationship between low incomes and female-headed households. This holds true both for white as well as black households, but is much more compelling for the latter group. As shown in Table 7, for example, all families in central cities in 1977 had money incomes of slightly under $14,000. Families with female heads, however, had incomes of less than half that ($6,658). For white families with female heads, total money income was $7,914. For black families, it was an abysmally low $5,125. And these ratios are degenerating over time, when contrasted with equivalent data for suburban areas.

For every category shown, the ratio between central city and suburban incomes from 1970 to 1977 has declined sharply. All central city families, regardless of their configuration, have incomes that are not keeping pace with equivalent configurations in suburbia, as well as declining in absolute dollars over time.

Table 5. Central City Household Type by Race: 1970 and 1977

	White				Black			
			Change: 1970 to 1977				Change: 1970 to 1977	
	1970	1977	Number	Percent	1970	1977	Number	Percent
Total	17,254	17,712	458	2.7	3833	4566	733	19.1
Primary families	12,665	11,870	−795	−6.3	2917	3212	295	10.1
Husband–Wife family	10,667	9,730	−937	−8.8	1891	1744	−147	−7.8
Male head (no wife present)	439	340	−99	−22.6	136	146	10	7.4
Female head (no husband present)	1,559	1,800	241	15.5	890	1322	432	48.5
Primary individuals	4,589	5,842	1,253	27.3	916	1354	438	47.8
Male	1,688	2,289	601	35.6	409	631	222	54.3
Female	2,901	3,553	652	22.5	507	723	216	42.6
Total	100.0	100.0			100.0	100.0		
Primary families	73.4	67.0			76.1	70.3		
Husband–wife family	61.8	54.9			49.3	38.2		
Male head (no wife present)	2.5	1.9			3.5	3.2		
Female head (no husband present)	9.0	10.2			23.2	29.0		
Primary individuals	26.6	33.0			23.9	29.7		
Male	9.8	12.9			10.7	13.8		
Female	16.8	20.1			13.2	15.8		

Source: Center for Urban Policy research analysis of data presented in U.S. Department of Commerce, Bureau of the Census, *Current Population Reports,* Special Studies P-23, No. 55, "Social and Economic Characteristics of the Metropolitan and Nonmetropolitan Population: 1977 and 1978," November 1978.
[a] Numbers in thousands; 1970 metropolitan definition.

Table 6. Percentage of Primary Families Headed by Females, by Race and Type of Residence: 1970 and 1977

Type of residence	Total (all races)			White			Black		
	1970	1977	Ratio[b] 1970–1977	1970	1977	Ratio[b] 1970–1977	1970	1977	Ratio[b] 1970–1977
U.S. total	11.0	13.4	1.22	9.2	10.7	1.16	28.0	36.8	1.31
Metropolitan areas	11.7	14.6	1.26	9.7	11.6	1.21	28.9	37.7	1.30
Central cities	15.7	20.5	1.31	12.3	15.2	1.24	30.5	41.2	1.35
Suburban areas	8.4	10.6	1.26	7.9	9.6	1.21	22.2	27.9	1.26
Central cities in Metropolitian areas of 1 million or more	17.1	22.5	1.32	13.1	16.0	1.22	30.8	41.7	1.35
Central cities in metropolitan areas of less tahn 1 million	13.9	18.3	1.32	11.5	14.4	1.25	30.0	40.1	1.34

Source: Center for Urban Policy research analysis of data presented in U.S. Department of Commerce, Bureau of the Census, *Current Population Reports,* Special Studies P-23, No. 55, ''Social and Economic Characteristics of the Metropolitan and Nonmetropolitan Population: 1977 and 1970,'' November 1978.

[a] 1970 Metropolitan area definition.

[b] Ratios computed from unrounded percentages.

Table 7. Total Money Income in 1969 and 1976: Families by Sex,
Race, and Type of Residence[a]

	Central cities (dollars)	Suburban areas (dollars)	Ratio of central city to suburban
Total all races			
All families			
1970	14,566	17,160	.85
1977	13,952	17,101	.82
Families with female head			
1970	7,586	9,351	.81
1977	6,658	8,539	.78
White			
All families			
1970	15,601	17,413	.90
1977	15,069	17,371	.87
Families with female head			
1970	9,014	9,842	.92
1977	7,914	8,985	.88
Black			
All families			
1970	10,188	10,745	.95
1977	9,361	12,037	.78
Families with female head			
1970	5,494	5,425	1.01
1977	5,125	5,789	.89

Source: Center for Urban Policy research analysis of data presented in U.S. Department of Commerce,
Bureau of the Census, *Current Population Report,* Special Studies P-23, No. 55, "Social and
Economic Characteristics of the Metropolitan and Nonmetropolitan Population: 1977 and 1970."
November 1978.

[a] Total money income in constant 1976 dollars. Families as of March 1977 and April 1970. 1970
metropolitan definition.

Female-headed households in central cities have shown the most
marked decline in real incomes over time. The selective migration of
black residents to suburbia undoubtedly underlies, at least in part, the one
substantial increment (and again these are data in constant dollars) of income accruing to families from 1970 to 1977: total black families in suburbia experienced an income gain of almost $1,300 from $10,745 in 1970
to $12,037 in 1977. The black income decline in the central city is clearly
linked with the selective migration of husband–wife families and the
residual dominance of female-headed households.

C. The Increasing Trauma of Rental Housing

In another context, reference has been made to the increasing problem
of rental housing in central cities—the issues of delinquency and foreclo-

sure, particularly in HUD-held guaranteed mortgages.[2] Within this context, it is important to focus on the data shown in Table 8, which shows median incomes of household types in central cities by race and tenure for 1973 and 1976. (These are not constant dollars).

Certainly there has been much more vigor of income growth among owners than holds true of renters, with the level of growth in the former triple that of the latter. And this holds true for blacks as well, but is much more extreme. Among the two-or-more-person black households who are owners, incomes increased 21.2 percent. Despite the declining value of the dollar over time, black renters experienced only a 1.5 percent income increase.

The latter ratio was very largely the result of a declining real income among renter families headed by females. For this category, there was an absolute decline of 11.3 percent in incomes. And this obviously would be even more accentuated if it were in constant dollars.

Increasingly, the central city is the focal point of the poor. Selective migration, and limited economic opportunities for advancement have produced this result.[3] It is mirrored in the next set of data to be presented here—that on poverty status.

D. Poverty Status

Nationally, poverty is declining in incidence. In the 1970 to 1977 period under consideration, there was a decline of 2.2 million persons who met the poverty criteria. Table 9 presents the data on individuals by family status who fell below the poverty level.

Every category was reduced except for females who were heads of families; in this group, there was an absolute increase of 710,000 individuals, nearly 40 percent. Indeed, almost a third of all females who head families fall into the poverty category.

The basic problem is much more clearly focused when the analysis is limited to central cities as shown in Table 10. Unlike the national pattern, there is an *absolute* increase in the number of persons in central cities who fall below the poverty line. While the total central city population declined by 4.6 percent, those in poverty status increased by 2.5 percent. This occurred despite a decline in poverty status among males who headed families and their wives. This gain was completely obliterated—and practically all of the total loss accounted for—by the increase in females who headed families, and by their children as well. In central cities, female family heads who were under the poverty line increased by 44.7 percent over the 7-year period. By 1977, 37.1 percent of such individuals were below the poverty line.

Male headed families and wives are climbing out of poverty. Female-headed families increasingly are subjected to all of its limitation and strictures.

Table 8. Median Income of Household Types in Central Cities by Race: 1973 and 1976[a]

	Total (all races)				Black			
			Change: 1973–1976				Change: 1973–1976	
	1973 (dollars)	1976 (dollars)	Number (dollars)	Percent	1973 (dollars)	1976 (dollars)	Number (dollars)	Percent
Owner occupied								
Two-or-more-person households	12,900	15,800	2900	22.5	10,400	12,600	2200	21.2
Male head, wife present	13,600	17.000	3400	25.6	11,700	14,700	3000	25.6
Other male head	12,800	14,000	1200	9.4	11,300	11,000	−300	−2.7
Female head	8,000	9,200	1200	15.0	7,000	7,200	200	2.9
One-person households	4,400	5,900	1500	34.1	3,900	4,100	200	5.1
Renter occupied								
Two-or-more-person households	8,300	8,800	500	6.0	6,500	6,600	100	1.5
Male head, wife present	9,600	11,500	1900	19.8	8,400	10,400	2000	23.8
Other male head	8,300	8,200	−100	−1.2	5,900	7,900	2000	33.9
Female head	5,800	5,300	−500	−8.6	5,300	4,700	−600	−11.3
One-person households	4,600	5,500	900	19.6	3,500	4,400	900	25.7

Source: U.S. Department of Commerce, Bureau of the Census, *Annual Housing Survey,* 1973, 1976.
[a] 1970 metropolitan definition.   1976 income is that received in 1975.   1973 income is that received in 1972.

Table 9.   Poverty Status in 1976 and 1969, Persons by Family Status,
U.S. Total All Races[a]

Family status	1970	1977	Change: 1970 to 1977		Percent below poverty levels	
			Number	Percent	1970	1977
All persons	27,204	24,975	−2229	−8.2	13.8	11.8
In families	21,250	19,632	−1618	−7.6	11.7	10.3
Head	5,500	5,311	−189	−3.4	10.8	9.4
Male	3,667	2,768	−899	−24.9	8.1	5.6
Female	1,833	2,543	710			
Wives	3,438	2,606	−832	−24.2	7.9	5.5
Related children under 18 years	10,560	10,081	−479	−4.5	15.3	15.8
Other family members	1,752	1,634	−118	−6.7	9.8	7.1
Unrelated individuals	5,954	5,344	−610	−10.2	37.1	24.9
Male	1,913	1.787	−126	−6.6	29.9	19.7
Female	4,041	3,557	−484	−12.0	41.9	28.7

Source: Center for Urban Policy research analysis of data presented in U.S. Department of Commerce, Bureau of the Census, *Current Population Reports* Special Studies, P-23, No. 55, "Social and Economic Characteristics of the Metropolitan and Nonmetropolitan Population: 1977 and 1970," November 1978.

[a] Families and unrelated individuals as of March 1977 and April 1970. Excludes unrelated individuals under 14 years old, members of the Armed Forces living in barracks, and college students in dormitories. Numbers in thousands.

The incidence of such groups, in turn, has strikingly impacted the fiscal vigor of central cities while increasing the stress on the social services provided to them. And, this is increasingly a problem that is falling on the black citizens of central cities. As shown in Table 11, the number of black persons in families in poverty status in central cities grew by more than one in nine (10.9 percent) from 1970 to 1977. Among unrelated individuals, there was an increase of one in six (17.7 percent). While there was a significant reduction of male heads and wives in poverty, it was more than overcome by the single largest poverty status growth group—that of female heads of families, which increased by nearly a quarter of a million (57.1 percent).

By 1977, more than half (51.1 percent) of the black females who headed households were below the poverty line. In turn, they substantially accounted for the 42.1 percent of all black-related children under 18 years within families who also met the poverty designation.

The urban crisis is not over—rather, it is entering on its most fearsome challenge. The demographic shifts within our society have left major urban areas increasingly as the focal point for the distressed—not merely the impoverished, but the increasingly impoverished. A thin facade of office structures and of new swinging groups distracts the eye from the functional reality.

Table 10. Poverty Status in 1976 and 1969, Persons by Family Status, Central Cities, All Races[a]

Family status	1970	1977	Change: 1970 to 1977		Percent below poverty level	
			Number	Percent	1970	1977
All persons	9247	9482	235	2.5	14.9	15.8
In families	6852	7302	.450	6.6	12.5	14.3
Head	1755	1961	206	11.7	11.1	12.6
Male	928	764	−164	−17.6	7.0	6.2
Female	827	1197	370	44.7	33.5	37.1
Wives	861	718	−143	−16.6	6.7	6.1
Related children under 18 years	3692	4017	325	8.8	18.4	23.9
Other family members	544	606	62	11.4	8.7	8.8
Unrelated individuals	2396	2180	−216	−9.0	33.1	24.6
Male	801	796	−5	−0.6	27.1	20.6
Female	1594	1384	−210	−13.2	37.3	27.7

Source: Center for Urban Policy Research analysis of data presented in U.S. Department of Commerce, Bureau of the Census, *Current Population Reports,* Special Studies, P-23, No. 55, "Social and Economic Characteristics of the Metropolitan and Nonmetropolitan Population: 1977 and 1970," November 1978.

[a] Families and unrelated individuals as of March 1977 and April 1970. Excludes unrelated individuals under 14 years old, members of the Armed Forces living in barracks, and college students in dormitories. Numbers in thousands.

Table 11. Poverty Status in 1976 and 1969, Persons by Family Status, Central Cities, Blacks[a]

Family status	1970	1977	Change: 1970 to 1977		Percent below poverty level	
			Number	Percent	1970	1977
All persons	3726	4167	441	11.8	29.1	31.0
In families	3196	3543	347	10.9	27.7	30.2
Head	725	908	183	25.2	24.9	28.0
Male	290	223	−67	−23.1	14.3	11.7
Female	436	685	249	57.1	49.1	51.1
Wives	260	194	−66	−25.3	13.9	11.3
Related children under 18 years	1940	2081	141	7.3	36.5	42.1
Other family members	271	360	89	32.8	18.9	19.8
Unrelated individuals	530	624	94	17.7	41.7	36.4
Male	197	274	77	39.1	32.6	31.6
Female	333	350	17	5.1	50.0	41.4

Source: Center for Urban Policy Research analysis of data presented in U.S. Department of Commerce, Bureau of the Census, *Current Population Reports,* Special Studies, P-23, No. 55, "Social and Economic Characteristics of the Metropolitan and Nonmetropolitan Population: 1977 and 1970," November 1978.

[a] Families and unrelated individuals as of March 1977 and April 1970. Excludes unrelated individuals under 14 yeras old, members of the Armed Forces living in barracks, and college students in dormitories. Numbers in thousands.

Table 12.   Income Losses in Central Cities due to Net Migration:
1970 to 1971 and 1975 to 1977, (1970 Metropolitan Definition)

A. Income in 1973 of Families and Unrelated Individuals 14 Years Old and Over Who
Migrated to and From Central Cities Between 1970 and 1974

Subject	Living in cities in 1970	Moved out of cities between 1970 and 1974	Moved to cities between 1970 and 1974	Net change between 1970 and 1974
Families (thousands)	16,823	3,363	1,563	−1800[a]
Mean income (dollars)	13,349	14,169	12,864	−1305[a]
Aggregate income (billions of dollars)	224.6	47.7	20.1	−27.6
Unrelated individuals (thousands)	6,975	1,066	926	−140
Mean income (dollars)	6,143	7,099	6,092	−1,007[a]
Aggregate income (billions of dollars)	42.8	7.6	5.6	−2.0

B. Income in 1976 of Families and Unrelated Individuals 14 Years Old and Over Who
Migrated to and From Central Cities Between 1975 and 1977

Subject	Living in cities in 1975	Moved out of cities between 1975 and 1977	Moved to cities between 1975 and 1977	Net change between 1975 and 1977
Families (thousands)	16,359	2,003	985	−1018
Mean income (dollars)	16,120	15,986	14,992	−994[a]
Aggregate income (billions of dollars)	263.7	32.0	14.8	−17.2
Unrelated individuals (thousands)	8,812	994	940	−54
Mean income (dollars)	7,388	8,055	7,612	−443[a]
Aggregate income (billions of dollars)	65.1	8.0	7.2	−0.8

Source: U.S. Department of Commerce, Bureau of the Census, *Current Population Reports*, Special
Studies P-23, No. 55, "Social and Economic Characteristics of the Metropolitan and Non-
metropolitan Population: 1974 and 1970," September 1975. U.S. Department of Commerce,
Bureau of the Census, *Current Population Reports*, Special Studies, P-23, No. 75 "Social and
Economic Characteristics of the Metropolitan and Nonmetropolitan Population: 1977 and
1970," November, 1978.

[a] Simple unweighted difference.

E. *The Aggregate Impact*

In Table 12, data are shown indicating the personal income loss in central cities due to net migration from 1970 to 1974 and 1975 to 1977.
Whether it is families or unrelated individuals, the pattern is similar. The
more affluent are leaving; the newcomers are less well endowed fiscally.
From 1970 to 1974, there was a reduction in aggregate resident income
within central cities of $29.6 billion due to migration. In the 2 years from
1975 to 1977, the equivalent figure was a loss of $18 billion.

In Table 13, these data have been converted into constant dollars (interpolating for 1974 to 1975, for which data are not available). This indicates an average annual net change (between 1970 and 1977) in 1976 dollars of $9.3 billion. Since these data are cumulative, by 1977 there has been a loss, in 1976 dollars, of $64.8 billion. So in the latter year, if no migration had occurred, $64.8 billion more in annual incomes would have accrued to central city households than was actually received.

The ramifications of these losses are of very significant magnitude. If we were to use the conventional rule-of-thumb of 25 percent of income allotted to rent, this represents a departure in excess of $16 billion. If we were to further view this decline in rent-paying capacity in terms of its impact on housing values, the results are evident. Assume that an efficient, well-managed apartment house sells for fives times its gross rent roll; the loss of $16 billion in rent-paying capacity translates into a $80 billion reduction in residential real estate values—and with it a proportionate decline in municipal income derived from real property taxation. There are equivalent implications, on basic retailing and service industries as well. The pattern of empty stores, of old fading central business districts, and of vacated downtown department stores is a reflection of this declining residential income base.

As best as we can analyze the data, this has been a sustained process with little sign of abatement. While much has been made of the relatively few cases of middle-class stabilization and/or return to the city (i.e., the "Capital Hill" phenomena and the like), as yet these are relatively trivial. A witness to the phenomenon is the accompanying data in Table 14 on the

Table 13. Derivation of Income Losses (1976 Dollars) in Central Cities Due to Migration: 1970 to 1977 (1970 Metropolitan definition)

Average annual net change, 1970 to 1974	−$7.4 billion (1973 dollars)[a]
Ratio of 1976 to 1973 consumer price index	$\dfrac{170.5}{133.1} = 1.28$[b]
Average annual net change, 1970 to 1974	−$9.4 billion (1976 dollars)[c]
Average annual net change, 1975 to 1977	−$9.0 billion (1976 dollars)[d]
Net change, 1974 to 1975	−$9.2 billion (1976 dollars)[e]
Total change: 1970 to 1977	−$64.8 billion (1976 dollars)[f]
Average annual net change: 1970 to 1977	−$9.3 billion (1976 dollars)[g]

Source: CUPR Analysis.
[a] Derived from Table 12.
[b] U.S. Bureau of Labor Statistics, *Monthly Labor Review*.
[c] 1.28 × $7.4 billion = $9.4 billion.
[d] Derived from Table 12.
[e] Mean of annual averages of two periods.
[f] Sum of annual averages of all periods.
[g] −$64.8 billion ÷ 7 years = −$9.3 billion.

Table 14.   Median Annual Income of Families and Individuals, by
Borough, in Constant (1967) Dollars, for Renter Households,
New York City, 1964, 1967, 1969, 1974, and 1977

Characteristics	*1964 (dollars)*	*1967 (dollars)*	*1969 (dollars)*	*1974 (dollars)*	*1977 (dollars)*	*Percent change 1974 to 1977*
Total: New York City	5900	6000	6500	5400	4800	−11.1
Borough						
Bronx	5600	5700	6000	4700	4000	−14.9
Brooklyn	5800	5800	6000	4900	4200	−14.3
Manhattan	5500	5600	6100	5400	5500	+1.9
Queens	7100	7500	8100	7000	5800	−17.1
Richmond	7100	6800	7700	7100	6100	−14.1

Source: Peter Marcuse.   1979 *Rental Housing in the City of New York.*   New York: Housing and Development Administration.

median annual income of families and individuals (in constant dollars) for
renter households in the boroughs of New York City.   The decline since
1969 in all cases has been most substantial, with the overall city median
declining from $6,500 to $4,800 over the 1969 to 1977 period.   This pattern
was largely paralleled from 1974 to 1977, with losses of one-seventh of
total income in the brief 3-year period.   The only exception is a relatively
minor 1.9 percent increase (again in constant dollars) in Manhattan.   A
new town may be evolving intown—the gentrified neighborhood—but it
is a relatively slender ray of light and is much too limited to support and
bring back with it the aging entities that we call central cities.

IV. CONCLUSION

The future implications of the poverty concentrations mirrored in the data
presented earlier are far from precisely definable at this writing.   Clearly,
in the past, we have had a demographic equivalent of Gresham's Law: the
presence of the poor tends to oust the more fortunate in our society.   The
decline in housing buying power of middle America that is clearly occurring may well cause the aborting of this phenomenon in the future.   The
decade of the 1970s however, has given little promise of mass revival in
the major central cities.

NOTES

1. Households are generally of two types: primary families and primary individuals.   Primary families comprise two or more related individuals and are usually subdivided into three

types: husband–wife families, male head (no wife present), and female head (no wife present). Primary individual households comprise either a single person living alone or two or more unrelated individuals. They are usually subdivided into male- and female-headed sectors. The Census Bureau, however, plans to replace the term "head" with "householder."

2. See George Sternlieb and Robert W. Burchell, "Multifamily Housing Demand: 1975–2000." A Study prepared for the use of the Subcommittee on Priorities and Economy in Government of the Joint Economic Committee, Congress of the United States. (U.S. Government Printing Office, Washington, D.C., 1978.)

3. See analysis in: George Sternlieb and James W. Hughes, "The Wilting of the Metropolis," Hearings before the Committee on Banking, Currency, and Housing, U.S. House of Representatives, *Toward a National Urban Policy* (U.S. Government Printing Office, Washington, D.C., 1977).

ALTERNATIVE DEMOGRAPHIC FUTURES AND THE COMPOSITION OF THE DEMAND FOR LABOR, BY INDUSTRY AND BY OCCUPATION

William J. Serow

ABSTRACT

This paper is an initial effort to demonstrate the effects of varying rates of population growth upon the industrial and occupational compositions of demand for labor. As such, the paper extends previous research activity that has demonstrated that changes in the composition of consumer demand are not sensitive to alternative rates of population growth. This paper begins with a replication of projections of consumer demand patterns under three alternative population projections and then transforms these results into projections of final demand by industrial sector, demand for labor by industrial sector, and demand for labor by occupational group. The results show that both labor force compositions are

Research in Population Economics, Volume 3, pages 209–223

ISBN: 0-89232-207-1

relatively insensitive to varying demographic patterns. However, while the industrial composition reflects a continuation of already existing trends, the occupational composition shows some tendency to move away from professional and highly skilled blue collar occupations, and towards service and clerical occupations. The final section of the paper reflects upon the implications of the results for higher education and labor force policy.

INTRODUCTION

The recent upsurge of interest in the macroeconomic consequences of declining population growth in industrialized nations has demonstrated that, contrary to the hypotheses advanced by various writers, (Robbins, 1929; Wander, 1978) there is not a great deal of difference in the distribution of household consumption expenditures between a relatively slowly and a quickly growing population. This conclusion seems to result from income effects (declining population growth yields a high worker-nonworker ratio and thus increases per capita income, *ceteris paribus*) counteracting the age distributional effects, which result from differing age-specific propensities to consume various bundles of goods and services. Overall, recent studies (Eilenstine and Cunningham, 1972; Resek and Siegel, 1974; Espenshade, 1978) show that, within reasonable bounds of future population growth, the pattern of consumer demand will vary but little, although that pattern will increasingly diverge from that of the present. For example, Espenshade finds that for two quite different population projections of the United States—specifically one with a three-child family (Series B) and one with a two-child family (Series E)—the share of total consumption expended on durable goods increases from 12–13 percent to 15 percent, the share expended on non-durable goods declines from 41–42 to 33–34 percent, and the share for service rises from 45–46 to 51–52 percent.

While these results are of extreme importance in their own right, they do lead directly to additional questions that have not yet been answered in the literature: given this pattern of change in the household sector, what are the corresponding patterns of change in total demand and, given the latter, what are the implications for the industrial and occupational composition of the demand for labor. The purpose of this paper is to provide some initial answers to these questions.

II COMPOSITION OF TOTAL DEMAND

While the household sector may provide the most visible portion of aggregate demand, it is by no means the only component. A great deal of industrial output is not directly consumed by households, but rather represents capital goods that are used by industry to produce other goods for final demand. Still other portions of industrial output are sold to the government (aircraft, for example). In 1975, gross national product (GNP) in the United States came to $1.5 trillion; of this, about two-thirds ($973 billion) was personal consumption, about one-eighth ($184 billion) was gross private investment (capital formation), and about one-fifth ($339 billion) represented government purchases of goods and services.

The approach taken here assumes that the household sector ultimately drives the entire economy—changes in the pattern of business and government spending are ultimately the consequences of changes in the level of consumer income and patterns of demand. The specific procedures taken are as follows.

Using techniques employed previously (Serow, 1972), projections of household consumption patterns are made for the United States for the period 1980–2020. The size and composition of the population and households are derived from U.S. Bureau of the Census Series I, II, and III projections [1975a,b];[1] from these, projections of size and composition of the labor force are derived utilizing Bureau of Labor Statistics' (Fullerton and Flaim, 1976) assumptions about labor force participation rates to 1990. Projections of average earnings per worker, in the aggregate, are taken from Bureau of Economic Analysis projections (U.S. Bureau of Economic Analysis 1972); these were disaggregated to allow for age–sex differentials using Denison's [1974] indices of earnings by age and sex. Thus, per worker earnings at any point in time are a function not only of time, but also of the age–sex composition of the work force. The level of earnings were translated into personal income by assuming constancy in 1969 ratios of earnings to total household income, by age of head of household (U.S. Bureau of the Census, 1973). After allowing for tax payments, the end result of these procedures are the projections of total and per household disposable income, in constant (1958) dollars, shown in Table 1.

Changes in the distribution of household expenditures over time are taken to be dependent upon the age composition of household heads and age-specific income elasticities of demand for various consumption categories. The 1972–73 Consumer Expenditure Survey (U.S. Bureau of Labor Statistics, 1976) provides age-specific *average* propensities to consume. More difficult to derive are *marginal* propensities to consume; that is, the pattern of distribution of expenditures for additional units of real income, holding all prices constant. In the absence of longitudinal data, the cross-sectional data from the 1960–61 Consumer Expenditure Survey were used along with the 1972–1973 data in an attempt to capture some temporal effects. It is assumed that the average increase in consumption for any good or service, across all income groups, for each age

Table 1.   Disposable Personal Income, Total and per Household
(1958 dollars)

Year and Series	Total (billions)	Per Household
1975	$ 581.4	$ 7,979
2000-I	1,443.1	14,011
2000-II	1,436.2	14,068
2000-III	1,431.2	14,109
2020-I	2,602.4	19,774
2020-II	2,364.5	19,716
2020-III	2,210.1	19,666

Source of basic data: Survey of Current Business, July 1976 U.S. Bureau of the Census (1977) *Current Population Reports.* Series P-60, no. 104 "Household Money Income in 1975 and Selected Social and Economic Characteristics of Households." Washington, Government Printing Office.

group, adequately represented the marginal propensity to consume that good or service for the age group. Unfortunately, there seems to be no clear-cut method of testing the validity of this assumption, although the results (Table 2) do not seem unreasonable, *a priori.*

The effects of changing income and age composition yield the changes in the distribution of household consumption summarized in Table 3. Generally, the results are quite consistent with the findings reported by previous investigators in that little difference is evident among the alternative projections. This is particularly true up to 2000, when demographic change has just begun to influence the number and age composition of households.

Table 2.   Estimated Income Elasticities, by Age of Household Head[a]

	<25	25–34	35–44	45–64	65+
Food	5.1	5.6	6.1	7.2	6.1
Fuels	7.7	8.0	7.3	6.1	6.5
Housing	17.7	18.4	16.9	14.1	15.0
Furnishings	19.5	20.3	18.6	15.5	16.6
Clothing	4.4	6.3	7.8	7.8	6.5
Personal care	1.1	1.3	1.6	2.0	1.9
Medical care	9.3	9.6	8.5	9.7	14.7
Vehicle purchase	16.3	10.9	12.0	14.9	13.4
Vehicle operations	7.8	5.2	5.8	7.1	6.4
Reading	1.1	1.5	1.4	1.3	1.0
Education	0.1	0.4	1.0	1.3	0.8
Gifts	3.4	3.8	4.4	5.1	5.1
Recreation	6.3	8.5	8.2	8.0	5.8

[a] Income elasticities are expressed in percent.

Table 3. Projected Distribution of Household Consumption, 2000 and 2020 (in percent, except for total)

	1975	2000-I	2000-II	2000-III	2020-I	2020-II	2020-III
Total (billions of 1958 dollars)	536.6	1303.0	1296.8	1292.3	2336.8	2123.2	1984.6
Food	20.4%	14.7%	14.6%	14.7%	11.5%	12.0%	12.5%
Fuel and utilities	4.6	5.6	5.7	5.9	6.4	6.2	5.9
Housing	24.6	20.7	20.8	21.0	17.7	20.1	22.4
Furnishings	5.2	10.7	10.6	10.5	13.5	12.9	12.2
Clothing	7.6	7.7	7.4	7.4	7.9	7.3	6.8
Personal Care	2.0	1.8	1.9	2.0	2.2	1.9	1.8
Medical Care	6.4	7.5	7.7	7.8	7.1	8.5	9.7
Vehicle Purchase	8.5	10.9	10.4	10.0	13.1	11.4	9.9
Vehicle Operations	8.8	8.0	7.7	7.3	7.7	6.7	5.8
Reading & Recreation	4.0	6.3	6.3	6.2	8.0	7.3	6.9
Education (private)	1.0	1.0	1.0	1.0	1.1	1.0	1.0
Gifts	4.4	5.1	5.9	6.2	3.9	4.6	5.0

Source of basic data: U.S. Bureau of Labor Statistics (1976)

These changes in consumer demand were then transformed into changes in total demand by the use of input–output analysis. This is an analytical technique that mathematically relates the quantity of output of each industry to the quantities of input from all industries that are required to produce this output. The specific data used are the 1967 table of total requirements, (U.S. Bureau of Economic Analysis, 1974) both direct and indirect, per dollar of delivery to final demand.[2] This table is an 82 by 82 matrix of industries, with each entry being a coefficient showing the dollar amount of input required, directly and indirectly, from each industry per dollar of delivery to final demand by the producing industry. For purposes of analysis, each of the producing industries is identified with a component of household consumption (or with total income or consumption)—this is in several cases, an arbitrary judgment. But, for the most part the linkage between the producing industry and the demand sector is obvious (see Appendix I).

The dollar value of household demand for each producer is multiplied by the coefficient for each supplier, yielding the dollar volume of output required of the supplier (for example, $D_1^H x_{1,1}; D_1^H x_{2,1}; \ldots D_1^H x_{82,1}$). When the process is repeated for each of the producing industries, the sum across all producing industries, for each supplying industry, equals total final output demanded from that industry (that is, $D_1^F = D_1^H x_{1,1} + D_2^H x_{1,2} + \ldots + D_{82}^H x_{1,82}$).

III. INDUSTRIAL COMPOSITION OF LABOR DEMAND

We view changes in the composition of final demand as an intermediate step in determining how the industrial composition of labor demand will respond to alternative demographic changes. Consequently, these re-results are not shown separately, but are available from the author upon request. In order to derive the demand for labor from final demand, it is necessary to make several additional adjustments. First of all, data showing the average annual increase in real productivity per worker [U.S. Bureau of Labor Statistics, 1975] for 1947–73 were used as industry-specific productivity indices. This measures the real (accounting for price changes) level of change in output per worker; for expository purposes it is assumed that this set of indices hold constant over the projection period. This is an important assumption, because embodied in it are assumptions of a constant trend, among industries, of technological change and factor substitution (between capital and labor). Thus far, the relationships between these variables and a changing demographic structure are uncertain, but are potentially of considerable importance [Kelley, 1972].

By comparing the average annual increase in demand for an industry's output with the productivity index of that industry one determines the relative change in the number of workers needed to produce this output. These changes, however, represent only the marginal changes on the demand side. Labor demand will also be influenced by the need to provide net replacements to an industry's labor force and by the influence of net foreign trade. The former influence is derived from age-sex specific work-life survival rates (Fullerton and Byrne, 1976); these reflect the fact that, *ceteris paribus,* replacement demand for labor in any industry will depend upon the age-sex composition of the workers. Thus, industries with a relatively large share of older workers at the beginning of the period will have, in the short run, a relatively high replacement demand; sometimes, as in the case of agriculture, this effect will mitigate relatively adverse employment effects of declining relative demand and/or relatively high productivity.

The latter influence recognizes that the demand for labor discussed thus far has been derived solely on domestic considerations but that, in many instances, international trade significantly augments (agriculture, chemicals, machinery, aircraft) or curtails (apparel, petroleum, footwear, motor vehicles) domestic production (U.S. Bureau of the Census, 1976). While foreign trade represents a fairly small share of the United States' Gross National Product (in comparison with most other industrial economies), the effects on selected industries can be quite significant.

To summarize, changes in the demand for labor in a given industry are determined by the change in demand for its output divided by its productivity index plus net replacement demand, all multiplied by a scalar factor equal to unity plus net exports of the industry as a percentage of total domestic production of the industry. The combination of these forces leads to the projection of demand for labor, by industrial sector, shown in Table 4. The data are shown in summary form, for reasons of ease of presentation and discussion. Complete data for detailed industries are available from the author upon request.

The essential congruence of the consumer demand projections for 2000 suggests that there will be but little difference in the composition of labor demand; this in fact proved to be the case, and table 4 shows comparative results only for the year 2020 (again, data for intermediate years are available from the author upon request). In the year 2020, there are some differences among projections in terms of the industrial composition of the labor force, but these are minor compared with the differences between those of the present and those of 2020. In other words, the principal changes in the industrial composition of the labor force which might be expected between now and 2020 are primarily the result of changes in economic structure consistent with recent trends, and only secondarily the

Table 4. Projection Industrial Composition of the Demand for Labor, 2020 (in percent, except for total)

	1975	2020-I	2020-II	2020-III
Total (Millions of jobs)	84.8	177.6	162.9	152.7
Agriculture	4.1%	0.9	1.0	1.0
Mining	0.9	0.5	0.5	0.5
Construction	5.9	2.7	2.5	2.3
Manufacturing	22.7	25.0	24.3	24.2
Food	2.2	0.9	0.9	1.1
Apparel	2.6	1.3	1.1	1.0
Furniture	1.4	1.8	1.7	1.7
Paper & publishing	2.2	2.5	2.4	2.2
Chemicals	1.3	1.0	1.0	1.1
Petroleum	0.3	0.1	0.1	0.1
Rubber	0.8	1.0	1.0	1.1
Leather	0.4	0.3	0.3	0.3
Stone	0.8	0.7	0.6	0.6
Primary metals	1.6	3.6	3.7	3.7
Fabricated metals	1.8	2.8	2.7	2.6
Non-electric machinery	2.7	3.3	3.3	3.3
Electric machinery	2.3	1.7	1.7	1.8
Transport equipment	2.5	4.0	3.8	3.6
Transportation and communication	6.6	5.8	5.7	5.7
Trade	20.6	18.6	19.0	19.6
Finance	5.5	8.6	8.5	8.5
Business	3.3	4.5	4.4	4.2
Personal services	4.3	6.5	6.5	6.4
Professional services	11.2	13.5	13.9	14.1
Government	13.7	13.6	13.4	13.4

Source of basic data: Employment and Earnings, March 1977

result of alternative demographic courses. Regardless of the demographic future, it seems likely that some manufacturing sectors (furniture, metals, printing and publishing, machinery, and transport equipment) and some service sectors (finance and insurance, business, personal, and professional sectors) will expand their shares of employment, with contraction occuring in the primary sector, some portions of the manufacturing sector (especially food and clothing), and in the trade sector.

If comparison is made among the 2020 projections, one finds that relatively high population growth favors relatively larger shares for construction, clothing, furniture, fabricated metals, printing, transport equipment, transport and communication services, and financial and business services. Most of these sectors can be seen as being positively affected by the greater increase in the number of households accompanying population growth.

On the other hand, relatively slower rates of population growth favor larger shares of employment in the trade and professional service sectors. The former may be an artifact reflecting to some degree the relative lack of growth in competing sectors, but the expansion of employment in professional services reflects the substantial increase in the demand for health care, which outweighs the relative decline in the demand for education (primarily reflected by the flatness of the government sector).

IV. OCCUPATIONAL COMPOSITION OF LABOR DEMAND

The final aspect of demographic change to be considered is the role that such change plays in the occupational composition of labor demand. This transformation is made simply by applying the 1970 matrix of detailed occupation by detailed industry of employment (U.S. Bureau of the Census, 1972) to the disaggregated results summarized in table 4. These basic data show, for example, that in 1970 2.9 percent of the persons employed in the agriculture, forestry and fisheries sectors were classified as professional workers, another 0.9 percent were classified as managers and administrators, and so on for all employing sectors. The results of this application yields the results for broad occupational categories summarized in table 5.

As was the case for industrial composition of projected labor demand, the principal differences to be found in the data are between the distribution of the present and that of the future, regardless of the demographic

Table 5. Projected Occupational Composition of the Demand for Labor, 2020 (in percent, except for total)

	1975	*2020-I*	*2020-II*	*2020-III*
Total (millions of jobs)	84.8	177.6	162.9	152.7
Professional	15.0%	14.2%	14.3%	14.4%
Managerial	10.5	9.0	9.1	9.1
Sales	6.4	7.7	7.5	7.6
Clerical	17.8	21.7	21.8	21.7
Crafts	12.9	11.9	11.8	11.6
Operatives	11.4	12.5	12.4	12.4
Transport operatives	3.8	3.6	3.5	3.4
Non-farm labor	4.9	4.0	4.0	4.0
Farm workers	3.5	0.7	0.8	0.9
Service workers	13.7	14.7	14.8	14.8

Source of basic data: same as table 4

path followed. However, unlike the changes in industrial composition, which generally reflect a continuation of the transition implicit in present trends, the projected occupational composition reflects some differences from the present which might be somewhat unanticipated.

The most striking difference is the relative decline in the proportion of professional and managerial workers relative to other (sales and clerical) workers. While the trend for white collar workers as a whole to grow relative to the labor force is projected to continue, the composition of this group will shift from 52 percent managerial and professional at present to about 44 percent in 2020. (Over the 1960–1975 period the proportion of white collar workers classified as professional and managerial has held constant at 51 to 53 percent). This result reflects the relative growth projected in three industrial sectors (finance, business services and professional services) which employ relatively large numbers of clerical employees.

The inclusion of professional services in the foregoing list may warrant further comment. In the aggregate, this sector employs a very high proportion (50.5 percent) of professional workers. However, there are notable differences between components of this industry, notably between health care and education (these account for about three fourths of professional services employment). As might be expected, the disaggregated data which underlie the results of tables 4 and 5 show substantial growth in health care employment relative to education, even in the case of Series I. In 1970, the occupational composition of the health care sector showed that some 38 percent of its workers were classified as professionals. For the education sector, the comparable proportion was 60 percent.

A similar type of change occurs for blue collar occupations. Regardless of the demographic future, the overall results point to a continuation of past trends suggesting a slight reduction in the proportion of workers falling into this broad classification. However, within this very broad category, all three projections point toward a decline in the relative numbers of workers employed at the highest skill levels (craft), with increases occuring at the semi-skilled or operative occupations. In 1975, crafts workers accounted for 39 percent of all blue collar employment (up from 36 percent in 1960): in 2020, they account for about 37 percent, regardless of projection. Such a result is probably the result of decline in the construction industry (more than half of whose employees were classified as craft workers in 1970), relative to several manufacturing sectors which employ operatives in comparatively large numbers.

Considering differences among the alternative projections to 2020, one finds that overall differences are minimal, although it should perhaps be noted that the overall share of professionals in the labor force is an inverse function of the rate of population growth, while the proportion of craft workers is a direct function. The role of demographic factors in the former case probably has elements relating to both the supply of and the demand for labor. In terms of supply, professionals on the whole, except for teachers, tend to be somewhat older than the average worker. Thus, an older labor force might well imply a larger proportion of professionals than a younger one, due simply to the comparative paucity of younger workers.

On the demand side, it will be recalled from the data in Table 4 that the slower growing populations have a higher proportion of workers engaged in professional services. Implicit in this is a greater shift toward health care and away from education than that found in the more rapidly increasing populations. Even though health care employs a lesser proportion of professionals than does education, the expansion of health care services (in Series III relative to Series I and II) and its attendant need for professional workers is large enough to outweigh the relative decrease in the demand for educational services.

The relatively large number of craft workers employed in the Series I projection is principally the result of the relatively large employment in the construction and transport equipment sectors found in this particular projection. In 1970, the overall employment in these sectors consisted of 56 and 27 percent craft workers.

V. IMPLICATIONS FOR HIGHER EDUCATION AND LABOR FORCE POLICY

The results presented above contain a variety of implications for policy considerations regarding higher education and the proper functioning of the labor market. The relative decline in the number of professional and managerial workers, who are presently most likely to possess a university degree, suggests that the outlook for conventional higher education might be even less bright than would be suggested by an inspection of trends in the size of the 18 to 24 year old population.[3] However, some mitigation of this possibly adverse trend is possible if the system of higher education proves sufficiently flexible to provide more occupational and retraining services than is presently true. Additionally, there has recently been greater attention paid in higher education circles to the provision of the needs of those individuals who pursue the education for purposes of what might be termed consumption or recreation rather than for strictly human capital formation. The continuation of such a trend could help offset the prospects for a relative diminution of demand for higher education due to labor market considerations.

There are a variety of labor market policy considerations which arise from the findings presented here. First, greater attention will have to be paid to the design of training programs intended to meet the need for specific occupations. Many of the clerical and service occupations, which all projections indicate will experience relatively rapid growth, are of the sort which require training supplemental to that offered by the typical secondary school curriculum. Such occupations might include physicians' assistants, para–legal workers, administrative aides, police and fire-fighters, data processing personnel, and the like. To a varying extent, these needs can be met through the utilization of existing higher education facilities.

A more pervasive difficulty will be in the adequacy of labor supply. Even with the growth of labor productivity and the continuing increase in female labor force participation that are assumed in these projections, the growth in the number of jobs during the first portion of the next century seems likely to occur at a rate exceeding that of labor supply. Our projections of total employment relative to the population aged 18 to 64 show ratios of .87, .92 and .96 for Series I, II, and III, respectively (1975 ratio = .68). Even allowing for an increased incidence of part-time employment and multiple jobholding, it seems likely that labor market policies will have to cope with the issue of increases in the rate of labor force participation. The large number (43 million in 2020) of persons aged 65 and over suggests that they are a potential source for much of this labor. Although many older persons might be uable or unwilling to work, others who wish to do so are hampered or prevented by institutional or contractual restrictions. Whether or not necessary changes, such as further restrictions on mandatory retirement or easing of the social security means test, would prove sufficient is a matter for additional research.

A precise evaluation of any potential inbalances should include an assessment of the effects of potentially mitigating circumstances, including variation in labor-force participation rates, the relative level of wages among industries, and the substitution of capital for labor. In this research, these relationships have been assumed constant, for expository purposes, but further research on this topic should explore the possibility of variation in these, and the ultimate consequences of this variation.

Another possible response to these potential supply-demand imbalances is a reconsideration of present immigration policies in order to permit larger numbers of migrants to enter the labor force [Neal, 1978; Wachter and Wachter, 1978]. Such a policy could induce further economic and demographic change, depending upon the size, age-sex composition, and duration of stay of the migrant population.

APPENDIX I

Assumed Linkages of Consumption Sector to Production

Consumption sector	*Producer*
Food	Agriculture, Forestry, Fisheries
Vehicle Purchases & Operations; Fuel & Utilities	Mining
Housing	Construction
Food	Food and Tobacco
Furnishings; Clothing	Textiles & Apparel
Furnishings	Lumber and Furniture
Reading	Paper & Publish.
Medical Care & Drugs	Chemicals
Vehicle Oper.; Fuel & Utilities	Petroleum
Furnishings	Rubber
Furnishings; Clothing	Leather
Housing	Stone, Glass, Clay
Vehicle Purchase; Housing	Primary Metals
Vehicle Purchase; Housing	Fabricated Metals
Total Income	Non-Electric Machinery
Total Income	Electric Machinery
Vehicle Purchase; Recreation	Transport Equipment
Total Income	Instruments
Fuel & Utilities; Recreation	Transportation, Communication
Total Consumption	Trade
Total Income	Finance, Insurance, Real Estate
Personal Care Products and Services	Personal Services
Total Income	Business Services
Medical Care; Education	Professional Services
Total Income	Government
Total Income	Other Services

ACKNOWLEDGMENTS

This research is supported by grant number 90-A-978 from the U.S. Administration on Aging. An earlier version was presented at the Population Studies Colloquium at Florida State University. The helpful suggestions of the editor and Professor Thomas Espenshade on the earlier draft are gratefully acknowledged.

NOTES

1. These projections imply ultimate completed family sizes of 2.7, 2.1, and 1.7, respectively. Accordingly, they differ in terms of age composition and rate of increase, as well. In the year 2020, the median age of the population under the three sets of assumptions is 30.8, 36.3 and 41.1 years for Series I, II, and III, respectively. The average annual rate of increase over the preceeding decade was 1.19, 0.54, and 0.07 percent.

2. Note that this use of the table freezes relative prices at their 1967 levels. Changes since then, especially for energy, may be expected to alter the coefficients to a varying, but at present unknown, degree.

3. For a somewhat different approach to this question, which yields a not dissimilar
result, see Dresch (1978).

REFERENCES

Denison, Edward F. (1974) *Accounting for United States Economic Growth, 1929–69.*
Washington, D.C.: The Brookings Institution.

Dresch, Stephen P. (1978) "Ability, Fertility and Educational Adaptation." *Research in
Population Economics 1:*37–68.

Eilenstine, D.C. and Cunningham, J. P. (1972) "Projected Consumption Demand for a Stationary Population." *Population Studies* 26 (July):223–231.

Espenshade, Thomas J. (1978) How the Trend Toward a Stationary Population Affects Consumer Demand." *Population Studies* 32 (March):147–158.

Fullerton, H. N. and Byrne, J. J. (1976) "Length of Working Life for Men and Women,
1970." *Monthly Labor Review* 99 (February):31–35.

——— and Flaim, P. O. (1976) "New Labor Force Projections to 1990." *Monthly Labor
Review* 99 (December):3–13.

Kelley, Allen C. (1972) "Demographic Changes and American Economic Development:
Past, Present and Future." Pages 9–44 in E. R. Morss and R. H. Reed (eds.), *Economic Aspects of Population Change.* Washington, Government Printing Office.

Neal, Larry (1978) "Is Secular Stagnation Just Around the Corner? A Survey of the Influ-
ences of Slowing Population Growth upon Investment Demand." Pages 101–125 in
T. J. Espenshade and W. J. Serow (eds.), *The Economic Consequences of Slowing
Population Growth.* New York, Academic Press.

Resek, R. W. and Siegel, F. W. (1974) "Consumption Demand and Population Growth
Rates." *Eastern Economic Journal* 1 (October):282–290.

Robbins, Lionel (1929) "Notes on Some Probable Consequences of the Advent of A Stationary Population in Great Britain." *Economica* 9 (April):71–82.

Serow, William J. (1972) "The Implications of Zero Growth for Agricultural Commodity Demand." *American Journal of Agricultural Economics* 54 (December):955–963.

U.S. Bureau of the Census (1972) *Occupation by Industry.* 1970 Census Subject Reports,
No. PC(2)-7C. Washington, Government Printing Office.

——— (1973) *Sources and Structure of Family Income.* 1970 Census Subject Reports, No.
PC(2)-8A. Washington, Government Printing Office.

U.S. Bureau of the Census (1975a) *Current Population Reports.* Series P-25, no. 607. "Projections of the Number of Households and Families:1975–1970." Washington,
D.C.: Government Printing Office.

——— (1975b) *Current Population Reports.* Series P-25, no. 601. "Projections of the Population of the United States: 1975 to 2050." Washington, D.C.: Government Printing
Office.

——— (1976) *Highlights of U.S. Export and Import Trade.* Washington, Government
Printing Office.

U.S. Bureau of Economic Analysis (1972) "Selected National Data on Economic Growth."
Pages 369–379 in E. R. Morss and R. H. Reed (eds.), *Economic Aspects of Population Change.* Washington, Government Printing Office.

——— (1974) "1967 Tables of Interindustry Transactions." *Survey of Current Business* 54
(February):50–55.

U.S. Bureau of Labor Statistics (1975) *Handbook of Labor Statistics-1975 Reference Edi-
tion.* Washington, Government Printing Office.

———— (1976) *Average Annual Expenditures for Selected Commodity and Service Groups Classified by Family Characteristics, 1972 and 1973.* Washington, Government Printing Office.

Wachter, M. L. and Wachter, S. M. (1978) "The Fiscal Policy Dilemma: Cyclical Swings Dominated by Supply Side Constraints." Pages 71–99 in T. J. Espenshade and W. J. Serow (eds.), *The Economic Consequences of Slowing Population Growth.* New York, Academic Press.

Wander, Hilde (1978) "Zero Population Growth Now: The Lessons from Europe." Pages 41–69 in T. J. Espenshade and W. J. Serow (eds.), *The Economic Consequences of Slowing Population Growth.* New York, Academic Press.

POPULATION CHANGES:
CONTEMPORARY MODELS AND THEORIES

Alfred Sauvy

I. INTRODUCTION

Rapid population growth in many developing countries has prompted a renewed interest in studies concerning the effect of population growth on economic development. This research takes one of two possible perspectives, which are the macroeconomic viewpoint, where the nation is the framework, or the microeconomic viewpoint, where the family is the framework. Regardless of the approach, most authors arrive at a pessimistic conclusion: population growth inhibits economic development because of the investments it requires. For expository purposes, we assume the macroeconomic viewpoint and present an example of such an investment.

Research in Population Economics, Volume 3, pages 225–238
Copyright © 1981 by JAI Press Inc.

ISBN: 0-89232-207-1

II. A SIMPLIFIED MODEL: HOUSING

Housing is the typical investment made by an individual. Hence, we take as a unit the housing-per-person (roughly one-third of the necessary amount of housing per family) and make our calculations using averages.

The construction of housing over a period of 1 year (excluding repairs and maintenance costs of existing facilities) fulfills three quantitative requirements without considering improvements to be made on future construction and net immigration from abroad. There are:

(1) remodeling of housing not presently in use;
(2) additional construction for supplementary inhabitants;
(3) additional housing requirements resulting from internal migration, especially from rural to urban areas.

Excluding the housing requirements for internal migration and assuming a stable population, per capita housing is given by

$$\frac{C_n}{P_n} = \frac{r}{100} \frac{e^{Dr/100}}{e^{Dr/100} - 1}$$

where

$r/100$ = rate of population increase

P_n = population at the beginning of year n

C_n = amount of housing constructed during year n

D = lifetime of a housing unit

If the lifetime of a housing unit is 100 years, as is usually the case in Europe, the above formula reduces to

$$\frac{C_n}{P_n} = \frac{r}{100} \frac{e^r}{e^r - 1}$$

Plotting C_n/P_n on the vertical axis and $r/100$ on the horizontal axis, a graphical representation of per capita housing is given in Figure 1. If OB is the bisector, the curve is always above OB. The difference between the curve and the bisector represents historical costs, while present costs are represented by the y values of the bisector.

Observation of Figure 1 leads us to conclude that total required construction cost increases less than proportionately with the population growth rate. However, the cost associated with a particular growth rate period (that is, the difference between the amount of housing required if the population increases at a rate of $r/100$ per year and the amount of nec-

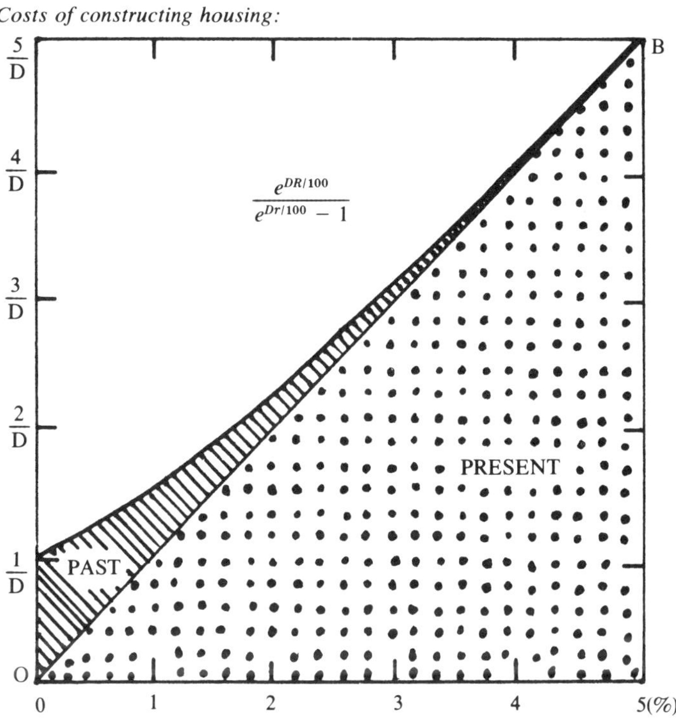

Figure 1.   Housing Costs According to
Annual Growth Rate of Population

essary construction if the population remains stationary) increases more than proportionately.

Housing is not the only investment for which the preceding methodology applies.   Nevertheless, the same conclusion is reached regardless of the type of investment: *growth is costly.*   A population decrease might be advantageous, since this decrease would enable the entire population to benefit from past capital accumulation.

Additionally, we may believe, *a priori,* that population growth is more costly for a developed country than for an underdeveloped country.   This belief may be attributable to the fact that the capital per person tends to be high in developed countries.   Any further increase in the population necessitates additional capital investments, thereby driving this ratio even higher.   However, investment is not the only factor that inhibits economic development.

III. LESSONS FROM EXPERIENCE

A. Primitive Populations

There are numerous "demographically primitive" populations that have undergone the process of overpopulation. Not only did these populations overstep the statistical optimum, but they also exceeded the maximum population allowed by the territory, given the technical conditions of the period. Stability in these economies was very rare; stationary or declining populations were under the threat of attack for their land by other too-numerous populations. The economic level and political power were inconsistent. Some examples of these populations are presented here.

1. Greece. Demographic growth in Greece was characterized by intensive colonization in the Mediterranean region. However, stability and eventual decline followed this growth period. The decline in natality was denounced by numerous writers such as Menander, Polybius, and Strabo and automatically led to the aging of the population. As a result of aging, decadence followed implacably.

2. Rome. From the time of Caesar, natality in Rome had fallen sufficiently to persuade Caesar Augustus to undertake pronatalist measures. These measures were both innovative and burdensome (in particular, the Papia Poppea). The decline in natality therefore, took place much earlier than the spread of Christianity or the era of decadence.

A century later, Nerva, and then Trajan, created the Alimentana. This was a type of allowance given to families for increases in the number of children born. From this we infer that population aging must have become even more pronounced. The question we must answer is, "Had it stretched to cover the rest of the Empire?" It is difficult to determine this. However, we do know that when the barbarians arrived at the frontiers, it was possible to find land to offer them, but no soldiers to resist them. What is more important is that aging occurred at the heart of the Empire. As in Greece, aging preceded decadence.

Thus, these two great historic phenomena of antiquity can be explained in the same way: population aging.

B. Spain in the Seventeenth and Eighteenth Centuries

Although it had driven out the Arabs, Spain (like most European countries) was overpopulated. Crises of subsistence were frequent: this was population control by famine. Consequently, a massive emigration to the New World took place. A method for increasing the standard of living appeared to be fewer people and more resources.

Despite its discovery of enormous riches, not only in terms of gold, but also spices, colonial provisions, etc., Spain grew steadily more impoverished. This appears paradoxical: all the models would have forecasted the opposite. According to people in the eighteenth century, "Spain has lost, in exchanging her men against metal." Although each Spaniard owned more land, the race as a whole grew poorer.

Psychological and sociological factors, excluded from mathematical models, play an important role here.

C. A Comparison: Development in Spain and Italy

Let's compare the North and South of Italy and the North and South of Spain. In both cases (i.e., Lombardy and Piedmont in Italy, Catalonia and the Asturias in Spain), the North, although much less prolific, developed at a faster rate. This difference seems to be in contradiction with the hypothesis regarding necessary population growth. However, the cause and effect must be clearly distinguished. The decline in natality began in the developed areas and was sufficiently long to allow this paradoxical result. Essentially, the industrialization of the northern parts of Italy and Spain caused a decline in natality; or even better, industrialization and the decrease in natality resulted from one and the same cause—the opening of civilzation in Western Europe. Therefore, in this example, we cannot draw a formal conclusion. However, we can see the importance of the difference in man's behavior.

It is precisely these different types of behavior that Mrs. E. Boserup observed during her various studies on agricultural countries: technology, she concludes, has varied under the influence of population pressure. A thinly scattered population squanders its land and abandons it to the effects of erosion. Black Africa and Southern Asia provide an excellent comparison of this.

D. Nineteenth Century Western Europe

This area of the world provides us with an experimental field of considerable interest. Isolation of the factor, the effect of which is to be measured, is satisfied here.

During the nineteenth century, the countries of Western Europe had the same culture and technology and relatively similar economic and political regimes. In contrast, population growth was rapid for all countries (from 1 to 3 percent, in general) except for France (from 1 to 1.5 percent). Moreover, France had the advantage of the immigration of young men. However, the other countries underwent emigration and hence, trained men but did not benefit from their skills.

According to the theories and models, we *should* observe the following conditions at the beginning of the twentieth century:

1. Since there were fewer French children (by almost one-third), they should have been better educated, better cared for, and healthier than those of other countries.

2. In a position to abandon less productive areas of land, (a result of its technical progress and low population density), French children should have had an advantage over the countries of higher average yields, per hectare or per man.

3. Having fewer children to bring up, and therefore fewer adults requiring services, the French should have been able to transfer their savings, investments, and efforts to economic investments and industries.

Therefore, the following should be true:

1. At the beginning of the twentieth century, per capita income should have been noticeably higher in France than in other countries. The application of analogous formulas, discussed previously, to the model presented here would yield a per capita income twice that of other countries (annual difference of 0.7 percent for the national income per inhabitant).

2. In particular, housing in France should have been superior to other countries.

However, neither of these results have been observed. At the beginning of the twentieth century, French children, although less numerous, were neither better educated, nor healthier than those in other countries. Infant mortality was even somewhat higher. Per capita income was more or less the same in all countries. Despite the abandonment of less cultivated lands, the average agricultural yield increased less in France than in other Western European countries. As an example, we can compare France and Germany: As the German population increased rapidly, the average yields in France should have increased more rapidly. The following table shows the increases of yield per hectare from 1880 to 1910:

	France	Germany
Corn	21%	63%
Rye	10%	97%
Barley	26%	55%
Oats	19%	71%
Potatoes	25%	75%

These results are contrary to logical expectations. Also, similar results hold for all sectors. Thus, slow population growth did not lead to the expected results. We show the explanation for this in Section IV.

E. Underdeveloped Countries

It is commonly said that underdeveloped countries suffer economically because of the too rapid growth of their populations.

If we determine the correlation between population growth and the increase in GNP from 1960 to 1975 for the 100 underdeveloped countries for which the World Bank records annual GNP (Figure 2), we should find a high negative correlation. However, the result of -0.114 is not significant.

The countries in which population increased most rapidly were not economically disadvantaged. Furthermore, their GNPs increased at least as

Figure 2. Growth of Population and Increase of GNP per Capita in Developing Countries from 1960 to 1975

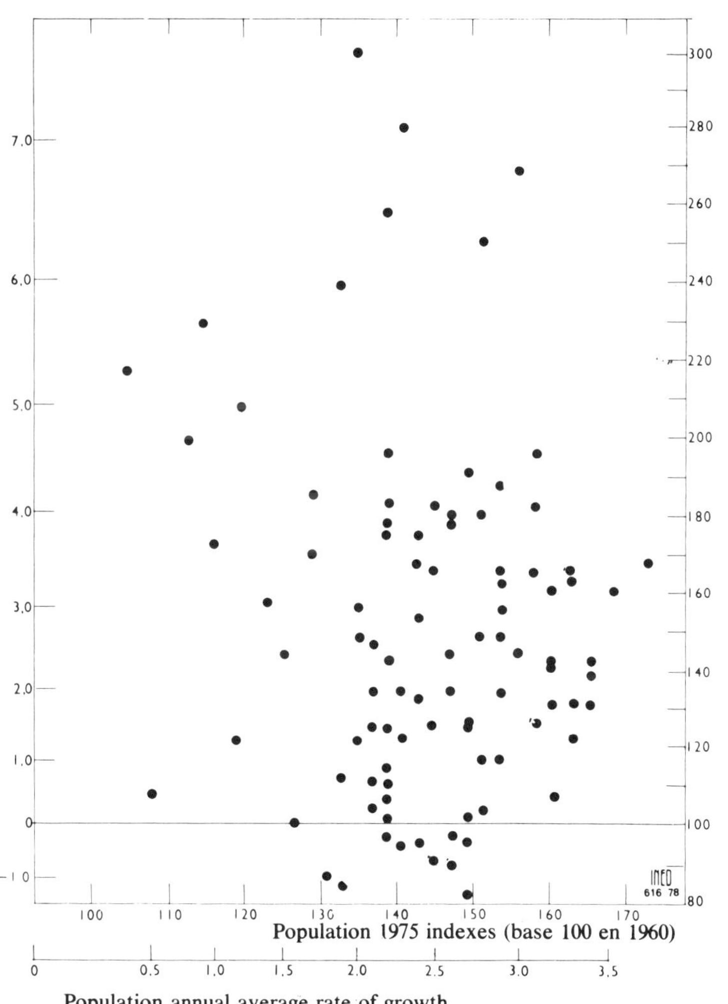

GNP per capita
Annual average rate of growth 1969–1975

Average GNP per capita
1975 indexes (base 100 en 1960)

Figure 3. Growth of Population and Increase of Agricultural Production per Capita in Developing Countries from 1961–1965 to 1971–1975 (base 100 en 1961–1965)

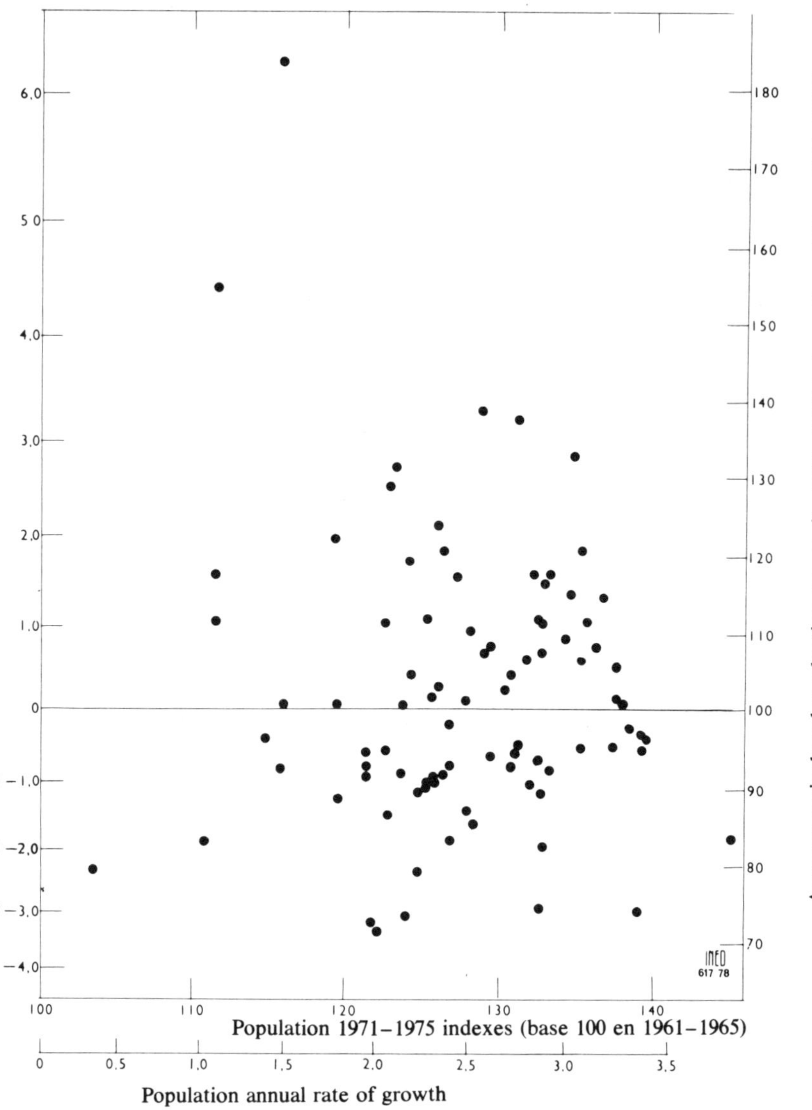

Average agricultural production per capita
Annual average rate of growth 1961–1965 to 1971–1975

232

much as that of countries undergoing slow population growth. Further calculations regarding this have been performed annually since 1969, and the results have been the same as those obtained previously.

If we use the growth in agricultural production per person instead of growth in GNP, we expect an even higher negative correlation, since agricultural production is affected by diminishing marginal productivity. However, this is not the case. The calculation over 10 years (1971–1975 average over 1962–1965 average) yields an insignificant correlation coefficient of 0.038. Instead of the expected downward slope, the graphical illustration is a shapeless cloud (Figure 3). However, these results should not be taken as a general rule. They do not preclude the fact that the rate of population increase may influence economic development in a favorable manner. Moreover, we believe that an increase of 2 or 3 percent per year cannot last for a lengthy period. The value of this analysis is different: it proves that the models that generally denounce the unfavorable influence of population growth do not, for the most part, have any value. They neglect various positive factors.

IV. POSITIVE FACTORS OF POPULATION GROWTH

While the literature describes factors regarding population growth, we prefer to emphasize two other factors that have been the focus of less study:

(1) a growing population's ease of adaptation,
(2) the human factor—man's behavior.

A. Advantages of Population Growth

1. Ease of Adaptation. In modern times, all populations find themselves in an environment of change and must therefore modify their structure, either geographically or professionally. In order to change the structure, it is easier to add something to the parts that must grow rather than take something away. Thus, a growing population adapts better to new conditions than does a stationary or declining population.

2. Advancement of Youth. Contrary to our *a priori* belief, a growing population is more favorable for the advancement of youth than a stationary population. It can be shown that the probability that a youth obtains a superior position in society during his lifetime is

$$\frac{1}{p} = \frac{r^9 - 1}{r - 1}$$

and increases as r increases.

To obtain this expression we employ the following assumptions:

(1) The population is stable and grows at the rate r over 5 years;
(2) There is no mortality between the ages of 20 and 65;
(3) A superior position in society is attained at 60 years of age, and
(4) D, the number of superior positions in society, is given by A/P, where A is the economically active population and P is a predetermined number.

3. Answer to Pressure and Difficulty—Man's Behavior. We have mentioned this phenomenon with regard to agricultural studies by Mrs. E. Boserup. Since little is known about nineteenth century France, we shall again examine this area. For example, why did agricultural yields increase more in other countries than in France? This occurred for reasons of conservatism and aging. Not only did France experience slow technological growth, but Parliament refused to establish agricultural educational facilities similar to those in other countries. The leader of the government, J. Mèline, went even further: on the eve of the 1914–1918 war, he suggested a return to the land. With its aging population, France refused to accept industrialization and *was doing an about face toward the past.* Additionally, cultivation of madderroot (red coloring) was encouraged—at the very time when the Badische Anilin was building factories to produce artificial colorings.

Additionally, the decline of the French Navy was more severe than in other countries. Under the influence of population aging, the French government and Parliament subsidized the Navy's sailing ships while other countries were adopting steam-powered craft.

Savings were undergoing the same phenomenon. Previously, savings had been substantial. However, the investment level had been constrained by the dominant influence of stockholding (in particular, State Loans), which tended to decrease the level of industrial investments.

B. Visibility of Benefits and Costs

At first glance, the cost–benefit balance is always against an increasing population. In reality, however, this is not necessarily the case, since costs, and in particular, expenditures, are much easier to measure than benefits. Arguments based upon unemployment, pollution, etc. easily lead to the belief in an excess of population. However, experience belies simplistic beliefs.

All forecasts made in the field of population have proven to be pessimistic. Events have always, without exception, developed more favorably, or less unfavorably, than forecast. A few examples follow:

1. In 1781, the Abbot Raynal, however progressive and optimistic he may have been, expressed concern regarding the United States. "If ten

million men ever find a sure source of subsistence in these provinces, that will be a lot . . . the country will be self-sufficient, as long as its inhabitants know how to gain happiness through thriftiness and moderation." New York alone now contains over 10 million people, who are neither particularly thrifty, nor, for the most part, live less than moderately.

2. In 1798, Malthus expressed great concern for Europe: population is increasing, he said, geometrically, while production is increasing arithmetically. Hence, population is increasing much faster than foreseen, while the production increase is slowing down spontaneously, *without any legislative steps being taken.*

3. In 1815, Governor Stamford Raffles considered Java, with its 4.5 million inhabitants, overpopulated. Today it contains 90 million people and *is* still overpopulated.

4. After World War II, concern was expressed for overpopulated Japan. In the words of Mr. J. Robin, from an article published in the journal *Population:* "Anxiety is felt thoughout Japan and one cannot help but think of the profundity of a great Chinese historian of the Classical period: 'You wished to seek misfortune; there it is; and the people departed, crying.'"

5. Around the same time, Germany (Federal Republic) was also the object of pessimistic feelings. Prior to the advent of Hitler, Germany was supposed overpopulated and had 4 million people unemployed. Furthermore, according to Morgenthau, Germany accepted 12 million immigrants. One can imagine the unemployment prospects! Additionally, its only resource was pastoralization. The result of this was that Germany not only integrated these extra inhabitants, but also received numerous immigrants from Eastern Germany and then undertook a massive immigration scheme. Subsequently, the number of farmers decreased. This turn of events has induced theorists to speak of the "German Miracle."

Just after the war, the general opinion regarding Italy was very pessimistic. Fascism, it was said, had only been able to curb unemployment as a result of its armaments industry and its colonization of Ethiopia. It was forecast that millions would be unemployed. However, Italy's economic progress outstripped all the forecasts and emigration came almost to a halt. Its present unemployment level is a result of untimely confusion and politics.

6. As a whole, Europe was supposed to suffer from serious unemployment as a consequence of overpopulation (see the emigration forecasts of Mr. Ole' Just). Austria was also supposed to suffer from mass unemployment. The loss of Indonesia by the Netherlands should have resulted in severe unemployment. For this reason, the country instituted a massive emigration plan. In 1980, the country's population is 14 million and the number of entries into the country outstripped the number of departures. Additionally, the unemployment rate is low, despite the oil crisis.

7. In 1951, the United Nations experts, Anglo-Saxon either by birth or training, stated that to raise per capita income in underdeveloped countries by 1 percent per year requires an annual investment of 10,710 million dollars, 6096 of which should be foreign investment. These figures do not include investments in education, health, roads, parts, etc. In actuality, investments in underdeveloped countries were less than half the figure quoted by the United Nations. Moreover, population increased by 2 percent per year, instead of the projected 1 percent. Under these conditions, the underdeveloped countries should have collapsed. Instead, per capita income increased by 1 percent per year.

8. The revival of natality in 1946 in France generated concern regarding unemployment. Since jobs were relatively scarce, projections indicated that unemployment would increase by 200,000 jobless persons each year.

In 1962, when repatriates returned from Algeria, the Committee of National Accounting projected that France should expect an additional 400,000 unemployed in one year. However, the 400,000 repatriated into France found gainful employment within a few months.

9. In 1965, forecasts indicated famine in India and the Far East in 1966, or at the very latest. 1967. Further research pushed the date into the future. In 1980, the situation was not worse, and the predicted famine had not occurred.

V. THE CONCEPT OF THE OPTIMAL RATE
OF GROWTH

Population growth results in certain costs and benefits. This section attempts to judge the overall effect of population growth. Since its acceleration or slow-down brings about a change in the age composition, we cannot follow a given population through time. However we can compare stable populations growing at different rates.

Figure 4 depicts one set of cost and benefit curves of population growth. Analysis of the concavity of these curves, and hence their relationship, provides us with some interesting information. First, we can neither measure nor precisely calculate the economic and sociologic benefits of population growth. However, we have an idea of their development. Figure 4 shows that benefits accruing to population growth are zero when the population growth rate is zero. Moreover, the benefits do not increase proportionately with the growth rate. Hence, neither the sociological advantages described nor the advantages of a supple structure stand to gain anything through rapid growth. Therefore, the function showing the benefits accruing to population growth is concave to the horizontal axis.

For expository purposes, we can utilize the cost function shown in Fig-

Figure 4.   Costs and Benefits of Population Growth, First Case

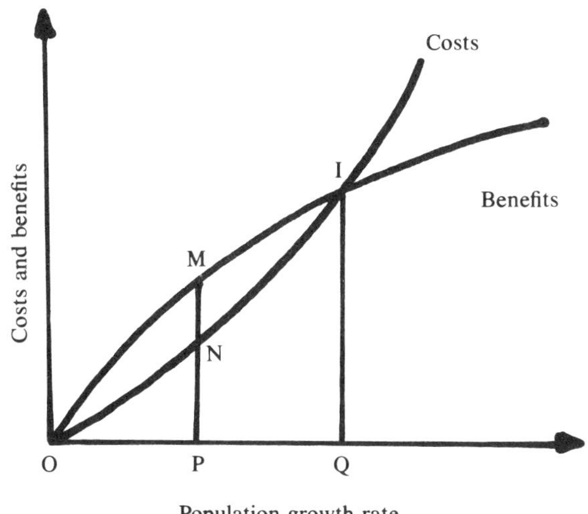

ure 1.   The cost due to growth is the total cost curve minus the cost accruing to zero population growth.   Hence, this curve starts at the origin and is convex to the horizontal axis.

The curves intersect because a tangent from the origin to the benefits curve has a steeper slope than one drawn to the costs curve.   Up to point *Q*, benefits exceed costs.   The net benefit is greatest at *P*, where tangents drawn to the curves are parallel.   The segment between these parallel tangents represents the largest distance between the curves.   The optimal growth rate is attained at point *Q* where benefits exactly offset costs.   It is difficult to measure this point of optimal growth.   However, it has been estimated that Western Europe had, during its most prosperous years (from 1950 to 1970) a growth rate slightly higher than 0.5 percent annually.

An optimal growth rate is desirable for a stable population.   Thus, if a stable population, growing at 0.5 percent annually, wants to increase its growth rate to the optimum of 1 percent per year, it would at the same time lose its "stability" and would recover this stability only after a very long time.

The basic difficulty in this type of analysis lies in measuring the benefits, and in particular, the tangent at the origin.   This is true because we could have a situation such as the one shown in Figure 5.   In this case, costs always exceed benefits.   This type of situation can be the consequence of a highly overpopulated country.   To provide food for one extra man would require a considerable amount of investments.   Therefore, zero growth is beneficial and, undoubtedly, a sharp decline in population

Figure 5.   Costs and Benefits of Population Growth, Second Case

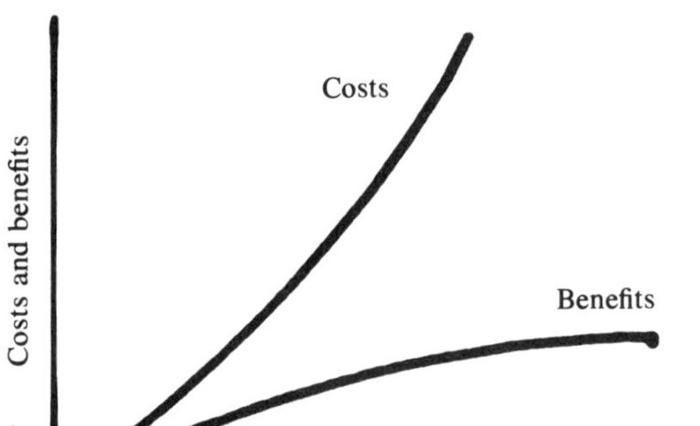

growth would increase per capita income.   However, there is no historic example of a country with a stationary or declining population over a sufficiently long period to support this conclusion.

VI. CONCLUSION

Since population growth has advantages and disadvantages, it is impossible to draw any generalizations.   While the costs of growth are usually quantifiable, the benefits rarely are, since these are, for the most part, sociological in nature.   For this reason, the benefits accruing to population growth are often omitted from mathematical models.   Specifically, the aging process, which, until the present, has been the subject of little research, is even more influential insofar as it has an analgesic effect on the population in question.   This is the field that should receive priority in research activities.

Government can slow population growth through action pertaining to natality.   However, this results in the aging of the existing population.   It can also act by modifying national consumption, that is, by encouraging those expenses that use little in the way of natural resources.   However, this type of policy applies to developed countries.

Economic science and its applications could make considerable progress in this area by applying to its analyses a method of interindustrial exchange (input/output) analogous to that of Leontief.   Using this procedure, the calculations would be made in terms of (1) status occupied in various professions, and (2) natural resources.   Due to the lack of information on these two points, our knowledge with regard to the relationship between the economy and the population is very limited.   Further research in this area is necessary.

POPULATION GROWTH AND PHELPS' TECHNICAL PROGRESS MODEL: INTERPRETATION AND GENERALIZATION*

Julian L. Simon and Gunter Steinmann

I. INTRODUCTION

The standard growth-theoretical assessment is that faster population growth yields a lower consumption level than does slower population growth (see, for example, Brems, 1973; Solow, 1970; Dixit, 1976). This is the outcome of the Solow–Swan model with exogenous technical progress, and it results from the need to devote more of total output to investment in order to equip additional new workers when labor force growth is higher.

Implicit in Phelps' (1966) model, however, is the surprisingly different result that higher population growth leads to a faster rate of growth and a

Research in Population Economics, Volume 3, pages 239–254

Copyright © 1981 by JAI Press Inc.

All rights of reproduction in any form reserved.

ISBN: 0-89232-207-1

higher level of consumption. To make that result explicit and bring it to the fore is the first purpose of this chapter. The second purpose is to show that Phelps' result with respect to population growth can be generalized to a much wider range of models than Phelps envisioned.

Before beginning on the analytic work, we wish to motivate our argument with some empirical data that show the production of knowledge and increase in productivity to be functions of population and market size, both of which are central elements in our theoretical analysis.

In 1682 William Petty commented:

> "As for the Arts of Delight and Ornament, they are best promoted by the greatest number of emulators. And it is more likely that one ingenious curious man may rather be found among 4 million than 400 persons . . . . And for the propagation and improvement of useful learning, the same may be said concerning it as above-said concerning . . . the Arts of Delight and Ornaments . . . ."

In an modern setting, Figure 1 shows the relationship between population size and size of scientific establishments (as measured by numbers of published authors) after per capita income is allowed for; the relationship is roughly proportional, which jibes with the common-sense idea that more heads produce more new ideas, ceteris paribus.

Figure 2 shows data on the relationship between output of great discoveries and population size (and population growth) in ancient Greece and

Figure 1

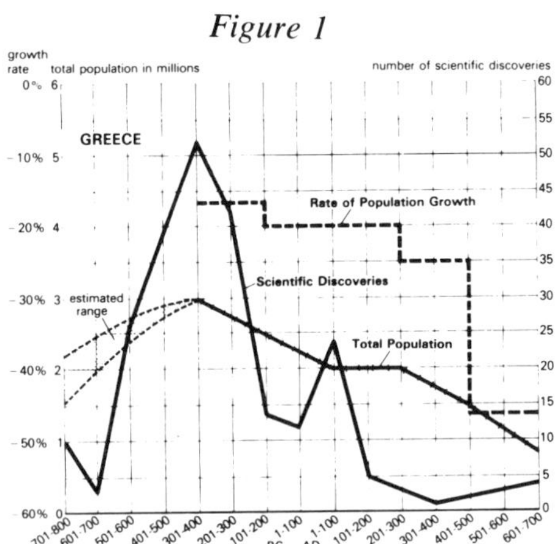

Sources: Sorokin, Pitinim. 1937. *Social and cultural dynamics.* 4 vols. Boston: Little, Brown & Company, p. 148; McEvedy, Colin and Richard Jones. 1968. *Atlas of world population history.* New York: Penguin; Clark, Colin. 1967. *Population growth and land use.* New York: St. Martins.

Figure 2

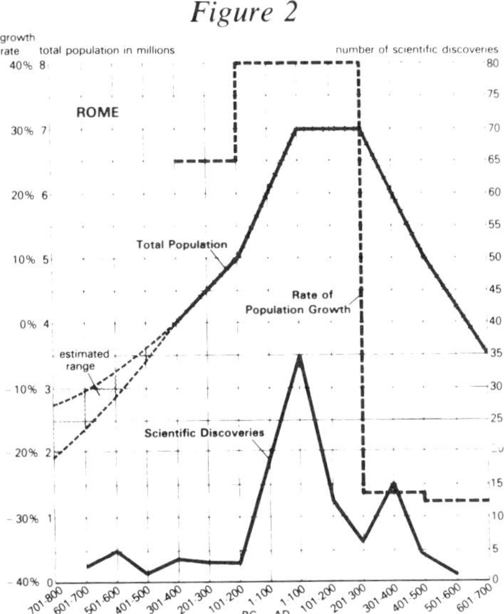

Sources: McEvedy, Colin and Richard Jones. 1968. *Atlas of world population history.* New York: Penguin; Sorokin, Pitinim. 1937. *Social and cultural dynamics.* 4 vols. Boston: Little, Brown & Company, p. 148; Clark, Colin. 1967. *Population growth and land use.* New York: St. Martins.

Rome. These data are germane to such assertions as that by Ansley Coale:

"[T]here is no warrant for the assumption that growth of knowledge is greater with a larger population . . . I have gifted and well-informed friends who seriously think that the intellectual heights achieved in classical Athens have never been equalled, and this was a community of a few thousand educated persons. The population of Florence at the time of the Renaissance was no greater than Trenton, New Jersey, yet Galileo was one of the key figures in the development of modern science: the Medici and their fellow bankers were pioneers in the development of modern banking, including double entry book-keeping; Dante is a figure in world literature rivalled only by Shakespeare and possibly Homer; Machiavelli is considered by some the godfather of political science, and in painting, sculpture, architecture and engineering the Florentines led the world. One could plausibly argue that this community of a hundred thousand persons did more for modern civilization in a few centuries than the U.S. has. Elizabethan London and Budapest between the two world wars (in fact, the Jewish community in Budapest) are other examples. (Personal communication, December 28, 1971)

These data seem, rather, to fit Kuznets's remark:

> "Population growth, under the assumptions stated, would, therefore, produce an absolutely larger number of geniuses, talented men, and generally gifted contributors to new knowledge" (1960, p. 388)

The incomp level of a society also influences the rate of scientific output in our theory. From a study by Love and Pashute (1978) Figure 3 shows that the size of the scientific establishment is a positive function of per capita income, with population size held constant. In a logarithmic regression with both and population size as independent variables, the elasticity of the number of scientific authors with respect to total population is 1.1 (indicating that the amount of science goes up at least proportionately with population size), and with respect to per capita income the elasticity is 1.9. Regressions with other specifications yield similar results, and these results agree with an earlier analysis by Price (1971).

Another element of our theory is that the size of the market influences the rate of change of productivity (though our format blurs technology and productivity). In Figures 4 and 5 we see evidence at the industry level that larger total output leads to higher productivity. These intercountry comparisons are designed to avoid the bias implicit in intracountry comparisons of various industries due to influence flowing from productivity change to output as well as the reverse. Of course the intercountry comparisons are not totally free of danger from this source. But specific important cases are reassuring. For example, it is clear that Canada's large production in the forest-products industry causes the high productivity in these industries; high productivity is not the reason that Canada grows many trees.

Figure 3

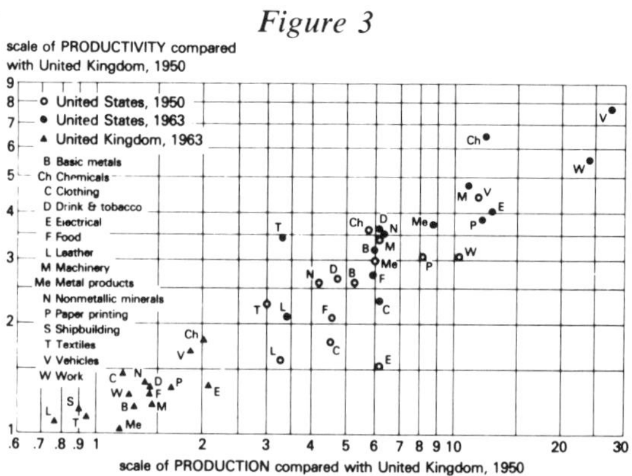

Redrawn from Colin Clark, *Population Growth and Land Use.* New York, St. Martins Press, 1967, p. 265.

Figure 4

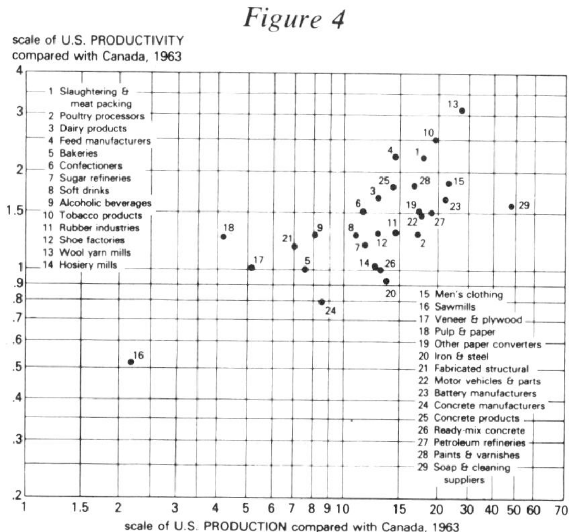

Source: E.C. West, *Canada–United States Price and Productivity Differences in Manufacturing Industries, 1963.* Ottawa: Economic Council of Canada, 1971, pp. 18–22.

II. THE IMPORTANT IMPLICIT IMPLICATION OF PHELPS' FUNCTION

A bit of background first: Various writers beginning with Kaldor (1957) and Arrow (1962) have made technical progress endogenous in growth models. But these writers have either said nothing about the effects of different rates of population growth or have concluded that it has a neutral or negative effect.[1]

Phelps proposed the technical progress function

$$\frac{A_t - A_{t-1}}{A_{t-1}} = \left(\frac{A_{t-w-1}}{A_{t-1}}\right) h \left(\frac{R_t}{A_{t-w-1}}\right) \tag{1}$$

where A = level of technology

R = number of researchers

and later K = the stock of capital

L = labor force

Y = total output

w = retardation factor

He makes $h(R_t/A_{t-w-1})$ a concave argument[2] because, he says, this assumption is necessary if "an exponential growth of researchers will produce an exponential increase of the level of technology" (1966:134). The number of research workers R may be considered proportional to the labor force, and w is a "retardation factor" to represent the delay in adoption of newly produced knowledge.

This function has the realistic properties that (a) more persons imply more knowledge, (b) there are diminishing returns at a given moment, and (c) a larger stock of knowledge leads to a larger increment of knowledge. And (d) it has the attractive theoretical characteristic that an exponential growth of researchers (or more simply for our purposes here an exponential growth of the labor force) produces an exponential increase in technical progress, and hence is consistent with the standard growth–theoretical notion of a steady state. Phelps' function and analysis is particularly interesting because—unlike earlier writers—he worked hard to justify the particular form of the function he used, and because his formulation has considerable plausibility.

Phelps deduced from his model the golden-age equilibrium that "consumption will grow at the rate 2λ" where λ is the rate of growth of the labor force, that is, per capita consumption will grow at the rate of growth of the labor force. He then goes on to derive an interesting golden rule for the amount of research, together with the amount of accumulation.

What is not mentioned by Phelps in this article—or to our knowledge by anyone else before or afterward, anywhere in the literature of population economics or of growth theory (except Eltis, 1973)—is the (for growth theory) startling implication that—contrary to the implications of standard growth theory and also contrary to the conventional wisdom—a higher rate of population growth leads to a higher rate of economic growth.[3] Also implicit in Phelps' model is that a population larger in absolute size will, *ceteris paribus,* have faster technical progress. Even Phelps himself, when discussing population growth and in a general way observing that more people mean more inventions (Phelps 1968, 1972), did not draw upon his 1966 model for a formal demonstration of the proposition.

There are, however, two important loose ends in Phelps' work:

1. There is no upper bound to the optimal population growth rate in Phelps' model (except, implicitly, fecundity). Economists are usually uncomfortable with such a theoretical outcome. But it is not obvious what reasonable economic force, if any, might be included in such a model that would yield a concave rather than a monotonic function for consumption level as a function of population growth.

2. Phelps' function indicates that technical progress should have become slower as population growth has declined in the twentieth century in the United States and in the western world generally.

In fact, technical progress has apparently been higher in the more recent decades than in the early decades of this century (Solow, 1957;

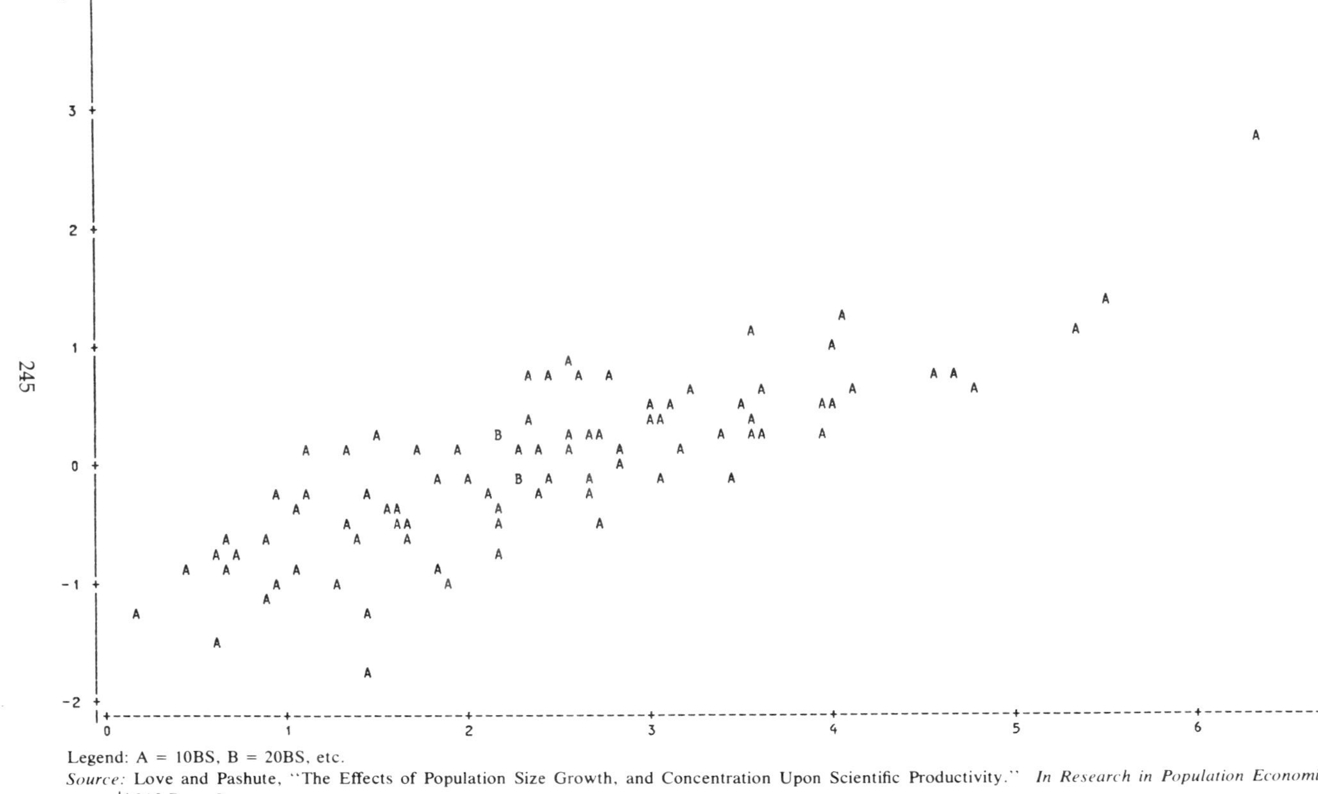

Figure 5. The Relationship of Scientific Activity and Population Size

Legend: A = 10BS, B = 20BS, etc.
Source: Love and Pashute, "The Effects of Population Size Growth, and Concentration Upon Scientific Productivity." *In Research in Population Economics,* vol. 1, JAI Press Inc.

Fellner, 1970). This empirical observation is consistent with technical progress being a function of the *total size* of the labor force (or R & D force). This dependence is not indicated in Phelps' equilibrium analysis. But a disequilibrium analysis with Phelps' function shows that between two populations of different sizes but growing at the same rate, the larger will have a higher technological level though the rate of productivity increase will be the same for the two populations. And higher population growth leads to a larger total population, *ceteris paribus*. Hence Phelps' function understates the contribution of population size and growth to the advance of economic welfare.

III. GENERALIZATION OF PHELPS' MODEL FOR MORE REALISM

We might rest here. But it should be interesting and useful to depart from Phelps' function to search for a function that more closely fits the historical facts and yields a more satisfying picture of population growth's effects.

In order to make it analogous to a production function,[4] Phelps' function may be written as

$$A(t) - A(t - 1) = A(t - w)h\left(\frac{R(t)}{A(t - w)}\right) \tag{2}$$

The factor $A(t - w)$ is reasonably equal to $A(t - 1)$ at all times. Hence the function boils down to (shifting to labor force L in place of R)

$$A(t) - A(t - 1) = A(t - 1)h\left(\frac{L(t)}{A(t - 1)}\right) \tag{3}$$

or

$$A_t - A_{t-1} = A_{t-1}h\left(\frac{L_t}{A_{t-1}}\right) \tag{3a}$$

This may be rewritten in the Cobb–Douglas form as

$$A_t - A_{t-1} = aA_{t-1}^\Delta L_{t-1}^\gamma \tag{4}$$

where $\Delta < 1$, $\gamma < 1$, and a is constant.

Implicit in Phelps' discussion is that $\Delta + \gamma = 1$ in Eq. 4, as seen in Phelps' requirement that the function be homogeneous of degree one, and his statement that "if the technology level should double we would require exactly twice the amount of research to double the absolute time rate of increase of the technology'' (Phelps, 1966:135).

Phelps' function is far more restrictive than it need be, however, even to satisfy his objective of golden-age steady growth. There are two directions in which this general framework may be generalized.

A. Generalization I

There is no need to assume that the function is homogeneous of degree one. As long as Δ is even slightly below unity, the result is the constant golden-age rate of growth of A and of consumption per capita that Phelps sought—even if there are increasing returns rather than the function being homogeneous of degree one that Phelps assumed was necessary. The reason for this interesting result can be seen intuitively as follows: rewrite Eq. (4) as

$$\frac{A_t - A_{t-1}}{A_{t-1}} = \frac{a A_{t-1}^{\Delta} L_{t-1}^{\gamma}}{A_{t-1}} \qquad \Delta, \gamma < 1 \tag{5}$$

If A rises at a rate greater than L, then A will grow large relative to L. As this happens, the denominator A_{t-1} on the right hand side (r.h.s.) grows faster than the term A_{t-1}^{Δ} in the r.h.s. numerator and hence tends to choke off the growth of the r.h.s.; at some point, a balance is reached and the r.h.s. is pushed downward by this force as hard as it is pushed upward by the sum of coefficients Δ and γ being greater than unity. So here we have a considerable generalization of Phelps' result that allows us to get closer to the observed empirical data mentioned earlier. A formal proof of this proposition emerges as a special result from our analysis of a technical progress with additional arguments, as discussed later.

B. Generalization II

In Phelps' function there is no purely economic argument, and hence technical progress proceeds without depending upon capital or output. This clearly is not realistic. The function also should include an argument that represents the amount of ''tools'' each potential knowledge creator is given, particularly the amount of education; this we may represent by the average level of output per worker (Y/L), which determines the average level of education. Furthermore, the total resources of an economy may influence its production of knowledge, as the total resources of the United States permit it to make space flights, whereas the total wealth and income of Sweden do not. We shall index total resources by total income, and then write the more general function

$$A_t - A_{t-1} = bL_{t-1}^{\gamma} A_{t-1}^{\Delta} Y_{t-1}^{\phi} \left(\frac{Y}{L}\right)_{t-1}^{\psi} \text{ with } b \text{ constant,} \quad \text{or} \quad (6)$$

$$A_t - A_{t-1} = bL^u A^{\Delta} Y^{\epsilon} \text{ with } M = \gamma - \psi \gtreqless 0 \text{ and } \epsilon = \phi + \psi > 0 \quad (6a)$$

The implications of this function were explored with a simple model composed of the following equations:

$$Y_t = K_t^{a}(A_t L_t)^{\beta} \qquad \alpha \text{ and } \beta \text{ are constants} \tag{7}$$

$$S_t = sY_{t-1} \tag{8}$$

$$K_t = sY_{t-1} + K_{t-1} \qquad 1 > s > 0 \tag{9}$$

Implicitly we have the short-run equilibrium condition that investment equals savings. Next, the exogenous labor force growth

$$L_t = L_{t-1} + dL_{t-1} \qquad d \text{ is constant} \tag{10}$$

The long-run equilibrium conditions are standard

$$\frac{A_t - A_{t-1}}{A_{t-1}} \simeq \frac{1}{A} \cdot \frac{dA}{dt} = \dot{A} = g_A \tag{11}$$

where g_A is a constant in equilibrium

$$\frac{Y_t - Y_{t-1}}{Y_{t-1}} \simeq \frac{1}{Y} \cdot \frac{dY}{dt} = \dot{Y} = g_Y \tag{12}$$

where g_Y is a constant in equilibrium

$$\frac{K_t - K_{t-1}}{K_{t-1}} \simeq \frac{1}{K} \cdot \frac{dK}{dt} = \dot{K} = g_K \tag{13}$$

where g_K is a constant in equilibrium. We begin by rewriting Eq. (6a) as

$$\dot{A} = bL^{\mu} A^{\Delta-1} Y^{\epsilon} \tag{6b}$$

Taking logs and differentiating, we get

$$\frac{1}{A}\frac{d\dot{A}}{dt} = \mu\dot{L} + (\Delta - 1)\dot{A} + \epsilon\dot{Y} \tag{14}$$

Using Eq. (11)

$$\frac{1}{A}\frac{d\dot{A}}{dt} = 0 \tag{11a}$$

This with Eq. (14) yields the following relation between the equilibrium values of g_Y, g_A, and g_L.

$$g_A = \frac{\epsilon}{1 - \Delta} g_Y + \frac{\mu}{1 - \Delta} g_L \tag{15}$$

Equations 7, 8, 10, 11, 12, and 13, plus the short-run equilibrium savings-equals-investment condition can be transformed and reduced into the well-known

$$g_A = \frac{1 - \alpha}{\beta} g_Y - g_L \tag{16}$$

Equations (15) and (16) contain only the arguments g_A, g_Y, and g_L plus constants. Therefore we can determine the equilibrium values of g_Y and g_A

$$g_Y = \frac{1 - \Delta + \mu}{\dfrac{1 - \alpha}{\beta}(1 - \Delta) - \epsilon} g_L \tag{17}$$

$$g_A = \frac{\left(\dfrac{1 - \alpha}{\beta}\right)\mu + \epsilon}{\dfrac{1 - \alpha}{\beta}(1 - \Delta) - \epsilon} g_L \tag{18}$$

For the special case of constant returns to scale in the production function [Eq. (7)], $\alpha + \beta = 1$, and we get the special results

$$g_Y = \frac{1 - \Delta + \mu}{1 - \Delta - \epsilon} g_L \tag{17a}$$

and

$$g_A = \frac{\mu + \epsilon}{1 - \Delta - \epsilon} g_L \tag{18a}$$

In this special case, the equilibrium value of the growth rate of per worker income[5]

$$g_{(Y/L)} = g_Y - g_L$$

(equals $g_{(Y/P)}$ if $g_P = g_L$, where Y/P is per capita income)

$$g_{(Y/L)} = \frac{\mu + \epsilon}{1 - \Delta - \epsilon} g_L = g_A \tag{19a}$$

Let us see what values of the parameters are possible and acceptable for Eq. (19a) to be consistent with our equilibrium conditions. First, we know that the numerator, $\mu + \epsilon$, must be positive because $\gamma + \phi > 0$, and $\mu + \epsilon = \gamma + \phi$. Next, the denominator must also be positive, or else there could be no equilibrium with positive growth rates of L, A, and Y. We can see in Eq. (6b) that $\Delta > 1$ or 8A would certainly increase with time, which violates an equilibrium condition. Furthermore, from Eqs. (17a) and (18a), we know that $\Delta + \epsilon > 1$ implies $g_A < 0$ and $g_Y < 0$ for $g_L > 0$. This solution is not only economically meaningless, but some simulation calculations also show that for all initial values of $\dot{A}$, $\dot{Y} > 0$ the condition $\Delta + \epsilon > 1$ causes the system to explode because $d\dot{A}/dt$ and $d\dot{Y}/dt$ are positive. Hence for positive population growth, a reasonable equilibrium exists only for $\Delta + \epsilon < 1$. What is most important, however, is that under these conditions there is an equilibrium.

Now to interpret our results. Given that both the numerator and denominator in Eq. (19a) are positive, a higher rate of labor force growth implies a faster equilibrium rate of growth of per capita income. And the mechanism is clear: We see in Eq. (18a) that a higher rate of growth of the labor force implies a faster equilibrium rate of growth of technology, and the multiplier is the same as in Eq. (19a). That is, more workers imply more technical change, and an increased rate of technical changes translates immediately into growth of per capita income that is faster to the same extent.

Phelps' model yields the same result because it is a special case of this model. This may be seen by simply setting $\epsilon = 0$ because neither Y nor (Y/L) is an argument in Phelps' model.

The extent to which an increment of population growth raises the equilibrium growth rate depends on the exponents (the "population elasticities") of the technical progress function in the linear function shown in Figure 6. This continues until $\Delta + \epsilon$ increases to unity, at which point the equilibrium system explodes and the rate of technical progress increases with time rather than remaining constant; this is by no means implausible economically however.

It seems remarkable to us that the elasticity of the labor force can be large without limit without causing the equilibrium system to explode, though continuing to raise the equilibrium rate of growth of per capita income. This is because the relationship between $\dot{L}$ and $\dot{Y}$ is unidirectional, whereas $\dot{A}$ and $\dot{Y}$ influence each other in a mutually reinforcing feedback relationship.

In brief, the macromodel with either Phelps' function or our more general function has the important implication—which is exactly the opposite of conventional growth theory with technical progress exogenous—that faster population growth implies a faster equilibrium rate of growth of the standard of living. It also has the pleasant property for theory and theorists that a realistic model of technical change and of the effect of population size and growth upon technical change may be comfortably embodied in growth-theoretical models without upsetting the basic structure of that theory.

IV. HISTORICAL MODIFICATION

Phelps' function and the generalized function described in Section III, do not differ for different historical ages. But the parameters of the tech-

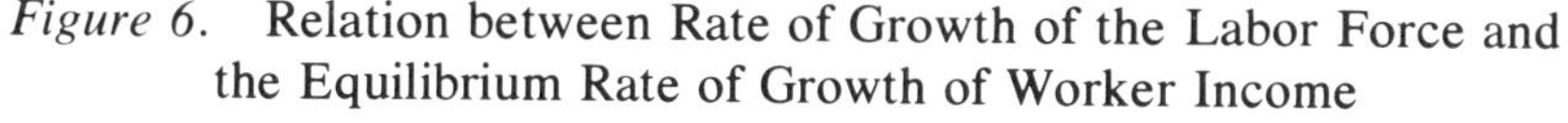

Figure 6. Relation between Rate of Growth of the Labor Force and the Equilibrium Rate of Growth of Worker Income

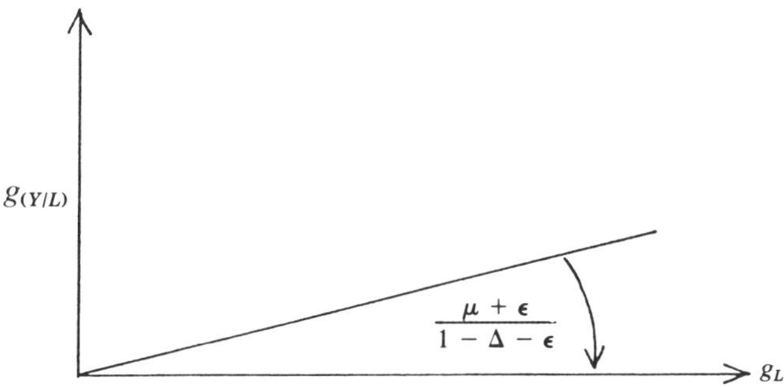

nical progress function clearly change as economic development proceeds. Consider the situation in 6000 B.C. There were relatively few new ideas for which both the intellectual basis and the need existed. Agriculture obviously was such an idea. And agriculture was independently invented in many different places, which suggests that an even larger number of potential inventors would not have increased the rate of knowledge creation. Of course, this invention repeatedly had to be made independently because of the lack of communication among groups and because of the lack of means to "store" the idea in writing. But these conditions are key characteristics of that earlier time when the stock of knowledge was much lower than now. Therefore we can say that Δ was large relative to γ at that time, perhaps approaching unity.

Now consider a moment such as the present. It would seem reasonable that the coefficients Δ and γ sum to at least unity; if we took the people and literature in half of the intellectual disciplines and industries on an odd–even random basis—chemistry but not physics, sociology but not psychology, French but not German, desks but not chairs, tires but not engines, and so on—and moved them to another planet, the sum of knowledge produced on this planet should diminish by half and should double when they return to this planet. If we assume for the moment that all ideas created in a given year are of equal value,[6] and if we assume that each new idea creates a much larger number of possible new ideas by combination with existing ideas than the number by which it reduces the pool of potential ideas when it is discovered,[7] then we can easily show that the pool of potential new ideas is increasing relative to the number of idea producers. The relative increase continues until the likelihood of duplicated inventions reaches zero. At that time, there no longer are diminishing returns to more researchers, and the operative constraint is only the idea-creating capacity of the individual. At that moment, Δ approaches unity and γ approaches zero.

To make the function more closely fit the flow of history we should also take into account the capacities of people to contribute as researchers, which includes education and the tools of research. After we pass into the time of writing, and until the amount of education that people receive is as much as they can profitably use, the effect of such an education-and-tools factor—which we may index with per capita income—will be positive, that is ψ, ϕ, and ϵ greater than zero. But at some time in the future, assuming income rises, the effect of this factor will approach zero.

The courses of these three factors may be functions of time, the level of knowledge, or—most reasonable—per capita income.

The effect of total resources, as indexed by ϕ, may continue to be positive indefinitely, however, and we are agnostic as to whether this exponent will rise or fall with the level of living.

V. SUMMARY

A faster rate of growth of labor force produces higher steady state consumption per capita than does slower labor force growth, with all functions that are similar to Phelps' and realistic in the sense of making the absolute amount of change in technical knowledge a function of the total size of the labor force and the technical level, and perhaps the level of income as well. As long as the exponents on the level of technique and total income sum to less than one in a Cobb–Douglas technical-progress-function formulation, constant exponential growth will appear—a much more general result than Phelps originally offered. And if the exponent on technical change is unity or above—as is suggested by the data on comparisons of markets of different sizes in various countries—the rate of change of technique and of consumption will increase rather than be constant.

ACKNOWLEDGMENTS

We appreciate useful conversations on this topic with Mark Browning.

The central proof shown in this paper appears in Steinnmann and Simon (1980). We found this analytic proof after this paper had been scheduled for publication with its conclusions based on evidence from computers simulations. The analytic proof is more compact and elegant, however, and hence we rely on it here.

NOTES

1. The single exception we have found is Eltis (1973:324–326), and he immediately qualified away the positive finding by reference to the negative effect of "living space" and other factors not included in his model. He also chose not to include the positive effect of population growth through knowledge creation in his steady-state model.

In earlier simulation work (1977:Chapter 6), Simon made the growth of technology endogenous using a model that he now judges inferior to Phelps'. If he had known of Phelps' work—or Kaldor's or Arrow's—when he first ran the simulation in 1970, or afterwards, he could have done better. But neither the standard literature, nor colleagues who work on growth theory whom he asked, made the connection between those models and population growth.

2. In Phelps' continuous notation, the function is

$$\frac{\dot{A}(t)}{A(t)} = \left(\frac{A(t-w)}{A(t)}\right) h\left(\frac{R(t)}{A(t-w)}\right)$$

where $\dot{A}$ = time rate of change of A.

3. For minority views, see Kuznets (1960), Clark (1967), and Phelps himself. In his literary discussion in 1967 and 1972, Phelps restates what may be called the Petty–Kuznets effect that a larger population implies more "ingenious men" who create economic progress, but he does not connect this up to his model. We find that the conclusion about the rate of population growth is also implicit in Kaldor's model (1957), though Kaldor does not see it this way, and also in Arrow's model (1962), which he describes as similar to Kaldor's. But a larger initial population *size* does not imply faster technical progress in Kaldor's model, or in the common interpretation of Arrow's model (see Sheshinski, 1967). In Simon (1977:Chapters 4–6) this effect is built into a general macromodel in which additional people come to have a positive effect on the incomes of others in the long run.

4. Leontief's point is particularly relevant here: "[I]n the actual process of scientific investigation, which consists in its larger part of more or less successful attempts to overcome our own intellectual inertia, the problem of proper arrangement of formal analytical tools acquires fundamental importance" (1966:59).

5. The general solution is

$$g_{(Y|L)} = \frac{(1-\Delta)\dfrac{\alpha+\beta-1}{\beta}+\mu+\epsilon}{(1-\Delta)\dfrac{1-\alpha}{\beta}-\epsilon}\, g_L \tag{19}$$

6. The fact that some ideas are of much higher value than others will not disturb this analysis as long as we observe that people differ considerably in their interests and capacities so that they will work on different ideas, and also that people have far less than perfect foresight about which projects will turn out to be the most valuable. The details of this argument are given in Simon (1980).

7. Machlup (1962) mentions this mechanism.

REFERENCES

Arrow, K.J. 1962. The economic implications of learning by doing. *Review of Economic Studies* 29:155–173.

Brems, Hans. 1973. *Labor, Capital and Growth.* Lexington, Mass.: Lexington Books.

Clark, Colin, *Population Growth and Land Use* (New York:St. Martins, 1967).

Coale, Ansley, Personal Correspondence, December 28, 1971.

Conlisk, John. 1969. A neo-classical growth model with endogenously positioned technical change frontier. *Economic Journal* 79:348–362.

Dixit, A.K. 1976. *The Theory of Equilibrium Growth.* New York: Oxford University Press.

Eltis, Walter A. 1973. *Growth and Distribution.* London: MacMillan.

Fellner, William. 1970. Trends in the activities generating technological progress. *American Economic Review 60:*1–29.

Kaldor, Nicholas. 1957. A model of economic growth. *Economic Journal 67:*591–624.

Kuznets, Simon, "Population Change and Aggregate Output," in Universities–National Bureau of Economics Research, *Demographic and Economic Change in Developed Countries* (Princeton: Princeton University Press, 1960).

Leontief, Wassily. 1966. *Essays in Economics: Theories and Theorizing.* New York: Oxford University Press.

Love, Douglas and Lincoln Pashute (pseud. for J. L. Simon), "The Effect of Population Size and Concentration Upon Scientific Productivity," in Julian L. Simon (ed.), *Research in Population Economics,* Vol. I Greenwich:JAI Press, 1978).

Machlup, Fritz, "The Supply of Inventor's and Inventions," in Richard R. Nelson (ed.), *The Rate and Direction of Inventive Acitvity* (Universities—Princeton University Press, 1962, pp. 143–170).

Petty, William, *Another Essay in Political Arithmetic,* in *The Economic Writings of Sir William Petty,* Charles H. Hull, editor (Cambridge: CUP, 1899).

Phelps, Edmund S. 1966. Models of technical progress and the golden rule of research, *Review of Economic Studies 33:*133–145.

Phelps, Edmund S., "Population increase," *Canadian Journal of Economics,* 1968, 1:497–518.

Phelps, Edmund S. 1972. Some macroeconomics of population leveling. *Economic Aspects of Population Change,* Elliott R. Morss and Ritchie H. Reed (eds.). Washington: U.S. Government Printing Office.

Derek de Solla Price, "Measuring the Size of Science," *Israel Academy of Sciences and Humanities Proceedings,* Volume 4, No. 6, 1971, pgs. 98–111.

Shell, Karl. 1966. Toward a theory of inventive activity and capital accumulation. *American Economic Review 51:*62–68.

Simon, Julian L. 1977. *The Economics of Population Growth.* Princeton: Princeton University Press.

Simon, Julian L. 1980. The technical progress function and labor force size: a micromodel fit to facts. Mimeo.

Sheshinski, E. 1967. Tests of the "learning by doing" hypothesis. *Review of Economics and Statistics 49:*568–578.

Solow, Robert. 1957. Technical change and the aggregate production function. *The Review of Economics and Statistics 39:*312–320.

Solow, Robert, *Growth Theory: An Exposition* (New York: Oxford University Press, 1970).

Steinmann, Gunter and Julian L. Simon, "Phelps's Technical Progress Model Generalized," *Economic Letters* (forthcoming).

West, E.C. 1971. *Canada-United States Price and Productivity Differences in Manufacturing Industries, 1963* Ottowa: Economic Council of Canada.

COMPUTING THE LEVEL AND DISTRIBUTION OF GAINS FROM FERTILITY REDUCTION

Andrew Mason and Daniel B. Suits

ABSTRACT

This paper describes and illustrates new procedures for measuring monetary gains from fertility reduction that can be applied to macromodels of population and development. A previously developed method for calculating the total monetary gain from averted births is reviewed. A new technique for distributing gains between birth-averting households and society at large is explained. The value of this technique is that spillover benefits are more policy relevant than total benefits and are less likely to be "infected" by nonmonetary benefits and costs (e.g., psychic value of children to their parents) of fertility reduction. A technique for evaluating alternative fertility reduction programs is described. Each of the methods is applied to a macromodel estimated from a cross section of countries.

Research in Population Economics, Volume 3, pages 255–272

ISBN: 0-89232-207-1

I. INTRODUCTION

In 1958, Coale and Hoover published their pathbreaking study of population growth and economic development. The subsequent 20 years have witnessed an enormous amount of research on specific aspects of population and economic growth and the development of large and intricate models that attempt to describe the full implications of rapid population growth for developing countries. Despite the effort, the usefulness of this research for evaluation and design of population policy has not yet been fully realized. One of the problems in applying this research is the difficulty of quantifying the benefits of population programs in a useful manner. There are a number of unresolved difficulties, e.g., the choice of an appropriate discount rate and treatment of psychic costs and benefits. Two of the major problems are addressed below.

A. How Should the Gains from Birth Control Be Measured?

The object of computing the value of an averted birth is to assign a monetary value to the associated increase in welfare to members of the society under study. Some of the effects of an averted birth are direct and amenable to measurement, e.g., an immediate reduction in consumption and a delayed reduction in labor force. Some of the effects of an averted birth are indirect but, in principal, easily measured. Population size may influence relative prices and wages (pecuniary externalities), thus changing the economic opportunities available to all members of society. Finally, a reduction in fertility may have ramifications that are very difficult, if not impossible, to measure. The psychic or nonmonetary benefits and costs of children to their parents may be substantial. There may be significant nonpecuniary externalities (e.g., environmental effects) associated with reduced population size (see Haveman, 1976; Williams, 1979).

Enke (1960, 1966, 1971) was the first to estimate the value of an averted birth. He measured the net benefit as the present value of the difference between lifetime consumption and lifetime earnings of a child were he born. As Simon (1969) and Krueger and Sjastaad (1962) have pointed out, a large portion of the costs (consumption) included in this measure are borne by the parents and may be offset by psychic benefits. In addition, neither pecuniary or nonpecuniary externalities are captured by the procedure suggested by Enke.

Simon (1969, 1970) has suggested that some of these limitations can be overcome by approaching the problem at the macrolevel. He measured the total gain as the discounted value of the increase in gross national product resulting from the reduction in childbearing. According to Simon, such an estimate includes neither costs nor benefits that accrue directly to birth-averting households, but the estimate does include pecuniary externalities. The method offered by Simon effectively deals with some of the problems described earlier, however, the use of gross national product as a measure of welfare is open to question. Per capita income is a much more widely used measure of improvements in welfare or differences in the standard of living between places (see Sauvy, 1969).

To this point, no satisfactory method has been developed for measuring either psychic costs and benefits or nonpecuniary externalities associated with fertility reduction. For example, there is little agreement about the effect of population growth and size on the environment or about how to measure the benefits of improvements in the environment. Although measuring psychic value of children may be equally difficult, Simon has pointed the way toward finessing the problem by distinguishing between benefits captured by birth-averting households and benefits that accrue to society as a whole. The second question discussed addresses this issue.

B. How Are the Benefits from Birth Control Distributed?

Simon was the first to discuss the importance of distinguishing the privately capturable benefits that accrue to birth-averting households from those benefits that spill over onto society at large. The distinction is important for a number of reasons. First, the principal justification for public intervention is the existence of externalities or spillovers from high fertility rates. If all benefits from an averted birth accrue to the birth-averting household, welfare may not improve at all from family planning programs, particularly in light of the nonmonetary or psychic costs that may accrue to birth-averting households. Second, the effect of birth reduction on the distribution of income has important policy implications. Enke has argued that quantifying spillovers from distributive programs, such as the payment of incentive bonuses, is unimportant. However, the evaluation of the distributive impact of these programs requires information on the distribution of the value of an averted birth. If benefits from birth control accrue entirely or primarily to birth-averting households, what justification is there for transfers to birth-averting households?

C. Approach

This paper describes procedures for answering each of these questions. Section III presents an alternative method for computing the monetary gains from an averted birth; this method was originally developed in Suits *et al.* (1975). Using an econometric model for a hypothetical developing country, the gains per averted birth are estimated to range from $90 to $9900, depending on choice of discount rate and number of births averted. In Section IV, total monetary gain is distributed between participating households and society at large. Because privately capturable benefits accrue much earlier than spillover benefits, the distribution is quite sensitive to choice of discount rate. Using a 5 percent discount rate, approximately 90 percent of the present value of an averted birth accrues to society at large, whereas at 15 percent, only about one-tenth is captured by society. At a discount rate as high as 20 percent, spillover benefits are slightly negative.

Section V describes a method for choosing among alternative population policies. One view is that there are high returns to a very rapid reduction in fertility. The alternative view is that returns are very long-term in nature and that population policy should pursue a gradual, but sustained, effort to reduce fertility. It is shown how the procedures developed in Sections III and IV, when combined with cost data, can be used to select among alternative population policies. However, before turning to the procedures for calculating the value of an averted birth, a brief description of the model used to illustrate the methods is given in Section II.

II. THE ECONOMETRIC MODEL

The estimates presented here were produced with the aid of an econometric model of economic growth and demographic change compiled by the authors. A full description of the model is available elsewhere (Suits and Mason, 1978a, 1978b) and a very brief sketch is sufficient at this point. The model consists of equations fitted to aggregate data drawn from a cross section of about 70 nations as of the year 1970. A highly schematic flow chart of the resulting system of equations is shown in Figure 1. As

Figure 1. Flow Chart of the Model

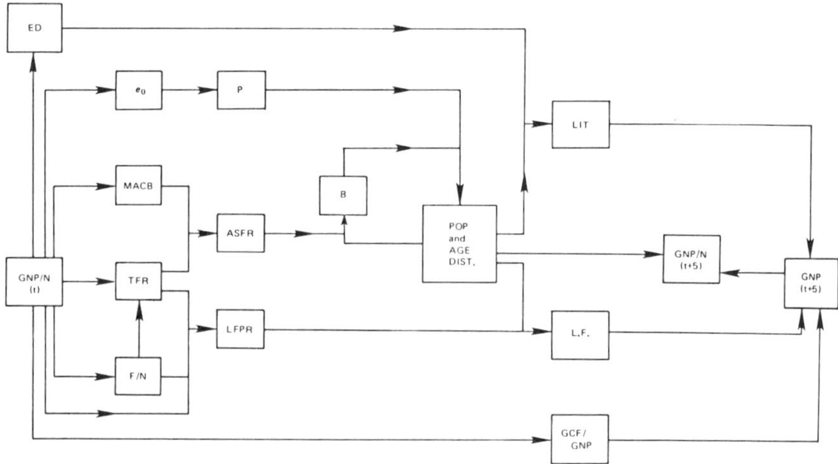

the chart indicates, per capita *GNP* directly impinges on the proportion of *GNP* devoted to gross capital formation (*GCF/GNP*), the percentage of population living on farms (*F/N*), and, along with the total fertility rate, the level of school enrollments (*ED*). In addition, per capita *GNP* enters three key demographic relationships, contributing to the determination of total fertility rate (*TFR*) (jointly with adult literacy and the urban–rural distribution of the population), mean age at child bearing (*MACB*), and life expectancy at birth (e_0). These demographic factors then combine to determine age-specific fertility (*ASFR*) and survival rates (*P*), which, together with the number and age distribution of the existing population, determine the number of births (*B*) and the number and age structure of the subsequent population. Lagged school enrollment ratios and the generated age distribution of the population determine the level of adult literacy. *GNP* per capita, the proportion of population on farms, and the total fertility rate also enter the determination of sex- and age-specific labor force participation rates, which, in turn, operate in conjunction with the population structure to determine the size of the labor force. The labor force together with literacy and capital formation contributes to determination of the *GNP* as of the next period. Dividing by population, we come full cycle to *GNP* per capita as of period $t + 5$.

Once conditions for an initial year are specified, the model generates a growth path whereby the values of all variables change over time. For example, given initial conditions that represent a nation with \$100 *GNP* per capita, with a total fertility rate (*TFR*) of 6200 per 1000 women and with a rate of natural increase in population of 2.3 percent per year, the model generates a simulated growth path as shown in Table 1. By the end of 100 years, real per capita *GNP* has grown to \$1472—an average rate of increase of 2.7 percent per year. The total fertility rate has fallen to 2600 and the rate of natural increase is down to 1.3 percent per year.

To employ the model for estimating the effects of reduced fertility on the path of economic development, the simulation of Table 1 is compared with a second simulation that begins with identical initial conditions, but in which, fertility is reduced to correspond to the impact of a specified family planning program. For this purpose, a simple scheme is devised that averts births in a fashion reasonably representative of family planning programs. This method involves establishing a target reduction in the total fertility rate by a specified data. In particular, results presented in Sections III and IV are based on a program that would reduce the *TFR* by 3600 (from 6200 to 2600) by year 50. It is also necessary to fix the time path by which fertility is reduced. In the examples used here, the difference between fertility under the birth control regime and the level that would otherwise prevail is increased linearly as shown in Figure 2. In other words, the program is designed to gain momentum with the passing of time.

Table 1.   Simulated Growth of a Poor Nation (GNP, GNP/N and
Population at Beginning of Period; Other Variables
are Interval Averages)

Year	GNP (billions)	GNP/N (dollars)	Population (millions)	Crude birth rate (per 1000)	Crude death rate (per 1000)	Rate of natural increase (percent)
0	1.00	100	10.0	40.75	17.63	2.3
10	1.60	127	12.6	38.90	16.90	2.2
20	2.53	160	15.8	36.60	15.92	2.1
30	3.96	203	19.5	33.72	14.63	1.9
40	6.21	262	23.7	31.13	12.92	1.8
50	9.78	343	28.5	29.12	10.92	1.8
60	15.45	453	34.1	27.53	9.07	1.8
70	24.50	596	41.1	25.74	8.25	1.8
80	38.49	784	49.1	23.63	8.42	1.5
90	60.09	1045	57.5	21.12	8.16	1.3
100	96.86	1472	65.8	—	—	—

It is important to note that action that reduces the number of births in any given year has a secondary effect in reducing births during subsequent years, partly because future population is lower than otherwise and partly because economic gains from the initial reduction in births contribute to future lowering of fertility rates. In calculating the number of births averted by the policy, only the number directly averted each year are counted. No "secondary" birth reduction is counted among the births averted by the program. In other words, the number of births counted as "averted" in any particular year is measured as the difference between the number of births for that year and the number of births that would have occurred in the absence of any program effort in that particular year.

The number of averted births each year, expressed as a percentage of the number of births that would have occurred in the absence of a program in that year, are charted in Figure 3. The percentage peaks in the fiftieth year and thereafter declines. The number of annual averted births reaches zero about year 90, since by that time the accumulated effect of past programs has already reduced fertility rates to the point where no more than 2600 births per 1000 women occur even in the absence of additional birth control effort. Indeed, the reduction in total fertility rate exceeds the original target level.

The accumulated economic and demographic impact of a program of these dimensions is substantial. By the end of 100 years, the rate of natural increase has declined to 0.5 percent per year as compared with 1.2 per-

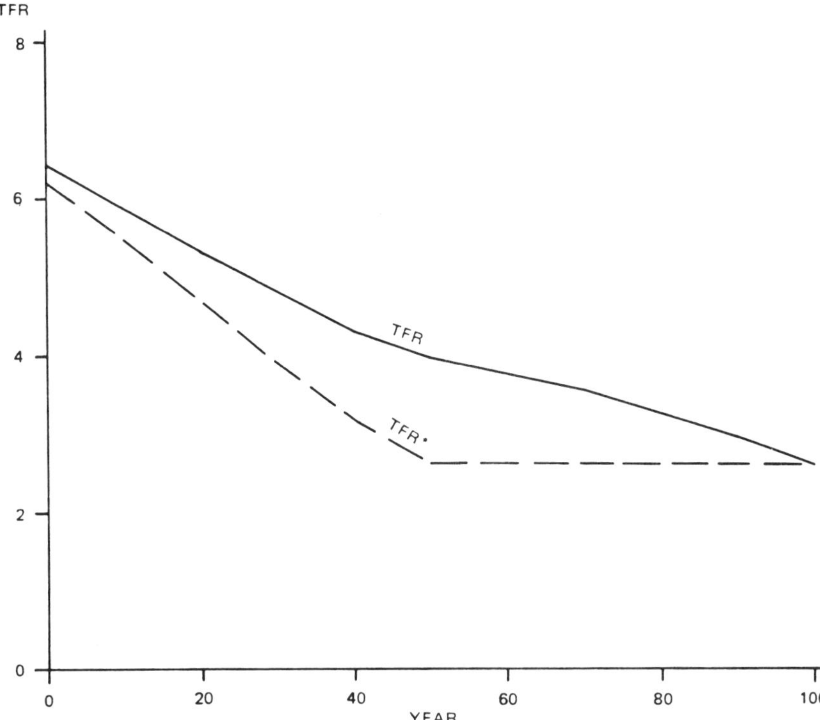

Figure 2. TFR without Birth Control (TFR) and Planned TFR (TFR*)

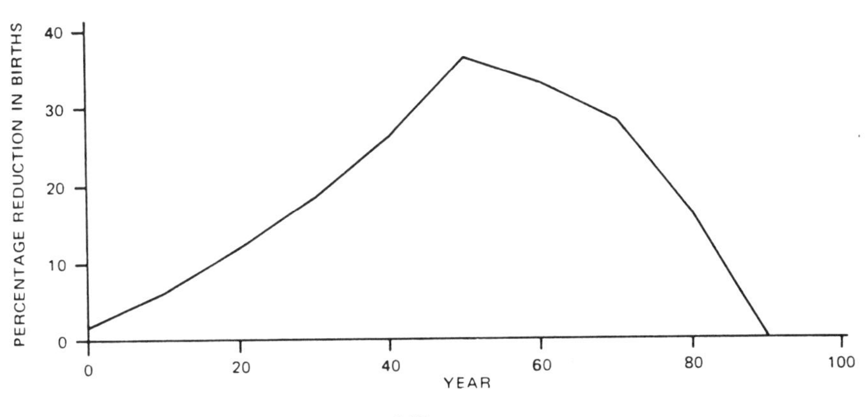

Figure 3. Percentage Reduction in Births from Birth Control in Each Year

Table 2.   Simulated Growth of a Poor Nation with Birth Averted
(GNP, GNP/N and Population at Beginning of Period;
Other Variables are Interval Averages)

Year	*GNP* *(billions)*	*GNP/N* *(dollars)*	*Population* *(millions)*	*Crude* *birth rate* *(per 1000)*	*Crude* *death rate* *(per 1000)*	*Rate of* *natural* *increase* *(percent)*
0	1.00	100	10.0	39.33	17.42	2.2
10	1.60	128	12.5	36.30	16.54	2.0
20	2.53	165	15.3	32.56	15.41	1.7
30	3.95	216	18.4	27.76	13.86	1.4
40	6.19	291	21.3	23.09	11.92	1.1
50	9.70	406	23.9	20.90	10.02	1.1
60	15.18	571	26.6	19.88	9.44	1.0
70	23.45	793	29.6	18.48	10.32	0.8
80	36.00	1115	32.3	18.18	10.13	0.8
90	57.95	1659	34.9	16.21	11.72	0.4
100	96.22	2574	37.4	—	—	—

cent in the absence of such a program. Over the century, the annual
growth rate of per capita *GNP* averages 3.3 percent per year as compared
with 2.6 percent were no births averted. By the end of the 100 year
period, *GNP* per capita stands at $2500, $1000 above the level achieved
in the absence of birth control. Table 2 provides a fuller description of
the simulation under the birth control regime.

III. THE VALUE OF AN AVERTED BIRTH

As measured by *GNP* per capita, the birth-averting program has raised
the material standard of living above that which would have been enjoyed
in the absence of a program. Comparisons of per capita income may
overstate the gain, because adults will make up a larger proportion of the
low fertility population and adults generally have higher "consumption
needs" than do children. To adjust for the differences in age structure,
the material standard of living is measured by *GNP* per equivalent adult,
that is, the number of persons in each age group is multiplied by consumption weights estimated by Meuller (1976). In symbols, the average material standard of living in any period t is $(GNP/A)_t$, where A is the number
of equivalent adults.

The economic gain from reduced fertility can then be measured as
follows. The standard of comparison is the *GNP* per equivalent adult
that the population would be expected to receive in any year t, in the absence of interference with fertility. Designate this standard as

$(GNP_s/A_s)_t$. Against this standard, we compare the material standard to be expected in the same year under the birth control regime: $(GNP_b/A_b)_t$. To measure the gain in any year, first calculate the GNP necessary to provide A_b equivalent adults with the standard of living they would expect in the absence of birth control. The required GNP is given by $(GNP_s/A_s)_tA_{bt}$. The gain from the birth control program is then defined as the excess of GNP_b over this amount. Thus the gain in year t is given as $GNP_{bt} - (GNP_s/A_s)_tA_{bt}$. In other words, the total monetary gain in any given year is defined as the amount of GNP that the population resulting from the birth control regime could give up during that year and still have a material standard of living equal to what would have prevailed in the absence of birth control.

Given the two simulations, this value is readily calculated for each year t. The total value of the birth control program is the sum of the entire sequence of annual values discounted to year zero. This present value, divided by the total number of births averted, similarly discounted, gives the gain per averted birth.

The calculated value of an averted birth is quite sensitive to the discount rate applied. Results are therefore presented for four discount rates: 0.05, 0.10, 0.15, and 0.20. A 15 percent rate was used by Enke (1971) and Simon (1970), although Simon argues that the value may be too high. On the other hand, interest rates and the return to capital are considerable in many developing countries. The rate of return to capital was calculated at nearly 20 percent for our econometric model.

The total monetary gain and gain per averted birth are shown in Table 3. The total gain ranges from \$14 billion (more than ten times the initial GNP) to \$8 million (.8 percent of GNP) and the gain per averted birth ranges from \$9934 to \$90 depending on the choice of discount rate. The gain per averted birth of \$215 for the 15 percent discount rate is surprisingly similar to Enke's estimates. The similarlity is misleading in two respects. First, the calculated gain depends upon the model used. The application of our method to the Coale and Hoover model yields a gain

Table 3.   Total Gain and Gain per Averted Birth

Discount rate	Total gain		Gain per averted birth
	Millions of dollars	*Percent of initial GNP*	
0.05	13,650	1365.0%	\$9,934
0.10	288	28.8%	830
0.15	32	3.2%	215
0.20	8	0.8%	90

per averted birth of over \$350. Second, the relationship of discount rate to benefits varies between methods. For the Enke procedure, the value of an averted birth declines with the discount rate because the value of foregone production increases relative to foregone consumption.

IV. THE DISTRIBUTION OF GAIN

The large gain per averted birth mirrors the substantial increase in the material standard of living caused by a reduction in fertility. All members of society may share in improved living standards, as average productivity rises in response to a higher rate of investment, improved educational attainment, and slower growth in the labor force. In addition, more rapid economic development induces additional reductions in fertility, a decline in mean family size, and additional increase in the average standard of living.

A substantial portion of the increase in the standard of living accrues directly to birth-averting households. The capturable gain from averted births consists of two parts: First, couples who avert births will have fewer children to support. Second, women who reduce their child-bearing will increase their employment, raising total household income above the level it otherwise would have been. The two components of capturable gain are computed in the following manner.

The extra *GNP* of all birth-averting households derived from smaller family size is measured by $(GNP_s/A_s)_t NAV_t$. NAV_t is the number of children, measured as equivalent adults, averted in year t. The number of children averted in year t equals the number of births averted during the preceding 15 years reduced by appropriate mortality rates.

The extra *GNP* of all birth-averting households derived from higher household income is measured as the product of the wage at time t and the change in female labor force due to averted births at time t. The labor force participation equations employed in our model indicate that, on average, an averted birth increases mother's total employment by about one-half year.

These two components are appropriately discounted and summed to obtain the total capturable gain and the capturable gain per averted birth. The difference between the total gain and the capturable gain gives the spillover benefits of the family planning program. The step-by-step procedures for computing the total, capturable, and noncapturable gains are given in the Appendix.

Table 4 shows the decomposition of total gain and gain per averted birth into its capturable and noncapturable components. The importance of the discount rate is immediately obvious. For a 5 percent rate, approximately 90 percent of the benefits are spillover. For the 10 percent rate,

Table 4.   Capturable and Non-Capturable Gain and
Gain Per Averted Birth

Discount rate	Total gain (*millions of dollars*)		Gain per averted Birth (*dollars*)	
	Capturable	Non-capturable	Capturable	Non-capturable
0.05	1,720	11,930	1,255	8,679
0.10	147	141	420	410
0.15	28	4	190	25
0.20	9	1	100	−10

the monetary benefits are about equally distributed between birth-averting households and society at large. As a higher discount rate is applied, the share of benefits that spill over declines substantially. For a 15 percent rate, about 10 percent of the monetary gain is noncapturable, whereas for a 20 percent rate, the noncapturable gain per averted birth is actually negative. In other words, an averted birth actually imposes costs on the rest of society.

The difference between the estimated spillover benefits and those computed by Simon are fairly large. Using a 15 percent discount rate, the noncapturable gain per averted birth is estimated to be \$25 as compared with Simon's estimate of over \$100. The difference reflects both the more favorable impact of fertility reduction on economic development predicted by the Coale–Hoover model used by Simon and differences in the methods for calculating benefits. If Simon's procedure is applied to the econometric model being used here, the spillover benefits are about −\$1 per averted birth. The difference in calculated benefits illustrates an important distinction between the method described here and the method proposed by Simon. The econometric model predicts a faster growth in per capita income but a slightly slower growth in total *GNP* resulting from averting births. In this situation, our method of measuring gain, in general, will produce positive benefits whereas Simon's will produce negative benefits.

The effect of the choice of discount rate on spillover benefits is striking. A decline in fertility has long-term effects on the growth of per capita income so that a substantial portion of the "extra" *GNP* is earned with a considerable lag. Of the three factors raising the rate of growth of *GNP*, an averted birth has an immediate impact only on investment but a delayed impact on the growth rate and the educational level of the labor force. In addition, an averted birth has indirect effects on per capita income that are long-term in nature.

The finding of negative spillover benefits at a high discount rate has a simple explanation. An averted birth increases the supply of labor, in the short run, through its effect on female labor force participation. Wages decline during the early stages of the birth control program, lowering per capita income of couples who do not avert births. At a high discount rate, these costs of an averted birth outweigh the subsequent benefits to society. Of course, the suggestion that the spillover benefits are negative depends on the relationship between labor force participation and fertility, about which there is considerable disagreement, little firm evidence, and considerable variation from country to country. In countries where there is a strong inverse relationship between labor supply and fertility, the existence of negative spillovers is a possibility, but the finding should not be generalized.

V. THE CHOICE AMONG POLICIES

To this point only one population policy has been considered, achieving a *TFR* of 2600 by year 50. The distribution of benefits between capturable and noncapturable components is not sensitive to variations in the population policy. However, the level of benefits varies considerably with the choice of program.

There are two dimensions of the class of policies to be considered. The first is the targeted reduction R in total fertility rate. The second is the number of years T required to achieve the targeted reduction in fertility. With each combination of R and T, there is an associated cost of the population program and an associated value. Alternatively, for any given population program budget, there exists a set of alternative policies that define an isocost curve and for any given value there is a corresponding isovalue curve. The points of tangency between the isocost and isovalue curves define the maximum gain for a given program budget or, taken together, the optimal expansion path for a family planning program.

Figure 4 illustrates the procedure. Years required to achieve a given reduction in total fertility are measured right to left so that as we move away from the origin, more rapid reductions in fertility are achieved, the cost of the program increases and, in general, the value of the program increases. (The possibility that the value associated with V_2 exceeds that of V_3 cannot be ruled out on *a priori* grounds. Reductions in fertility can be too rapid. The set of viable policies consists of those for which the value increases as we move away from the origin.) The zero isocost curve (C_0) and the zero isovalue curve (V_0) coincide as they represent the costs and gains from not implementing a program. Each point on this curve gives the reduction in fertility from the initial *TFR* that can be expected in the absence of a family planning program.

To operationalize this procedure, the macromodel is simulated repeatedly, varying the parameters of the birth-averting program, R and T. For

Figure 4. Illustration of Iso-Curve Analysis; C_i are Iso-Cost Curves V_i are Iso-Value Curves

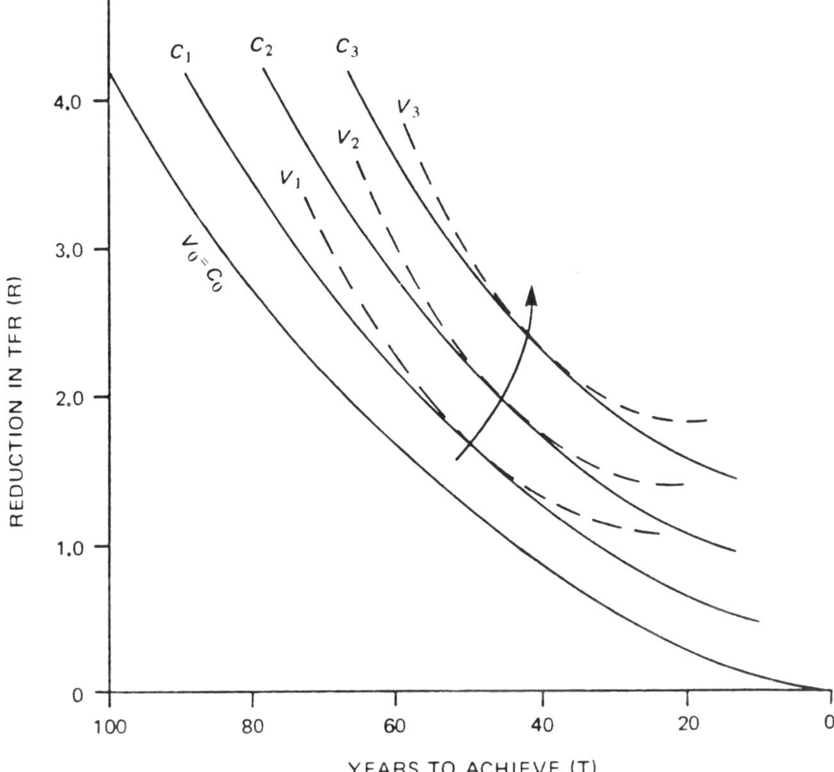

each combination of R and T, the total discounted noncapturable gain V and the discounted number of births averted C are calculated using a 10 percent discount rate. In order to approximate the isocost curves, it is assumed that the price of an averted birth is independent of R and T. Consequently, the isocost curves can be approximated by the discounted number of averted births. The implications of relaxing this assumption are discussed later.

Figure 5 illustrates the difference between two policies on the same isocost curve. Each program averts about 500,000 discounted births. The first program reduces *TFR* by 3 births per woman to 3.364 by year 30. The second program reduces *TFR* by close to 4 births per woman to 2.586 by year 40. The first program averts more births between year 0 and year 30 and fewer births thereafter than the second program. Likewise, the first program achieves a lower total fertility rate for the first 35 to 40 years

Figure 5. Annual Births Averted for Two Programs of Similar Size

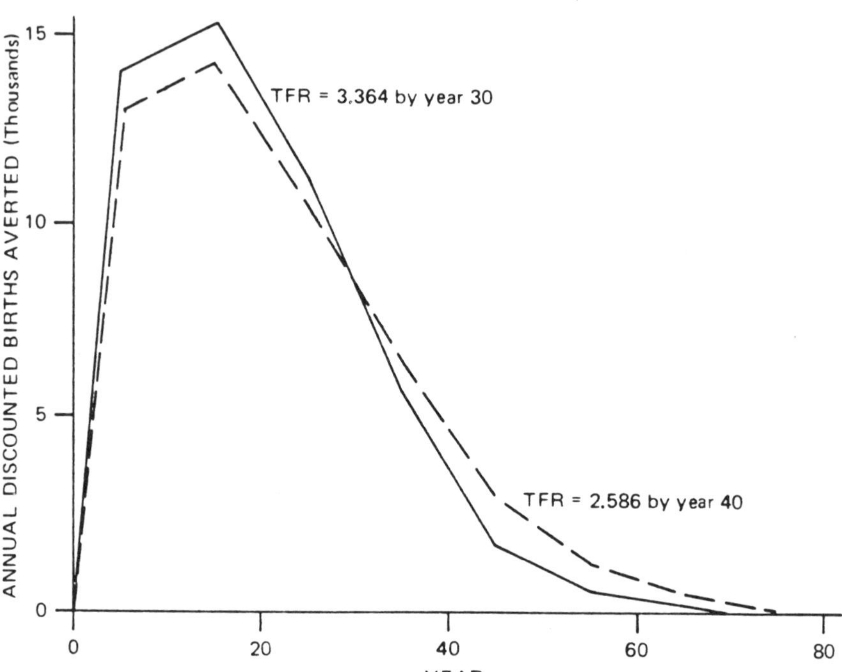

of the simulation. Thereafter, the fertility rate is above that achieved with the second program.

The isovalue and isocost curves are approximated by regressing the spillover benefits *V* and the number of averted births *C* on the parameters of the birth averting program, *R* and *T*. The estimated relationships are

$$V = 0.0517 - 0.0017T^\star + .000023(T^\star)^2 + .0474R^\star + .00013R^\star T^\star \quad (1)$$

for $N = 35$; "R^2" = 0.9959

$$C = 1.2747 - 0.0435T^\star + 0.00038(T^\star)^2 - 1.2290R^\star + 0.0825R^\star T^\star \quad (2)$$

for $N = 35$; "R^2" = 0.9888

where $T^\star = 100 - T$

$$R^\star = R - R(T,0)$$

The transformation of T, $T^\star$, conforms to the practice of measuring T from right to left in Figure 4. $R(T,0)$ is the reduction in *TFR* in the absence of any family planning program. $R^\star$ is the reduction in *TFR* at time T attributible to the family planning program. The transformed variable allows a closer approximation but need not do so in general.

Rearranging terms, the isovalue and isocost curves are given by

$$R_V = \frac{V - 0.0517 + 0.0017T^\star - 0.000023(T^\star)^2}{0.0474 + 0.00013T^\star} \tag{3}$$

$$R_C = \frac{C - 1.2747 + 0.0435T^\star - 0.00038(T^\star)^2}{-1.2290 + 0.0825T^\star} \tag{4}$$

It is also possible to solve Eqs. (3) and (4) for the expansion path. Equating the partial derivations with respect to $T^\star$ and solving for R gives

$$R_E = -0.0028 - 0.1045T^\star + .0114(T^\star)^2 \tag{5}$$

Of course, R_E gives the locus of points for which the first-order conditions are satisfied. The second-order conditions are not satisfied for values of T less than 100 years. In other words, we have a corner solution. For a given program size (measured by discounted births averted), the noncapturable gains are maximized by achieving the greatest total reduction in *TFR* at the expense of achieving a more rapid initial decline. Several isovalue and isocost curves and the corresponding expansion path are shown in Figure 6.

Figure 6. Estimated Iso-Value and Iso-Cost Curves; C_i are Iso-Cost Curves, V_i are Iso-Value Curves

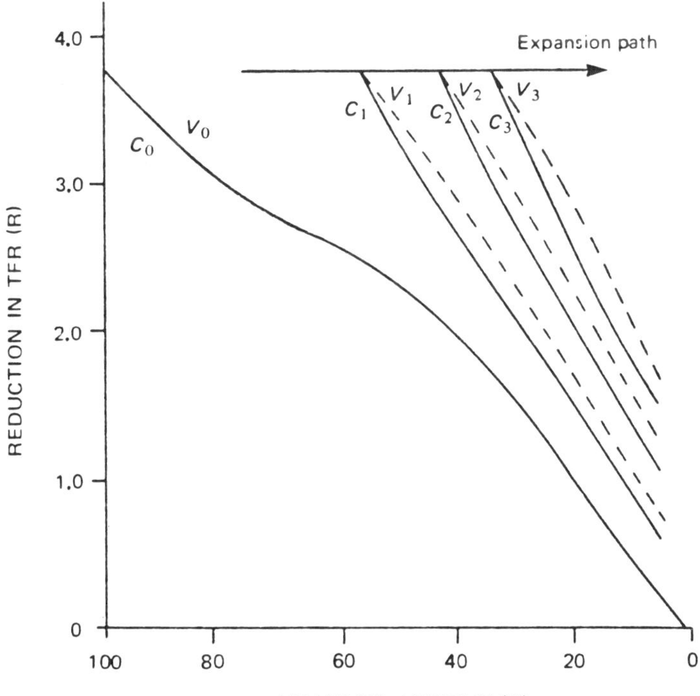

It cannot be overemphasized that this example is illustrative and not in-tended to support any particular policy at this point. It is doubtful that our knowledge about costs of family planning programs are sufficient to support this analysis. The price of an averted birth probably increases with the reduction in *TFR* and decreases with the time required to achieve a given reduction. This probability implies isocost curves that are more convex than those estimated earlier and may push the expansion path toward the interior.

Likewise, were the procedure applied to a different macromodel, the shape of the isovalue curves might be considerably different. For ex-ample, if threshold effects play an important role in the relationship between population and development, the payoffs to large initial reduc-tion in fertility could be substantial. Isovalue curves corresponding to such a model would be steeper than those shown in Figure 6 and the asso-ciated expansion path would be pushed downward.

VI. CONCLUDING REMARKS

Research that attempts to value the gains from fertility reduction is exceedingly ambitious and suffers a number of shortcomings. Evaluating conclusions requires a clear understanding of the limitations both of methods for valuing the gains and of the models of population and devel-opment that underlie calculated values. The sensitivity of results to choice of discount rate, to the method employed in measuring monetary gain, and to key population and development relationships is evident in the results reported here.

The entire effort to represent the development process is fraught with problems. A considerable part of "development" is the commer-cialization and modernization of activities previously carried out in the home. Industrial production counts whereas home production does not. When a mother enters the labor force, not only are her wages included in *GNP*, but the wages of the babysitter, the housekeeper, and the chef, who are merely replacing work she previously carried out in the home.

The choice of an appropriate welfare measure such as income per equivalent adult is a troubling problem. An alternative approach to the one taken here is to treat children as consumption goods and argue that two households with equal income but different number of children are equally well off. The standard of living would be measured as income per household or income per adult. This approach does have its drawbacks, however. It is inappropriate to populations with large numbers of un-wanted births. Further, it presupposes complete consumer sovereignty of parents over their children.

Finally, compressing all of the implications of reduced population growth into a single number conceals a great deal. There is no mention of the distribution of the spillovers to society. Who benefits from these gains? All of the members of society? The rich and the poor? Surely, understanding the impact of reduced population growth on the distribution of income is as important as calculating the total gain.

APPENDIX

Steps for Computing the Monetary Gains from Averted Births

A. To Compute the Total Gain (GAIN)

1. Compute the equivalent numbers of adults in each year for the standard simulation A_s and the birth averting simulation A_b: w, equivalent adult consumer units; N, population.

$$A_s = \sum_a w_a N_{as}$$

$$A_b = \sum_a w_a N_{ab}$$

2. Compute the difference in *GNP* per equivalent adult between the two simulations in each year.

$$GNP_b/A_b - GNP_s/A_s$$

3. Compute the *GNP* that the birth control regime population could give up and still maintain the *GNP* per equivalent adult of the standard simulation population in each year.

$$GAIN_t = A_b(GNP_b/A_b - GNP_s/A_s)_t$$

4. Compute the total discounted gain over the entire simulation interval; r, discount rate.

$$GAIN = \sum_{t=0}^{125} (1 + r)^{-t}GAIN_t$$

B. To Compute the Capturable Gain (CG)

1. Compute the number of averted children of each age in each year; p_a is the probability of surviving from birth to age a; B^*_{t-a} is the number of births averted a years ago.

$$C_a = p_a B^*_{t-a}; \quad a = 0 \text{ to } 15$$

2. Compute the number of equivalent adults averted in each year.

$$NAV = \sum_{a=0}^{15} w_a C_a$$

3. Compute the "extra" *GNP* from reductions in family size in each year attributable to averted births.

$$X = (GNP_s/A_s)NAV$$

4. Compute the discounted capturable gain from smaller family size over the entire simulation interval.

$$CG_1 = \sum_{t=0}^{125} (1 + r)^{-t}X_t$$

5. Compute the increase in woman-years worked in each year due to averted births. (Based on estimated female labor force equation.)

$$\Delta L_t = .49B^*_{t-5}$$

6. Compute the additional income received by birth-averting households due to averted births in each year.

$$\Delta Y_t = wage_{bt} \Delta L_t$$

7. Compute the discounted capturable gain in *GNP* from increased employment over the entire simulation interval.

$$CG_2 = \sum_{t=0}^{125} (1 + r)^{-t}\Delta Y_t$$

8. Compute the entire discounted capturable gain; Eq. (4) + Eq. (7).

$$CG = CG_1 + CG_2$$

C. To Compute the Noncapturable Gain (NCG)
    1. Subtract the discounted capturable gain from $NCG = GAIN - CG$
the discounted total gain.

D. To Compute Any Gain per Averted Birth
(Any GAIN)
    1. Divide gain by discounted total of averted $Any\ GAIN/\Sigma(1 + r)^{-t}B_t^*$
births.

ACKNOWLEDGMENT

We express our appreciation to Linda Martin, Gayle Uechi, and Sandra Ward for their assistance.

REFERENCES

Coale, Ansley and Edgar Hoover. 1958. *Population Growth and Economic Development.* Princeton: Princeton University Press.

Enke, Stephen. 1960. The gains to India from population control. *Review of Economics and Statistics 42*:175–181.

Enke, Stephen. 1966. The economic aspects of slowing population growth. *Economic Journal 76*:44–56.

Enke, Stephen. 1971. The economic consequences of slowing population growth. *Economic Journal 81*:800–811.

Krueger, Anne O. and L. A. Sjastaad 1962. Some limitations of Enke's economics of population. *Economic Development and Cultural Change 11*:246–248.

Haveman, Robert. 1976. Benefit–cost analysis and family planning programs. *Population and Development Review 2*:37–64.

Mueller, Eva. 1976. The economic value of children in peasant agriculture. *Population and Development: The Search for Selective Intervention*, Ronald G. Ridker (ed.). Baltimore: John Hopkins University Press.

Sauvy, Alfred. 1969. *General Theory of Population.* London: Weidenfeld and Nicolson.

Simon, Julian. 1969. The value of avoided births to underdeveloped countries. *Population Studies 23*:61–68.

Simon, Julian. 1970. Family planning prospects in less developed countries and a cost–benefit analysis of various alternatives. *Economic Journal 80*:58–71.

Suits, Daniel B. and Andrew Mason. 1978a. Gains from population control: results from an econometric model. *Papers of the East–West Population Institute,* Honolulu: East–West Center.

Suits, Daniel B. and Andrew Mason. 1978b. Measuring the gains to population control: results from an econometric model. Presented to annual meeting of the Population Association of America. April 13–15.

Suits, Daniel B., Ward Mardfin, Srawooth Paitoonpong, and Te-Pei Yu. 1975. Birth control in an econometric simulation. *International Economic Review 16*:92–111.

Williams, Anne D. 1979. The economic value of life. Presented to the Workshop on Modeling Population Change and Economic Development, Tenth Summer Seminar in Population, East–West Population Institute, East–West Center, Honolulu.

WHAT DOES "OPTIMUM POPULATION" MEAN?

David D. Friedman

I. INTRODUCTION

One weakness in the discussion of population policy that has raged for the last decade has been the almost unanimous failure of the participants to consider seriously by what criterion alternative futures containing different numbers of people ought to be judged—what, in other words, is meant by the term "optimum population."[1] A striking example is the collection of essays entitled *Is There An Optimum Level of Population?* published in 1971 by the Population Council (Singer, 1971). Most of the contributors use, explicitly or implicitly, "per capita welfare" as their criterion, apparently blissfully unaware of the arguments with which Meade, more than 20 years ago, demonstrated its implausibility (Meade, 1955:82–88). Of the two who actually discuss whether a per capita criterion is appropriate, one dismisses the question with the remark that "most of us would prefer" a per capita measure, and the other with the assertion "surely, what we want to do is to maximize the per capita share." Neither provides any arguments for his position. Of the three

Research in Population Economics, Volume 3, pages 273–287
Copyright © 1981 by JAI Press Inc.
All rights of reproduction in any form reserved.
ISBN: 0-89232-207-1

contributors who clearly do not see per capita welfare as the appropriate criterion, two assert, again without argument, that the appropriate criterion is the survival (for one author short-term and for one long-term) of the human race; the third wishes to maximize world brain and individual potentiality, both (fortunately) undefined.

The purpose of this article is to repair this omission in the literature, not by demonstrating that there is one clear and unambiguous criterion for optimum population to which all reasonable men must agree, but by showing the inadequacy of the criterion of per capita welfare and discussing some alternatives.

In discussing optima in ordinary economic questions, where the population is treated as given, there are three common approaches. The utilitarian approach assumes that individual utility functions are in principle knowable and comparable across individuals so that one can say whether a proposed change injures one set of people by more or less than it benefits another. A second approach uses the Pareto criterion; because interpersonal utility comparisons are assumed impossible, one alternative is said to be superior to another only if it is preferred by some and opposed by none; this has the unfortunate difficulty of providing only a very partial ordering, hence leaving many pairs of alternatives incomparable. The third approach attempts to impose reasonable conditions on an (unknown) social welfare function which is to be maximized in order to permit arguments that do not depend on the precise form of the function but do depend on its having certain characteristics. This may also assist the search for the "true" social welfare function by eliminating some, most, or (in the case of the Arrow Theorem) all of the alternatives.

Since my purpose is to illuminate those problems peculiar to population decisions, I prefer to assume away, at least initially, all other problems of defining optimality. I therefore begin by assuming, with Meade, that there exist individual utility functions that are interpersonally comparable, and discuss, in that context, the two alternatives he considered: maximizing per capita utility (in his terms, "welfare") and maximizing total utility. Having done so, I will then discuss the possiblity of some Pareto-like criterion for population decisions, and lastly consider what general conditions one might impose on possible social welfare functions designed to permit comparisons of alternative futures with different populations, and then examine how well the criteria I have considered meet those conditions.

II. PER CAPITA UTILITY AND TOTAL UTILITY

Consider two alternative futures with different populations. If our criterion is per capita utility, we compare the two futures by taking, for each, the sum of the utilities received by its inhabitants divided by their number; the higher figure defines the better society. Assuming that our utility function is defined in the sense described by Von Neumann and Morgenstern (1944:15–30), this corresponds to saying that the better society is that in which a person would prefer to be randomly placed; a "lottery" consisting of an equal chance of living any one of the society's lives will itself have a utility equal to the average of the utilities of those lives. This seems, at first glance, an unobjectionable criterion.

It involves, however, a fallacy of composition. Consider two alternative futures, each with a population of one hundred; in future A, the average utility is 80 utiles per person and in future B, it is 100. Suppose we wish to compare, not A and B, but A and A′, and B and B′, where A′ and B′ are created from A and B, respectively, by adding, in each case, one more person with a utility of 90 utiles. We assume that the additional person is in precise utility balance with the rest of his population; nobody else is helped or hurt by his existence. Imagine, if you like, that he is born, lives, and dies on a desert island without ever seeing another human being.

If our criterion is average utility, it follows that A′ is superior to A, but B′ is inferior to B. Whether it is desirable or undesirable for a particular life to be lived then depends, not merely on what that life is like, but on what the lives of a set of people totally uninfluenced by the additional person are like. This is, surely, an unsatisfactory result.

It may be objected that in practice people are affected by each other—an additional person living a below average life will make other people miserable, either because they feel obliged to help him at a cost to themselves or because they receive negative utility from the knowledge that someone else is less happy than themselves. If this is so, then that fact should be included in defining the utility functions of our hypothetical populations. There still remains the question of how, in principle, we choose among such populations; if our criterion is to be one of average utility then even if, after taking account of all such effects, the additional person imposes no harm on the rest of the population (perhaps because they receive benefits from his existence that balance the costs) we must still judge his existence to be undesirable because it brings down the average, even though it does so without injuring anyone.

Meade made the same argument in a somewhat different form:

> Suppose two communities A and B to exist. Suppose that neither has any appreciable economic dependence on the other so that the disappearance of A would not appreciably affect the standard of living in B nor the disappearance of B the standard of living in A. Suppose, further, that the standard of living in B is somewhat lower than in A, though both communities are properous and enjoy high standards. The strict application of the objective of maximizing welfare per head would lead to the conclusion that the world would be a better place if community B ceased to exist,

since output per head for all citizens of A and B would certainly be increased if that section of the community with the somewhat lower standard were to cease to exist (Meade, 1955:87).

Following Meade's line of argument, it is worth noting that a strict application of the per capita criterion implies that everyone who is less happy than the average ought to be painlessly killed (or at least, to avoid the question of means versus ends, that it would be a good thing if they all dropped dead) unless he not only benefits other and happier people, but benefits them by enough to outweigh the "injury" he imposes on the average level of utility by his existence. It also implies, given the belief of most writers on population that people in poor countries are on average much less happy than people in rich countries, that an epidemic that depopulated the poorer parts of the world would be an unambiguously good thing. While few of those who support such a criterion would be willing to carry it that far, some do seem to accept similar conclusions of a less drastic sort—in particular, the conclusion that holding down the reproduction of the poor is a good thing in itself, independent of whether the existence of poor people harms or helps the not-poor.

The obvious alternative to maximizing per capita utility is to maximize total utility; this is the alternative Meade chooses. In order to define what this means, we must first define zero utility. This was not necessary when we were concerned with per capita utility because the addition of a constant to everyone's utility function[2] results in adding the same constant to the average, hence that population that has the higher average utility before the transformation will have a higher utility after as well. This is not true for total utility; the lower the level that we define as corresponding to zero utility, the more favorable the total utility criterion is to larger populations. Going back to our previous example of A and A′, the question now is whether the additional person brings with him positive or negative utility—or, if we drop the assumption that his existence does not influence others, whether the difference between his own utility and the net reduction he causes in the utility of others is positive or negative. This depends crucially on what standard of life corresponds to zero utility.

Meade recognized the problem and so defined what he called a "welfare subsistence level":

> A man may be above the basic "physical subsistence" level and yet his existence may be considered so wretched as to count as a minus quantity from the point of view of economic welfare. He must attain something appreciably above the bare physical subsistence level before he can be said to be counted as a positive contribution to economic welfare (Meade, 1955:88).

This states the problem but does not answer it; how, in principle, does one decide where the welfare subsistence level is? The answer, I think, is that since utility functions are observable in the form of choices, and since negative utility is by definition that utility below which existence is worse than nonexistence, the zero point of the utility function is that point below which a person, given the choice, would prefer not to exist. But people have that choice; for many of us, suicide is not only possible but inexpensive—all it costs is our life. For others, it is possible but expensive—those, for example, who believe that suicide, being a sin, imposes serious post mortem costs or those who value the welfare of others who would be injured by their death (dependent children, for instance).[3]

Following the principle of consumer sovereignty to its somewhat grisly conclusion, it seems natural to say that if a person, having access to means for killing himself, refrains from doing so, it must be because his utility for living is greater than for dying. Making allowance for costs of dying (other than the opportunity cost of not living) such as pain, injury to others, and the price of the bullet, we than have a definition of zero utility; a person's utility is zero when he is exactly indifferent between committing a costless suicide and not doing so or when he would be indifferent to committing a costly suicide or not doing so, were his utility from living to be lowered by an amount corresponding to the costs of suicide (or were he to be offered additional benefits from suicide, such as someone else taking care of his orphaned children, with canceled the costs).[4]

This definition of zero utility, which seems to be the only one consistent with the usual economic approach to human behavior, makes the criterion of maximum *total* utility very favorable to large populations; if zero utility is defined as the suicide point then even in a very poor society additional children bring with them into the world substantial positive utility. More precisely, if we consider two societies D and E with populations $P_D > P_E$, E will be more attractive only if a person choosing between a lottery that gives him a $1/P_D$ chance of living each of the lives in D and one that gives him a $1/P_D$ chance of living each of the lives in E and a $(P_D - P_E)/P_D$ chance of dying, would prefer the latter. Introspection suggests that if P_D is substantially larger than P_E, E must be very much more attractive than D for that to happen.

We have seen that the criterion of maximizing per capita utility leads to the highly counterintuitive conclusion that the desirability of a particular life existing depends on the accident of whether the other people who happen to exist at the same time are better or worse off then the person who lives the life, so that the existence of a particular life will be judged desirable in one future and undesirable in another even if it has no interaction at all with those to whom it is being compared. It also leads, if taken seriously, to some rather unattractive recommendations for action. We now see that the alternative criterion of maximizing total utility is likely to lead to the conclusion that a world of 24 billion people living at the edge of subsistence is superior to a world of 4 billion living in prosperity—it seeming unlikely that an Indian peasant would be willing to play a game of Russian roulette with five chambers loaded, even if offered the opportunity of emigrating to the United States if he survived. The true utilitarian may reply that the result seems wrong only because we, having been brought up in affluence, fail to appreciate that the difference in utility between an Indian peasant and an American suburbanite is small compared to the difference between an Indian peasant and a corpse. Those of us who remain unconvinced may want to look for yet another criterion.

III. EXPANDED PARETO CRITERION

A. Principles

To do so, I replace the assumption that utility functions exist and are interpersonally comparable with the weaker assumption than an individual can in principle compare the attractiveness to him of his life with that of being another person living another life in some alternative future. While this may seem somewhat strained, it is difficult to see how we can make any statements at all about the relative attractiveness of different futures inhabited by different people without something of the sort.

Our new criterion should be chosen to avoid the problems generated by both the per capita utility and total utility criteria. It should avoid the fallacy of composition by which below average lives are treated as if, by bringing down the average, they inflicted a positive injury on the rest of the population. And it should reflect at least a decent agnosticism concerning the superiority of a future with large numbers of less happy people to one with fewer numbers of happier people. The cost of this avoidance, by analogy with the ordinary Pareto criterion, will be the failure to provide a complete ordering; some, perhaps many, pairs of alternative futures will be incomparable.

As a first try, based on the Pareto criterion and my previous argument about how zero utility should be defined, let us say that a larger society D with population P_D is superior to a smaller society E with population P_E if D contains a subset d of size P_E for which there exists a one-to-one mapping between D and E, such that each person in E is mapped into a person in d whose life he regards as at least as attractive as his own,[5] provided that the individuals in $(D - d)$ have a utility of at least zero in the sense defined earlier. In other words, a larger society is more attractive if it contains enough ''spaces'' for the population of the smaller society which the members of that society consider at least as attractive as the spaces they presently occupy, and if the remaining members of the larger society are at least sufficiently happy to prefer life to costless suicide.

Applying the same principle in the opposite direction, we could say that the smaller society is superior if it contains ''spaces'' for all the members of the larger society that they regard as at least as attractive as those they now occupy, where the "excess spaces" corresponding to the difference in the two populations each consist of a "life" of not living.

There are some difficulties with this. To begin with, it implies that a smaller society will never be found superior to a larger, however attractive the smaller may be, unless the larger contains a number of people, equal to the difference in the populations, who would rather be dead than alive. This seems, to put it mildly, unlikely. It further implies that a larger society will never be found superior as long as it contains at least $P_D - P_E + 1$ lives that nobody in the smaller society prefers to his own. In eliminating our previous problems, we have come up with an ordering so partial as to be virtually nonexistent.

The situation can be improved by altering the criterion in a way that allows the attractiveness of one life to balance the unattractiveness of another. Consider two alternative societies, each of which has only two members. The better-off member of society B (call him b_1) is much better off than the better-off member of society A (a_1); the worse-off member (b_2) is slightly worse off (than a_2). Under our criterion as so far given, A and B are incomparable. They are equally incomparable under the conventional Pareto criterion, if we think of a_2 and b_2 as corresponding to two different alternatives for the same person, and a_1 and b_1 similarly. "Going from" A to B makes one person better off and one worse off; hence neither it nor the reverse change is a Pareto improvement.

But in the context of population we are comparing, not two different futures for the same set of people (as in the conventional Pareto case), but two different futures for two different populations—different in who is in them even if the two populations happen to be of the same size. *A priori,* there is no more reason to compare a_2 to b_2 than to compare him to b_1—or to a mixture of the two. Suppose the relative attractiveness of different roles in the different populations is such that a_1 would prefer a lottery made up of a .9 chance of being b_1 and a .1 chance of being b_2 to his present life, and that a_2 would similarly prefer a .1 chance of being b_1 plus a .9 chance of being b_2. There then exists a mapping, not of people into people but of people into probability mixes of people, which uses up all of the "places" in both (equal-sized) populations, and which maps each person in A into a preferred alternative (a lottery among possible places) in B. It seems reasonable to say that if this is the case, then B is preferable to A, in a sense analogous but not identical to the normal Pareto criterion. By extension, we can say that a larger population future is superior to a smaller population future if there exists some mapping from the latter to the former that maps each individual into a probability mix of lives (a lottery with probabilities for living each of one or more of the lives lived in the larger society) such that the total probabilities in each lottery add up to one, and the sum of the probabilities with which different people are mapped into the same life adds up to no more than one, where each individual regards his lottery as at least as attractive as his present life, and where any life in the larger society for which the summed probabilities do not add up to one corresponds to a person in the larger society whose utility is not less than zero, in the sense defined earlier. A smaller society is superior to a larger society in the same sense, with the "missing spaces" corresponding, as earlier, to nonexistence. Mathematically, we require that:

E is preferred to D iff $\exists\, p_{ij}$, $(i = 1, \ldots, P_{D}; j = 1, \ldots, P_{E})$ such that $\forall_i$, $\Sigma_j p_{ij} U_{ij} \geq U_{i0}$, *and* for some i, $\Sigma_j p_{ij} U_{ij} > U_{i0}$, *and* $\forall_j \Sigma_i p_{ij} \leq 1$, *and* $\forall_i \Sigma_j p_{ij} \leq 1$, *and* $\forall_j$ such that $\Sigma_i p_{ij} < 1$, $U_{0j} \geq 0$.

Here p_{ij} is the probability with which person i in D is mapped into life j in E, U_{ij} is the utility to i in D of living life j in E, U_{i0} is the utility to i in D of living his own life, U_{0j} similarly for j in E. Note that these utilities need not be interpersonally comparable.

If, however, we assume that every life has the same utility to everyone, this reduces to

E is preferred to D iff for every $d \subset D\ \exists\, e \subset E$ such that $\Sigma_{i \in e} U_{0i} \geq \Sigma_{i \in d} U_{i0}$ *and* $\text{Min}_{i \in (E-e)} U_{0i} \geq 0$ *and* $|e| \leq |d|$ (i.e., set of lives e in E contains no more lives than set of lives d in D).

I have now at least reduced the difficulties presented by the first attempt at a Pareto-like criterion. In order for a smaller society to be judged superior, the "surplus" members of the larger society need not all prefer nonexistence to existence; it is sufficient if enough members of that society are willing to accept some risk of nonexistence (in exchange for a probability of a much more attractive life in the smaller society if they win their gamble), so that the summed probabilities of nonexistence add up to the difference between the two populations. This is a difficult requirement, but not an impossible one, if the smaller society is sufficiently attractive. I call this the expanded Pareto criterion.[6]

In some ways, this criterion seems very similar to Meade's preferred alternative of total welfare, since by the definitions of Von Neumann–Morgenstern utility, the utility of a lottery is the sum of the utility of the outcomes weighted by their probabilities. The difference is that under my Pareto-like criterion, lives may be mixed but not added; there is no way that two less happy people can "add up to" one happy person.

B. *Application*

Of the three criteria for optimal population that I have discussed, two (per capita and total utility) have been discussed elsewhere in this literature. The third (the expanded Pareto criterion) is not only (to the best of my knowledge) novel, it is also less easy to understand intuitively. The reader may find it useful to consider some hypothetical alternative futures and see how they would compare under the various criteria. For purposes of simplicity, I will assume that each life can be assigned a utility, such that a person choosing between two alternative lives will always prefer the one with the higher utility. I will further assume that these are Von Neumann–Morgenstern utilities—that is to say, they are so defined that a person choosing between two lotteries will choose that lottery for which the expected value of the utilities of the outcomes is higher. These assumptions are not essential for the criterion—it is sufficient that individuals can compare their lives to alternative lives and to lotteries among alternative lives—but they greatly simplify exposition.

Consider the alternative futures f, g, and h shown in Table 1. Comparing f and g, each of which has a population of 3, we observe that g is higher in total (hence also per capita) utility. Under a conventional Pareto criterion the two are incomparable, since person 6 in g is worse off and person 4 is better off than anyone in f. To apply the expanded Pareto criterion, note that a lottery involving a 50 percent chance of being 4 and a 50 percent chance of being 6 has an expected utility of $(0.5 \times 7) + (0.5 \times 2) = 4.5$. Future g can be thought of as made up of two such lotteries (giving a total of 1 chance of being 4 and 1 chance of being 6) plus a certainty of being 5. Persons 1 and 2 would each prefer the lottery to his

Table 1.   Comparison of Futures

Future	Person	Utility	Total utility	Per capita utility
f	1	3	9	3
	2	3		
	3	3		
g	4	7	12	4
	5	3		
	6	2		
h	7	6	14	2.8
	8	3		
	9	2		
	10	2		
	11	1		

present state; person 3 is indifferent between his present state and becoming person 5, hence by the expanded Pareto criterion g is superior to f.

What about h? In terms of total utility, it is the best of all; in terms of per capita utility, it is the worst. To apply the expanded Pareto criterion for comparison of h with f, note that a lottery consisting of a 50 percent chance of being 7 and a 50 percent chance of being 9 has an expected utility of $(0.5 \times 6) + (0.5 \times 2) = 4$. Persons 1 and 2 would each prefer one such lottery to his present condition; person 3 is indifferent between his present position and "being" person 8. We hence have a mapping that maps each person in f into a life or lottery of lives that he regards as at least as good as his own, and at least one person (actually two) into a life or lottery of lives that he prefers to his own. The remaining lives in h (10 and 11), which nobody from f is being mapped into, have utility greater than zero, hence persons 10 and 11 "are better off alive than dead" and their presence in h cannot be held to make it a worse future than if they did not exist. So, by the expanded Pareto criterion, h is better than f.

In comparing h to g, on the other hand, we note that there is no way to construct three lives or lotteries of lives in h (remembering that each life can be used only once) that 4, 5, and 6 would prefer to their own. There is also no way to transfer the population of h into the lives of g with satisfaction for all concerned. Persons 8 and 9 would be willing to take lives 5 and 6, respectively, and person 7 would prefer life 4 to his own. But that would leave 10 and 11 with no choice but nonexistence, which they do *not* prefer to their present circumstances. Nor is there any way of combining the lives of g (including two "empty spaces"—call them 6' and 6", each a life of nonexistence with utility zero) to give a set of lotteries that the inhabitants of h would all be willing to exchange for their present lives. Hence g and h are incomparable under the expanded Pareto criterion.

C. *Multiple Generations*

So far this discussion has been put in terms of comparing two futures as if they were future instants; while we have considered people living lives (which presumably takes time to do), we have not explicitly considered that the population that is being optimized consists not of those alive at some instant but of the entire path of population from the present to the end of time, i.e., the entire set of people who will ever live.[7] If we do so, we see another disadvantage of the per capita criterion in comparison with either of the other alternatives. If we are to average over the people alive at any one time, surely we should also average over those who live at different times, and it is then that grand average that is to be maximized. If we include in our average all who have ever lived, there is a strong case for trying to make future populations large; even if their members are not very well off, they are probably better off than the approximately 55 billion people who have already lived and died,[8] so increasing their numbers is likely to pull up the average. If we do not include those already dead, we have a criterion that changes at every instant; we may correctly maximize the average today and be told, 50 years hence, that we acted wrongly; by *their* criterion, the welfare of those who lived in the intervening period should be given no weight at all.

It is also interesting to note that if our criterion is the average welfare of everyone who will ever live, another objective suggested by some—the survival of our species—is not obviously desirable. If future survival must be purchased at the cost of present abstention, why should we want it? Why not burn up our resources in one burst of glory, providing a high level of utility for ourselves and our children and arranging, by appropriate contraceptive measures, that they will have no children to pay the bill? If, as many now argue, the reduction of the spacial extension of our species is entirely unobjectionable—hence desirable if it implies any increase at all in the average welfare of its members—the same ought to be true of its temporal extension as well.

IV. GENERAL CONDITIONS ON OPTIMALITY CRITERIA

Having discussed some specific optimality criteria for population, it is worth asking, in the spirit of the "social welfare function" approach, what general conditions any such criterion ought to meet. I begin by defining a "future" as a set of lives to be lived, including a complete description of all facts relevant to those lives. An optimality criterion is then an ordering (partial or complete) of futures, or in other words a set of ordered pairs (f,g) where f and g are different futures. If such an ordering includes the pair (f,g) we will say that f "is at least as desirable as" g. If it also includes (g,f) we will say that f "is equivalent to" g; if it does not include (g,f) we will say that f "is preferred to" g. If the ordering contains neither (f,g) (g,f) we will say that f and g "are incomparable" (under that ordering).

The first condition one might expect such an ordering to meet is transitivity; if f is at least as desirable as g and g is at least as desirable as h, then f is at least as desirable as h. This is necessary in order to make the ordering correspond to our normal intuitive ideas about "as good as," "better than," and so forth. It has the further useful consequence that cycles are impossible: a set of futures f, g, and h such that f is preferred to g, g is preferred to h, and h is preferred to f must violate transitivity.

A second condition that seems reasonable is that the ordering be what Nozick (1974:209) calls "aggregative" and Sen (1973:39–41) "additively separable.'' To see what this means, consider decomposing a future (containing, say, 5 lives) into two subfutures (say, 2 lives and 3 lives). Since each subfuture is itself a future, it must include a description of all facts relevant to the lives it contains, hence a future containing, say, lives a and b, must also include a *description* of lives c, d, and e, insofar as they affect a and b. One may perhaps think of such a subfuture as a future in which a and b exist as people, while c, d, and e are robots, identical to people insofar as any effect they have on a and b, but of no normative significance in themselves. A "partitioning" of a future is then a set of subfutures in which each life of that future appears once and only once. A "natural partitioning" is one none of whose subfutures contains a description of any life included in any other of its subfutures; in other words, it partitions the future into sets of lives that *in fact* do not interact with each other—as in the desert island example given earlier.

An ordering is aggregative if and only if, for any two futures f and g, *if f* and g can each be partitioned (into $f_1, f_2, \ldots, f_n; g_1, g_2, \ldots, g_n$) in such a way that for each i, f_i is at least as attractive as g_i, *then f* is at least as attractive as g. *And if* for each i, f_i is at least as attractive as g_i, and for some i f_i is preferred to g_i, *then f* is preferred to g.

These two conditions correspond reasonably well to some of those conventionally applied to social welfare function. I would like to add one more condition of a rather different nature, which I call "microrationality." It is that the criterion that is to be applied to judging entire futures be one that people in fact apply, at least approximately, in judging that part of the future most relevant to themselves, i.e. the lives of themselves, those near and dear to them, and their descendants. There are two arguments for requiring this. The first is that in constructing such a criterion we are trying to generalize our normative intuitions; we feel that certain principles are appropriate in dealing with those we know and care about, and since we have no reason to believe that those we know and care about are in fact any different from other people, we believe that ideally those principles should somehow be broadened to include everyone.

The second argument is methodological rather than philosophical. In constructing optimality criteria (whether for different populations, or more conventionally for different alternatives for the same population) we usually find ourselves trying to maximize something (total utility, for instance) that we have no possible way of measuring. This seems at first impossible; if we cannot measure what total utility would be under each of several alternatives and compare them in order to choose the best, how can we make any use of the criterion "maximize total utility" (or any other such criterion)? The conventional solution is to choose a criterion that in some approximation (no externalities or zero transaction costs for the conventional Pareto criterion, for instance) is automatically maximized by the separate decisions of the individual actors. We then observe in what respects the real world deviates from that approximation and take actions that either remove the deviations or compensate for them (effluent taxes to compensate for externality effects of pollution, for example). In this way, we can hope to move the world closer to optimality without ever having to measure the quantity we are trying to optimize.[9]

It is possible, of course, that there is a "morally correct" criterion for optimum population and that this criterion is not microrational. What this argument suggests is that if this is so, this criterion is unlikely to be very useful for generating policy recommendations. It may therefore be prudent, in trying to construct a criterion, to limit ourselves to those that are microrational as well as transitive and aggregative.

Of the criteria we have considered, both per capita and total utility are obviously transitive. In order for the expanded Pareto criterion to be transitive, we must assume that in deciding whether or not I prefer my present life to some life (or lottery of lives) in a hypothetical alternative future, I can abstract away from the particular tastes I actually have and make the decision in some "objective" fashion. Otherwise it would be possible for person i in future f to prefer life j in future g to his own, for person j in g to prefer life k in future h to his own, and for person k in future h to prefer life i in future f to *his* own—each of the three having, of course, different tastes. Supposing that each of the three alternative futures has a population of one, h is then preferred to g, g is preferred to f, and f is preferred to h, which contradicts transitivity. We must therefore assume, in order to guarantee transitivity, that the comparison among lives can be done in some way independent of which person is doing it.

Are the criteria we have considered aggregative? Per capita utility is not (this is the point of Meade's criticism). Total utility and the expanded Pareto criterion are. Are they microrational? Casual examination of individual reproductive behavior suggests that it is not aimed at maximizing the total utility of parents plus descendants (my previous discussion of that criterion suggests that doing so would probably involve raising the reproduction rate to its biological maximum), hence that criterion is not microrational; it is at least arguable that both maximization of per capita utility (remembering that up to some point additional children may raise the utility of their parents even if by diluting the pool of resources available to the family, they lower that of their siblings) and the expanded Pareto criterion are.

APOLOGIA

To many readers, especially those who are not economists, this article may seem both irrelevant and flippant, with its discussions of zero utility, suicide points, and the desirability or otherwise of killing off most of the human race. I can only protest that ideas do have consequences, and different ideas have different consequences. If we accept, as I believe we should not, a criterion that views every below average life as presumptively evil, entitled to exist only if it pays its way by providing some benefit to offset the "harm" it does by lowering the general average, we will be led to conclusions that are, I think, both morally and intellectually indefensible.

NOTES

1. The only exceptions I know of are two articles by Julian Simon (1970) and (1975, revised in 1977, Chapter 18). In the latter, he refers to a previous discussion of mine that was in a circulated draft of Friedman (1972) but not, as he incorrectly assumed, in the published version. There is also a brief mention of the problem in Meade (1967:236).

2. The Von Neumann–Morgenstern utility function for a single person is arbitrary with regard to linear transformations; the assumption of interpersonal comparability makes the set of utility functions arbitrary with regard to a single linear transformation applied to all utility functions simultaneously.

3. This argument applies only to those who are dependent on the potential suicide, not those who merely care about him; in the context of the economic theory of altruism (Becker, 1976:282–294) the latter should be benefited by the suicide of someone whose utility is negative, since it raises his utility and hence theirs.

4. A very similar definition of zero utility is given by Ng (1975:561–562).

5. More precisely, it is necessary that the alternative be as attractive to everyone and more attractive to at least one person; for purposes of simplicity I omit the latter qualification throughout the discussion, but it should be considered implicit in both of my Pareto-like criteria.

6. This term seems to have been first used by Simon (1975) to describe a special case of my "first try" at a Pareto-like criterion—the case where one of the two societies being described is created from the other by adding an additional person.

7. This point is discussed in Simon (1970).

8. This estimate is from unpublished work by Gerald Feinberg.

9. For an attempt at treating population decisions in this way, see Friedman (1972).

REFERENCES

Becker, Gary. 1976. *The Economic Approach to Human Behavior*. Chicago: University of Chicago Press.

Friedman, David. 1972. *Laissez-Faire in Population: The Least Bad Solution*. New York: An Occasional Paper of the Population Council.

Meade, J.E. 1955. *Trade and Welfare*. London: Oxford University Press.

Meade, J.E. 1967. Population explosion: the standard of living and social conflict. *The Economic Journal* 77:233–256.

Ng, Yew-Kwang. 1975. Bentham or Bergson? Finite sensibility, utility functions and social welfare functions. *Review of Economic Studies* 42:545–569.

Nozick, Robert. 1974. *Anarchy, State and Utopia*. New York: Basic Books, Inc.

Sen, Amartya. 1973. *On Economic Inequality*. Oxford: Clarendon Press.

Simon, Julian. 1970. The per capita income criterion and natality policies in poor countries. *Demography* 7:369–378.

Simon, Julian. 1975. The welfare effect of an additional child cannot be stated simply and unequivocally. *Demography* 12:89–105.

Simon, Julian. 1975. *The Economics of Population Growth*. Princeton: Princeton University Press.
Singer, S. Fred (ed.). 1971. *Is There An Optimum Level of Population?* New York: McGraw-Hill.
Von Neumann, John and Oskar Morgenstern. 1944. *The Theory of Games and Economic Behavior*. Princeton: Princeton University Press.